Structural Change *and* Strategy of Development

Structural Change
and
Strategy of Development

Resource-Industry Linkages in North-East India

Edited by
Gurudas Das

Akansha Publishing House
New Delhi - 110059 (India)

Akansha Publishing House
R 37-B, Vani Vihar, Uttam Nagar
New Delhi-110059
E-mail: ektabooks@yahoo.com

Showroom
4649/21B, Ansari Road
Darya Ganj
New Delhi-110002
Ph. : 23263193 / 9811582579

Structural Change *and* Strategy of Development

First Published : 2005
ISBN 81-87606-63-0

(The responsibility for the facts stated, conclusions reached etc. is entirely thatof the Author. The publisher is not responsible for them, whatsoever.)

Printed in India

Published by M. P. Misra for Akansha Publishing House, New Delhi-110059.
Printed at *Tarun Offset Printers* Delhi-110053.

Contents

Introduction

Neither structural change in the economies of developing countries strictly follow Clarkian framework, developed in the 1940s, nor do they meticulously follow Kuznets transformation, conceived during the 1960s and 70s. It appears that there is no single stylized path towards economic development. There are instances where countries are striving towards development without Kuznets transformation in relation to their sectoral performances. Of course, there is no dearth of instances as well where economic development has been the outcome of sectoral transformation along Kuznets line. In fact, Kuznets' observations are based on the development experiences of the developed countries. However, the opening up of the national economies and their ever increasing interdependence have created a condition in the global economy where sectors across the national boundaries may get interlinked and a country may experience economic development without showing structural change of Kuznets variety. There is no denying the fact that economic development accompanies structural change, but the fact is that this change may or may not conform to the Kuznets transformation.

One may view economic development both in short term as well as in long term perspectives. Conformity between economic development and change in the structure of an economy may not be realizable, although desirable, in the short term. But it is desirable in the long term as the question of sustainability is involved. After all, the resiliency of an economic structure depends largely on the inter-sectoral linkages. As the different sectors of an economy draw upon each other in a variety of ways, the stronger the inter-sectoral linkages the higher is the resiliency of the structure and vice versa. Thus, Kuznets transformation may be regarded as an indicator of resilient long term development of an economy.

It is in this context that the authours in this volume have looked into the sectoral performances of the economies of the states of north east India and the changes in sectoral share of labour force in them. Although similar studies are available at country level, this volume attempts to fill the gap at the regional/local level. The need for such a venture has been felt for long as the economic policy making in these states has been suffering from lack of systematic analysis of structural transformation in them and the implications of this change for policy interventions. Apart from structural change, the contributors have also looked into the resource base and its linkage with the industrial structure in the states of north east India. These exercises enable us to locate the strengths and weaknesses in each of the economies and find out alternative options for policy formulation for promoting development in them.

It has been observed that the share of primary sector in Net State Domestic Product (NSDP) is on the decline in all the states of north east India. But the decline in the corresponding share of labour force engaged in this sector lags far behind. This allows one to infer about the overcrowding and consequent declining labour productivity in agriculture and increasing pauperization of the rural life. This brings into the fore the urgency of expanding non-farm sector in all the states in the region.

Within a three tier sectoral classification, Kuznets transformation talks about increasing shift of income and labour from primary to secondary and then to tertiary sector. It has been, however, observed that the secondary sector in these states either remained stagnant or has experienced deceleration over time in terms of both income generation and employment of labour. A further segregation of the secondary sector show that much of the income generated in this sector is coming from construction activities rather than manufacturing. In fact, the contribution of the manufacturing activities to the share of secondary sector is on decline in majority of the states in the north east. This is, no doubt, a major cause for concern as far as the long term resiliency of these economies are concerned. This has led to the weak resource-industry linkages in all the states.

However, the rise in the share of the tertiary sector in NSDP has compensated the fall in the share of primary sector. In all the states, the contribution of the tertiary sector to NSDP is increasing over time. It has been observed that within the tertiary sector, public administration is contributing the most. Thus, it is the government expenditure that generates income in this sector. This is another major cause for concern. This leads one to conjecture that market forces are not strong enough to mobilize local resources and generate income in these economies.

Thus, unlike Kuznets transformation, there has been a distinct movement of these economies from primary to tertiary sector bypassing the secondary sector. The weak linkage between the primary and secondary sectors has made the transition of the former from tradition to modernity difficult. Moreover, the poor growth of the secondary sector has weakened the base of the tertiary sector. The grafted growth of the tertiary sector not only suffers from lack of self-sustenance but also breeds socio-political tensions as the labour force trained in it could hardly be absorbed in non-agricultural sector.

Contributions in this volume may be categorized into two types. There is a set of state-specific studies which have looked into these issues in depth at the state level. P.K. Kuri has covered Arunachal Pradesh. He has observed that the poor growth of the secondary sector in Arunachal Pradesh may be due to the very low plan allocation for this sector. His analysis of structural change in Arunachal economy and distribution of plan allocation make a *prima facie* case in favour of this hypothesis which may be taken up further for rigorous exposition. Besides bringing this hypothesis into fore, he also analysed the causes of poor industrial growth in the state. M.A. Salam, in his supplementary observation, also has argued to establish strong intersectoral linkages for promoting industrial development in Arunachal Pradesh. While covering Assam, Kishor Singh Rajput has observed that structural change in the economy of Assam has bypassed the secondary sector. This has crippled the economy of the state, which is showing the signs of deceleration for last five decades. Archana Sharma, in her supplementary observation, has noted the weak resource-industry linkages in Assam. Amar Yumnam has looked into the economy of Manipur. He has observed that the structural change that Manipur is being experiencing is absolutely different from the Kuznets transformation. He has pointed out that the increase in the share of the secondary sector in NSDP in Manipur is not because of the growth of manufacturing activities *per se* rather due to the better coverage of the unorganized activities which were not covered earlier. Rajesh Dutta has dealt with the economy of Meghalaya. His analysis shows that the structural transformation has bypassed the secondary sector and the resource-industry linkage is very weak in Meghalaya. Nirankar Srivastav has also observed very little change in the structure of the secondary sector in Meghalaya. Santanu Ray has made similar observation in relation to the economy of Mizoram. He has pointed out that construction activities contribute far more to the share of secondary sector than manufacturing activities. Gorky Chakraborty, in his supplementary, has pointed out the importance of people's participation while considering the options for strengthening resource-industry linkages in Mizoram. B. K. Jamir has studied the economy of Nagaland. She has also pointed out that contribution of construction activities to secondary sector is much higher than manufacturing. E. Bijoykumar Singh has commented on the need to study structural change in terms of more disaggregated sub-sectors. Anil Bhuimali and Kanak Kanti Bagchi have studied the economy of Sikkim and come out with similar observations. The Sikkimese economy also exhibits a movement from primary to tertiary activities. Manufacturing is almost non-existent. K. S. Chakraborty has looked into the economy of Tripura. Tripura is also experiencing a movement from primary to tertiary activities. The resource-industry linkages remain very weak in the economy of Tripura.

Another set of contribution focus on the region as a whole. These contributions have looked into the issues from a broader perspective. Utpal Kumar De has noted that although the percentage contribution of the primary sector across the states of the region is on decline, it still plays the predominant role in generating income and employment for the people. B. Mishra has studied the impact of public expenditure across the different sectors of the economies of Meghalaya and Nagaland. The hypothesis forwarded by P.K. Kuri and B.K. Jamir has been testified in Mishra's contribution. He observed that public expenditure is done more on social services compared to economic services. This has resulted in the disproportionate growth of the service sector in both Meghalaya and Nagaland. B.S. Butola has viewed the problems of development of the region from "other" perspective. He has made a critique of the "traditional" way of looking at the problems through resource-industry linkages. Instead, he forwarded a view to look into these problems through "culture-society-economy-environment interlinkages". Rabindra N. Bhattacharya has identified a number of problem areas relating to the long term development of the region. He has observed that given the socio-political uncertainty, the firms extracting the renewable as well as non-renewable resources in the region will unlikely to take into account the future expectations (opportunity cost) into its cost calculation and hence likely to overuse these resources. This may lead to catastrophic consequences for the economies of the region in the long run. He has observed further that the take-off into higher growth rates and sustainable economic development will be directly related to the ability of these economies to manage their natural resources efficiently and sustainably over the medium to long term. At the end, I have tried to touch upon the political economy of underdevelopment and some policy options for promoting development in the region.

This exercise was initiated in 2002 under the patronage of ICSSR-NERC, Shillong. Contributors worked throughout the year. During March 20-21, 2003, a seminar was organized at the North Eastern Hill University (NEHU), Shillong, where all the contributions were presented and discussed. We thankfully acknowledge the generous financial contributions from the Ministry of Development of North Eastern Region, Government of India, New Delhi, and the Indian Council of Social Science Research (ICSSR), New Delhi, without which it would have been difficult for us to bring out this volume.

I am thankful to C.J. Thomas, Director, ICSSR-NERC, who has taken all the trouble to organize the studies that made up the volume, and yet given me the opportunity and pleasure of editing it.

Shillong
October 15, 2004

—Gurudas Das

Contributors

Kanak Bagchi [Ph: 0353-580178 (R), e-mail: kkbagchi@hotmail.com] is Reader in Economics at the University of North Bengal. He writes on agrarian issues in West Bengal.

R. N. Bhattacharya [Ph: 033-24303152 (R), e-mail: rnbeco@yahoo.com] is Professor of Economics at Kalyani University. He has written extensively on resource economics. He edited and co-authored *Environmental Economics: An Indian Perspective* (2001, Oxford University Press, New Delhi)

Anil Bhuimali [Ph:0353-580177 (R), email: anilbhuimali@hotmail.com] is Reader in Economics at the University of North Bengal. He writes on the economic issues relating to North Bengal.

B. S. Butola [Ph: 011-6193515 (R), email: butolajnu@yahoo.com] is Reader at Jawaharlal Nehru University in the Centre for Studies in Regional Development. He has written on social, political and economic issues relating to north eastern region.

Gorky Chakraborty [Ph: 0373-2310223 (R)] teaches Economics at Doom Dooma College, Assam. He writes on the economic issues relating to northeastern region.

K. S. Chakraborty [Ph: 0381-2517711 (R), email: rd_agartala@rediffmail.com] is Regional Director, Indira Gandhi National Open University, Agartala. He authored *Anatomy of Overtrading* (2003, Mittal, New Delhi).

Gurudas Das [Ph: 0364-2233856 (R), 9436111533, email: gurudas_das@yahoo.co.in] is Reader in Economics at the North Eastern Hill University. He works on the society, polity and economy of north east India. His recent publication (co-edited and co-authored) is *Dimensions of Rural Development in North East India* (2004, Akansha, New Delhi). Presently he is working on "The Security and Development in India's North East".

Rajesh Dutta [Ph: 0364-2211347 (R), email: raj_datt 333@rediffmail.com] teaches Economics at St Edmunds's College. He writes on the economic issues relating to Meghalaya. Presently he is studying the linkages between social capital and economic development in Meghalaya.

Utpal Kumar De [Ph: 94361-02066(m) email: de_u@yahoo.com] is Reader in Economics at the North Eastern Hill University. He writes on issues relating to agriculture and environment. He authored *Economics of Crop Diversification*, (2003, Akansha, New Delhi)

B. Kilangla Jamir [Ph: 0369-227322 (R), email:bkj amir@yahoo.co.in] is Reader in Economics at Nagaland University. She writes on economic issues relating to Nagaland.

P. K. Kuri [Ph: 0342-2557566 (R), email: Pravatkumarkuri@rediffmail.com] is Reader in Economics at the University of Burdwan. He served the University of Arunachal earlier. He wrote extensively on the economy of Arunachal Pradesh. He co-authored *Land Reform in Arunachal Pradesh* (2001, Classical, New Delhi)

B. Mishra [Ph: 0364-2550391 (R), email: bmishra_nehu@hotmail.com] is Reader in Economics at the North Eastern Hill University. He gives courses on Public Finance and writes on issues relating to this area.

K. S. Rajput [Ph: 0364-2504802 (R)] teaches Economics at St. Anthony's College, Shillong. He writes on economic issues relating to the north eastern region.

Santanu Ray [Ph: 0389-2335794 (R), email: santanuray1@rediffmail.com] is attached with the Department of Economics at Mizoram University. He writes on the economic issues relating to Mizoram.

M. A. Salam [Ph: 03782-222052 (R)] teaches Economics at Bomdila College. He writes on issues relating to Arunachal Pradesh.

Archana Sharma [Ph: 0361-2571673 (R), email: sharmaarchana@yahoo.com] is Reader in Economics as well as Honorary Director (In-Charge) in Women's Studies Research Centre at Gauhati University. She writes on economic and gender issues relating to north eastern region.

E. B. Singh [Ph: 0385-2220979 (R), email: elangbambksingh@yahoo.co.in] is Professor of Economics at Manipur University. He writes on economic issues relating to the north eastern region.

N Srivastav [Ph: 0364-2550087 (R), email: nirankarsrivastav@yahoo.com] is Professor of Economics at North Eastern Hill University. He writes on economic issues relating to the north eastern region. He authored *Survey of Research in Economics on North East India 1970-1990* (2000, Regency, New Delhi)

Amar Yumnam [Ph: 0385-2455107 (R), email: yumnam1@yahoo.co.uk] is Professor of Economics at Manipur University. He has written extensively on the economic issues relating to Manipur as well as the north eastern region.

1

Changing Economic Structure and the Prospects of Resource Based Industrialization in Arunachal Pradesh

—Pravat Kumar Kuri

INTRODUCTION

Structural transformation is inevitable in the process of economic development. It is, in fact, an inseparable concomitant of economic development/industrialization (Kuznet, 1966). Colin Clark is said to be the first thinker to theorise the structural change that takes place in a tri-sectoral economy. He identifies a negative association between per capita income and the share of the primary sector in labour force, and a positive association between per capita income and the share of the secondary and tertiary sectors in labour force (Clark, 1940). In the economy of Arunachal Pradesh structural transformation is a recent phenomenon. At the time of Independence, this state lagged far behind the other parts of the country in terms of development indices. The economy of the State was a mono-economy characterized by traditional slash-and-burn method of agriculture and few small and cottage industries (Roy, 1995). Modern sectors, both tertiary and secondary where production is organized at the non-household level did not emerge then. After independence, the Government followed Nehru-Elwin Policy of isolation, the policy which encouraged the autonomous development of tribal population (Elwin, 1959). However, this policy witnessed a serious set back during the Chinese aggression in 1962 and was replaced by an active policy which aimed at removing the economic disparities between Arunachal Pradesh and other parts of the country. Heavy investments were made to develop the infrastructure - road, communications and other facilities - and administration was decentralized by locating different offices inside the State. Since independence the development of this state has been rapid and the socio-economic disparities between it and other parts of the country reduced significantly (Roy and Kuri, 2001). The literacy rate, which was negligible at the time of independence, increased to 54.74 per cent in 2001, a rate that is comparable to other parts of the country. Economic development along with government-sponsored urbanization has brought about significant changes in the structure of the economy.

TRENDS IN NET STATE DOMESTIC PRODUCT

Net State Domestic Product (NSDP), which is considered to be the most important single indicator of the overall performance of the economy, multiplied nearly 7.5 times in Arunachal Pradesh from Rs.13140 lakhs in 1970-71 to Rs. 98025 lakhs in 1999-2000 with an average annual exponential growth rate of 7.55 per cent at 1993-94 prices. The decadal decomposition of growth rate reveals that the state experienced the highest

Table 1 : Annual Exponential Growth Rates of NSDP and Per Capita NSDP in Arunachal Pradesh during 1970-71 and 1999-2000 (at 1970-71 base prices)

	1970-71 to 1999-2000	1970-71 to 1979-1980	1980-81 to 1989-1990	1990-91 to 1999-2000
NSDP	7.55 (51.19)	7.07 (9.66)	7.81 (27.20)	4.88 (7.21)
Population	2.87 (132.86)	3.04 (73.43)	3.21 (50.01)	2.49 (260.87)
Per Capita NSDP	4.68 (33.21)	4.02 (5.33)	4.70 (15.17)	2.39 (3.53)

Note: Figures in the parentheses are the 't' values

Source: Linking Series Estimates of SDP of Arunachal Pradesh: 1970-71 to 1999-2000, Directorate of Economics and Statistics, Government of Arunachal Pradesh, Itanagar.

rate of growth in 90's during which NSDP grew at the rate of 7.81 percent per annum. Compared to 90's, the last decade of the 20th Century witnessed a 40 per cent fall in the annual exponential growth rate of NSDP. The growth rate was observed to be 4.88 per cent per annum during 1999-2000.

Per capita income is commonly used as an index of the standard of living of the population of a country/state. The rate of growth of per capita income, by definition, is the rate of income (GNP/NSDP) and the rate of growth of population. In Arunachal Pradesh, the rate of growth of population is high, in fact, much higher than the national average. During thirty years period from 1970-71 to 1999-2000, the population of Arunachal Pradesh grew at the exponential rate of 2.87 per cent per annum. The decadal segregation reveals that in the 80's annual exponential growth rate of population was 3.04 per cent, which further increased to 3.21 per cent in the 90's. On the other hand the last decade of the twentieth century witnessed a relatively smaller rate of growth of population (2.39 per cent annum). However, this rate is still much higher than the national average of 1.93 per cent per annum. Therefore a larger proportion of income growth is absorbed by a significantly higher rate of growth of population in Arunachal Pradesh. In effect, in spite of a relatively higher rate of growth of income, the per capita income of the state grew rather modestly. During the thirty years period since 1970-71, the per capita income grew at the rate of 4.68 per cent per annum. The trend growth rate of per capita NSDP was observed to be 3.04 per cent, 3.21 per cent and 2.49 per cent during 80's, 90's and the last decade of the 20th century respectively. The State experienced a significant deceleration in both the NSDP and per capita rates of growth in the recently concluded decade. The performance of Arunachal economy also slowed down in relation to the National economy. To substantiate this point an attempt has been made to compare the per capita NSDP of

Arunachal Pradesh vis-à-vis the national average. For this purpose the per capita NSDP of Arunachal Pradesh as percentage of the per capita National income (at 1993-94 prices) has been regressed on time. The result for different time periods is shown in table-2 below.

During 1970-71 to 1999-2000, the per capita income of Arunachal Pradesh vis-à-vis the national average increased at

Table-2 : Trends of per-capita NSDP of Arunachal Pradesh relative to National Average during 1970-71 to 1999-2000 and decadal sub-periods at 1993-94 prices

1970-1971 to 1999-2000	1970-71 to 1979-1980	1980-81 to 1989-1990	1990-91 to 1999-2000
Y=56.08+1.70t	Y = 52.71 + 1.91t	Y = 75.89+1.53t	Y=108.21-1.52t
$\overline{Y}$=82.46	$\overline{Y}$= 63.20	$\overline{Y}$ = 84.3	$\overline{Y}$= 99.88
R^2=0.08	R^2 = 0.74	R^2 = 0.66	R^2 = 0.29
N = 30	N = 10	N = 10	N = 10

Note: (i) Y=Per Capita NSDP of Arunachal Pradesh as percentage of per capita national income at 1993-94 prices. (ii) t = time period (iii) N= number of observations (iv) $\overline{Y}$= mean per capita income

Source: (i) Linking series Estimates of SDP of Arunachal Pradesh: 1970-71 to 1999-2000, Directorate of Economics and Statistics, Government of Arunachal Pradesh Itanagar. (ii) Economic Survey, 2001 - 2002, Government of India.

the rate of 1.70 per cent per annum. The average relative position of per capita income during the period stood at 82.46 per cent of the national average. In the 80's the relative per capita income of Arunachal Pradesh grew at the rate of 1.91 per cent per annum, which declined to 1.53 per cent in 90's. However, the decade, 1990-91 to 1999-2000, experienced a reverse situation during which the per capita NSDP of Arunachal Pradesh declined while at the same time there was an increase in national average. As a result regression co-efficient took the negative sign (-1.52). Therefore, it can be asserted that in the growth performance of per capita income, Arunachal Pradesh slipped down the national average in the last decade of the twentieth century. In terms of relative per capita income (see Appendix table-I), Arunachal occupied 20th position in 1980-81 among all the states and Union Territories of the Country in 1880-81 and 4th among the States of North East India (next to Tripura, Nagaland and Meghalaya). Her position improved to be 12th in 1990-91 among the States and Union territories and second among the States of North East India, only next to Nagaland. She maintained her ranking unchanged in 1997-98 among the states of North East India but dropped to 15th position among all the States and Union territories of the country.

SECTORAL GROWTH IN NSDP

To have a deeper insight into the growth of NSDP, the analysis has been further carried out at more disaggregated level, that is, for different sub-sectors of the economy and the result is presented in table- 3 below.

Among the different sub-sectors of the primary sector, fishery showed the fastest growth rate (20.60 per cent) during 1970-71 to 1999-2000, followed by mining and quarrying (17.60 per cent), agriculture (6.80 per cent) and forestry and logging (3.33 per cent). It is to be noted that the high growth rates of fishing and mining and quarrying were simply due to their low base values. The highest decadal growth rates in all the sub-sectors of the primary sector were observed in 90's. However, growth rates in all the sectors slowed down sharply in the last decade. In fact, mining, forestry and logging experienced a negative growth rates during the period. The negative growth rate of the forestry and logging is the outcome of the Supreme Court ban imposed on December 12, 1996 putting restrictions on non-forest activities in the forest of the country.

Table-3 : Annual exponential Growth rates of NSDP under different sectors and sub-sectors during 1970-71 to 1999-2000 and decadal sub-periods in Arunachal Pradesh(base price: 1970-71)

NSDP under Sectors/sub-sectors	1970-71 to 1999-2000	1970-71 to 1979-1980	1980-81 to 1989-1990	1990-91 to 1999-2000
Primary	6.18 (24.37)	4.61 (8.28)	8.34 (11.19)	1.33 (1.19)
Secondary	8.01 (24.26)	8.03 (3.89)	6.71 (6.03)	6.21 (3.47)
Tertiary	9.52 (44.63)	11.40 (7.19)	7.64 (19.89)	8.14 (11.59)
Agriculture	6.80 (29.72)	6.40 (11.38)	8.85 (15.02)	2.19 (2.69)
Forestry & logging	3.33 (5.28)	3.20 (0.32)	4.67 (1.67)	-4.58 (-1.06)
Fishery	20.60 (28.13)	14.30 (6.75)	32.80 (10.78)	10.40 (13.61)
Mining	17.60 (8.57)	14.30 (1.99)	36.40 (3.02)	-0.63 -0.17)
Manufacture	13.10 (11.61)	14.20 (16.44)	15.00 (3.66)	-4.18 (-1.96)
Construction	7.32 (18.75)	7.70 (3.45)	6.04 (4.42)	5.12 (2.26)
Banking	17.90 (15.88)	28.70 (6.77)	18.60 (8.37)	8.70 (4.78)
Communication	4.83 (5.30)	10.10 (7.66)	-1.82 (-0.58)	12.90 (4.26)
Trade	2.53 (7.12)	10.50 (8.06)	2.77 (6.45)	-0.50 (-0.37)
Estate	6.68 (3.98)	-3.59 (-6.95)	10.30 (1.34)	-11.20 (-4.72)
Administration	-0.48 (-1.11)	3.75 (3.08)	-4.56 (-2.68)	5.97 (3.87)
Other services	10.60 (23.76)	9.57 (2.91)	8.58 (7.28)	6.82 (3.56)

Note: Figures in the parentheses are the 't' values
Source: Linking series Estimates of SDP of Arunachal Pradesh: 1970-71 to 1999-2000, Directorate of Economics and Statistics, Government of Arunachal Pradesh Itanagar.

Among the different sub-sectors of the secondary sector, the registered and un-registered manufacturing sector showed the highest growth rate of 13.10 per cent per annum, followed by construction (7.32 per cent). However, in spite of government's earnest efforts to extend a number of facilities to the intending industries and entrepreneurs, the manufacturing sector failed to maintain a positive rate of growth in the last decade of the 20th century.

In tertiary sector, banking service registered the highest growth rate of 17.90 per cent per annum during 1970-71 to 1999-2000 followed by other services (10.60 per cent) and communication (4.83 per cent). The trend growth rates improved significantly in the 80's in all the sub-sectors but slowed down in the 90's. In fact, during the 90's communication sector experienced a negative trend rate of growth.

CHANGING STRUCTURE OF THE ECONOMY

The analysis of the sectoral composition of NSDP over time gives an idea of the relative position of different sectors of the economy along with its changing structure. The standard tri-sectoral classification of the economy is adopted to identify the relative importance of

Table-4 : Sectoral Contribution of NSDP and Main Workforce Participation in Arunachal Pradesh : 1970-71,1980-81, 1990-91 and 1999-2000(Base price-1993-94)

Year	NSDP	Per capita NSDP	NSDP(in lakh) from			No. of Main Workers in			
	(in Rs. Lakh	(in Rs.)	Primary Sector	Secondary Sector	Tertiary Sector	Primary Sector	Secondary Sector	Tertiary Sector	Total Workforce
1	2	3	4	5	6	7	8	9	10
1970-71	13140	2808	7778	2672	2690	216823	1196	51523	269542
			(59.19)	(20.34)	(20.47)	(80.44)	(0.44)	(19.12)	(100)
1980-81	24889	4001	11767	5528	7594	23595	27960	49525	313436
			(47.28)	(22.21)	(30.51)	(75.28)	(8.92)	(15.80)	(100)
1990-91	58876	6902	27192	12695	18989	263666	33859	93451	390976
			(46.19)	(21.56)	(32.25)	(67.44)	(8.66)	(23.90)	(100)
1999-	98025	9170	34586	21446	41993	-	-	-	-
2000(Q)			(35.28)	(21.88)	(42.84)				

Source: (i) Linking series Estimates of SDP of Arunachal Pradesh: 1970-71 to 1999-2000, Directorate of Economics and Statistics, Government of Arunachal Pradesh Itanagar.

(ii) Figures in the parentheses are the percentage of total NSDP/Workforce

(iii) Census of India, 1971, 1981 and 1991

different sectors in NSDP of Arunachal Pradesh during 1970-71 to 1999-2000. Let us first confine our analysis to the discrete level i.e. on four different points of time during the reference period as indicated in column 1 of table 4.

A close reading of table-4 reveals some important facts about the sectoral aspects of the structure of the economy of Arunachal Pradesh. A horizontal reading of column 4,5 and 6 for all the four points of time shows that the share of the primary sector in State's total NSDP has been declined continuously since 1970-71. In 1970-71, the primary sector claims 59.19 per cent of the NSDP; the secondary sector 20.34 per cent while the tertiary sector contributes 20.47 per cent. In the same year, primary sector's share of main workforce exceeds 80 per cent, which is more than four times the share of workers in the tertiary sector. In 1970-71, the secondary sector accounts only 0.44 per cent of the total workforce of the economy. That is to say, in 1970-71, the economic structure of the State is dominated by the primary sector. Like 1970-71, in 1980-81 and 1990-91 also the primary sector dominates the economic structure of the state. However, there is a gradual decline in the importance of the primary sector and a compensatory rise in the importance of secondary and tertiary sectors both in terms of the sectoral contribution to NSDP and total workforce. In 1990-91, the primary sector dominates the economic structure of the state by claiming 46.19 per cent of the NSDP and 67.44 per cent of the workforce. The situation changes in 1999-2000. The tertiary sector dominates the economic structure by claiming 42.84 per cent of the NSDP. However, the primary sector continues to occupy the dominant position in terms of workers absorption ratio. So far as the non-primary sectors are concerned, in all the four points of time, the tertiary sector has higher NSDP and workforce compared to the secondary sector.

Therefore, the data in table-4 help us to identify the relationships between the level of economic development, as measured by per capita income (column 3), and the sectoral composition of income and workforce. Along with the increase in per capita income, there is a clear shift away from the primary sector to the non-primary sectors. The shift is more pronounced in the case of NSDP than in the case of workforce. The change in the share of different sectors in NSDP and in workforce participation is better explained in table-5.

It is evident from table 5 that the positive changes in the per capita NSDP (column-8) are accompanied by negative changes in the share of the primary sector (column-2) and positive changes in the share of the secondary sector (column-3; except in 1980-81 to 1990-91) and tertiary sectors (column-4) at different points of time. The percentage change in the share of workforce in the primary sector has been declined consistently over the period (column 5) along with matching increase in the secondary and tertiary sectors (column 6&7). It is interesting to note that the percentage change in the share of NSDP or workforce of all the sectors together is, in fact, *a zero-sum-game.* The sum of the changes of any two sectors is having equal magnitude but opposite signs when compared to the third sector (columns 2-4 and columns 5-7). This signifies that one sector expands at the cost of others and there is a clear indication that structural change in the economy of Arunachal Pradesh has led to a significant decline in the contribution of the primary sector to NSDP and /or workforce participation and a matching increase in the contribution of secondary and tertiary sectors. However, the change in the tertiary sector has been lopsided. Tertiary sector has been expanded at much faster rate than the secondary sector.

Table-5 : Changes in the Economic Structure of Arunachal Pradesh

Period	% Change in the share in NSDP of the			% Change in the share in the Workforce of the			% Change in per capita NSDP
	Primary sector	Secondary sector	Tertiary sector	Primary sector	Secondary sector	Tertiary sector	
1	2	3	4	5	6	7	8
1970-71 to 1980-81	-11.91	1.87	10.04	-5.16	8.48	-3.32	+42.49
1980-81 to 1990-91	-1.09	-0.65	1.74	-7.84	-0.26	8.10	+72.51
1990-91 to 1999-2000	-10.91	0.32	10.59	-	-	-	+32.86
1970-71 to 1990-91	-13.00	1.22	11.78	-13.00	8.22	4.78	+145.80
1970-71 to 1999-2000	-23.91	1.54	22.37	-	-	-	+226.57

Source: (i) Linking series Estimates of SDP of Arunachal Pradesh:1970-71 to 1999-2000, Directorate of Economics and Statistics, Government of Arunachal Pradesh Itanagar.
(ii) Census of India, 1971, 1981 and 1991

The existence of fluctuations over time implies that we cannot generalize about underlying trends on the basis of comparisons between selected end points, No doubt, our estimates for these selected years confirm the direction of change between these particular end points and accord well within the predictions of development theory. However, there is a danger of using such comparisons for any assessment of the underlying trends. This can only be done on the basis of time series as a whole. Accordingly, a linear time trend is fitted to the extent of share of each sector and sub-sectors in NSDP. For the sake of comparison, the same exercise is done for the national economy with reference to GNP. The resulting estimates are reported in table-6.

There is clear evidence of a significant negative time trend in the share of primary sector both at state level and the national level during 1970-71 to 1999-2000. Arunachal Pradesh experienced the decline of her primary sector at the rate of 0.66 percentage points[1] per annum compared to 0.67 percentage points decline experienced by the country (the results of the linear time trend of the sub-sectors of the economy are given in appendix table-II). The decline in the contribution of primary sector to NSDP has been compensated by the combined rise in the contribution of secondary and tertiary sectors both at the state and national economy, however, at varied rates. In Arunachal Pradesh, the contribution of secondary sector increased at the insignificant rate of 0.09 percentage points[2] while the tertiary sector rose at the significant rate of 0.56 percentage points per annum[3]. The tertiary sector replenished around 86 percent of the fall of the primary sector, remaining 14 per cent by the secondary sector. In the national economy, tertiary sector replenished around 72 percent of the fall of the primary sector, remaining 28 per cent by the secondary sector. Thus the tertiary sector of the economy of Arunachal Pradesh made its headway at a faster rate than that of the national economy. The secondary sector is the weak sector of the economy. Decade-wise analysis reveals that there is uniform pattern of structural transformation in the national economy: the contribution of the primary sector has been declined over the last three decades while there is an increase in the contribution of secondary and tertiary sectors. In contrast to national economy there are decadal fluctuations in the pattern of structural transformation in Arunachal Pradesh. However, one point is common in both the national economy and the economy of Arunachal Pradesh that over the years the structural change has brought about a slow and steady shift away from the primary sector towards and secondary and tertiary sectors and the tertiary sector has gradually been appearing as the dominant sector of the economy.

To sum up, the primary sector is found to be the most dominant sector in the economy of Arunachal Pradesh both in terms of its share in the NSDP and workforce. The structural change in Arunachal Pradesh shows a slow and steady shift away from the primary sector towards the secondary and tertiary sectors. However, what is unusual in the structural change of Arunachal Pradesh is that the service sector expanded at the expense of the secondary sector[4]. In recent years, tertiary sector is found to emerge as the dominant sector of the economy lagging much behind the secondary sector.

NEED FOR SECTORAL RE-ADJUSTMENT IN THE STATE PLAN

The formal planning process in Arunachal Pradesh started since the fourth five year plan with a meagre allocation of only Rs. 17.99 crores for the entire State. The plan allocation increased steadily over the successive five year plans: 63.30 crores in the fifth plan, 212 crores in the sixth plan, and 400 crores in the seventh plan. In the draft tenth

Table-6 : Structural transformation in Arunachal Pradesh vis-a-vis India: Linear time trend- 1970-71 to 1999-2000 and decadal sub-periods (1993-94 prices)

Year	Arunachal Pradesh			India		
	Primary sector	Secondary sector	Tertiary sector	Primary sector	Secondary sector	Tertiary sector
1970-71 to	P=60.23–0.66t	S=19.40+0.09t	T=20.37+0.56t	P=48.71–0.67t	S=19.81+0.19t	T=31.49+0.48t
1999-2000	=50.04	=20.85	T=29.12	=38.40	=22.67	=38.93
	R^2=0.70	R^2=0.09	R^2=0.75	R^2=0.97	R^2=0.91	R^2=0.96
1970-71 to	P=63.10–1.29t	S=19.14+0.24t	T=17.76+1.06t	P=48.33–0.66t	S=19.58+0.23t	T=32.09+0.42t
1979-1980	=55.98	=20.46	=23.57	=44.72	=20.87	=34.41
	R^2=0.50	R^2=0.07	R^2=0.71	R^2=0.76	R^2=0.64	R^2=0.73
1980-81 to	P=49.09+0.33t	S=21.26–0.28t	T=29.65–0.06t	P=43.20–0.80t	S=21.18+0.26t	T=35.63+0.54t
1989-1990	=50.91	=19.74	=29.35	=38.81	=22.61	=38.58
	R^2=0.14	R^2=0.15	R^2=0.03	R^2=0.91	R^2=0.92	R^2=0.86
1990-91 to	P=51.38–1.49t	S=20.76+0.29t	T=27.86+1.20t	P=36.29–0.84t	S=23.96+0.10t	T=39.75+0.74t
1999-2000	=43.22	=22.35	=34.44	=31.66	=24.53	=43.81
	R^2=0.76	R^2=0.54	R^2=0.54	R^2=0.95	R^2=0.22	R^2=0.93

Note : P stands for primary production as percentage of NSDP(GDP) of AP(INDIA) is the mean percentage rate

S stands for secondary production as percentage of NSDP(GDP) of AP(INDIA) is the mean percentage rate

T stands for tertiary production as percentage of NSDP(GDP) of AP(INDIA) is the mean percentage rate

R^2 is the correlation of determination

Source: (i) Linking series Estimates of SDP of Arunachal Pradesh: 1970-71 to 1999-2000, Directorate of Economics and Statistics, Government of Arunachal Pradesh Itanagar.

(ii) Economic Survey, 2001-2002, Government of India.

five year plan the proposed allocation for Arunachal Pradesh has been fixed Rs. 4627 crores over Rs. 3569.89 crores in the Ninth plan and Rs. 1155 crores in the Eighth plan. Throughout the planning process three sectors namely Transport & Communication, Service and Agriculture & Allied sector have received priority status in Arunachal Pradesh. In the fourth five year plan transport and communication got the highest priority. It was followed by agricultural & allied services and the social & community services. Industry and minerals received a meagre sum of only Rs. 0.99 crores of the total outlay. Over the fifth, sixth, and seventh five year plan periods some old sectors have been divided into smaller sub-sectors to provide special attention to some of these sub-sectors. However, the predominance of transport, services, and agriculture in receiving high allocations has remained more or less intact. Sectoral allocation of Plan outlay since sixth five year plan is given in table 7.

Since the eighth five year plan the Government of Arunachal Pradesh has been following a uniform pattern of sectoral priorities. In the eighth five year plan, service sector got the highest priority having received 32.05 per cent of the plan outlay. It was followed by the transport and communication sector which received 29.78 per cent, and agricultural & allied services including rural development, special area program, irrigation and flood control, forestry and wild life got 22.89 per cent. Industry and minerals received only 2.12 per cent of the plan outlay. This pattern again followed in the ninth and draft tenth plans. In the ninth five year plan social and community services has received the highest allocation being 38.58 per cent of the proposed total outlay. The second position has gone to the transport and communication sector with an allocation of 26.04 per cent. The combined allocations of agriculture and allied sector including rural development and irrigation and flood control amount to 21.00 per cent of the total plan outlay. In recent years specifically seventh plan onwards energy sector has been receiving much attention in terms of plan allocation. In the ninth five year plan the allocation to energy sector was 13.09 per cent of the proposed outlay.

The trends of the plan allocation to industries and minerals show that Arunachal Pradesh has never considered industrialization to be the priority area in any of the previous plan periods. It is interesting to note that plan allocation in Arunachal Pradesh to industry and minerals has never crossed even five per cent of the total plan outlay. The relative share of industry has either remained constant or declined over the successive plan periods. In the ninth plan proposed allocation was only 1.29 per cent of the total outlay.

The allocation towards service sector is very high in Arunachal Pradesh. This sector is being received on an average more than one third of the total plan outlay since the eighth five year plan. In the absence of rudimentary government services in the remote areas of the state, higher allocation to the service sector seems to be appropriate. Moreover, ever since the introduction of planning in Arunachal Pradesh, the main focus has been attached to the construction activities and building up of infrastructure. Given the accidented topography of the state, this priority to the development of infrastructure again seems to be quite relevant. It is to be noted in this context that higher capital formation in these sectors have been made at the cost of other developmental activities. With the meager allocation to industry and mineral sector one cannot expect any worthwhile industrialization in the State. There should be a balance between agriculture, industry, trade and service sector for bringing about all round economic development in the State.

Table-7 : Sectoral Plan Outlay in Arunachal Pradesh (Rs. in crores) since sixth five year plan

Plan Period	Agriculture & Allied	Industry & Minerals	Transport & communication	Energy	Services	Total
Sixth	78.52	10.26	56.10	-	67.12	212.00
(1980-85)	(37.04)	(4.84)	(26.46)		(31.66)	(100)
Seventh	118.05	9.50	127.15	36.90	108.40	400.00
(1985-90)	(29.51)	(2.38)	(31.79)	(9.22)	(27.10)	(100)
Eighth	264.38	24.49	343.93	151.96	370.24	1155.00
(1992-97)	(22.89)	(2.12)	(29.78)	(13.16)	(32.05)	(100)
Ninth	749.69	46.10	929.51	467.13	1377.46	3569.89
(1997-02)	(21.00)	(1.29)	(26.04)	(13.09)	(38.58)	(100)
DraftTenth	1100.79	82.57	1161.56	595.38	1686.70	4627.00
(2002-07)	(23.79)	(1.79)	(25.10)	(12.87)	(36.45)	(100)

Notes:(i)Agriculture and allied sector includes agriculture, rural development, special area program, irrigation and flood control, forestry and wild life. The service sector includes general economic services, social service, education, general services and science, technology and environment. (ii) Figures in the parentheses are the percentage of total

Source: Directorate of Planning and Development, Government of Arunachal Pradesh, Itanagar.

NATURAL RESOURCES IN ARUNACHAL PRADESH

In any judicious and rational planning resource survey is of fundamental importance. Natural resources exist in the environment as stock from which economic activity draws flows of inputs. Optimal utilization of natural resources is the pre-condition for sustained economic development of any region or country. The existence of vast resource base creates conditions for comparative cost advantage in economic activities. Arunachal Pradesh has a wide and varied natural resource. Since the days of NEFA administration attempts have been made to identify the resource base of this region. National council of applied economic Research (NCAER) in its techno-economic report (1967) identified forests and hydropower as two important resources in the region that have tremendous potential for development. However, the survey team felt that the region is not well endowed with mineral resources that can be effectively utilized for any worthwhile industrialization programme in the region (Datta, 1991). The exploitation of natural resources involves enormous initial investment. The cost of exploitation becomes exceptionally high if we include social and environmental cost associated with it. No cost benefit analysis has yet been undertaken in this state to estimate the available resources in value terms. Under the circumstances, we like to have a glance on the physical features of some of the important resources in Arunachal Pradesh

LAND

Arunachal Pradesh is basically a hilly State, only a very small proportion of its geographical area is plain. Exactly 3.35 thousand hectares, which constitutes around 4 per cent of the total geographical area, is plain. Out of total geographical area of about 84 thousand square kilometers, 70 per cent constitutes broad and narrow valleys, 10 per cent foot hills and flat areas and remaining 20 per cent constitutes snow clad peak area. The area of agricultural operation confined to only 4.18 per cent of the total geographical area (Govt. of Arunachal Pradesh, 2000). The reported area for land utilization was 54950 sq. km in 1995-96, which constituted around 66 per cent of the total geographical area. Out of which 94 per cent was under forest cover and only 3.37 per cent was under net sown area (Basic Statistics, NER 2000, p.32). However, the percentage of net sown area to total operational area tended to show a rising trend. In 1970-71, 23.56 per cent of the total operated area was under net-sown area that increased to 28.29 per cent in 1976-77, 35.19 per cent in 1980-81, 43.37 per cent in 1985-86 and further to 47.33 per cent in 1990-91.This was made possible mainly through the reclamation of culturable wasteland. Over the years, a substantial proportion of culturable wasteland was brought under cultivation. The culturable wasteland, which was 30.41 per cent in 1970-71 declined to only 9.43 per cent in 1990-91(Basic Statistics NER, 2000).

Two types of agriculture are prevalent in Arunachal Pradesh: shifting cultivation or slash-and-burn method of cultivation which is locally known as jhumming; and the permanent cultivation. Because of the high environmental costs associated with shifting cultivation, efforts have been made by the government to wean away the farmers from shifting cultivation to permanent cultivation. Due to sustained efforts made in this direction, the net sown area under permanent cultivation has steadily increased in the State. In 1970-71, 75.69 per cent of the net sown area was under jhumming remaining 24.31 percent was under permanent cultivation. However, the situation changed significantly in 1990-

91 during which around 56 per cent of the net sown area was under permanent cultivation and the remaining 44 per cent was under jhumming.

Per-capita availability of land resource is an important policy variable. In Arunachal Pradresh, because of the smaller size of population the per capita availability of land is high and above the national average. In 1970-71, the per capita availability of usable land in Arunachal Pradesh was 0.93 hectares. It declined continuously in all subsequent Agricultural censuses and reached to 0.31 hectares in 1990-91. The land-man ratio of Arunachal Pradesh is still much higher than the all India average of 0.23 hectares. In fact, Arunachal Pradesh occupied 4th position in northeast India in terms of per capita availability of land next to Mizoram, Meghalaya, and Nagaland (Bhattacharya, 2000). However, compared to its total geographical area, per capita availability of agricultural land in Arunachal Pradesh is low because of its hilly terrain and a vast area of land is under forest cover. With limited agricultural land and rising population, operational holding in the state has tended to show a declining trend.

Table-8 : Per-capita availability of Agricultural Land in Arunachal Pradesh (in hectares)

Year	Available land for use ('000')	Population ('000')	Land per-capita
1970-71	433	468	0.93
1976-77	326	566	0.58
1980-81	246	632	0.39
1985-86	267	727	0.37
1990-91	263	865	0.31

Note: Total land available for use has been estimated by adding net sown area, current fallow, fallow other than current fallow and culturable wasteland.

Source: *Agricultural 1990-91*, Extracted from table 2-13.3 P.4, Agricultural Census Division, Department of Agricultural, Arunachal Pradesh

In 1970-71, the average size of operational holding in Arunachal Pradesh was 6.19 hectares, it declined continuously in all the successive Agricultural Censuses and reached to 3.71 hectares in 1990-91.Moreover, during the 20 years period from 1970-71 to 1990-91, there was significant fragmentation in agricultural landholdings.

The number of small and marginal holdings (area less than 2 hectares), which was 19.63 per cent of total agricultural land holdings in 1970-71, increased to 36.25 per cent in 1990-91.The small size of holding is economically unviable. It acts as a hindrance to agricultural mechanization and so incapable to generate agricultural surplus.

FOREST

Arunachal Pradesh is rich in forest resources. The state covers only 0.11 per cent of the population while its geographical area constitutes 2.5 per cent of total area of the country. As high as 61.55 per cent of the total geographical area of the state is under forest cover as against 22.8 per cent for the country as a whole. Total forest cover of the state is 51540 sq. km, which is largest among the states of North East India and second highest among the states of India only next to Madhya Pradesh(Forest Statisticse,(2000-2001).

According to legal status, there are seven fold classification of forests in Arunachal Pradesh. The estimate of the latest forest statistics is shown in table-9 below.

Table-9 : Legal forest Status in Arunachal Pradesh-2000-2001

Sl. No.	Legal Classification	Area (sq.km.)	% of recorded forest	% of geographical area
1	Reserved forest	9722.69	18.86	11.61
2	Protected forest	694.30	1.35	0.82
3	Anchal Reserve forest	329.38	0.64	0.39
4	Village forest	300.24	0.58	0.36
5	National Parks	2468.24	4.79	2.94
6	Wild life sanctuary	7059.75	13.70	8.43
7	Unclassified State forest	30965.39	60.08	36.90
	Total	51540.00	100	61.55

Source: Forest Statistics, 2000-2001, Department of Environment and Forest, Itanagar Arunachal Pradesh.

For the scientific management and sustainable use of forest produce, around 19 per cent of the forest cover of the State has been brought under the category of reserve forests. The unclassed state forest constitutes the highest 60.08 per cent of the total forest area of the State. Only 0.64 per cent of the forest cover is under Anchal Reserve forest. National Park and Wildlife Sanctuary together constitutes 18.49 per cent of the total forest cover of the State.

As per the satellite imaginary data, the forest cover of the State is much higher than what has been reported in the forest statistics. One such estimate conducted by FSI, Derhradun. As per the assessment in 1999, the total forest area of the State is 68,847 sq.km, which constitutes 82.21 per cent of the total geographical area. Out of total forest area, 83.89 per cent accounts for dense forests while the remaining 16.11 per cent under open forests. By occupying 10.80 per cent of the total forest cover, Arunachal Pradesh ranked second among the States of India next to Madhya Pradesh, which covered 20.71 per cent of total forest area of the country.

The per capita availability of forest area is significantly higher in Arunachal Pradesh compared to the national average of only 0.12 hectares. In Arunachal Pradesh the per capita availability of forest area is 6.31 hectares (Forest Statistics, 2000-2001). This high per capita availability of forest area is mainly due to the low population size in the State. With a geographical area of 83,743 sq.km, the density of population is only 13, which is lowest in the country (Census, 2001). It is interesting to note that under Inner Line Regulation Act 1873 which is still in operation in the state, no migrant people have any rights in the natural resources-land, forest etc. Therefore, an average autochthons of this state enjoys around 9.91 hectares of forest area[5]. This figure is one of the highest in the country.

Forest is an important source of revenue in the State. In 1992-93, the forest revenue contributed 66.34 per cent of the state revenue while the plan allocation to forestry sector was only 4.06 per cent. During 1992-93 to 1995-96, forest sector alone contributed on an average 60 per cent of the state revenue per annum. Thereafter there was a sudden decline of forest revenue in 1997-98; from 60.81 per cent in 1996-97 to only 18.15 percent in 1997-98.This sudden decline is mainly due to the imposition of a ban on the extraction of forest and forest production by the Supreme Court in 1996. It is also evident from the table that in the recent years of along with the decline of forest revenue, the plan outlay of the forest sector tended to show a declining trend. This is really a cause for concern. This trend needs to be altered, and fund allocation in the forestry sector must be increased substantially so that more investment in forestry sector could be made to increase the productivity of forests.

Table-10 : Forest Revenue and Plan Outlay in Arunachal Pradesh

Year	Revenue (in lakh)	% of State Revenue	Forest Plan Outlay	% of State Plan
1990-1991	2157.95	NA	674.35	4.00
1991-1992	2594.48	NA	862.12	4.16
1992-1993	2847.79	66.34	956.00	4.06
1993-1994	3964.54	66.37	996.00	3.77
1994-1995	3488.77	49.96	1182.00	3.55
1995-1996	4904.39	72.18	1377.79	3.14
1996-1997	2523.60	60.81	1271.00	2.78
1997-1998	753.17	18.15	1471.00	2.86
1998-1999	1243.47	39.96	1071.00	2.31
1999-2000	1544.17	34.18	1572.00	3.12
2000-2001	1299.72	NA	1093.50	1.70

Source: Forest Statistics, 2000-2001, Department of Environment and Forest, Itanagar, Arunachal Pradesh

HYDRO-ELECTRIC POWER

Arunachal Pradesh is considered to be the storehouse of huge hydroelectric power potential of the county. Almost all major rivers of the State are perennial and most of them provide ample scope of hydroelectric power. There are various estimates of hydroelectric power potential in Arunachal Pradesh. It is estimated that out of 84044 MW (at 60 pr cent load factor) hydropower potential of the country, 26747 MW i.e. 32 per cent is available in Arunachal Pradesh(Draft tenth five year plan document, p.58). This figure is 30,000 M.W as per State Government's estimate (Economic Review, 1999) and 27000 M.W as per the estimates of Tata Consultancy Service (p.68). Arunachal Pradesh occupies top most position in the country in terms of hydroelectric potential (TCS-1997, P.3-2). The total hydropower potential available in the State is estimated to be one third of the entire hydro potential of the country. If a part of the available hydro-power potential is explored, the State will not only be self sufficient in fulfilling the power requirement of the state but at the same time it can take care of the power demand of the entire region. Thus, "the hydropower potential of the State offers not just local opportunities but a promise of national solution and wider regional prosperities through inter-country grid connection and exchange" (Shukla Commission Report, 1997).

In spite of the immense potentiality of hydroelectric power, only a small part of it has been tapped so far. The low harness rate in the State is mainly due to three reasons: (i)

hydropower project is capital intensive in nature. Harnessing of hydel power potential requires a huge capital investment;(ii) steep hilly topography and inaccessible terrain act as deterrents to undertake any major hydel power plant in the state; (iii) Arunachal Pradesh falls under seismically high sensitive zone. The setting up of hydel projects requires construction of large dams. There is a possibility of considerable submerger and displacement associated with the establishment of hydroelectric power plant. It is estimated that at the beginning of the tenth plan the total power demand of the State will be of the order of 94 MW. As of now there are 43 small hydel projects with an aggregate installed capacity of 32.12 MW (the most important among them are Tago(4,500KW), Mai I & II (3,000KW), Dirang(2000KW), Dibang Vally (1350KW), Yambung(2000KW), Along(1200KW), Lohit(1000KW), Khonsa(1000KW)).Thus, shortfall at the beginning of Tenth Plan is around 62 MW. Currently this shortfall is partially met through diesel generation (9.68) and partly by importing power (about 22 MW) from Central sector generating projects located in other states of North East. Arunachal Pradesh is badly placed in terms of installed capacity and power generation. Tata Consultancy Services placed Arunachal Pradesh at 20th position among the states of India in terms of power-installed capacity. In 1999-2000, total installed capacity in hydel electric power was 30.57 MW.

Table-11 : Source- wise Installed and Generated Capacity of Electricity in Arunachal Pradesh

Year	Installed capacity (M.W)			Generated (M.U)		
	Total	Hydel	Diesel	Total	Hydel	Diesel
1993-94	39.35	23.55	15.80	60.10	48.35	11.75
1994-95	39.53	23.65	15.88	68.53	50.81	17.72
1995-96	48.88	23.83	25.05	66.67	49.77	16.90
1996-97	48.88	23.83	25.05	88.55	68.55	20.00
1997-98	53.88	23.83	30.05	89.29	69.25	20.04
1998-99	55.51	30.74	24.77	66.89	54.35	12.54
1999-2000	65.57	30.57	35.00	62.21	52.10	10.11
Total change (1993-94 to 1999-2000)	26.22	7.02	19.20	2.11	3.75	-1.64
Percentage change (1993-94 to 1999-2000)	66.63	29.81	120.52	3.51	7.76	-13.96

Source: *Statistical abstrat*,2000, p. 55, Directorate of Economics and Statistics, Government of Arunachal Pradesh.

Out of total power installed capacity of 65.57 MW, diesel power accounts for 35.00 MW which is around 53 per cent of the total installed capacity in 1999-2000. The installed capacity of hydel power in the State has increased by 30 per cent during 1993-94 to 1999-2000. While the installed capacity of diesel power has increased significantly from 15.80 MW in 1993-94 to 35.00 MW in 1999-2000, the increase is about 121 per cent during the period. Further, table-11 indicates that the consumption of electricity has been increasing steadily in the State. Total power installed capacity and generating capacity has increased by 66.63 per cent and 3.51 per cent respectively during seven years period 1993-1994 to 1999-2000.

In recent years the state government has emphasized on the development of hydro-power sector, which has taken a firm footing by the setting up of National Hydro electric Power Corporation (NHPC), the North Eastern Electrical Power Corporation (NEEPCO) and the Brahmaputra Board in the State . The Ranganadi project being built by NEEPCO and NHPC on the right bank of Dikrong river, which is on the verge of completion, is expected to be generated 405 MW of electricity. With the completion of this project Arunachal Pradesh will become a surplus state in generating hydel power. Moreover, the State has undertaken a number of new projects to harness its vast hydroelectric potential.

Table-12 : Ongoing and New Hydel Projects in Arunachal Pradesh

Projects	Capacity(MW)	Total Costs (in crores)
Ongoing		
Ranganadi Phase-I	405	920
New		
Kameng	600	1,785
New Subansiri	7,300	16,435
Noa Dihang (cascade)	20,000	31,215
Ranganadi, Phase-II	100	544
Dikron	100	298
Domwe	520	2200
Total	29,025	53,397

Source : Shukla Commission Report(1997). Extracted from annexure table-8, p.76A

With the persistent efforts of the State Government, the Central Government has approved the first feasibility report submitted by NHPC on Middle Siang(1000MW), Middle Subansiri(1600 MW), Upper Subansiri(2000 MW) and Lower subansiri(2000) hydro power projects. Construction of these projects will start during the Tenth Plan period and scheduled to be commissioned by the end of the Eleventh Plan. For construction of Ranganadi Hydro Electrical Project Phase II of 100 MW, a MoU was signed with the NEEPCO and the project would be commissioned during the Eleventh Plan period. Moreover, NEEPCO has been entrusted to undertake survey and investigation works on Kameng river, Tawang river and Pare river in Papumpare district. The Brahmaputra Board has also been entrusted to start survey and investigation works on Lohit, Noa dihang and Tirap river basins.

MINERALS

Minerals occupy a position of strategic importance from the point of view of planning for economic development. The mineral resource deposits of the State have not yet been fully assessed. Preliminary survey and studies conducted by the Geological Survey of India and other various organizations like Oil India Limited; Mineral Exploration Corporation Limited etc. have indicated the occurrences of rich mineral resources in Arunachal Pradesh. But, till date this state is geologically least explored. For scientific exploration and utilization of mineral wealth of the State, a Mineral Development and Trading Corporation (APDMTC) has been set up in the State in 1991. Moreover, for exploitation of mineral resources, the State Government has created a Department of Geology and Mining in the year 1995. There are large varieties of minerals that exist in the natural environment of Arunachal Pradesh. The total value of mineral production in Arunachal Pradesh was Rs. 11 crores in 1994-95 registered a decline of 30 per cent compared to Rs. 16 crores in the previous year. Petroleum (crude) accounted for 99 per cent of value of mineral production in Arunachal Pradesh in 1994-95. Coal, dolomite, limestone, graphite, marble, oil and natural gas, lead, zink and other minerals occur in the State. Important minerals, their reserves and locations are given in appendix table-III. Remote location of the mineral deposits and lack of infrastructures hamper the development of State's mineral sector. The harnessing of potential requires heavy capital investment. Many of the mineral reserves are under forest cover and commercial exploitation of these may affect the fragile economic system of the State adversely.

HUMAN RESOURCES

Human resource generally means total quantitative and qualitative human aspects in a society. The term human resource development may be defined as a process of organizing and enhancing the physical, mental and emotional capabilities of individuals for productive works. An efficient and satisfied workforce is the main significant factor in organizational effectiveness and managerial excellence and so a deciding factor in economic development.

POPULATION TREND

As per Census 2001, the total population of Arunachal Pradesh is 10.91 lakhs. The decadal growth rate of population has come down from 36.83 per cent in 1981-91 to 26.21 per cent in 1991-2001.Along with the growth rate of population, the percentage of tribal population has been declined steadily over the decades; it has declined from 88.67 per cent in 1961 to 63.66 per cent in 1991. Sex ratio, on the other hand, is an important aspect of population characteristics. It has an important bearing upon socio-economic status of people. There is a considerable improvement in sex ratio in the State in 2001 with 901 females per 1000 males as against 859 in 1991.

Table-13 : Growth of Population, Density and Literacy Rate in Arunachal Pradesh: 1961-2001

Year	Population (in Lakhs)	%of Tribal Population	Decadal growth rate (%)	Literacy Male	Literacy Female	Literacy Person	Sex ratio (per '000' male)	Density (per sq. km.)
1961	3.37	88.67	-	12.24	1.42	7.23	894	04
1971	4.68	79.02	38.91	17.82	3.71	11.29	861	06
1981	6.32	69.82	35.15	28.94	11.32	20.79	862	08
1991	8.65	63.66	36.83	51.10	29.37	41.59	859	10
2001	10.91	NA*	26.21	64.07	44.24	54.74	901	13

Note: *figure for 2001 is not yet available.

Source: Census of India, 1961,1971,1981,1991and provisional population total of 2001 Census.

LITERACY RATE AND EDUCATION

Education is an important component of human resource. It is considered as a kind of capital i.e. a stock, embodied in human beings that will yield the future income stream. It is, in fact, a sound investment in man. The modern education is a post independence phenomenon in Arunachal Pradesh. At the time of independence formal education was almost unknown to the indigenous people of the State. There were only two primary schools in the entire state prior to 1947 and the literacy rate was almost negligible. However, with the successive plan efforts, Government made significant progress in the spread of education in Arunachal Pradesh. Educational institutions, mainly schools, were established, funded and nurtured by the Government. In effect, educational institutions grew at a very fast rate in the State. There are as many as 1849 educational institutes including one University and a Technical Institute in the State as on 31.03.2000 (Govt. of Arunachal Pradesh, 2000). During the last forty years, the literacy rate of the State has increased more than 7.5 times from 7.23 per cent in 1961 to 54.74 percent in 2001. There is no doubt that the State has achieved tremendous success in education sector. Still, the literacy rate in Arunachal Pradesh is much below the all India average of 65.38 per cent. One of the reasons for low level of literacy in the state is the high dropout rate at the primary level. To combat this problem government has undertaken a number of incentive schemes like free supply of textbooks, school uniforms, providing hostel facilities etc. Government's efforts have led to a gradual decline of dropout rate in the state. The primary dropout rate in the State that was as high as 66.14 per cent in 1984-85 has declined to 49.50 per cent in 1998-99.

TECHNICAL SKILLS

In Arunachal Pradesh institutional facilities for technical education is very poor. North Eastern Regional Institute for Science and Technology (NERIST) established in 1986 is the only major institute in the State for imparting training in technical education. Apart from NERIST there are only a few Institutes in the State e.g. the Rural Industrial Development Centre at Dirang in West Kameng, Industrical Training Institutes (ITI) at Roing and Taborijo for imparting training in technical education. Trades like draughtmenship, TV/radio repairing, secretarial practices, blacksmithy, tinsmithy, automobile servicing, welding etc. are being taught in these institutes. There are no institutes in the State to study the technical disciplines like medicine, veterinary, pisciculture, etc. Since 1991 to 1999, 2798 students have been sent to other States to study various technical disciplines like Medicine (363), Agriculture (232), Veterinary (117), Horticulture (4), Enginee-ring (2050, both for degree and diploma), Pisciculture (7) and Handloom technology and Sericulture (25)(Government of Arunachal Pradesh, 1999).

TRADITIONAL SKILLS

Most of the tribes in the State have expertise in the manufacture of various handloom and handicrafts items. The major items for traditional handicrafts are- (i) Weaving, (ii) Cane and bamboo works (iii) Pottery, (iv) Black smithy, (v) Metal and ivory works and (vi) Wood carving and carpentry etc. (Das, 1995). These traditional skills of the indigenous people are considered to be an important aspect of human resources of the State.

INDUSTRIAL STRUCTURE IN ARUNACHAL PRADESH

Arunachal Pradesh is one of the industrially backward States in India. The State has a very unique industrial structure; it has no heavy industry and no large industrial structure. Since Independence, industrial activities in the state are mainly concentrated to the small scale village and cottage industries. In the whole State there are only 18 medium scale industries, out of them, 13 are located in three districts namely Lohit, Changland and Tirap. Almost all the medium scale industries are forest resource based e.g. saw mills, veneer mills, plywood industry etc. In the industrial structure of cottage and small scale units, crafts and sericulture constitute main activities of trades. The people of Arunachal Pradesh have a tradition of artistic craftsmanship in a variety of crafts such as weaving, painting, smithy work, basket making, woodcarving etc. Handloom is a household occupation throughout the State. The major handloom products are carpet, galley, jacket, shawl, galuk, wall hanging, cane hat etc. There are 4694 registered village and small scale industrial units in the State, out of them, only 1764 units are operative (Government of Arunachal Pradesh, 2000).

The existing industries in Arunachal Pradesh can broadly be classified into eight categories: (i) weaving and textile, (ii) wood & wood products (iii) trade (iv) services (v) Printing (vi) engineering (vii) agro-based & (viii) mineral based industries (TCS, 1997). Weaving and textile include weaving centers, knitting centers and small garment making centers, these centers fulfill the local demand for weaving & textile. The wood and wood based industries comprises manufacturing of furniture, plywood from veneer etc. On the other hand, photocopier shops, photographic studio's and other small shops constitute the sub-sector of trade industries. Service related industries form another important sub-sector. It comprises repairs mostly motor repairs, and services of transport operators. The important sub-sector is agro-based industries. It comprises fruit processing units and rice de-husking units. The engineering industries include forging and moulding industries. They also include wire fabrication units and wire drawing units. Industries based on minerals mostly include stone crushing, bricks making, candle making and cement manufacturing. The sectoral analysis of investment as presented in table-14 reveals that wood and wood based product category attracts highest level of investment (53.25 per cent) followed by service sub-sector (16.53 per cent), agro-based industries (13.21 per cent) and mineral based industries (7.15). Other sectors attract small proportion of investment for industrial activities.

SMALL SCALE INDUSTRIAL DEVELOPMENT IN ARUNACHAL PRADESH

Ever since the planning era, the efforts of the government were mainly confined to the promotion of traditional handicrafts, handloom and village and cottage industries. With the sustain efforts of the Government, the small Scale and cottage industry achieved significant growth in the State of Arunachal Pradesh. In order to asses the performance of the small scale industries we have considered three basic parameters- the number of units, employment and total annual production over three points of time during 1990 to 2000. The changes that have occurred over the time in each of these in Arunachal Pradesh are recorded in table -15. The table shows that (i) the number of SSI units has risen over the years; as compared to 1990, the number has increased more than eleven times in 2000; (ii) total annual production has also registered a continuous increase; as compared to its level in 1995, it has increased almost five times in 2000; (iii) as compared to 1990, total employment of SSI units has increased a little more four times in 2000;

Table-14 : Sector and District wise Distribution of Investment in Arunachal Pradesh

(in lakhs)

Districts	Weaving & Textiles	Wood & Wood Products	Trade	Services	Printing	Engine-ering	Agro Based	Mineral Based	Total
Lower Subansiri	1.67	82.33	1.50	17.91	4.82	38.63	84.49	3.00	235.35
West Siang	1.20	26.50	2.00	4.00	2.70	15.20	30.00	5.00	86.60
Dibang Valley	-	55.15	-	1.14	-	-	4.16	-	60.45
East Kameng	-	246.05	-	162.47	1.89	12.31	-	58.49	481.21
Tawang	-	-	-	8.45	1.20	2.30	3.92	-	15.87
West Kameng	2.50	49.53	2.41	4.51	-	7.76	15.30	10.70	92.71
Changlang	-	179.84	-	-	2.42	17.91	19.74	8.71	228.62
Total	5.37	639.40	5.91	198.48	13.03	94.11	158.61	85.90	1200.81

Source: Tata Consultancy Service (1997), *Perspective Plan for Arunachal Pradesh* Phase- II, Table No. 4.3, p. 4-4.

(iv) the average size of employment per SSI unit has declined over the years; it has declined from about nine persons per unit in 1990 to about four persons in 1995 and further declined to three persons per unit in 2000[6]; (v) SSI units are mainly concentrated in four districts namely Lower Subansiri, East Siang, Lohit, and Papumpare.

It is to be noted that significant percentile change as observed in the number of registered units, in employment and in total value of production of SSI units is mainly due to the low base values. Being the major industrial activities of the State, the growth of SSI units cannot be treated as impressive one. Among the small scale industrial activities in the state, sericulture and handicrafts together comprise the major industrial activity. Four important varieties of silk are produced in the State: Mulberry, Eri, Muga and Oak Tasar. In 1999-2000, there are 27 sericulture demonstration centers in the state including 222 sericulture village and 20 reeling units. In terms of number of rearers, the silk variety Eri occupies first place (3620), followed by Mulberry (1394), Muga (125) and Oak Tasar (30). Moreover, Arunachal Pradesh is having rich heritage of traditional handloom and handicraft activities. In 1999-2000 there are 88 crafts centers in the State. During last thirty years, the annual out-turn of craft centers was raised at an average annual rate of 23.81 pr cent from Rs. 3.49 lakh in 1970-71 to Rs. 27.59 lakhs in 1999-2000. The sale proceeds of Emporium and Showroom cum Sales Counter have increased at an annual rate of 34.14 per cent from its very low level of Rs. 2.89 lakhs in 1970-71 to 31.50 lakhs in 1999-2000.

AGRICULTURAL AND NON-AGRICULTURAL ENTERPRISES

The Directorate of Economics and Statistics, Government of Arunachal Pradesh so far conducted four Economic Censuses (1977, 1980, 1990 and 1998). These census reports reveal the structure and characteristics of the agricultural and non-agriculture enterprises in Arunachal Pradesh. Agriculture enterprises are those engaged in any of the activities relating to livestock production, agricultural services, trapping and game propagation, forestry, logging & fishing. While, the non agricultural enterprises are those which are engaged in any of the activities pertaining to (i) mining and quarrying (ii) manufacturing (iii) electricity, gas & water (iv) construction (v) whole sale trade (vi) retail trade (vii) restaurants & hotel (viii) transport (ix) storage and ware housing (x) communication (xi) financial insurance, real estate, and business services (xii) community, social and personal services and (xiv) other activities. As per Fourth Economic Census, 1998, there are altogether 20,69 enterprises in the sample. Out of which 200 i.e. 0.97 per cent are engaged in agricultural activities while the remaining 20,493 i.e. 99.03 per cent are engaged in non-agricultural activities. Moreover, out of total employment of 80,536 persons, 733 persons (i.e. 0.91 per cent) are engaged in the agricultural sector while remaining 79,803 persons (i.e. 99.09 per cent) are usually working in non-agricultural sector. So far as activitywise participation of enterprises is concerned, the highest participation is observed in the activity group retail trade having 44.85 per cent (9190 in numbers) followed by the activity group community, social and personal services having 32.56 per cent (6672 in numbers). The lowest participation is found in the activity group mining and quarrying being only 0.11per cent (3 in numbers).

Table-15 : Growth of Small scale Industries in Arunachal Pradsh

Districts	No. of Units Registered as on			Total No. of Employment		Total annual production		(Rs. In lakh)
	31.3.1990	31.3.1995	31.3.2000	31.3.1990	31.3.1995	31.3.2000	31.3.1995	31.3.2000
Tawang	10	92	223	23	428	709	3.20	235.47
West Kameng	23	216	169	228	641	622	5.84	294.52
East Kameng	2	92	145	64	105	345	11.80	131.91
Papumpare	-	244	1088	-	1501	3968	350.00	3334.04
Lower Subansiri	57	485	667	470	1000	114	1.00	128.09
Upper Subansiri	12	160	213	93	150	480	15.00	37.01
West siang	64	370	260	545	425	1160	120.39	541.21
East Siang	39	324	481	330	1275	1095	70.50	3094.91
Upper siang		21	132		75	245	10.00	850.91
Dibang Valley	77	322	250	443	1767	602	656.59	1478.38
Lohit	93	441	477	690	2177	1841	1185.70	2103.06
Changlang	22	123	283	476	2000	2056	580.00	3145.05
Tirap	16	256	306	249	761	1801	712.10	2212.88
Arunachal Pradesh	415	3146	4694	3611	12305	15038	3722.12	17586.92

Source: Statistical Abstract, 1990,1995,2000, Directorate of Economic and Statistics, Government of Arunachal Pradesh

PUBIC SECTOR INITIATIVES TO INDUSTRIALISATION IN ARUNACHAL PRADESH: A TESTIMONY OF FAILURE

In the first two and half decades after independence, the Government of Arunachal Pradesh did not take any major initiative for industrial development in the state. Efforts for industrialization initiated only in 1970's. However, due to its geographical location, poor physical infrastructure, under developed markets and demand constraints, the State could not attract much private investment for her industrialization; the public sector had to play the leading role in this regard. Public sector initiatives so far undertaken for industrialization in the State can broadly be divided into two groups: State sponsored schemes and programs and Centrally sponsored schemes and programs[7].

Among the State sponsored programs, the first bold step towards industrialization has been the establishment of Arunachal Pradesh Forest Corporation (APFC) in 1977 under the Company Act, 1955. Since its inception APFC has undertaken a number of industrial ventures e.g. establishment of saw mills, veneering mills, Plywood industries etc. In the field of cash crop cultivation, the corporation raised coffee plantation, cardamom plantation and tea plantation. However, almost all the industrial units set up by APFC (of course, excepting a few) are reported to have been running under loss in recent years. The situation has become worse after the Supreme Court's Verdict on December 12, 1996 imposing restrictions on the exploitation of timber and timber products. Many forest based industries established by APFC have forced to closed down due to recurring loses in recent years.

The boldest step towards industrialization was the establishment of Arunachal Pradesh Industrial Development and Finance Corporation (APIDFC) in 1978.This Corporation was established with a view to act as a catalytic agent of industrialization by extending finance to small scale entrepreneurs, organizing training program for skill formation & entrepreneurial development and developing marketing network. APIDFC directly established a number of medium sized plants: a cement plant, a T.V assembling plant, a roof sheet unit, a printing press, a furniture unit, a raw material bank and a few others. However, due to the absence of any financial discipline, commercial competitiveness, undeveloped marketing network, unskilled workforce etc. APIDFC failed to function efficiently to achieve the desired goals. In effect, a number of industrial ventures undertaken by APIDFC started yielding negative balance and subsequently some of these plants became economically unviable and forced to close down like Mini Cement Plant at Tezu, Arunachal Pradesh Horticultural Processing Industries Limited (APHPIL) at Nigmoi etc.

Over the years due to recurring loses, all the public sector Corporations namely APFC, APIDFC and APDMTC, which were to play the pioneering role in the industrial development of the State, have been reeling under the burden of heavy financial debt. They have lost their effectiveness and created huge liabilities to the Government. As a result, in a restructuring move, the Government of Arunachal Pradesh in a Cabinet meeting on May 31, 2002 decided to close down all these three Corporations[8]. It is reported that APFC was having maximum Rs. 9.9 crores negative balance, APIDFC having 57 lakhs and APMDTC Rs. 1400 negative balance (Arunachal Times, June1, 2002). This decision of closing down all the three Corporations marked an end of the well-planned vision of industrial development through public sector undertakings in the State of Arunachal Pradesh. It is to be noted in this context that in a counter move the employees of all these three Corporations had gone to the court for justice against the Cabinet decisions. Till date the matter is under judicial verification, and all the three Corporations are still operative in the State.

In view of the unsatisfactory performance of the public sector units, the Government of Arunachal Pradesh announced the New Industrial Policy 2001 with a new thrust to industrialization: "(i) the state government will encourage the establishment of industrial undertakings in the private and co-operative sectors for the sustainable development of the state. (ii) investors from outside the state will be encouraged to invest in the State. Hundred percent equity ownership of an industrial unit by entrepreneurs will be allowed for a maximum period of thirty years by the end of which, such equity holding will be reduced to 49 per cent, the remaining 51 per cent will be held by local Arunachal tribal entrepreneur or a group of local entrepreneurs or the state government, if it considers necessary to do so. (iii) outside entrepreneurs may be allowed to hold land on lease for a period of thirty years, after which the lease may be renewed for a further period of thirty years. (iv) development of all kinds of industries will be encouraged. To begin with, the following industries will have priority: (a) industries based on agriculture, horticultural and plantation produce; (b) industries based on locally available raw materials; (c) textile (handlooms and power looms) and handicrafts;(d) electronics and knowledge based industries;(e) industries based on non-timber forest produce; and (f) infrastructure such as power and communication"(Industrial Policy, 2001).

RESOURCE-INDUSTRY INTERLINKAGES

Several studies have been conducted so far to assess the natural resource endowment and industrial potential in Arunachal. The studies by NCEAR (1967), TCS (1997), IIE (1996) have identified several resource base industries that would have tremendous potential for development in the State. The broad industrial categories as identified by these study groups are:

(i) agro-based industries such as agricultural processing industries.
(ii) industries based on forest, horticulture and plantation
(iii) commercial production of hydro-electricity
(iv) mineral based industries &
(v) development of tourism industry.

However, there is a big gap between potential industrial options and actual achievements in the State of Arunachal Pradesh. In spite of having tremendous potential for resource based industrialization, Arunachal Pradesh is one of the least industrialized States in India. One of the reasons may be that Arunachal Pradesh has started late in the process of planned economic development. The first industrial policy aiming at all-round industrial development has come only in 1994. The New industrial policy 2001, which is under operation, is the second in the row.

There are several dimensions to inter-sectoral resource flows. The direction and magnitude of resource flows between agricultural and non-agriculture is an important determinant of the pattern of development. Agriculture is the pre-dominant economic activity in the State. Agriculture and industry are expected to act complementary to each other for overall development of the economy. Agriculture and industry linked most obviously through the provision by former to the latter of surplus at the beginning of the development process. Agricultural productivity and surplus generating capacity of the state is low. As a result, agricultural input supplying and output using industries have not come up in the State. There is a dire necessity of agricultural resource base industries in the State. The poor linkage between agriculture and industrial activity has led to slow down the overall rate of growth of the economy.

The broad pattern of industrialization in the State has been the mere extension of forest extraction activities. Out of 18 medium scale industries in the state barring three (one mini cement plant at Tezu, one horticulture processing industry at Nigmoi, and a tea industry at Pasighat) all the fifteen medium scale industries are forest resource based like saw mills, veneering mills and plywood industry. After the imposition of ban imposed by Supreme Court, the prospect of forest based industries received a serious set back; a number of saw mills and veneering mills have closed down in recent years. The lone mineral based cement industry at Tezu had a life span of only eleven years. It was sick and running under lose and finally closed down in 1995.The horticulture processing industry, which was established in 1982, also shut down in 1995. Other than forest based industry, resource based manufacturing activities in the State include stone crushing, flour milling, candle manufacturing, aromatic oil extraction, and agro-processing.

The geo-climatic condition of the state is conducive for the development of horticultural products. But, the horticultural product based industries like orange squash, pineapple squash and slices, canned mushroom and bamboo shoots, jam-jelly, dried ginger and ginger powder, spices floricultural and horticultural garden, tissue culture etc, did not make much headway in Arunachal Pradesh.

Tourism has been declared as an industry in the State. With picturesque landscape, turbulent rivers, deep gorges and lofty mountains, snow-clad peaks, thousand of species of flora and fauna, Arunachal Pradesh presents ample scope for the development of tourism industry. There are a number of important tourist spots in the State like wild life sanctuaries at Namdapha, religious and historically important places like Tawang (Buddhist Monastry), Parasuram Kund (Tezu), Malinithan, the places of scenic beauty like Tawang, Bomdila and Tipi, adventurous tourist places like Along, Zero, Bhalukpong etc. Tourism industry in the State is still in the nascent stage. Infrastructure for the development of tourism industry like hotel, road, transport, communication, etc. has not yet been developed in the State. Only in the ninth plan the Government of Arunachal Pradesh has undertaken a comprehensive master plan for the development of tourism industry in the state.

Thus the State has failed to translate the vast resource base of the region into productive industrial activities. This has led to a very low efficiency of State resources and resource-industry interlinkage has been found to be very weak. The industrial activities in the State have been carried out without generating much forward and backward linkage in economic activities. The main constraints strangling industrial growth of the State are:

Infrastructural Facilities: One of the important constraints in the development of industries in Arunachal Pradesh has been an utter lack of infrastructural facilities like proper land, transport and communication, power, banking facilities, schooling, health and medical care etc. and a consequent absence of a proper investment climate in the State. In the absence of these, it becomes difficult to provide the necessary logistic support to industrial activities. The lack of these basic industrial infrastructures discourages entrepreneurs coming from outside.

The flow of Fund: The flow of investible fund in Arunachal Pradesh is very poor.

The availability of institutional finance to this sector has not been commensurate with their needs nor in proportion to the volume of activity generated by the sector. In fact, it is conceded that inadequate finance has been one of the major causes for industrial sickness in the State. The financial agencies are not coming up to finance industrial activities because of the poor recovery rate.

Technology: The state of industrial technology in Arunachal Pradesh is very poor. The development and application of technology appropriate to the local conditions has been very limited in Arunachal Pradesh. Identification of technology needs and delivery mechanisms for existing technology are virtually non-existent in the State. Entrepreneurs shy away from technologies that are high risk, not cost effective or that involve high transfer costs. It is to be noted here that local resource based small scale industries can survive only if they are in a position to meet the market demand, on the basis of technological efficiency and low costs.

Marketing infrastructure: Marketing has been considered as one of the critical constraints faced by the industrial units in Arunachal Pradesh. Arunachal economy is still in the transitional phase. Different communal economies of the state are in the process of integration with the market economy. The competitive and efficient market structure that is necessary for economically viable industrial activities is almost non-existence in the State. Moreover, marketing network with the neighboring States has not been developed much because of poor transport communication system. On the other hand, the size of the local market is very narrow in Arunachal Pradesh. The products are mainly produced to absorb the local demand. Any surplus generated in the process creates the problem of disposal. The marketing support given by the government and some government agencies has been found to be limited to only a few products like handlooms, handicraft and some of the products of village and khadi industries. However, the proportion of the produce marketed through these agencies is also very limited.

Inner line regulation: The British Policy of isolating the hill people from the plain, which was implemented through the Inner Line Regulation Act 1873, is still in operation in Arunachal Pradesh. The spirit of innerline regulation is that employment of migrants should be discouraged or at least minimized in Arunachal Pradesh. As an automatic corollary of Inner Line Regulation, is the restriction on the free flow of goods and services in Arunachal Pradesh. In the absence of locally available enterprising man-power, this regulation has in fact imposed restrictions to industrial activities in the Sate both by contracting factor as well as commodity markets. In the presence of Inner Line Regulation, the industries that require mainly migrant lobourers and marketing outside the State need to be discouraged.

Property Rights: The indigenous populations of Arunachal Pradesh have got the exclusive property rights in land. The outside entrepreneurs cannot purchase any land for industrial purpose. This type of land tenure system in Arunachal Pradesh is acting as a major obstacles to resource base industrialization in the State specially plantation based industries like horticulture etc. that requires large tracks of land. Unless the land laws for setting up industrial units are relaxed, industrialization in Arunachal Pradesh will continue to suffer.

Lack of Tribal Entrepreneurship: Entrepreneurship and skills so necessary for success in industrial ventures are mostly conspicuous by their absence in Arunachal Pradesh. With the growth of secondary and tertiary sectors of the economy some entrepreneurship has come into being, but non-locals or migrant people has provided a greater part of this entrepreneurship. Arunachalee element in the whole spectrum of entrepreneurship is very insignificant. Lack of education and training facilities for imparting technical and managerial sills have come in the way of development of local entrepreneurs. Moreover, the local people have shown a tendency not to face the competition of the market aggressively. They are risk avoider and hire out their license, building, machinery etc. to the outside entrepreneurs and they collect mainly the rent and interest. As a result most of the existing industrial and business venture are being operated by non-locals, but on paper they are owned by the tribals(Roy and Kuri, 1998).Only in recent years some local people started taking interests in business ventures and a neo-merchant class of local origin has tended to emerge in the State.

ROLE OF THE MARKET AND STATE

The proximity of market is an important pre-requisite to industrial development. Because of the late starter in the process of economic development, the market, an important institution of modern industrial societies is underdeveloped in Arunachal Pradesh. The lack of proper market infrastructure acts as a disincentive to the producers to generate any surplus production. The productions are organized mainly to fulfill the home demand or in accordance with the demand in the local markets. Any surplus generated in the process goes mostly waste as it cannot be marketed outside the locality due to poor transport and communication system. There are only few regulatory markets in the State. The market supporting infrastructure like cold storage, warehouses, godown etc. has not yet been developed in the state. Unless the marketing infrastructure is created the industrial sector will continue to remain undeveloped in the State.

There are many areas where the government should encourage investment and creation of markets. The importance of market has been multiplied in recent years because of the ongoing process of liberalization and globalization of the national economy. There cannot be anything like selective liberalization or partial globalization except when one wants to protect a preferred community. At least in the present state of the economy where a large number of people have been struck in the road to development, it is government's duty to attract the internal and external capital to energies the rural economy, aggressively penetrate the economy of the surrounding States and country, and keep competition on its main agenda. It must create opportunities for local people not only in terms of creating jobs but also in undertaking business venture.

Given the low level of entrepreneurship, underdeveloped marketing infrastructure and low skill base of the state, Government would have to play a pioneering role in fostering industrial growth in the State. For industrialization, the role of the Government can be of three folds: promotional role, developmental role and regulatory role. The promotional role is to be performed by the State by providing the various direct incentives, such as cash subsidies, tax concession, building of infrastructure, provision of financial assistance etc. and indirect incentives like provisions of an environment conducive for investment in the industrial sector. The developmental role includes the preparation of industrial policy, identification of thrust areas and announcement of incentive package to attract investment in the industrial sector. To overcome the industrial sickness, appropriate revival packages are to be effectively implemented to revitalize the industrial sector of the State. The Government should undertake entrepreneurship development programmes and provide technological training through establishment of industrial training institutes, polytechnices, and engineering colleges. It must also co-ordinate with banks and financial institutions to help entrepreneurs in getting loans and finances. As a regulator, the Government must apply rules so that industry does not conduct itself in a manner that is prejudicial to the interests of the society. The State needs to come forward to protect the interests of small investors and bankers by checking defaults and misappropriation of funds by the management of public and private sector companies.

THE CONCLUDING REMARKS

Agriculture is the dominant economic activity in Arunachal Pradesh. Even after more than thirty years of economic planning, the primary sector constitutes to claim substantial proportion of the workforce and income in Arunachal Pradesh. However, the structural transformation is found to be biased towards the development of secvice sector. In spite of having tremondous potential for resource-based industrialization, the secondary sector has failed to make any significant headway in the State. Notwithstanding the definite and determinant role that agriculture has in the process of economic development, it is to be borne in mind that industrialization alone can cause the creative structural disequilibrium necessary for achieving the higher level of output and employment. Economic development in the modern sense cannot be conceived without reference to industrialization that involves an inevitable shift away from the primary sector to the secondary and tertiary sectors. Since it is desirable to have a balanced development of both the primary and non-primary sectors in the process of economic development, it is necessary to develop the secondary sector deliberately so as to initiate and accelerate the structural change necessary for attaining higher level of development.

The State is endowed with rich natural resources, but is still economically underdeveloped. The State's efforts for resource-based industrialization have not been fructified into any noticeable success. The available vast potential of agriculture, horticulture, forest and hydel power demands a comprehensive approach for the creation of a climate conducive for industrial development in the State. However, as mentioned above, the industrial options of the State are constrained by many factors and the operational hindrances arising out of these constraints have brought about a situation of *low level equilibrium trap* in industrial activities. Under the circumstances, the Government will have to provide *a big push* to break this *trap*. For this, first of all, there is a need for sectoral adjustment in the State plan, more allocation are to be provided to the industrial sector. Only after the creation of necessary industrial infrastructure, the State will be able to attract the private investment for industrialization. The State's infrastruc-ture and resource endowment should be developed in areas comparatively better suited for investment. In the present state of the economy, if the Government does not play the instrumental role, the prospect of resource-based industrialization in the State will remain merely as a theoretical possibility for years to come.

Since independence the industrialization in the State has mainly been confined to the development of small scale village industries. The policies and programmes towards the development of these industries so far have been passive and protective. No thrust has been given on the modernization and diversifications of industrial activities. Initiatives for medium scale resource based industrialization have not been succeeded mainly due to the lack of industrial infrastructure and ineffective market forces. Moreover, industrial activities in the State have failed to generate much inter-sectoral linkages in economic activities. In effect, the State of Arunachal Pradesh has been passing through a prolonged phase of *industrial recession*. In view of the current industrial sickness of the State, the concerted efforts must be made by the government to improve the efficiency and productivity of the industrial units. This can be achieved by a series of measures that include, first and foremost, a revamping of management and management objectives. In the absence of private investment, the Government must act as a facilitator to the industrial development. In this context, it may be mentioned that three public sector Corporations namely APIDFC, APFC and APMDC are to be revived, restructured and provided with greater autonomy to undertake industrial venture in the State. On the other hand, the industrial policy of a State has a direct bearing upon the functioning as well as the growth of industries. The new industrial Policy 2001 provides a wide range of incentives aimed at promoting industrial growth in the State. Enhancement of supply of infrastructural facilities, establishment of more industrial estates etc. is commonly held priorities in the State. Initiatives have to be taken to shift the priority from physical domain to the institutional domain. Appropriate institutional reform can bring about economic efficiency in the use of resources and act as the most potent force of development in Arunachal Pradesh.

Notes

1. The contribution of agriculture to state income has steadily declined in Arunachal Pradesh (appendix table- II). On an average the contribution of agriculture to state income has declined at the rate of 0.26 percentage points per annum while the contribution of forestry declined at the rate of 0.48 percentage points.
2. In the secondary sector, manufacturing and construction are two main sub-sectors. The contribution of construction sub-sector to state income has declined at the insignificant rate of 0.04 percentage points. On the other hand, the contribution of manufacturing sub-sector to state income has increased at the insignificant rate of 0.15 percentage points per annum. As a result the contribution of the secondary sector tended to increase at the insignificant rate of 0.09 percentage point per annum over the 30 years period. Of course, there are decadal fluctuations to these results (appendix table-II).
3. In the tertiary sector, trade is an important sub-sector, which has grown at the significant rate of 0.10 percentage point per annum during 1970-71 to 1999-2000 (appendix table- II).
4. Clark (1940) and Fisher (1939) provided one of the earliest, but still persuasive hypothesis on the development of service sector. They argued that countries could be expected to move mainly from primary to secondary and secondary to service production during the period of economic development. Because high-income elasticities are associated with many service activities, it is argued that this sector only becomes large after the basic necessities of the primary sector are provided and most demand for manufacturing goods are satisfied. This process as come to be known as the Clark-Fisher hypothesis. However, many sectoral theorists including Bour and Kamey (1965) questioned the validity of the Clark-Fisher hypothesis. They argued that such generalization is erroneous and misleading. Arunachal Pradesh, for example, is a case where there has been overlapping development of the tertiary sector. Tertiary sector developed at a faster rate than the secondary sector during the period of structural change of the economy.
5. In the calculation of per capita forest resource in Arunachal Pradesh, satellite imaginary data for forest area has been used while population figure has been taken from the latest population census, 2001. While, in the calculation of per capita forest area of the autochthons, tribal population figure has been taken from census 1991. This is because final census report 2001

containing decomposition of total population into tribal and non-tribal category is yet to be published.

6. The size of the employment per unit has been calculated with respect to total registered small scale units. It is to be noted that at present more than fifty percent of these registered units are not functioning. So, the size of the employment per operative unit is much higher than that has been given in the text. For example, on 31.03.02, out of 4694 registered units, 1764 units are functioning with an average employment of nine persons per unit. But, one point is true that over the years the average size of employment per unit has shown a declining trend.

7. Two important centrally sponsored schemes that have been implemented in Arunachal Pradesh are: the establishment of Industrial Estates (IE) and District Industries Center (DIC). Industrial Estates have been established to attract new industries in the state since 1977-78. These IE's offer developed land, constructed sheds, power, developed road, banking facilities and other infrastructure that is essential to promote the establishment and growth industries. As on 31.03.2000, there are 14 industrial estates spreading over 10 districts of the State. In East Kameng, West Siang and Upper Siang there are no Industrial Estates. On the other hand, DIC's were introduced in the state in 1978 to assist tiny cottage and village industries. During the eighth plan this DIC scheme was transferred to the State. Apart from these two schemes, a number of other centrally sponsored schemes like Central Investment Subsidy Scheme, Central Transport Subsidy Scheme, Central Infrastructure Assistant Scheme, Establishment of Export Promotion Industrial Park, establishment of Colled Rolled Steel Plan, etc. were introduced in Arunachal in various plan periods. However, the success records of these centrally sponsored schemes are not satisfactory in the State.

8. More than 500 employees would be affected due to the proposed decision of the closer of these three corporations. However, Cabinet decided to extend the facilities to the employees under Voluntary Retirement Scheme (Arunachal Times, June 1, 2002).

APPENDIX

TABLE-I : Relative Per capita Income (RPI) of States of India and Union Territories

States/Union Territories	RPI 1980-81	Rank	RPI 1990-91	Rank	RPI 1997-98	Rank
Arunachal	87.41	20	97.50	12	92.25	15
Assam	76.32	27	82.60	23	62.69	26
Monipur	80.17	25	72.91	26	71.25	23
Meghalaya	88.32	19	92.15	17	75.37	20
Mizoram	80.34	24	90.51	19	91.82	17
Nagaland	92.29	17	109.84	9	102.72	11
Tripura	94.47	14	79.03	24	68.05	24
Sikkim	88.73	18	97.16	13	89.12	18
Andhra Pradesh	84.25	21	89.76	21	91.94	16
Bihar	58.69	28	55.28	28	43.34	28
Delhi	238.04	2	211.97	1	231.30	1
Goa	183.77	4	166.85	3	191.31	3
Gujrat	119.97	9	118.22	8	133.46	8
Haryana	139.95	7	143.91	5	137.46	7

contd.

Himachal Pradesh	104.52	12	97.72	11	93.11	13
Jammu & Kashmir	123.59	8	86.18	22	74.69	21
Karnataka	94.41	15	92.73	16	98.96	12
Kerala	105.38	11	95.24	14	111.09	10
Madhya Pradesh	92.40	16	89.94	20	72.67	22
Maharashtra	143.11	6	141.87	7	151.69	5
Utter Pradesh	80.51	23	73.38	25	63.52	25
West Bengal	110.55	10	94.53	15	92.26	14
Andaman & Nicobar Island	261.18	1	181.33	2	180.06	4
Chandigarh*	-	-	-	-	265.21	-
Pondichary	183.83	3	142.71	6	202.39	2
Orissa	77.64	26	59.01	27	61.63	27
Punjab	150.98	5	152.41	4	148.44	6
Rajasthan	81.78	22	91.01	18	87.57	19
Tamil Nadu	95.68	13	103.27	10	120.89	9
Country	100		100		100	

Notes: (i) RPI denotes state per capita income as percentage of National per capita income
(ii) * Excluded Chandigarh in the ranking (for the sake of comparison).
Source: Economic Survey 2000-2001

TABLE-II : Structural Transformation in Arunachal Pradesh : Linear time trend of the sub-sectors of the Economy

Activities	1970-71 to 1999-2000	1970-71 to 1979-80	1980-81 to 1989-90	1990-91 to 1999-2000
Agriculture	A=40.49-0.26t Â =36.49 R^2=0.39	A=39.49-0.24t Â =38.17 R^2=0.09	A=36.12-0.40t Â =38.33 R^2=0.28	A=37.86-0.89t Â=32.98 R^2=0.68
Forestry and logging	F=19.85-0.48t F=12.40 R^2=0 .72	F=25.53-1.08t F =17.62 R^2=0.75	F=12.92-0.33t F=11.11 R^2=0.15	F=11.76-0.80t F=8.48 R^2=0.32
Manufacturing	M=1.70+0.15t =4.01 R^2=0.02	M=0.91+0.09t =1.41 R^2=0.76	M=4.38+0.26t =5.82 R^2=0.30	M=7.05-0.41t =4.80 R^2=0.70
Construction	C=18.73-0.04t C=18.12 R^2=0.02	C=18.33+0.16t C=19.21 R^2=0.03	C=18.34-0.30t C=16.75 R^2=0.17	C=18.17+0.04t C=18.41 R^2=0.002
Trade	T=3.05+0.10t =4.62 R^2=0.69	T=1.69+0.36t =3.67 R^2=0.87	T=3.92+0.13t =4.61 R^2=0.86	T=5.68-0.02t =5.57 R^2=0.02

Notes: 'A' stands for proportion of agricultural income to state income
'F' stands for proportion of forestry and logging income to state income
'M' stands for proportion of manufacturing income to state income
'C' stands for proportion of construction income to state income
'T' proportion of income from trade to state income
Source: Linking series Estimates of SDP of Arunachal Pradesh: 1970-71 to 1999-2000, Directorate of Economics and Statistics, Government of Arunachal Pradesh Itanagar.

Table-III : Minerals Deposits in Arunachal Pradesh

SL. No.	Minerals	Reserves (Million tones)	Location
1	Coal	84.23	Namchick,Namphuk, Changlang District
2	Dolomite	154.13	Rupa, Kaspi, chilipam, Dedza, Jamin,West Kameng District (In addition, specific locations of the occurrences of dolomite have been found in Siang river and in between Pasighat and Pangin. However, reserves not yet been estimated).
3.	Lime stone	409.35	Pangen-Boleng,East Siang District, Tiding, Lohit District, Hunli, Dibang Valley, Menga, Upper Subansiri District
4.	Graphite	3.26	Bopi, Khetabari, taliha, Upper Subansiri Dostrict (a preliminary estimate indicates that the reserve of graphite rock near tail village is West Siang may even go up to 10.35 MT)
5.	Marble	76.12	Tezu, Lohit District;Dora river Hunli, Pyuli, Dibang vally,
6	Crude Oil	30	Khumchali Jairammpur, Kharsang, Changlang District
7.	Natural gas	Exact quantities have not yet been ascertained. However 30 million cubic meter of natural gas are extracted annually.	Kharsang, Kumchi, Changland District
8.	Sulphide	Not yet estimated	Potin, ranga Valley
9.	Pyrito	Not yet estimated	Potin, ranga Valley
10.	Mineral water	Not yet estimated	Various places throughout the state
11.	Lead Zink	Not yet estimated	Shergaon, West Kameng,Namchick, Namphuk, changland District
12.	Quartzite	3.13	Kalak tang, Kameng District
13.	Rock Minerals, Glass, Sand, Lime Stone and Marbles	Not yet estimated	Tenga Valley, Teja Valley, Dora river
14.	Gold	Not yet estimated	Subansiri and Dikrong
15.	Iron Ore	Not yet estimated	Yomcha and adjacent areas
16.	Clay	Scanty data available	Yazali and adjacent areas

Source: Arunachal Pradesh Mineral Department and Trading Corporation Limited and Draft tenth five year plan, Government of Arunachal Pradesh

REFERENCES

Basic Statistics North -Eastern Region (2000), Shillong.

Bhattacharjee R.P. (2000): *Economic Development of Arunachal Pradesh*, Himalayan Publishers, Itanagar.

Bour, D.T and B.S Kamey (1965): *The Economics of Underdeveloped Countries*, Cambridge University Press.

Clark, Colin (1940): *The Conditions of Economic Progress*, Macmillan.

Das, G (1995): *Tribes of Arunachal Pradesh in Transition*, Vikas Publishing House, Pvt. Ltd. New Delhi.

Datta, P.S. (1991): *Economic Development of Arunachal Pradesh- A Case Study of North Eastern Council's Role*, Har-Anand Publications, New Delhi.

Elwin, V (1959): *A Philosophy for NEFA*, Directorate of Research, Government of Arunachal Pradesh,

Fisher, A.G.B. (1939): 'Production: Primary, Secondary and Tertiary', *Economic Record*, Vol. 15, June.

Government of Arunachal Pradesh(1998, 2000): *Statistical Abstracts*, Directorate of Economics and Statistics, Itanagar.

————————————(1970-71, 1980-81, 1985-86, 1990-91): *Agricultural Censuses*, Directorate of Agriculture, Naharlagun.

————————————(1994,2001): *Industrial Policy*, Department of Industries, Itanagar..

————————————(2000-2001): *Forest Statistics, Arunachal Pradesh,* Department of Environment and Forests, Itanagar.

————————————(1997,1999): *Economic Review*, Directorate of Economics and Statistics, Itanagar.

————————————(1951-2002): Various five Year Plans of Arunachal Pradesh, Department of Planning and Development, Itanagar.

————————————(2001): *Linking series Estimates of SDP of Arunachal Pradesh: 1970-71 to 1999-2000*, Directorate of Economics and Statistics, Itanagar.

Government of India (2001-2002): *Economic Survey*

Institute of Industrial Entrepreneurship (1996): 'Arunachal Pradesh: Its Resources and Industrial Prospects', Guwahati

Kuznet (1966): *Modern Economic growth- Rate, Structure and Speed*, Yale University Press, New Haven.

National Council of Applied Economic Research (1967): *Techno-Economic Survey of NEFA*, New Delhi.

Roy, N.C.(1995): 'Growth and Structural Changes in the Economy of Arunachal Pradesh', *Arunachal University Research Journal*, vol. 1, Itanagar.

————and P.K.Kuri(1998): 'Risk, Transaction Cost and Entrepreneurship Development in Arunachal Pradesh, In: B. Datta Ray and Prabin Baishya(ed). *Sociological Constraints to Industrial Development in North East India.* Concept Publications, New Delhi.

————————(2001): *Land reform in Arunachal Pradesh.* Classical Pulishing House, New Delhi.

Shukla, S. P. et al. (1997): *Transforming the Northeast*, High Level Commission Report to the Prime Minister, New Delhi.

Tata Consultancy Services (1997): *Perspective Plan for Economic Development (final report)- phase I*, Department of Planning, Government of Arunachal Pradesh.

————————(1997) *Development of Planning, Government of Arunachal Pradesh (Final Report)-phase II*, Department of Planning, Government of Arunachal Pradesh.

Supplementary Observation

Changing Pattern of Industrialization in Arunachal Pradesh : Some Basic Issues

— M.A. Salam

Development can be understood as a process of expanding the real freedom enjoyed by the people (Sen, 1999). Development requires the removal of major sources of unfreedom, for instance,

- Economic poverty, which begets hunger, malnutrition, inadequate clothing and sheltering and lack of basic sanitary facilities;
- Lack of opportunity in regard to get education, to go for employment as per choice and availability of health facilities;
- Socio-cultural-political tyranny.

All these unfreedom can be reduced to two sets of unfreedom besetting to the people where, (i) they live, i.e., to their self-being and (ii) they work, i.e. to their agency.

Hence the development is a process of growth of income and over all change. This change entails the transformation of society over the stages in whatever way we like to perceive:

- Traditional, pre-requisites, take-off, drive to maturity, mass consumptions.
- Pre-capitalist, capitalist and post-capitalist.

Development, therefore, cannot be equated conceptually with rise in per capita income or with industrialization, or with acquisition of technology, or with modernization. Nevertheless in this paper we take the growth of per capita income as a close equivalence of development for two reasons: (i) to corroborate the proposition with some empirical data and (ii) growth rate is a necessary condition for expanding the freedom enjoyed by the people. And we take industrialization not as an end in itself but a strategy to have better growth rate.

Table 1 is self-explanatory. In Arunachal Pradesh growth rate has been recorded systematically from the 4th plan onward. The performance of the economy has picked up from the seventies. It was satisfactory during the 1980s and the 1990s. The decadal growth rate of the three subsequent decades were 61.5%, 78.7% and 74.9%, while the per capita

Table 1

Years	Growth (%)	Per capita growth	Plan wise growth (%)	Per capita (%)	Decadal Growth (%)	Per capita (%)
1970-71	-	-	4th Plan (1969-70 to 1974-75) 4.3	1.0		
1971-72	7.7	4.2				
1972-73	1.7	-1.5				
1973-74	3.2	-0.2				
1974-75	4.5	1.3				
1975-76	4.4	1.2	5th Plan (1975-76 to 1979-80) 8.9	5.8		
1976-77	12.2	8.9				
1977-78	18.1	14.6				
1978-79	13.6	10.6				
1979-80	-3.9	-6.3				
1980-81	6.2	5.0	6th Plan (1980-81 to 1984-85) 8.3	5.3	6.15	3.27
1981-82	15.2	11.2				
1982-83	3.4	0.4				
1983-84	7.1	3.7				
1984-85	9.6	6.4				
1985-86	12.8	9.4	7th Plan (1985-86 to 1989-90) 7.4	4.1		

contd.

Table 1. ***(Continued)***

Years	Growth (%)	Per capita growth	Plan wise growth (%)	Per capita (%)	Decadal Growth (%)	Per capita (%)
1986-87	6.8	3.5				
1987-88	6.5	3.2				
1988-89	8.2	4.8				
1989-90	2.9	-0.4				
1990-91	18.4	14.6	16.3	12.9	7.87	4.72
1991-92	14.3	11.2				
1992-93	2.6	0.0	8th Plan (1992-93 to 1996-97) 5.2	2.7		
1993-94	14.4	11.8				
1994-95	0.4	-2.0				
1995-96	14.8	12.1				
1996-97	-6.0	-8.4				
1997-98	3.2	0.7	5.3	2.2		
1998-99	0.9	-3.4				
1999-2000	11.9	9.7			7.49	4.63

Source: Linking series estimates of state domestic product of Arunachal Pradesh 1970-71 to 1999-2000(Q), SDP Section, Directorate of Economics and Statistics, Government of Arunachal Pradesh, Itanagar.

decadal growth rate for the same periods were 32.7%, 47.2% and 46.3%. Provided that the poverty line has not gone up on the scale of population distribution and the gini coefficient has not increased then one can safely decipher from the table that at least the material requisites of the well-being in the state has been doubled in every 15 years. In other words, the people of Arunachal Pradesh are enjoying the higher range of economic freedom over the periods of time.

Industrialization is a process whereby the structural transformation in the economy takes place. It takes place in two accounts: (a) the proportion of the total income from non-agricultural sector increases; (b) there is a shift of working population from agricultural sector to non-agricultural sector (Bagchi 1988). Tables 2 and 3 reveal the facts about the industrialization in Arunachal Pradesh.

From Table 2 we get the impression that the relative importance of primacy sector goes down over the plan periods and the relative importance of secondary sector remains almost the same. And the tertiary sector has gained. From Table 3 we receive the information that there is a considerable shift of the working force from agricultural activities to non-agricultural activities. Agricultural sector was engaging around 80% of the total work force in 1971, which has gone down gradually, i.e. 69% in 1981 and 64% in 1991. The trend approves that industrialization and structural transformation are taking place in the economy of Arunachal Pradesh.

Table 2

(Rs. in lakh)

Sector	4th Plan	5th Plan	6th Plan	7th Plan	8th Plan	9th Plan (upto 2000 only)
Primary Sector	32920 (58.21)	53065 (55.41)	74986 (50.10)	116021 (51.82)	187282 (46.33)	99398 (36.27)
Secondary Sector	11785 (20.84)	18724 (19.55)	30617 (20.45)	42462 (18.97)	92731 (22.94)	61268 (22.36)
Tertiary Sector	11848 (20.95)	23979 (25.04)	44101 (29.45)	65402 (29.21)	124213 (30.73)	113391 (41.37)
Total	56553	95768	149704	223885	404226	274057

Figures in bracket indicate percentage.

Source: Linking series estimates of State Domestic Product of Arunachal Pradesh (1970-71 to 1999-2000) (Q), SDP Section, Directorate of Economics and Statistics, Government of Arunachal Pradesh, Itanagar.

III

Arunachal communities have evolved over the ages. They have made use of natural endowments through expending the communal or individual labour power (as the case warranted). To assist the labour power they have developed indigenous technology. The total produce has been consumed quite often within the community. Hence, every community practiced an elaborate allocational procedure of resources and distributional method of produce (Haimendorf 1980). For a background understanding here we constrict our discussion mainly to understand the modus operandi of the resource flow, i.e. how resources are effected (mobilized and allocated for the production process in pre-independence phase of Arunachal Pradesh).

Table 3

(Numbers in lakh)

Indicators	Census		
	1971	1981	1991
Total workers	2.69	3.33	4.00
Cultivators	2.11 (78.43)	2.23 (66.96)	2.36 (59.00)
Agricultural labourers	0.05 (1.85)	0.08 (2.40)	0.20 (5.00)
Non-agricultural labourers	0.53 (19.70)	1.02 (30.63)	1.44 (36.00)
Total non-workers	1.98	2.99	4.65
Work participation rate (from total population)	57.60	52.69	46.24
Non-workers participation rate	42.40	47.31	53.76
Decadal percentage rise of total workers	-	23.79	20.12
Decadal percentage rise of cultivators	-	5.69	5.83
Decadal percentage rise or agricultural labourers	-	60.00	150.00
Decadal percentage rise of non-agricultural workers	-	92.45	41.81

Source:Economic Review of Arunachal Pradesh 2000, Directorate of Economics and Statistics, Government of Arunachal Pradesh, Itanagar.

Capital may be construed as the portion of resources, which are oriented for carrying the production cycle. These resources may be material (seeds and technology etc.) may be immaterial (technical knowledge, skill and experiences etc.). In pre-capitalist society there is a problem of valuation of these resources in some monetary unit. My contention is that there exists capital at embryonic stage even in pre-capitalist societies, however, in different forms. The essence of capital lies in three functions; it is a productive asset; it affords a control over the purchasing power, it is a fund per investment (Firth and Yamey 1963). Productive assets involve seeds, dao, digging sticks, baskets etc. Control over purchasing power includes grains or cooked food or clothes, which are served to the workers engaged in production operation. It is a type of working capital. And also sometimes these items are transferred to some households and the recipients feel obligation to reciprocate either with the same goods or rendering services later on. Such borrowing (borrowing for consumption) does not yield any interest. If borrowing is to meet the requirements of production operation, lender may share a portion of the produce. Loan is also obtained on mortgaging a land where usufruct goes to the lender. And there is symmetry of power relation in the community with the accumulation of these resources (Elwin 1965). Important thing is that production is done in advance not only to meet the family requirements (consumption goods) but also to meet the production expenditure (capital goods). Hence, adequate amount is accumulated and saved which is invested at various stages of production.

In general society categorizes the items of assets according to the degree of liquidity (Firth & Yamey 1963); food items and other subsistence goods; cattle, clothes and metal objects; ornaments and rights over land.

Further these communities did not leave in seclusion. They used to trade in the market place with other contiguous communities (Das 1995).

Industrialization as a method of development requires deliberate strategy for the backward region. The path towards industrialization is more like an obstacle race than a journey on a highway. It is obstructed by various conflicts and contradictions. Institutional arrangements, cultural pattern, value system, interlinkages of resource flow, power relation etc. come on the way as obstruction. Proceeding at a snail pace rate through bit-by-bit will not generate the same effect as if we generate through giving a single bit of big push, which would overcome such circumstantial constraints. After independence and more specifically after the Sino-Indian conflict, Government has realized and initiated the development process on the line of big push. As a result in a decade a substantial amount of social overhead capital has been formed and it has kept rising in various forms like (i) in the form of infrastructure facilities such as bridges, roadways, other means of communication, power generation etc; (ii) in the form of human social capital through education and health services; (iii) in the form of institutional network such as administrative unity, banking system, etc. Government undertook this project of big push because each one of the aforementioned activities is indivisible, lumpy and requires a long gestational investment. The Table 4 gives the government outlay and expenditure over the plan periods.

One may easily visualize that there is a shift in the strategy of industrialization from the 1970s. Hence in the post independence phase of Arunachal Pradesh we have two strategies of industrialization, however, to a greater extent they are complementary.

Strategy upto the 1970s

The initial phase of industrialization basically involves the development of traditional skill with the use of locally available materials. Hence, the industrial strategy of NEFA was mainly to promote handicraft and village industries. This has two purposes (i) the people would earn a subsidiary income in addition to the normal agricultural works; (ii) to preserve the indigenous crafts and to help the people to grow in the traditional line through using the local available raw material. Consequently, raw material procurement and production sale units (emporium) and Crafts Training-cum-Production Center (CTPC) has been set up. These two organizations have co-ordinated in imparting trainings and producing the output, and marketing them. Government has provided tools at 50% subsidy and 50% of the cost was to be raised in easy installment either in cash or in kind (finished products supplied by the trainees) during 3 years (Das 1995).

Such strategy is appropriate only during the initial years for the non-monetised underdeveloped region. The craft centers and village industries were producing the output which were required by the majority of people, i.e. goods were not alien to them. They were produced by labour intensive method using the local technology with minimum amount of investment. In strict sense of the term this was not a commodity production because no amount of commodification and alienation are involved. And therefore it carries the germs, which would have defeated the purpose namely market remains stagnant. The sale proceeds hardly cover the costs leaving meagre margin, which does not generate sufficient incentive to go for expanded production.

Table 4

Plan Periods (5-Year Plan)	1st FYP	2nd FYP	3rd FYP	Three Annual Plans (1966-69)	4th FYP	5th FYP	Annual Plan (1979-80	6th FYP	7th FYP	Annual Plans (1990-91 to 1991-92	8th FYP
Outlay	3.00	5.01	7.15	8.57	17.99	63.30	23.41	222.90	551.61	375.49	1728.62
Expenditure	2.01	3.57	9.20	8.32	21.58	60.86	22.51	205.85	550.51	372.70	1714.62
Regular employment generated	1774	2444	3269	1665	2970	4588	99	4305	33993	2180	39819

Source:50 Years Space of Development in Arunachal Pradesh (1947-1997), Directorate of Economics and Statistics, Government of Arunachal Pradesh, Itanagar.

Strategy from the 1970s

Since the 1970s, there has come a change in the industrial pattern of Arunachal Pradesh. There are several reasons which we can be put under two heads: the political reasons, and the economic reasons. During the 60s and early 70s, the underlying assumption of compatibility between growth and employment has been questioned on empirical ground. Hence, growth through industrialization may not create employment and because of concentration and centralization of resources, inequality of individual as well as of regional emerges. Unemployment and regional inequality have a high bargain for the pressure group under democratic set up. As a result Central Government has formulated a policy to develop the backward region through accelerating the rate of industrialization. The North East Region has come under the economically backward region. Further, Central Government has a policy to develop the hilly and tribal regions. And by that time Arunachal Pradesh has received the status of the Union Territory. Hence, the State has enjoyed the advantageous positions on many grounds: (i) being the Union Territory its development project has come directly under the Centre; (ii) Arunachal Pradesh is a part of the NER. Hence the NEC also considers its problems; (iii) Arunachal Pradesh is a hilly state and is inhabited by the various recognized tribes. So it receives the benefits of these two also; (iv) further Arunachal Pradesh enjoys the status of strategic state for its international boundaries. Furthermore, sufficient time has passed and Government has already poured sufficient amount of money in the form of investment in social overhead which has increased the real income of the employees and contractors and so middle class, however thin in numbers, has emerged. And they were creating the demand for industrial produce.

The industrialization phase of the 70s contains three-pronged strategy:

(i) to develop the industrial estates in the vicinity of urban area through which a firm can enjoy the benefits of external economies and also the benefits of linkage effect in the form of relatively regular power supply, higher mobility of skilled labour and inputs within the firms, demand generation and a better transportation and communication facilities, etc.

(ii) To provide the fund for investment at some concessional rate with subsidy the financial institutions (like Arunachal Pradesh industrial Development and Financial Corporation Ltd. APIDFC) have been established. Central Government has initiated many schemes of subsidy e.g. Central Investment Subsidy Scheme (CISS), Central Transport Subsidy Scheme (CTSS) etc. To accelerate the industrial growth and other incentives for example price preference, a subsidy on the training of manpower, industrial housing, exemption from sale's tax and registration fees etc. are provided to boost up the entrepreneurship within the State.

(iii) To provide a link between the resource potential of the district and entrepreneurial capability of the people and the specialized developmental institutions, the District Industries Centre (CDIC) have been set up. This provides the organizational platform for the execution of various policies.

As a result of these steps, the small-scale industries have flourished in the State. Its number has increased from 11 in 1971 to 4596 in 1999. Further 18 medium scale industries have come up.

Some Basic Issues

One basic problem of industries in Arunachal Pradesh is presumed that it suffers from inadequate demand, which is because of the small size of population. Hence demand is not sufficient to stimulate the production. Further the urban agglomeration of territory is flooded with the goods supplied from plain areas.

Basically this is a false presumption that demographic factor determines the demand and so the rate and level of industrialization. Had this been the case, the industrialization would have been limited to the developing nations where around 80% of the world population resides. This is the size of market, which is important, and size of market depends upon:

1. Distribution of income: the higher the distribution is egalitarian the wider will be the middle classes who are the effective consumer because they have both aspiration and affordable capacity.
2. The specialization of industrial structure, i.e., the more the firms are specialized, the more the market expands and the higher will be the inter-linkages.
3. The level of wage rate; the higher will be the wage structure the more demand will come forth and market expands.
4. Market of commodity is prone to change. Hence it cannot be stagnant.
5. Market of industry depends on the decay of handicrafts and artisan production. Proto-industrialization is necessary.
6. Fiscal effect is also significant, i.e., market is created through Government expenditure.

Another set of problems in regard to industrialization in Arunachal Pradesh are often recorded as:

- There are two types of entrepreneurs in most of business activities. One is the real entrepreneur who is mostly non-local and second is the trading permit holder. There is an attitudinal difference between these two types of entrepreneurs, which hampers the growth of firm.
- The entrepreneurs are interested in availing the subsidies and concessional loans. And the funds are misallocated because they are used for some other purposes (not in the industrial proposal, which are registered).
- The government agency stresses more upon the relevant paper documents rather than the viability and feasibility of the proposed firms. And they are in the pressure of fulfilling the target. In order to fulfill the target and viability of their projects.

Let us reduce these events to the psychological plane of an individual. The whole behaviour of an individual can be classified under two categories.

1. Behaviour intending for the self-being, i.e., a teleogical approach.
2. Behaviour intending for his/her agency, i.e., a deontological approach.

If the teleogical approach prevails upon the deontological approach in the behaviour, this leads to the possessive individualism. And when the deontological approach prevails in the behaviour, this gives rise to the developmental individualism i.e., when whole develops automatically parts receive benefits.

Since there is a demand constraint and there is blockade in the factor flow across the sectors, the general business psycho-logy (i.e., expectation) is that sufficient proceeds will not come forth. One expected profit happen to be less than the benefits firms receive in he form of various subsidies and other incentives. The firms would like to bank upon the benefits of these facilities than to go for production. Hence its logical corollary follows; the higher the amount of incentives will be the more frequently such events will occur. This action of the entrepreneur makes the instrumental organ (government agency) to make ready at least the documents for record sake. This calculation of entrepreneur is more tilted towards the teleological approach and in this framework he is swayed away with acquisitive motive. Thus, unless the motive is checked on psychological plane such events cannot be stopped. And no amount of incentives would bring industrialization in the State.

The next basic issue I raise here that how far industrialization becomes an agent for the development of the society as a whole. Most of the backward regions face the problems of dual economy where we have two sectors; modern industrial sector and traditional agricultural sector. It is presumed that the benefit of industrialization must revolutionize the traditional agricultural sector, i.e., industrialization must be an agent for the development of society as a whole but instead it gives rise to inequality between the two sectors.

The benefit can be transferred if there are some linkages. The two sectors can be linked through two flows; the factor flow and the product flow.

Among factors, land is perfectly immobile. It carries significantly high importance in agriculture but it is of negligible significance in industrial sector. Capital and entrepreneurship have a unilinear trend of mobility because their movement is mainly governed by the return consideration. Labour is the only mobile factor across the two sectors. Further there exists organizational asymmetry between the two sectors, for instance, productivity is the basis of distribution in modern industrial sector then the conventional norm is the basis of distribution in the traditional agricultural sector. If surplus of labour in agriculture means that marginal productivity of labour is close to zero then competitive allocation is not possible because in agriculture if wage is so determined then hardly marginal peasants and agricultural labourer would survive. And if the prevailing wage rate of modern industrial sector is taken as a rate to clear all wage bills in agriculture then system will collapse for the proceed will hardly cover the cost due to price structure of agricultural products. Labour is the only equilibrating flow but still the two sectors cannot be brought in equivalence for products of labour are not equal across the sectors because of institutional asymmetry. In factor flow such asymmetry and rigidity hamper significantly the flow of benefits of industrialization to the agricultural sector. In product flow, products of both sectors flow smoothly across the sectors. But the terms of trade goes against agricultural sector. Hence industrialization has not served so significantly to the society as a whole as it is expected.

REFERENCES

Amartya Sen, 1999, *Development as Freedom*, Oxford University Press, New Delhi.

Amiya Kumar Bagchi, 1988, '*Industrialization*', *The New Palgrave*: *A Dictionary of Economics*, Vol.2, The Macmillan Press Ltd., London.

Christoph von Fürer-Haimendorf, 1980, *A Himalayan Tribe*: *From Cattle to Cash*, Vikas Publishing House Pvt. Ltd., New Delhi.

Raymond Firth and B.S. Yamey, 1963, *Capital Saving and Credit in Peasant Societies*, Aldine Publishing Company, Chicago.

Verrier Elwin, 1965, *Democracy in NEFA*, Directorate of Research, Government of Arunachal Pradesh, Itanagar.

Gurudas Das, 1995, *Tribes of Arunachal Pradesh in Transition*, Vikas Publishing House Pvt. Ltd., New Delhi.

"Linking Series Estimates of State Domestic Product of Arunachal Pradesh 1970-71 to 1999-2000 (Q)", Directorate of Economics and Statistics, Government of Arunachal Pradesh, Itanagar.

"Economic Review of Arunachal Pradesh", 2000, Directorate of Economics and Statistics, Government of Arunachal Pradesh, Itanagar.

"50 Years Space of Development in Arunachal Pradesh (1947-97)", Directorate of Economics and Statistics, Government of Arunachal Pradesh, Itanagar.

2

A Study of Sectoral Development of Assam : Retrospect and Prospect

—Kishor Singh Rajput

Geographically, Assam is surrounded by Bhutan and Arunachal Pradesh on the North, Nagaland and Manipur on the East, Meghalaya and Mizoram on the South and Bangladesh, Tripura and West Bengal on the East. Since independence many changes have taken place in Assam. In fact, Assam is now a shadow of its former self (Hazarika 1999). In 1948, the North East Frontier Agency (NEFA), present Arunachal Pradesh, was separated from Assam. In 1957, Nagaland was carved out of Assam as a Centrally Administered Area and was formally accorded the statehood in 1963. Meghalaya was created in 1970 as an autonomous state and it became a full-fledged state in 1972. In the same year, Mizoram came into being as a Union Territory and finally declared as a state in 1987, along with Arunachal Pradesh.

Demographically, over the years, population has continuously increased in Assam, thereby giving it the distinction of being the most populous state in the North East India with a total population of 2.66 crore in 2001. It accounts for 2.4 percent of total geographical area of the country and 2.6 percent of the country's population.

Economically, out of the seven sisters of the North East, Assam is the most developed state. But when we compare Assam with states like Maharashtra, Gujrat and Tamilnadu, we find that Assam lags far behind in almost all economic spheres.

STRUCTURAL CHANGES

a) Trend in the Growth of State Domestic Product of Assam

The growth of a state's gross domestic product or net domestic product and its sectoral composition and the changes in it over the years very much portray the structural changes taking place in it. Table 1 shows the growth of the Gross State Domestic Product at Factor Cost and the Net State Domestic Product at Factor Cost of Assam at both current and constant prices. The GSDP at current prices rose from Rs. 215 crore in 1950-51 to Rs. 21336 crore in 1997-98, whereas the GSDP at constant (1980-81) prices, during the same period, rose to Rs. 4784 crore from Rs. 1002 crore. On the other hand, the NSDP at current prices increased from Rs. 204 crore to Rs. 18865 crore and the NSDP at constant (1980-81) prices from Rs. 956 crore to Rs. 4302 crore during the period of 1950-51 to 1997-98.

Table 1 : SDP of Assam at Factor Cost at Current and Constant (1980-81) Prices

Year	GSDP at Factor Cost (Rs. Crore)		NSDP at Factor Cost (Rs. Crore)	
	At Current Prices	At Constant Prices	At Current Prices	At Constant Prices
1950-51	215	1002	204	956
1960-61	393	1293	365	1217
1970-71	912	1882	844	1760
1980-81	2516	2516	2298	2298
1990-91	10621	3769	9498	3426
1997-98(Q)	21336	4784	18865	4302

Source: Basic Statistics of Assam 2000 and Statistical Handbook of Assam 1999 Q = Quick Estimate

However, during the period of 1950-51 and 1997-98, though the NSDP at constant prices increased by 4.5 times, it was slower than the increase of the NNP at constant (1980-81) prices which multiplied by 6.7 times. The slow growth of India's NNP itself is a big concern and further slow increase in Assam's GSDP and NSDP should to be a bigger concern for the policy makers.

Looking at the growth of the real GSDP, we find that the growth rates in both the primary and secondary sectors declined during the period of 1980-81 to 2000-01 (Table 2).

Table 2 : Percentage Annual Growth in Real GSDP and Its Three Main Sectors

Period	*Primary Sector*	*Secondary Sector*	*Tertiary Sector*	*GSDP*
1980-1990	2.16	4.13	4.37	3.34
1991-2001	1.89	3.88	4.52	3.27
1980-2001	1.81	3.80	4.57	3.25

Source: Assam Development Report 2002

The tertiary sector has only shown a slight upward trend as the growth rate increased from 4.37 percent during 1980-1990 to 4.52 percent during 1991-2001. As a result of the poor performance of the primary and secondary sectors during this period, the percentage annual growth of the real GSDP declined from 3.34 percent to 3.27 percent. Therefore, in real terms, the economic growth process in the state has decelerated in recent years.

If we look at the percentage distribution of NSDP by Industry of Origin, then we find that the share of the primary sector, as expected, declined from 48.07 percent in 1980-81 to 40.85 in 1997-98, with the share of the agriculture sector declining from 44.21 percent to 34.59 percent. On the other hand, the share of tertiary sector has shown an upward trend as its percentage share in the NSDP increased from 40.39 in 1980-81 to 47.76 in 1997-98. However, within the tertiary sector, trade, hotels and restaurants as well as transport, storage and communication, showed a stagnant or very little growth. The sub-sectors of the tertiary sector that showed an upward trend in their share in Assam's NSDP were the community and personal services, and finance and real estate. Contrary to this, in the transitory phase, it is always expected that infrastructure, trading activities, etc. expand and so is their share in the State's NSDP.

Likewise, the secondary sector's share in the NSDP has remained almost unchanged, thereby showing total failure on the part of the economic planning to initiate rapid industrial development in the state. The share of the manufacturing sector even declined over the period of 1980-81 to 1997-98. In other words, the development process of Assam has totally bypassed the secondary sector of the economy.

Table 3 : Percentage Distribution of NSDP at Factor Cost by Industry of Origin at 1980-81 Prices

Industry	1980-81	1997-98
PRIMARY	**48.07**	**40.85**
Agriculture	44.21	34.59
Forestry, Logging, Mining, etc.	3.86	6.25
SECONDARY	**11.54**	**11.38**
Manufacturing	6.53	4.97
Registered	4.16	3.56
Unregistered	2.37	1.41
B. Construction, Electricity, etc.	5.01	6.41
TERTIARY	**40.39**	**47.76**
A. Transport, Storage and Communication	2.62	3.25
B. Trade, Hotels and Restaurants	11.73	11.66
C. Finance and Real Estate	12.69	15.75
D. Community and Personal Services	13.35	17.10
NSDP	100.0	100.0

Source: Statistical Handbook of Assam, 1999

Not only the sectoral composition of the state's NSDP shows features of backwardness, the inter-sectoral linkages in the economy are also very poor. The 64 × 64 Input-Output table prepared for 1982-83 (Dept. of Economics, G.U. 1987-88), which still holds true as the basic character of the economy of Assam has not changed very much, brought out the following features:

- The inter-sectoral dependence of the Assam economy is very low, about 70 percent of the cells being empty. Agriculture, petroleum and tea industries, in that order, were the three most important dominant sectors in the Assam economy.
- The inter-sectoral production linkage is very weak, intermediate consumption being only 35 percent of the gross value of the output.
- Except for 17 commodities/sectors such as sugarcane, jute, tea, crude oil, petroleum products, plywood, silk textiles, etc. Assam is heavily dependent on net imports for meeting her internal demand.

Furthermore, the Per Capita Income, a better indicator of economic development than the NSDP and NNP, of Assam has also shown an upward trend over the years. The Per Capita NSDP, both at the current and constant prices rose from Rs. 251 and Rs. 1173 in 1950-51 to Rs. 7335 and Rs. 1673 respectively in 1997-98 respectively. But these very figures become discouraging when we compare them with the growth of the Per Capita NNP.

Table 4 : Per Capita NSDP of Assam (in Rs.)

Year	1950-51	1960-61	1970-71	1980-81	1990-91	1997-98
At Current Prices	1173	1140	1221	1284	1544	1673
At Constant Prices (1980-81 Prices)	251	342	585	1284	4281	7335

Source: Basic Statistics of Assam 2000 and Statistical Handbook of Assam 1999

Table 5 : Per Capita Income of Assam and India at Constant (1980-81) Prices

Year	1950-51	1960-61	1970-71	1980-81	1990-91	1998-99
Assam	1173	1140	1221	1284	1544	1708
India	1127	1350	1520	1630	2222	3132
Difference	+46	-210	-299	-346	-678	-1424

Source: Basic Statistics of Assam 2000 and Assam Development Report 2002

As the Table 5 shows, in the beginning, Assam had a higher Per Capita Income than the national average. In 1950-51, Per Capita income at constant prices for Assam and India stood at Rs. 1173 and Rs.1127 respectively with a positive difference of Rs. 44 for Assam. However, during the succeeding years of economic planning, this trend was reversed as the National Per Capita Income rose above the Per Capita Income of Assam. As a result, the Per Capita Income of India as a whole stood at Rs. 3132 in comparison to Rs. 1708 of Assam in 1998-99, thereby showing a negative difference of Rs. 1424 for Assam. These figures, therefore, invariably reflect the point that during the last 50 years of economic planning, the country as a whole has grown faster than Assam. In other words, the economic planning of last 50 years in the country has not benefited Assam as much as it has some other parts of the country. In fact, the state has decelerated in recent years (Bezbaruah 2002).

b) Trend in the Occupational Distribution of Population of Assam

There is a close relationship between development of an economy on the one hand, and occupational structure on the other and economic progress is generally associated with certain distinct necessary and predictable changes in occupational structure (Clark 1940). In other words, we may say that in every progressive economy there has been a steady shift in employment and investment from the essential primary activities to secondary activities of all kinds and to a still greater extent into tertiary production (Fisher 1945).

Table 6 : Percentage Occupational Distribution of Population of Assam, 1971-2001

Sector	1971			1991		
	Person	Male	Female	Person	Male	Female
Primary Sector	**83.98**	**83.83**	**85.57**	**73.99**	**71.00**	**86.50**
Cultivators	61.31	65.33	16.22	50.91	50.90	50.93
Agricultural Labourers	10.82	11.18	6.71	12.08	12.10	12.02
Livestock, Fishing, etc	11.85	7.32	62.64	11.00	8.00	23.55
Secondary Sector	**3.75**	**3.50**	**6.45**	**5.56**	**6.09**	**3.34**
Household Industry	0.26	0.27	0.15	0.88	0.57	2.17
Other than House-hold Industry	2.84	2.53	6.11	3.11	3.61	1.02
Construction	0.65	0.70	0.19	1.57	1.91	0.15
Tertiary Sector	**12.28**	**12.67**	**7.98**	**20.45**	**22.91**	**10.16**
Trade and Commerce	3.36	3.60	0.67	6.84	8.23	0.99
Transport, Storage	1.14	1.24	0.10	2.50	3.04	0.28
& Commun. Other Services	7.78	7.83	7.21	11.11	11.64	8.89

Source: Census of India 1971 and Statistical Handbook, Assam, 1999

We have already seen how the last 30-40 years of economic transition process of Assam has bypassed the secondary sector. As the Secondary sector grew at a slower rate than the service sector over the last few decades, the shift in the occupational distribution is also bent more towards the tertiary sector. Because of the rapid population growth in Assam, still a very high percentage of the people are dependent on the agriculture sector and those who are moving out from the primary sector are being absorbed mostly in the tertiary sector. In other words, as the industrial activities have not expanded, more and more people are looking for gainful employment in the unorganised segment of the tertiary sector.

A distinct feature of the change in the occupational distribution of the population of Assam (Table 6), during the period of 1971 and 1991, is that the percentage of female workers engaged in activities like livestock farming, fishing, etc. and in the secondary sector declined significantly, whereas the percentage of female cultivators and agricultural labourers jumped from 16.22 percent and 6.71 percent to 50.93 percent and 12.01 percent respectively.

A high percentage of people engaged in a backward agriculture sector invariably means prevalence of large-scale seasonal and disguised unemployment, low per capita productivity and widespread poverty. The percentage of people engaged in the secondary and tertiary sector is low in Assam. This is because the industrial development in Assam concentrated in few industries of tea, coal, and petroleum has had very little forward-backward linkages and multiplier effect and, hence, virtually no effect on the occupational structure. So did fail the rural development strategy of the government to create adequate number of non-farm employment opportunities in the rural areas.

Therefore, in order to bring forward the desired change in the occupational pattern of population of Assam, along with a check on the population growth, an effective non-farm employment policy has to be in place.

Table 7 : Sectorwise Percentage Distribution of Plan Outlay of Assam

Sector	1st Plan	2nd Plan	3rd Plan	4th Plan	5th Plan	6th Plan	7th Plan	8th Plan	9th Plan
Agriculture and Allied Services	19.01	13.79	10.52	18.49	18.70	15.90	19.0	11.04	11.9
Rural Development	5.43	12.01	9.79	3.65	2.37	2.00	1.7	4.05	8.2
Industry and Minerals	0.53	8.86	8.13	9.05	5.90	4.50	4.9	6.91	4.6
Irrigation, Flood Control and Power	23.73	7.68	28.98	32.08	27.93	50.00	39.1	33.55	18.4
Transport and Communication	15.69	13.33	8.46	13.94	7.16	8.00	7.7	6.31	10.2
Social Services	35.60	40.71	33.03	21.48	17.68	19.10	23.9	35.36	42.3
General and General Economic Services	-	-	-	-	0.54	0.60	3.0	2.32	3.7
Unallocated/Others	-	3.61	1.09	1.31	19.72	-	0.7	0.45	0.7

Source: Basic Statistics of North-Eastern Region 2000; Statistical Handbook of Assam 1968 and 1974

SECTORAL ALLOCATION OF PLAN OUTLAYS OF ASSAM

Sectoral allocation of plan outlays very much shape the future direction of an economy. From the Table 7 it can be seen that the state's plan outlay for industry and minerals has remained stagnant. This low level of plan outlay earmarked for the industrial sector over the various plans is the reason why the state public sector has failed to take the lead role in the field of industrial development, at least as it was expected in the initial phase of economic development. The share of plan outlay for the social services has, however, increased sharply from17.7 percent during the Fourth Plan to 42.3 percent during the Ninth Plan. The increased investment in various social services like education, medical care and social security measures is very much laudable as it benefits the society in the long run. But being predominantly an agricultural state and agriculture being a state subject with little assistance coming from the Central government, a decreasing share of plan outlay for the agriculture sector is very much questionable.

In an economy like Assam where establishing a large-scale industrial base looks very difficult, the economy has to revolve around a modern agricultural and service sector. So the need is to strengthen the agriculture sector so that both production and productivity increase. This can definitely be very beneficial for the state on many counts. On one such count, as many development theories suggest, increased productivity in the agriculture sector can generate not only surplus foodgrains for the non-farm population, but can also generate valuable internal savings needed for various productive activities. However, in an excess populated state like Assam, a modern viable agriculture sector also invariably calls for an effective rural non-farm employment strategy.

Popular political compulsion in economic decision making is a bane. As a result, on many occasions, the planned measures are directed to meet the immediate concerns of the general public rather than looking at the crucial areas of long-term sustained economic development of the state. Lack of sustainability of various economic policies has also been a big problem. Therefore, unanimity among the political parties on certain crucial economic areas is a must for the sustenance of the core and important development policies.

However, in order to effect desired occupational distribution in the economy, the state must focus, more than ever before, on the aspects like raising agricultural productivity, implementation of an effective rural non-farm employment policy with emphasis on the development of the cottage and village industries. Last but not the least, the government has to ensure the best and optimum utilisation of whatever meagre amount of financial resources that it has at its disposal.

RESOURCE BASE OF THE STATE

The state of Assam is well-endowed with natural resources required for rapid and smooth industrial development. In other words, the nature has been very kind on her as far as the availability of these resources is concerned. Let us have a cursory look at the key resources available in Assam.

a) Human Resource

The total population base and the growth rates in it over the years has ensured significantly the advantage of availability of cheap and adequate supply of labour force for the economy of Assam. For example, the total population of Assam increased from 8.02 millions in 1951 to 26.64 millions in 2001, i.e., more than 3 times increase in her population. During this period, of course, the country's population also almost increased by three times. However, during the decade of 1991-2001, Assam's popu-lation growth rate has been found lower than the national figure, unlike the decades of 1950s and 1960s. Though the decadal growth rates for Assam are coming down over the years, but this decline is not good enough to see any chance of obtaining the goal of stabilisation of population in the state in near future.

Table 8 : Total Population and Its Decadal Variation in Assam and India, 1951-2001

Year	Total Population (in millions)		Decadal Variation (in %)	
	Assam	India	Assam	India
1951	8.02	361.09	-	-
1961	10.83	439.23	34.98	21.51
1971	14.62	548.16	34.98	24.80
1981*	18.04	683.33	23.36	24.66
1991	22.41	846.30	24.24	23.85
2001**	26.64	102.70	18.85	21.30

Source: Various Census Reports and India 2002.
* 1981 Census was not held in Assam. So interpolated figures are used. ** Provisional figures.

Table 9 : Density, Sex Ratio and Urban Population of Assam and India, 1951-2001

Year	Assam			India		
	Density	Sex Ratio	% of Urban Population	Density	Sex Ratio	% of Urban Population
1951	-	868	4.29	117	946	17.3
1961	97	869	7.21	142	941	18.0
1971	186	896	8.82	178	930	19.9
1981*	230	910	9.88	216	934	23.3
1991	286	923	11.10	267	927	25.7
2001	340	932	12.72	324	933	27.78

Source: Various Census Reposts and India 2002
* Interpolated figures for Assam, as the Census could not be held in 1981.

Because of the rapid population growth, the size of the labour force has also increased in Assam. For example, the percentage of workers in total population increased from 27.96 percent in 1971 to 35.88 percent in 2001 (Provisional figure). When we consider the increase in the population during this period along with this increase in the percentage of workers, then we definitely have to say that the increase in the absolute size of the labour force is quite significant.

Table10 : Work Force Participation Rate in Assam (in %)

Year	Total Workers	Main Workers	Marginal Workers	Non-Workers
1971	27.96	-	-	72.04
1991	36.09	31.20	4.89	63.91
2001	35.88	26.59	9.29	64.12

Source: Various Census Reports

But, enough strong agro-industrial base in Assam has not been created to absorb this growing labour force. The fact that 1524616 people were registered with the Employment Exchanges in Assam in 2001, a significantly deflated figure, speaks about the volume of the problem and not to mention about the incidence of seasonal and disguised unemployment problem. There are certain grey areas as well in the existing human resources of Assam. For example, despite the increase in the literacy rate of population of Assam over the years (Table 11), a further rapid improvement in this regard is urgently called for. This is because even a cent percent literacy rate is not a very accurate yard stick to measure the true quality of the population, because of the very definition adopted in the Census to define a literate person. There is also the mismatch between the demand and supply of human resources. On the one hand, we have large number of educated unemployed persons, we lack a true class of entrepreneurs in the society, on the other. But it is also true fact that a cent percent literate society can very well create the base for bringing in the required qualitative changes in the labour force as well as in the society at large in future.

Table11 : Percentage of Literates in Assam and India, 1951-2001

Year	Assam			India		
	Total	Male	Female	Total	Male	Female
1951	18.50	-	-	16.60	24.9	7.90
1961	27.20	37.60	15.3	28.29	40.38	15.10
1971	28.14	36.68	18.63	29.48	39.52	18.70
1981	-	-	-	43.67	56.50	29.85
1991	52.89	61.87	43.03	52.21	64.13	39.29
2001	64.28	71.93	56.03	65.38	75.85	54.16

Source: Various Census Reports and India 2002; Statistical Abstract of Assam 1967-68 and 1978

36.09 percent of the population of Assam lives below the poverty line. So a large number of the labour force living below the poverty line and a significant number above the poverty line also fail to get the required amount of nutritional supplement in their daily diet. The result is the weak and somewhat inefficient labour force working in the economy. So we can say that the labour force in Assam is large and cheap, but not healthy and efficient. The figures of life expectancy at 55.7 years and infant mortality rate at 76 per thousand (CSO 2000) and figure of 63.2 percent children suffering from anemia (NFHS 1998-99), etc. leave a reminder of the hard work lying ahead of Assam.

Table 12 : Percentage of People below the Poverty Line

Year	Rural	Urban	Combined
1973-74	52.67	36.92	51.21
1993-94	45.01	7.73	40.86
1999-00	40.04	7.47	36.09

Source: Economic Survey 2001-02, Government of India

b) Land and Agricultural Resources

Assam is the second largest state of North East India in terms of geographical area. Agriculture forms the backbone of the Assam's economy. According to a 1991 census, about 69 percent of the total workforce of the state were engaged in agriculture and allied activities. The contribution of the agriculture sector to the NSDP was 35.09 at current prices in 2000-01 (NEDFi 2002). For Assam, the land utilisation statistics is provided in the Table 13 and the area and production of foodgrains and non-foodgrains in Table 14.

Table 13 : Land Utilisation Statistics of Assam (in ha.)

Sl. No.	Classification	1990-91 Census	1995-96 Census	% Variation
1	Geographical area	7843800	7843800	-
2	Area under operational holding	320500	325300	1.5
3	Average size of holdings	1.27	1.24	-0.02
4	Net area sown	2781000	2744000	-1.3
5	Area sown more than once	1181000	1245000	5.4
6	Total gross cropped area	3962000	3989000	0.007

Source: NEDFi Databank Quarterly, Vol.1, Issue 1, 2002

Table14 : Area and Production of Foodgrains and Non-Foodgrains in Assam. (Area in hectare and Produc-tion in tonnes)

Year	Foodgrains		Non-Foodgrains		All crops	
	Area	Production	Area	Production	Area	Production
1951-52	1634158	1430349	302692	957700	1936850	2388049
1960-61	1804237	1667773	325568	1135927	2129805	2803700
1970-71	2095886	2039552	361410	1264101	2457296	3303653
1980-81	2474469	2635439	542538	1870625	3017007	4506064
1990-91	2755221	3441905	693707	3887295	3448928	7329164
1998-99	2700870	3433978	728945	3956554	3429815	7390532

Source: Some Basic Statistics of Assam 2000

The above table clearly shows that the production of all crops in Assam increase from 23.9 lakh tonnes in 1951-52 to 73.9 lakh tonnes in 1998-99, i.e., a three time increas However, during this period, production of non-foodgrains increased faster than th foodgrain production, i.e., non-foodgrains production increased by 4.1 times as compare to 2.4 times increase in foodgrains production.

c) Mineral Resources

Assam is quite well endowed with the mineral resources. Among these, petroleu (crude), natural gas, coal and limestone occupy important place.

Table 15 : Reserves of Important Minerals of Assam

Minerals	Estimated Reserves (in million tonnes)
Coal	371
Limestone	463
Sillimanite	50
White clay (Fuller's earth)	20
Quartzite	17
Granite (billion cubic metre)	10
* Petroleum (Crude)	156.2
* Natural gas (billion cubic metres)	151.7

Source: NEDFi Databank Quarterly, Vol.1, Issue 1, 2002; Profiles of States, EIS, CMI, March 1997

Besides the above-mentioned mineral deposits, other minerals found in Assam are feldspar, china clay, fire clay, and iron ore.

(d) Forest Resources

With the separation of various districts of Assam as full-fledged states during the 1950s and 1960s, the total forest area in Assam declined from 4951575 hectares in 1953-54 to 2613057 hectares in 1999-2000. At the end of the March 2001, the forest area constituted about 34.14 percent of the total geographical area of Assam (Economic Survey, Assam 2002-03). Assam possesses the percentage of forest cover as prescribed by the National Forest Policy of 1998. But it is also a fact that, among the North Eastern states, Assam ranks last in terms of forest cover (Basic Statistics of NER 2000).

Table 16 : Total Forest Area of Assam, 1953-54 to 1999-2000. (in hectare)

Year	1953-54	1960-61	1971-72	1980-81	1990-91	1999-00
Area	4951575	2529159	1753200	2062400	2141224	2613057

Source: Some Basic Statistics of Assam 2000

This extensive forest area of Assam is full with various rich flora and fauna. The forest products of the state mainly comprised of industrial wood, fuel wood, bamboo, stone, thatched cane, sand, etc. The out turn of industrial wood and fuel wood, two main forest products of the state, were 33.73 thousand cubic metre and 31.58 thousand stack cubic metre respectively during the year 1998-99.

Table 17 : Revenues Earned by the Forest Department in Assam (in Rs. crore)

Year	Timber	Others	Total
1991-92	10.86	6.67	17.53
1995-96	11.03	6.73	17.76
2000-01	2.86	8.51	11.37

Source: ADR 2002

As far as the revenues earned by Assam's Forest Department is concerned, then we find that the revenue earned from timber declined sharply after the Supreme Court imposed ban on felling of trees in 1996. However, the revenues earned on other items have shown a gradual upward trend.

One of the most attractive features of the State's forestry sector is its colourful wildlife comprising variety of animals, reptiles, birds and fishes. Assam is famous all over the world as the home of great one-horned rhinoceros. The highly endangered species of the world found in Assam are hollock gibbon, the stumped-tailed macaque, the capped languor and golden languor monkeys, the pigmy hog, the clouded leopard, the golden cat, the white winged wood duck, etc. So Assam is definitely an attractive destination where tourists can encounter a great variety of wildlife in her 5 National Parks, 20 Wildlife and Bird Sanctuaries (Economic Survey 2002-03).

However, the state has failed to reap large-scale benefits from this sector. The figures for the tourist flow to Assam in 2000 stood at just 10,01,577 for the domestic tourist and 5,959 for the foreign tourist.

Table 18 : Tourist inflow to Assam (in numbers)

Year	Indian	Foreign
1995	3,48,532	2,575
1998	9,39,721	3,843
2000	10,01,577	5,959

Source: ADR 2002

As a result of low tourist inflow, the revenue earned in this regard is also very low. For instance, in 1999-2000, the total revenue earned from tourists was just Rs. 63.98 lakhs. This revenue earned is quite insignificant compared to its vast potential.

e) Water and Fishery Resources

The fact that Assam is richly endowed with water resources can not be exaggerated. The large number of perennial rivers and their tributaries offer vast scope for irrigation and hydroelectric power facilities. Though the installed capacity of all power generating plants increased from 141.5 M.W. in 1980-81 to 572.4 M.W. in 2001-02, the share of hydel plants stands at just 2 M.W. It also clearly speaks about the inability of both the Central and state governments to invest required amount of fund in this critical area. Similar is the case with the irrigation facility.

Likewise, Assam is well endowed with fishery resources with 1.5 lakh hectares of inland water bodies and 5500 km. long river stretches. Though the fish production in Assam increased from 76.02 thousand million tonnes in 1990-91 to around 160 thousand tonnes, Assam still imports around 20,000 tonnes of fish annually, the value of which is estimated at around Rs. 80 crores (Dept. of Fisheries 1997-98).

INDUSTRIAL STRUCTURE

The present industrial state of Assam very well typifies the paradox of 'poverty amidst plenty'. The state has remained poor amidst huge and rich natural resources. In fact, the most striking feature of Assam's development is that it is falling behind the rest of the country (ADR 2002).

When we look at the growth of the industrial sector in Assam over the plan period, then we see some progress. For example, the number of registered factories increased from 119 in 1953 to 1861 in 1997-98. But the bottom line is that many other states in India progressed much faster than Assam and, hence, the gap between them widened.

Table 19 : Growth of Numvber of Factories in Assam, 1953-1997

Year	Number of Factories Registered	Number of Persons Employed (in '000)
1953	119	7
1961	1275	78.20
1970-71	1484	89.90
1980-81	1583	225.96
1990-91	1548	199.83
1997-98	1861	278.49

Source: Basic Statistics of Assam 2000

Also when we look at the type of the registered factories, then we find that most of these factories are dealing with agriculture, forest and mineral based products. For instance, in the year 2000, out of the 2406 registered factories, 1055 were the manufacturer of food and beverages, 421 were manufacturing wood and wood products, 405 were the manufacturer of other non metallic mineral products and few others engaged in related activities (Assam Statistical Handbook 2002). In true sense, therefore, the manufacturing base of the state is very much centred around the agriculture sector. In other words, a modern manufacturing base is very much absent in the Assam economy.

Table 20 : Index of Industrial Production in Assam (base-1971=100)

Industry	1995	1998
Sawing and Paneling of Wood	140	0
Manufacturing of Plywood	314	164
Manufacturing of Matches	87	0

Source: Directorate of Economics and Statistics, Assam as reported in the ADR 2002

However, it should be noted that after the Supreme Court ban of 1996, the number of wood based industries declined sharply from 634 in 1995 to 421 in 2000. The effect of the Supreme Court ban on forest based industries can be seen from the Table 20 of Index of Industrial Production in Assam. Therefore, it seems that development of forest based industry at the present juncture is not a viable proposition, given the fact that Assam just fulfills the norm of the forest cover prescribed.

Table 21 : Production, Sales and Employment of Khadi and Village Industries, 2000-01

(Rs. in lakh)

Industry	Value of Production		Total Sales		Employment	
	1988-89	1997-98	1988-89	1997-98	1988-89	1997-98
Khadi & Village Industry	1411.90	4066.55	1350.00	3468.73	1.10	1.11

Source: Basic Statistics of NER2000

A comprehensive rural development strategy will always call for the proper and speedy development of the village and khadi industries. Particularly, for agriculture sector like that of Assam which is characterised by the existence of the problem of seasonal and disguised unemployment, the development of these rural based industries is a must. Though the various figures of the khadi and village industries have shown an upward trend (Table 21), a lot still remains to be done, particularly in the context of efforts to link khadi and village industries in the overall tourism development strategy.

In terms of the SSIs also, the situation is not that encouraging. Already 1732 units of the SSIs have closed down due to various reasons. Even the presently working units of 4430 are beset with many problems. The dismally low capacity utilisation of this overall sector at 19.31 percent, the lowest figure even among the seven sisters of the North Eastern region, is a reflection of their various problems. The recent removal of the Quantitative Restrictions (QRs) under the WTO regime will put a mark on the question of their very survival.

Table 22 : Position of SSIs in Assam (as on 31.03.1998)

Closed Units	Working Units	Employment	Production (Rs. in lakh)	Capacity Utilisation (%)
1732	4430	34475	30325	19.31

Source: Basic Statistics of NER 2000

According to the Basic Statistics of the North Eastern Region 2000, the number of large and medium industries stood at 128 as on 31.03.1998, thereby accounting for 72.3 percent of the total large and medium industries in the region. But because of the lack of diversification in the industrial structure, the state has developed almost an enclave type of economy. Tea industry is very much a part of this pattern of growth, which came into existence during the British period itself.

Table 23 : Growth of Tea Industry in Assam

Year	No. of Tea Garden	Area under Tea (in hectares)
1951	785	155,674
1961	744	162,367
1971	750	-
1981	777	203,038
1991	848	233,284
1997	2472	229,843

Source: Basic Statistics of Assam 2000; Assam Statistical Handbook 2002

Table 24 : Annual Survey of Industries (Factory Sector) of Assam and Maharashtra, 1997-98

States	No. of Factories	Fixed Capital (Rs. crore)	Working Capital (Rs. crore)	Productive Capital (Rs. crore)	Workers Engaged ('000)	Net Value Added (Rs. crore)
Assam	1861	4255	1574	5829	125	1268
Maharashtra	20542	76281	34071	110352	1041	33792

Source: Statistical Abstract, CSO, 2000

The number of tea gardens in Assam increased from 785 in 1951 to2472 in 1999. The recent jump (1991to 1997) experienced in the number of tea gardens is basically due to the setting up of small tea gardens in almost every parts of Assam. However, this industry is also passing through a very difficult phase. Stiff competition in the international tea market from countries like Sri Lanka, China and Kenya, declining productivity and quality, growing unrest among the workers, etc. are few ails plaguing the tea industry of Assam.

As a whole, the industrial structure of Assam is quite backward in comparison to states like, say, Maharashtra. A comparative picture of industrial structure of these two states is provided in Table 24.

Table 24 shows that there is sea difference in the industrial structure of these two states. The productive investment (summation of the fixed and working capital) was Rs. 110352 crore in Maharashtra in comparison to Assam's figure of Rs. 5829 crore. Because of this disparity in the level of productive investment, the figures of number of factories in Assam and Maharashtra stood at 1861 and 20542 respectively. Likewise, the net value addition in Maharashtra's economy was as high as Rs. 33792 crore, contrary to Assam's figure of Rs. 1268 crore.

REASONS OF POOR LINKAGES

From above discussion, it is quite clear that the planned efforts of more than 50 years in Assam failed to create a progressive, modern and a well- diversified industrial structure that too amidst availability of plenty of resources. What are the reasons of poor resource - industry linkages in Assam? An in-depth study of the existing findings, reports, research papers, comments of the experts, etc. point basically towards the following factors:

a) Lack of Infrastructure: First let us have a look at the level of infrastructure that exists for the development of the agriculture sector. The irrigation potential created in Assam in 1995-96 stood at just 480078 hectares and the percentage utilisation of this potential was as low as 23.6 percent. This is one reason why the irrigation area for rice, the most important food crop in Assam, is only 21.1 percent in comparison to 99.2 percent in Punjab and 48.8 percent in India as a whole. This is also one of the reasons, along with the problem of floods, why paddy area under HYV seeds and fertiliser consumption is quite low in Asam in comparison to all-India figure as shown in table 26.

Table 25 : Irrigation Potential and Utilisation

Year	Irrigation Potential in Assam			Rice Area under Irrigation (%)		
	Created (ha.)	Utilised (ha.)	Utilisation (%)	Assam	Punjab	All-India
1983-84	280274	165199	58.9	23.0	98.7	42.3
1995-96	480078	113088	23.6	21.1	99.2	48.8

Source: ADR 2002

Notes:a) Data on irrigation potential created are as on March of every year and do not refer to the potential created during the year.

b) Data on irrigation potential utilised are for each year.

Table 26 : Paddy under HYV seeds and Fertiliser Consumption

Year	Paddy Area under HYV Seeds (%)		Fertiliser Consumption (kg./ha.)	
	Assam	India	Assam	India
1980-81	25.4	45.4	2.8	31.9
1995-96	49.9	73.2	13.5	74.4

Source: Fertiliser Statistics (Various Issues) as reproduced in ADR 2002

Likewise, in the absence of a proper network of regulated markets in Assam, the farmers have failed to reap benefits from the agriculture sector. In general, they are often forced by the village traders and other middlemen to sale their produce at lower than the market prices/ minimum support prices. For example, as on 31-3-1994, there were 34 regulated markets in Assam in comparison to 667 in Punjab.Lack of adequate storage facilities add to the problems of the farmers. They often have to go for distress sale of their produce. At the end of March 1999, there were only 46 warehouses of both State and Central Warehousing Corporations with a total capacity of 2,94,000 tonnes, which can fulfill the storage requirement of the state agriculture sector only partially.

Similar is the situation in terms of credit advanced to the agriculture sector of Assam. Table 27 tells us that the institutional sources have clearly failed to meet the credit requirement of the farmers. The credit advanced to farmers in Assam in terms Rs. per hectare is quite lower than Punjab and all-India figure.

Table 27 : Credit Advanced to the Agriculture Sector at 1980-81 Prices. (Rs./ha.)

Year	Assam	Punjab	All-India
1988-89	343.2	989.7	592.4
1996-97	237.9	1053.1	788.2

Source: ADR 2002

In fact, the credit advanced to the agriculture sector of Assam during the period of 1988-89 to 1996-97 came down from Rs. 342.2 per hectare to Rs. 237.9 per hectare. But as the corresponding all-India figure has gone up during the same period, the declining credit supply to this sector is not an all-India trend as it is evident from the figures of Punjab.

With these poor infrastructural facilities, when we add other constraints affecting agriculture sector of Assam like frequent and damaging waves of floods, severe attack of pests and insects due to hot and humid conditions, etc., finding an answer to the question of persistence backwardness of the agriculture sector of Assam does not look difficult.

In the field of industrial infrastructure also, the state is far from a healthy situation. The transport bottleneck is a major problem in this regard. The disruption of the partition not only increased transportation costs but it also dislocated traditional markets of the North East India. The road distance to the rest of the India increased, connectivity through road became poor, and lack of access to the port of Chittagong meant international markets also became less accessible (ADR 2002).

Even last 50 years of planned development efforts have not changed the situation much. In fact, as Table 28 shows, in terms of road density of surfaced road, Assam is far behind the all-India figure and the gap is increasing. Though investment has been made in this field in recent years to clear the backlog, the situation has not changed. Even the maintenance and the quality of the existing have suffered. In case of railways, the mighty Brahmaputra is creating a big problem. It runs through Assam dividing it into two parts. So just three bridges are not enough to facilitate comprehensive railway connectivity in Assam.

Table 28 : Density of Surfaced and Unsurfaced Roads (km. Per' 000 sq. km.)

Year	Surfaced Road		Unsurfaced Road	
	Assam	India	Assam	India
1990-91	127	312	709	297
1996-97	148	424	724	326

Source: CMIE: Infrastructure, Various Issues as reported in the ADR 2002

Electricity consumption is one of the lowest in the country with the figure of 116-kwh/ person/year at present. This is so in spite of the fact that Assam has huge power potential. The persistence power shortages have left power intensive industries helpless. Along with this, the increased power tariffs have rendered these and many other industries uncompetitive. And in the present national and international industrial environ-ment, the weak and the uncompetitive industries will perish. Likewise, though the telephone direct exchange lines have increased from 2.2 per 1000 persons in 1991-92 to 8.4 in 1998-99, the telephone density in Assam is still only about 40 percent of that in India.

In the financial sector, though the number of bank offices has increased from just 69 in June 1969 to 1263 in March 2000 along with deposit mobilisation from Rs.3,429 crore to Rs. 8,44,415 crore, the credit deposit ratio remains one of the lowest in the country. The figure of credit-deposit ratio just increased from 27.3 in 1969 to 32.0 in 2000. How has then the nationalisation of banks benefited the economy of Assam? Therefore, the conclusion we can draw from this is that in the money market of Assam, the informal segment is still dominant and flourishing. The presence of the capital market, which can help mobilising long term money for the industries, is almost negligible, though the Guwahati Stock Exchange exists in the state. However, the growth of industries and the capital market is somewhat a two-way traffic and neither of them is moving. And equity culture is very much lacking in almost whole country and so not surprisingly in Assam too.

(b) Natural resources themselves cannot guarantee industrial development. They have to be utilised properly. The Red Indians, the natives of America, lived for centuries in poverty amidst huge resources. The situation changed drastically once European skills and capital migrated there after the discovery of America by Columbus. So we have to learn to utilise these resources in the best way we can. For that we need the services of co-operant factors like adequate supply of capital and relevant technologies. Neither we have adequate supply of indigenous capital and technology nor we have succeeded in attracting these from outside Assam. In other words, the very factors that link resources with their ultimate use are in short supply in Assam.

Lack of indigenous entrepreneurial ability has also affected the pace of development in the state. It is also a fact that a plethora of financial institutions have emerged in Assam over the years to suit entrepreneurial requirements. Banks are flushed with funds but their problem is the low credit deposit ratio. But banks argue that proper demand has not been made by the users (Raghaviah and Das, 2001).

(c) Dearth of resources at the disposal of the government has been another reason. The state was expected to act as the initiator of the industrial growth. Lack of resources and its lower than optimum uses over the years have made the state deficient in certain critical areas. In an imperfect underdeveloped economy, market forces do not always give the best result. That is why state's intervention to guide the economy in the right direction is needed.

But in the past, mistakes were made in economic field by the government. That is one reason why finances of the state government are in shambles at present. Finances were not managed and invested properly in right channels during the last 50 years. Instead of becoming a self-propelled economy, it has become almost a stagnant economy. Assam spent 78 percent of total expenditure in 2000-01 in salary, pension, interest payments and repayment of loans (Bezbaruah 2002). But the seeds of this problem were planted long back.

PROBABLE POLICY OPTIONS / FUTURE STRATEGIES

At the sectoral level, as the ADR suggests, Assam's development needs to be centred around the following activities. In the primary sector, agriculture and its allied activities, including fishery, should get due attention. There is an urgent need to promote rabi season as an engine for agricultural growth in Assam. The kharif season is beset by the problem of floods and, hence, the farmers follow a kind of risk averting policies as they fear to loose their money invested in the costly inputs of HYV seeds and chemical fertilisers. No surprise that 92.5 percent of the cultivated land in Assam is flood prone.

Likewise, commercialisation of the agriculture sector is the need of the hour. Hence, the emphasis has to shift from production for self-consumption to market and production of crops, which have a high commercial value as well as compara-tive advantage vis-à-vis, other parts of the country. Following is such a list of crops, suggested by the ADR, on which Assam can focus on.

Furthermore, many processed food products like chips, juices, jams, spice preparations, etc. can be produced with these crops. These processed food products also have storage and transportation advantage over raw materials. They also fetch higher prices and help enlarging markets- both internally and externally. We have to remember here that all the North Eastern states are food importers from other parts of India, which involve heavy transportation cost. Therefore, Assam's rapid progress in the agricultural field can definitely help her to capture the food markets of at least this part of India. For this to happen, however, massive investment is required for developing the infrastructural facilities.

Table 29 : Crop Categorisation.

	Assam important in All-India agricultural map	Assam unimportant in All-India agricultural map
Acreage share>1% in total cropped area in Assam	Rice, Rapeseed and Mustard, Jute and Mesta, Tea, Potato and Arecanut.	Wheat and Pulses
Acreage share< 1% percent in total cropped area in Assam	Sweet potato, Banana, Papaya, Chillies, Turmeric, Cabbage, Cauliflower, Brinjal, Lemon, Orange and Pineapple.	Sugarcane

For enhancing fish production in the state, in the short run, the state must ensure efforts to popularize modern aquaculture practices, introduction of integrated and intensive farming, revitalisation of the extensive machinery and provision of credit support to the fish farmers. The long-term measures include scientific development of the water bodies, exploitation of the fisheries in the low-lying areas and regeneration of the unsuitable agricultural land to pisciculture activities. Scientific and healthy rearing of the fingerlings is also an important requirement for obtaining optimum fish production in the state.

In the secondary sector, industries with higher forward and backward linkages should get topmost priority. Past research studies (Dept. of Economics, G.U.) have identified the following industries as having higher forward and backward linkages: non-ferrous metal products, other metal products, iron and steel, other wood products, cotton textiles, other non-electrical equipments, paper and paper products, construction, electricity, petroleum products and chemical products. Though inter-sectoral linkages are important considerations for investment, the other factors like demand and competitive advantage should duly be taken into account. So resources in the future, mainly from the public sector, should be diverted towards these industries as they have higher multiplier effect.

In the tertiary sector, tourism and IT based activities hold much promise for the state. But again for encashing the vast potential of the tourism sector, a sound level of infrastructure facilities and a tourist friendly environment are basic pre-requisites. So a concrete and comprehensive tourism policy aimed at addressing issues like creating the required level of infrastructure base, developing the required pool of tourists guide, coordinating the works of various concerned departments, etc. can and will help this sector immensely in the long run.

As a whole, the following measures need to be initiated to improve the industrial scenario in Assam:

i) An industrial development conducive atmosphere needs to be created by solving the long- pending insurgency problem. Though it is a difficult task, but a whole hearted sincere effort can definitely make a difference in this regard.

(ii) The government of Assam will have to play, notwithstanding the problem of resource constraint, an important role in the development of socio-economic infrastructure facilities as well as ensuring good governance in the economy. For this, however, the state must have to improve its fiscal health sooner than later.

(iii) With better understanding with Bangladesh, the state must open and develop the waterways so that the water connectivity between the state and Kolkata as well few other foreign countries improve greatly.

(iv) Exploring the marketing opportunities for the products of the state in the neighbouring countries with diplomatic initiatives and better understanding. Also the state must try to extend the market for Assam's industries by making the various Central departments located in the state to purchase their requirements within the state through proper negotiation with the Central government.

REFERENCES

Assam Development Report 2002, Planning Commission, Government of India, New Delhi.

Basic Statistics of North Eastern Region 2000. North Eastern Council, Government of India, Shillong.

Bezbaruah, M.P. (2002): *Tourism and Economic Development of Assam.* North East Economic Association, Guwahati, Assam.

Clark, C. (1940). *The Conditions of Economic Progress.* Quoted in, *Indian Economy,* Datta and Sundharam.

Datta and Sundharam (2000). *Indian Economy*, S. Chand and Company Ltd., New Delhi-55.

Dept. of Economics, Gauhati University and ISI, Delhi Centre (1987-88). The Structure of Assam Economy (1982-83) and A Perspective Plan of Assam upto 2000 A.D.

Dept. of Fisheries (1998): *Status Report on Fisheries Development in Assam 1997-98*, Government of Assam.

Economic Survey (2002-03). Directorate of Economics and Statistics, Government of Assam, Guwahati.

Economic Survey (2001-02), Government of India, New Delhi.

Fisher, A.G.B. (1945). *Economic Progress and Social Security.* Quoted in *Indian Economy* Datta and Sundharam.

Government of Assam (White Paper), (1999), *State Finances: The Factual Position*, Finance (Economic Affair) Department, December.

Hazarika, B. (1999): Ananlysis of In Migration in Assam. Term paper presented as a partial requirement for the fulfillment of the Master of Population Studies, IIPS, Mumbai.

India 2002, Ministry of Information and Boardcasting, Government of India, New Delhi.

Lekhi, R.K. (1995). *The Economics of Development and Planning*, Kalyani Publishers, Ludhiana-110055.

National Accounts Statistics of India 1950-51 to 1995-96, EPW Research Foundation, Mumbai, October 1997.

NEDFi Databank Quarterly, Vol. I, Issue I, July 2002.

NEDFi: Resources and Investment Potential in North Eastern Region, Highlights.

NFHS-2: 1998-99, India, International Institute for Population Sciences, Mumbai-88.

Profiles of States, EIS, CMIE, March 1997.

Raghaviah, J. and Das, S. (2001). *Performance of National Equity Fund Scheme in the NE Region - A Preliminary Enquiry,* working Paper No.- 001- 2001. N.E.I.B.M., Guwhahati-22.

Selected Socio-Economic Statistics, India 2000, Central Statistical Organisation, Government of India, New Delhi.

Some Basic Statistics of Assam (2000), Directorate of Economics and Statistics, Government of Assam, Guwahati.

Statistical Abstract of Assam (1967-68 and 1978), Directorate of Economics and Statistics, Government of Assam, Guwahati.

Statistical Abstract: India 2000, Central Statistical Organisation, Government of India, New Delhi.

Statistical Handbook of Assam (1968,1969,1999 and 2002). Directorate of Economics of Statistics, Government of Assam, Guwahati.

Supplementary Observation
Economy of Assam : Resource-Industry Linkages

—Archana Sharma

INTRODUCTION

Assam is a state rich in natural resources like natural oil, natural gas, coal, rubber, tea and some minerals like granite, limestone and kaolin. The present state is much smaller than what it was forty years ago. It is still the largest economy in the North East. But unfortunately, what the NCAER commented about the State's economic progress in the early fifties remains the same at the end of the twentieth century ,the same compliment about the natural resources and the lament for not having made sufficient progress, with a note of consolation that it has the potentiality of making progress provided there is good governance. The present paper analyses the movement of the SDP and the share of the secondary sector in SDP over time. It gives a brief description of the major resources available in the State and the industries based on those resources. It analyses the industrial situation in Assam and attempts to find out the factors affecting a proper resource industry linkage.

MOVEMENT OF SDP

At present, the State is far behind the rest of the country in terms of different indicators of economic development. Whereas in the early fifties the State had a higher per capita income than the all India average, it started falling since the sixties and the fall continued (Table 1). In the post liberalisation period (Table 2), the distance of the per capita SDP and per capita NNP only widened to reach as high a value as Rs. 4,097 at constant prices.

Table 1 : Distance between Per Capita SDP and Per Capita NNP at constant (1980-81) Prices

Year	Distance between Per Capita SDP and Per Capita NNP
1950-51	+47
1960-61	-210
1970-71	-299
1980-81	-346
1990-91	-698
1995-96	-1002

Source: Vision Assam, 2025

Table 2 : Per Capita Income of Assam and India(in Rupees)

Year	At Current Prices		At Constant Prices	
	Assam	India	Assam	India
(1)	(2)	(3)	(4)	(5)
1993-94	5,715.0(-1983.2)	7,698.0	5,715.0(-1983.2)	7,698.0
1994-95	6,493.0(-2,383.4)	8,876.4	5,737.0(-2,350.6)	8,087.6
1995-96	7,001.0(-3,159.3)	10,160.3	5,760.0(-2,738.5)	8,498.5
1996-97	7,394.0(-4,206.9)	11,600.9	5,793.0(-3,242.9)	9,035.9
1997-98	7,966.0(-4,805.5)	12,771.5	5,796.0(-3,491.9)	9,287.9
1998-99	8,826.0(-5,886.4)	14,712.4	5,664.0(-4,069.1)	9,733.1
1999-2000	9,720.0(-5,842)	15,562.0	5,978.0(-4,089)	10,067.0
2000-01	10,198.0(-6,289)	16,487.0	6,157.0(-4,097)	10,254.0

Note: Figures in brackets indicate distance between Per capita SDP and Per Capita NNP
Source: Government of Assam: Economic Survey,2001-2002

The Net State Domestic Product at constant (1993-94) prices registered an annual growth rate of 4.21 per cent during 2000-2001, which was a decline compared with the growth rate of 6.9 per cent during 1999-2000. The growth rate in per capita real SDP was 2.99 per cent in 2000-2001 against 5.54 per cent in 1999-2000.Compared to the all India average rates, the growth rates for Assam have however been quite good during these two years (Table 3).

Table 3 : Growth Rates of Real Per Capita NNP and Real Per Capita SDP

Year	Growth rates(%)			
	ASSAM		INDIA	
	NSDP	Per Capita SDP	NNP	Per Capita NNP
1999-2000	6.9	5.54	6.4	4.4
2000-2001	4.21	2.99	3.7	1.9

Source: Government of Assam: Economic Survey, 2001-02 and Government of India: *Economic Survey*, 2001-02

SECTORAL DISTRIBUTION OF SDP

The share of the secondary sector

The large resource base leads to the expectation that the contribution of the secondary sector to SDP will be quite high. However, it is not true in case of Assam. The share of the secondary sector in State Income was 20.2 per cent in 1955-56 at current prices and 17.2 per cent at constant (1948-49) prices. No definite trend in the share of the secondary sector has been perceptible, with the share increasing to as much as 23.6 per cent in 1975-76, but dwindling between 13 and 15 per cent in the nineties (Table 4).

Table 4 : Share(%) of Secondary Sector in Net State Domestic Product

Year	1993-94	1995-96	1996-97	1997-98	1998-99	1999-2000	2000-01
(1)	(2)	(3)	(4)	(5)	(6)	(7)	(8)
At Current Prices	13.36	13.32	13.93	14.72	14.46	18.09	18.32
At Constant (1993-94) Prices	13.36	13.47	13.84	14.03	13.41	15.65	15.17

Source: Government of Assam: Economic Survey, 2001-2002

THE RESOURCES

Nature has really been gracious enough to shower her blessings bountifully on this north-eastern part of the country. Each of the seven North Eastern States and even the new eighth member has vast reserves of natural resources, although some of those are available only in small quantities. While counting the resources of Assam, tea and petroleum obviously come first, although the forest resources are also of no less importance.

TEA

Tea plants used to grow naturally in the Upper Brahmaputra valley. The existence of tea plants in the Brahmaputra valley is said to have been discovered and publicised by Mr. C.A. Bruce, an official of the British Empire, way back in1826. Since then tea industry flourished in Assam. This led to the establishment of a Tea Research Centre at Toklai in Jorhat. Although it was established after nearly ninety years of discovery of tea in the State, i.e. in 1911, the Centre has rendered valuable service towards developing more scientific and fruitful methods of cultivating tea plants, applying fertilizer, testing soil, selecting sites for garden and processing tea leaves. In 1974 an Instant tea project was also established at the Tea Research Centre of Toklai Experimental Station. A Tea Auction Centre - Guwahati Tea Auction Centre - was established in 1970 at Guwahati.

At present, tea is grown both in the Brahmaputra and Barak plains. Tinsukia, Dibrugarh, Sibsagar, Jorhat, Golaghat, Nagaon and Sonitpur are the districts where tea gardens are mostly found. Assam produces 51% of the tea produced in India and about 1/6th of the tea produced in the world.

PETROLEUM

Assam is the third largest producer of petroleum (crude) and natural gas in India. Petroleum and natural gas production is nearly 16% and 8% respectively of the total production in the country. In 1999, production of crude oil was 5001 thousand MT, and of natural gas was 1333 million cubic meters. The Digboi Moran and Rudra Sagar oil fields are the major source of oil and gas. The first commercial discovery of crude oil in the country was made in 1889 at Digboi near Brahmaputra valley in Assam. After the discovery of Digboi well No. 1, systematic drilling began in 1891. In 1899 a new company, Assam Oil Company was formed. In 1921, Burmah Oil Company of U.K. joined the exploration of oil fields in Assam. In 1953, a new oil discovery was made at Naharkatia near Digboi and then Moran in 1956. In 1959 Oil India Pvt. Ltd. was incorporated for the production and development of the oil fields. In 1981, Oil India Limited (OIL) became a wholly owned Government of India Enterprise for the management of oil fields in Assam. (www.eastindiavya-par.com)

NATURAL GAS

Like petroleum, natural gas is a valuable source of power and various other chemical by-products. In Assam, almost all the petroleum producing areas of the Brahmaputra Valley, especially Naharkatia, Moran, Lakuwa and Rudrasagar, contains 'associated natural gas'. The important industries so far built up on the basis of the natural gas of Assam are Namrup Fertilizer Factory, Namrup Thermal Power Project, Production of Carbon Black, Assam Petrochemicals and Assam Gas Company, which provides liquified petroleum gas for domestic use. There are LPG bottling plants at Duliajan, North Guwahati, Silchar etc. The BRPL also uses natural gas as raw material to produce various chemicals.

COAL

Assam has large reserves of coal too. The State is said to contain about 1200 million tonnes of coal reserves. The first coal mining in the region was started in 1865 at the Makum coal-fields by the erstwhile Assam Railway and Trading Company and now it is mined by the North-Eastern Coal-Fields. Makum coal field includes four major mines: Namdong Colliery on the western end. Borgolai Colliery at the central portion. Ledo colliery at the central portion. Tippong colliery on the eastern extremity of the coal field. The coal belt extends from Dilli-Joypur in the west to Tipok in the east. The entire coal in this region is unique in the sense that it is highly volatile (36% - 42%), has low ash content (3%-15%) and possesses high crackling index (10%-29%). Coal is found also in Koilajan, Sheelvetta in Karbi Anglong, Khota-Arda Dithor, located near Umrangshu, N.C.Hills. Saraipung-Tarajan located 5 km. south west of Bhadoi Panch Ali of Tinsukia district. Garampani, within the Kopili reservoir area and Singrimari, Halliday Gunj in Dhubri.

CLAY

Assam is endowed with fairly large reserves of sedimentary white clays as well as Kaolin or 'China clay', which forms an important basic raw material for ceramic or refractory industries. Scientific surveys indicate the sporadic occurrences of china clay, fire clay, fuller's earth (white clay) and sedimentary clay deposits throughout Assam. China clay is found to occur at many places in the Karbi Anglong district. This clay is quite suitable for the manufacture of medium to low-grade white wares and other ceramic products like stoneware pipes, sanitary ware, glazed tiles and bricks.

White fire clay is found in Sheelveta and Kailajan in Karbi Anglong covering an area of 0.21 sq. km. Scattered deposits of fuller's earth (white clay) occurs along the bank of Pagladia river at Subankhata and Bhutan Khuti areas in Nalbari. White coloured sedimentary clay in Irangmara, situated at the southern part of Silchar, Cachar.

IRON ORE

Occurrences of banded-iron ore have been located in the Chanderdinga hills and Abhayapuri areas in Goalpara district and in the Aradanga-Rangchapara areas on the border of Kamrup.

COPPER

Copper minerals occur in the Mahamaya hills in Goalpara district.

GOLD

Gold is reported to occur in sands, gravels and alluvial terraces along some of the rivers in the Lakhimpur, Sibsagar and Darrang districts of Assam.

GYPSUM

Gypsum in the form of selenite crystals and disseminated in shale beds occur at a few places in Karbi Anglong.

FELSPAR

Felspar is a common mineral found to occur in association with granites. Recently workable felspar deposits have been recorded near the Hahim area in Kamrup district.

GRANITE

Light coloured granite in Mahamaya hills in Goalpara district, Agiathuri and Dudhkuri hills in Kamrup district and at a few places in Karbi Anglong. Black granite is also found at a few places in n Goalpara and Nagaon.

LIME STONE

State Directorate with the help of IBM proved a reserve of 30 million tons of cement grade lime stone at Koilajan Deposit in Karbi Anglong Dilai parbat deposit, Sainilango at 28 km East of Bokajan, Sheelbhetta deposit, about 40-km from Diphu railway station, Panimur deposit, Umrangshu deposit, New Umrangshu deposit, Tumbung deposit in North.Cachar Hills etc., have proved reserve of cement grade of different quantities.

QUARTZITE

Jiajuri Hill and Thanajuri Hills in Karbi Anglong, southern part of Nowgong district Barhola and Chapanala deposits in Nagaon, have different varieties of Quartzite reserves like feldspathic quartzite and kaolinized quartzite.

SILIMANITE

Chippinala, connected with Phuloni at N.H. 36 by a 9 km. long road. Phuloni is again connected with Diphu, the district head quarter of Karbi Anglong.

FOREST RESOURCES

Valuable timber (Sal, Bansum, Gamari, Sishu, Sonaru, Titasapa, Khokan, Simalu, etc., available in the entire State. Particularly in Kamrup, Nagaon, Goalpara and Darrang districts. These can be used for producing railway sleeper, plywood boards, hard board, etc., building materials, furniture, other timber frames, icons, paper pulp and fuel.

Medicinal plants (Arjun, Aswagandha, Ashok, Molar, Silikha, Amlakhi, Bel, Sewali, Jaba, Sarpagandha, Teteli, Boira, Thekera, Salmugra, Olatkambal, Ou, Bakul, Jamu, Amara, Tulasi, etc. and hundreds of herbs and creepers) are also available in the entire State. These medicinal plants are useful for preparing medicine oil and scent and also medicines. Cane (Raidang, Patidoibet etc.) and Bamboo (Bhaluka, Jati, Kotah, Nal, Kekoa, etc) are also available in plenty.

Cane is found all over the State particularly Upper Assam and Cachar and bamboo is grown all over the State. Both the items are used for making furnitures. Bamboo is a popular building material and is also used for making agricultural implements. It is an important ingredient for making paper pulp. Other utility plants like Khoir, Nahar, Agor, Majankari, Som, Era, Sowalu, Barhamthuri, Majathi, Indigo, Bata, Khagari, Kher, Takeu, Tara, etc. are also found in the entire State and are useful for preparing non-edible oil, Muga and Eri cocoon rearing , building materials scent and other utility goods like, khoir, gum, dye, jaju, etc. (Gazetteer of India: Assam, 1999).

These resources are supplemented by the rare animal and birds of different varieties, and the vast water resources, and the agricultural resources like paddy, maize, wheat, jute, cotton, sugar cane, arecanut, coconut, fruits, vegetables & spices: banana, pineapple, orange, potato, sweet potato, papaya, cabbage, onion, tapioca.

THE INDUSTRIAL SCENARIO

The State has a number of industries based on local resources. There are a number of traditional industries viz., weaving in country looms, pottery, blacksmithy, village carpentry, bamboo and cane works, spinning of endi, mug and mulberry silk, vegetable dying, wood carving, hand pounding of rice, manufacture of ivory products etc. Many of these industries are however decaying and have not been able to stand the tough competition thrown by machine made goods due to lack of capital and marketing facilities (Gazetteer of India, Assam State, 1999). Sometimes even because of the reluctance of the new generation to take up such painstaking, low earning trades.

The mining and heavy industries in the State are: petroleum, industries based on natural gas, coal industry and cement industry. Assam today has four refineries altogether at Digboi, Noonmati (Guwahati), Bongaigaon and Numaligarh, while a host of other industries have followed the petroleum industry, by and large depending on it. These include the fertiliser industry at Namrup, and the Assam Petrochemicals Ltd. also at Namrup, both dependent on natural gas. Besides there are series of polyester textile units, these being downstream units to the Bongaigaon Refinery and Petro-Chemicals Ltd. Two giants of the oil industry in the country, Oil India Ltd, and Oil & Natural Gas Corporation Ltd., carry out massive exploration and drilling activities in the State, while the state-sector Assam Gas Company and the public sector Gas Authority of India Ltd. handle the transportation of natural gas to the different industries (Dhingra, B.S.: Knowing India 3: Assam: PIB, GOI).

Among the large scale and medium industries, the foremost one is the Tea industry. Tea industry has contributed substantially to the economy of Assam. About 17 percent of the workers of Assam are engaged in the tea industry. Paper Industry and its associated industries viz. Caustic Soda and Chlorine Plant, India Carbon limited and Assam Carbon limited can be placed next. Match factories, Chemical and Spinning Units, Sugar Industry, Spun Silk mills, Jute Mills, Asbestos Cement Industries, Industrial Gas Units, LPG Units, Metal Industries and Railway Workshops are some of the medium scale industries in the State. Some of these industries utilise forest resources. The Small Scale Units are mostly agro based. These are: Rice Mills, Flour Mills, Saw Mills, Ginning Mills, Plywood Industries,

Soap Factories, and Oil Mills etc. Although this makes a long list of industries, many of these industrial units have been identified as sick units and some of these are also defunet.

NUMBER OF REGISTERED FACTORIES IN THE STATE & THEIR PERFORMANCE

The statistics on the number of registered factories in the State for the period 1995-97 show that the highest number of registered factories is manufacturers of food products. But there is a decrease in the number of such units also between 1996 and 1997. Other manufacturing units which showed a decline between 1995 and 1997 are: Textile units, wood and wood products and paper producing units (Table 5).

Table 5 : NUMBER OF REGISTERED FACTORIES IN ASSAM:1995-97

Industry Code (Maj-Gr)	Type of Industry	1995	1996	1997 (Provisional)
20-21	Manf. of food products	1036	1041	1034
22	Manf. of beverage, Tobacco and Tobacco products	6	4	6
23	Manf. of cotton textiles	23	21	17
24	Manf. of wool, silk and synthetic fibre textiles	13	14	15
25	Manf. of jute , hemp and mesta textiles	5	5	5
26.	Manf. of textile products(including wearing apparel of the than footwear	4	5	4
27	Manf. of wood and wood products,furniture and fixtures	634	624	584
28	Manf. of paper and paper products and printing ,publishing and allied industries	34	34	32
29	Manf. of leather and leather and fur products(except repair)	2	2	2
30	Manf. of rubber ,plastic petroleum and coal products	53	54	53
31	Manf. of chemicals and chemical products (except petroleum and coal)	34	39	38
32	Manf. of non-metelic mineral products	421	320	400
33	Manf. of basic metal and alloys	78	78	78
34	Manf. of metal products and parts (except machinery and transport equipments	79	82	77
35	Manf. of machinery machine tools and parts (except electrical machinery)	25	29	31
36	Manf. of electrical machinery apparatus appliances and supplies and parts .	12	12	9
37	Manf. of transport equipments and parts .	5	5	4
38	Other manufacturing industries	1	1	2
39	Repair of capital goods	31	35	32
40	Electricity	18	18	19
41	Gas and steam	8	9	9
42	Water works and supplies	3	3	3
70	Land transport	3	3	3
74	Storage and warehousing	13	13	18
75	Communication services	1	1	1
92	Education, scientific and research services	3	3	3
96	Personal services	2	2	2
97	Repair services	54	54	50
	Grand Total 2601	2511	2526	

Sources: Chief Inspector of Factories, Assam.

Table 6 : INDEX NUMBER OF INDUSTRIAL PRODUCTION IN ASSAM: 1994-1997 (Base:1970=100)

Industry Group	1994	1995	1996	1997	% change over '94 to' 95	% change over '95 to 96	% change over '96 to 97
1. Grain Mill Products	100	86	118	54	-14.00	37.21	-54.24
2. Manu. Of refining of Sugar	15	26	13		73.33	-50.00	-100.00
3. Manu.of other edible Oils and fats	57	35	32	50	-38.60	-8.57	56.25
4. Tea Processing	188	188	200	201	0.00	6.38	0.50
5. Manu.of Cotton Textiles	107	82	101	104	-23.36	23.17	2.97
6. Manu. Of Jute Textiles	302	312	294	394	3.31	-5.77	34.01
7. Sawing and Planning of wood (other plywood)	115	140	128	3	21.74	-8.57	-97.66
8. Manu.of veneer plywood and their products.	454	394	314	178	-13.22	-20.30	-43.31
9.Mau. Of fertilizers and pesticides	47	103	76	76	119.15	-26.21	0.00
10. Manu.of matches	76	80	70	7	5.26	-12.50	-90.00
11. Petroleum refinery Products	265	272	294	316	2.64	8.09	7.48
12.Petroleum products NEC	77	39	46	20	-49.35	17.95	-56.52
13. Alluminium Products	188	142	131	86	-24.47	-7.75	-34.35
ALL INDUSTRIES	204	202	210	202	-0.98	3.96	-3.81

Source: Government of Assam: Directorate of Economics and Statistics

Table 7 : Annual Survey of Industries (Summary Results):Assam:1993-94-1994-95

Item	Unit	1993-94	1994-95	%age Share in the all India Total(1994-95)	%age changein 1994-95 over 1993-94
(1)	(2)	(3)	(4)	(5)	(6)
1.Factories	Number	1435	1514	1.23	5.51
2.Fixed Capital	Rs.Crores	1519.05	1936.87	0.70	27.51
3.Working Capital	-do-	806.44	918.69	0.78	13.92
4.Invested Capital	-do-	2184.49	2791.69	0.72	27.80
5.Outstanding Loan	-do-	1,410.12	2,526.45	NA	79.17
6.Total Works	Number	94,832	1,01,371	NA	6.90
7.Total Employees	-do-	1,13,562	1,24,095	0.36	9.28
8.Wages to Workers	Rs. Crore	130.40	172.90	NA	32.59
9.Total Emoluments	-do-	188.12	254.78	0.72	35.43
10.Total Input	-do-	2,695.07	3,170.49	0.81	17.64
11.Value of Products	-do-	3,506.80	4,122.85	NA	17.57
12.Value of Output	-do-	3,682.89	4,315.85	0.83	17.19
13.Depreciation	-do-	128.07	158.85	0.85	24.03
14.Value Added	-do-	859.75	986.51	0.90	14.74
15.Net Income	-do-	785.28	730.10	NA	-7.03

Source:Government of Assam: Directorate of Economics and Statistics, Statistical Handbook of Assam, 1999

Table 8 : ANNUAL SURVEY OF INDUSTRIES(SUMMARY RESULTS): ASSAM:1997-98 to 1999-2000

Item	Unit	1997-98	1998-99	1999-2000	% change in '99-98over 97-98	% change in '99-00 over 98-99
(1)	(2)	(3)	(4)	(5)	(6)	(7)
1. Factories	Numbers	1855	1424	2339	-23.23	64.26
2. Fixed Capital	Rupees in lakh	423929	226719	244803	-46.52	7.98
3.Working Capital	Rupees in lakh	154033	87735	135898	-43.04	54.90
4. Invested Capital	Rupees in lakh	562960	327263	382707	-41.87	16.94
5. Total Employees	Numbers	153541	112546	113799	-26.70	1.11
6. Value of gross output	Rupees in lakh	740046	807850	870991	9.16	7.82
7. Net fixed Capital formation	Rupees in lakh	NA	3074	11503	NA	274.20
8.Net value added	Rupees in lakh	142129	152439	263861	7.25	73.09
9.Net income	Rupees in lakh	120820	137890	246273	14.13	78.60

Source: Government of Assam: Directorate of Economics and Statistics,Economic Survey:Assam 2001-2002

The index number of industrial production figures of the various industries (Table 6) shows that compared to 1970, only Manufacture of Jute Textiles, Petroleum and Refinery Products, Tea Processing, Manufacture of Plywood and Veneer Products and Manufacture of Cotton Textiles showed upward movement, but that too was only marginal in case of Plywood and Veneer Products and Cotton Textile. Between 1994 and 1997, the production of these industrial units showed a negative trend along with the remaining ones in the list.

From the Annual Survey of Industries (Summary Results) (Table 7), it can be seen that the position of the State in the industrial map of the country is abysmally low. This can be gleaned from all the variables representing the industrial scenario of the State. The total number of factories in the State account for only 1.23 percent of the country's total. The total value added by the factories is only 0.9 percent of the total value added by the same sector at the all India level.

The indicators reflecting the various aspects of the industrial sector do not even reflect any perceptible improvement over time. While the number of factories increased by 5.5 percent between 1993 -94 and 1994-95, and there is also an increase in fixed, working and investible capital, the overall scenario is gleam as there is a negative turn in the net income but a very high rate of increase in the outstanding loan.

The same indicators for the period 1997-2000 (Table 8), however, show a much improved picture. Particularly the change between 1999-2000 is very encouraging.

Table 9 : SALE OF ELECTRICITY BY TYPE OF CONSUMERS IN ASSAM (M.U.) : 1980-81 to 1997-98

Period	Total Units Sold to Ultimate Consumer	Domestic	Commercial	Industry		Public Lighting	Free Supply	Irrigation	Public Water Works	Tea Garden	Bulk Supply in the State	Outside State	Rural Industry
				Low and Medium Voltage	High Voltage								
(1)	(2)	(3)	(4)	(5)	(6)	(7)	(8)	(9)	(10)	(11)	(12)	(13)	(14)
1980-81	638.9	65.0	30.0	61.1	245.0	8.0	-	15.0	4.0	9.7	-	-	-
1990-91	1636.0	180.0	115.0	149.0	440.0	14.0	10.0	26.0	27.0	240.0	165.0	218.0	50.0
1995-96	1782.3	464.3	172.7	51.6	477.8	11.7	-	43.9	54.5	246.8	286.7	-	-
1996-97	1960.4	575.5	168.9	261.1	260.4	10.8	-	45.6	35.1	251.4	246.5	42.5	62.5
1997-98	1877.0	449.6	159.5	203.8	628.4	6.0	-	25.3	34.8	NA	253.4	5.3	-

Source: Government of Assam: Directorate of Economics and Statistics, Statistical Handbook of Assam, 1999.

REASON FOR CONCERN

The overall industrial scenario in the State has created concern not because the position of the State is lower than that of the Indian average, nor because the share of the secondary sector is low, because such situations are very likely to occur in case of some of the States, particularly those which are predominantly agricultural. Assam is also a predominantly agricultural State, but that situation is rather by default and not by choice. Moreover, the State has not been able to catch up with the rest of the country in the pace of agricultural growth as well because of various constraints, floods and lack of modernisation of agriculture being the two main reasons.

The main reason for the concern regarding the slow rate of industrial development of the State is that the State still have enormous unused potential, and utilisation of those resources, through the forward and backward linkages, will surely be able to trigger off the rate of growth of the State economy.

Table 8 : ANNUAL SURVEY OF INDUSTRIES(SUMMARY RESULTS): ASSAM:1997-98 to 1999-2000

Item	Unit	1997-98	1998-99	1999-2000	% change in '99-98over 97-98	% change in '99-00 over 98-99
(1)	(2)	(3)	(4)	(5)	(6)	(7)
1. Factories	Numbers	1855	1424	2339	-23.23	64.26
2. Fixed Capital	Rupees in lakh	423929	226719	244803	-46.52	7.98
3.Working Capital	Rupees in lakh	154033	87735	135898	-43.04	54.90
4. Invested Capital	Rupees in lakh	562960	327263	382707	-41.87	16.94
5. Total Employees	Numbers	153541	112546	113799	-26.70	1.11
6. Value of gross output	Rupees in lakh	740046	807850	870991	9.16	7.82
7. Net fixed Capital formation	Rupees in lakh	NA	3074	11503	NA	274.20
8.Net value added	Rupees in lakh	142129	152439	263861	7.25	73.09
9.Net income	Rupees in lakh	120820	137890	246273	14.13	78.60

Source: Government of Assam: Directorate of Economics and Statistics,Economic Survey:Assam 2001-2002.

Among the major constraints in the path of industrial growth of the State, infrastructural constraints like disruption of communication both within the State and with the rest of the country, marketing disadvantages, power constraint and inefficient management ,lack of local entrepreneurial skill, lack of funds, have been identified as the major ones. Particularly low availability of power comes first. The present power position of the State shows that the per capita power consumption in the State is very low, 116 Kwhr against the all India average of 479 Kwhr, in 1996. The major portion of the power is used for domestic purposes. The latest trend however shows that power consumed by high voltage industrial units is on the rise (Table 9).

Table 9 : SALE OF ELECTRICITY BY TYPE OF CONSUMERS IN ASSAM (M.U.) : 1980-81 to 1997-98

Period	Total Units Sold to Ultimate Consumer	Domestic	Commercial	Industry: Low and Medium Voltage	Industry: High Voltage	Public Lighting	Free Supply	Irrigation	Public Water Works	Tea Garden	Bulk Supply in the State	Outside State	Rural Industry
(1)	(2)	(3)	(4)	(5)	(6)	(7)	(8)	(9)	(10)	(11)	(12)	(13)	(14)
1980-81	638.9	65.0	30.0	61.1	245.0	8.0	-	15.0	4.0	9.7	-	-	-
1990-91	1636.0	180.0	115.0	149.0	440.0	14.0	10.0	26.0	27.0	240.0	165.0	218.0	50.0
1995-96	1782.3	464.3	172.7	51.6	477.8	11.7	-	43.9	54.5	246.8	286.7	-	-
1996-97	1960.4	575.5	168.9	261.1	260.4	10.8	-	45.6	35.1	251.4	246.5	42.5	62.5
1997-98	1877.0	449.6	159.5	203.8	628.4	6.0	-	25.3	34.8	NA	253.4	5.3	-

Source: Government of Assam: Directorate of Economics and Statistics, Statistical Handbook of Assam, 1999.

The State is grossly dependent on outside sources for power supply (Table10) inspite of the enormous hydro power potential. Only 4.49% of the total water resources in the State have so far been utilised (NEDFI: NE Data Bank).

REMEDIES

Several expert Committees have probed into the causes of slow progress of the State and suggested remedies (Jain Committee, Shukla Committee, Planning Commission). The expert Committees are unanimous in their opinion regarding the necessity of improving infrastructure, particularly power, road and rail connectivity.

In 1997, a new industrial policy was announced for the NE Region. The Government of Assam also announced a new Industrial policy.

INDUSTRIAL POLICY

The Policy aims at maximizing the utilisation of locally available resources, promote domestic and foreign investment, develop local entrepreneurial skills especially those of women, focus on the development of key sectors like food processing, handloom and textiles and rural non-farm sector. The policy also aims at revitalizing the sick Public Sector Undertakings and move towards a broad industrial base with appropriate forward and backward linkages (Eco Survey: Assam:2001-02).

INCENTIVES

Development Subsidy upto 10% of fixed capital upto Rs. 0.3 million per unit, for all sector of industrial units where fixed investment does no exceed Rs. 50 million. Special state capital subsidy of 30% of cost of main plant and machinery, upto Rs. 3 million, for industries, till the Central Capital Investment.

Subsidy scheme is re-introduced

Additional state capital subsidy of 5% of fixed capital investment for pioneer units, subject to a ceiling of Rs. 1 million.

Assam Finance Tax on industries lowered from 12% to 4%.
50% subsidy on power consumption of upto 1MW (Max. Rs. 0.5 million,) 30% between 1 MW (Max.Rs.1.5 million) and 20% above 5 MW (Max Rs.3 million).
Subsidy on manpower development to compensate for cost of training.
Equity participation in medium-and large-scale units and SSIs by AIDC and ASIC respectively.

STATE IDENTIFIED PRIORITY SECTORS

Coal & Hydro-Elecric Power, Plastic Processing,
Rapid Transport System, Textiles, Urban Infrastructure Development

CONCLUSION

The overall industrial scenario induces one to conclude with the same old statement of potentials sans utilisation. However, the figures analysed above for the period after 1997, had shown some improvement. This is however too early to say, whether this is an impact of the new industrial policy and the measures taken on the basis of the suggestions made by the expert Committees, particularly when the data are not available even for five years after the actions have been taken. Moreover, many of the provisions suggested by the expert Committees have not as yet been complete.

The economy has faced several shocks during the post liberalisation period, viz., the shock on the timber industry due to the Supreme Court ban, large scale unemployment due to financial crunch of the State Government and also as a measure for assuring good governance, the large bouts of floods and the problems of internal turmoil like insurgency.

Moreover, the State is still predominantly rural and unfortunately the perennial problem of floods, which have crippled the rural economy, has not yet been tackled properly. The water resources, which could have been the source of joy and the foundation stone of growth of the economy, have been turned into sorrow. For a proper resource industry linkage, the right kind of rural urban linkage also must be established through proper road connectivity, marketing facilities etc., to ensure the flow of resources to the industries and the flow of finished goods to the market. It is already too late for a new industrial policy for the State; such delays may once again halt even the little progress that has been made.

Efficient management at every step is the call of the time, whether downsizing the government, which has become the key word now, is the panacea or whether better means for utilising the manpower more efficiently need be evolved is also a question.

3

Development Experience of Manipur: A Framework for Industrialization

—*Amar Yumnam*

Introduction

The development experience of a province in a country can be appreciated in two ways. First, we may compare its position *per se* in an initial period with that at a terminal period. Secondly, we may compare its position with that of other provinces or the national average at a point of time or over a period of time. The present paper is an attempt of the first variant. It tries to give basically the evolution of the economy during the last few decades and its possible ramifications on the industrialization scenario.

Macro-Economic Profile of Manipur

Geographical Setting

Given the prevailing technology and orientation for development interventions so far, geography seems to have been destiny in so far as the development of Manipur in a larger context is concerned. With this understanding in mind we provide a brief geographical setting of the State here, the economic implications of this would be discussed later.

Manipur is a land-locked isolated, hill-girt, State having a geographically distinct identity. It is situated in the eastern most part of North-Eastern hilly region of India. It lies between 93°58' and 94°45'E longitudes and 23°50' and 25°42'N latitudes. The State is almost rectangular in shape. According to physical features, she can broadly be divided into two natural regions, viz. the hills and the valley. The hills encircling the valley stretch from the north to southern direction with an average height ranging between 1,500 to 1,800 metres above the mean sea level. The hills on the northern part of the State are higher and measure around 3,000 metres above the mean sea level. The hills have sub-temperate to temperate climate. The valley in the centre is surrounded by rows of hills on all sides. It covers an area of about 2,238 sq. km. constituting only about 10 percent of the state's total area. The average elevation of the valley is 790 m above the mean sea level. The valley, which is considered to be the "rice bowl" of the State, has sub-tropical to sub-temperate climate.

The climate in the State has distinct winter, warm humid and rainy seasons. The average rainfall during the last 10 years was 1482.2 mm. with heavy precipitation during the months of June, July and August.

Manipur has two important rivers viz., the Imphal river (Manipur river) and the Barak river with many small rivers. The Loktak Lake in the southern part of the valley is the biggest fresh water lake in the North-Eastern region of India. During rainy season the lake covers an area of about 260 sq. kms. and during dry season the size of the lake reduces to 60 sq. kms. There are also a number of smaller lakes in the southern portion of the valley.

Village Population

Whereas the absolute population size, coupled with the domestic product figures, has implications about the size of the market for investment, it is ultimately the scope for exploiting the benefits of "snowball effect" of agglomeration economies that decide the diversification and growth of a regional economy. *Ceteris paribus*, this scope for agglomeration economies would initially determined by population concentrations. So we give a picture of the population concentration in the State in Table-1[1] It is clear from the tale that, as at the national level, the maximum concentration of population is found in the villages of populations ranging from 2,001 to 5,000 persons. It is also clear that as high as 36.49 percent of the State's total population live in villages of less than 1,000 persons, which is a proportion higher than the national average by 10.66 percentage points. In a similar comparison it can be seen that about 58 percent of the State's total population reside in villages of less than 2,000 persons as compared to the national average of 52 percent. These, along with the low absolute size of the population, speak volumes about agglomeration economies nature of development interventions to be undertaken and technological orientation to be adopted.

Table 1 : Distribution of Population by Village Size Categories, 1991

Region/Size Category	<=500	501-1000	1001-2000	2001-5000	>=5001
India	5,13,58,103	9,06,63,035	13,99,04,991	15,83,61,739	6,89,40,345
	(9.52)	**(16.81)**	**(25.94)**	**(29.73)**	**(18.35)**
Manipur	2,22,242	1,76,674	2,30,598	3,65,534	98,050
	(20.33)	**(16.16)**	**(21.1)**	**(33.44)**	**(8.97)**

Source: *Census of India*

Note: Figures within parentheses indicate percentages of the relevant totals.

Expenditure Categories

The above scenario of the scope for agglomeration economies would be clearer if we examine the expenditure categories of the population. Table 2 is a picture of the distribution of households by per capita monthly expenditure groups. It reveals the following:

a) the urban scenario is much worse in the State than at the national level in as much as 90 per cent of the households in the urban areas of the State belong to the expenditure class of less than Rs.300 per month;

b) the rural scenario is better in the sense that most of the households belong to the middle categories or Rs.235-Rs.455; and

c) the proportion of households in the highest category is much lower in the State than at the national level.

Table 2 : Distribution of Households and Population by Monthly Per Capita Expenditure Groups, 1993-94 (in %)

Expenditure	groups	Region Manipur	Households All India	Population Manipur	All India
Rs.235	Rural	19.1	44.5	21.2	49.0
	Urban	62.3	41.0	71.5	48.7
Rs.235-300	Rural	35.8	20.5	37.0	20.4
	Urban	29.7	20.3	23.6	20.5
Rs.300-455	Rural	38.5	21.9	36.9	20.2
	Urban	7.1	23.9	4.4	20.2
Rs.455 and above	Rural	5.9	12.2	4.4	9.8
	Urban	0.4	13.8	0.3	9.5

Source: *National Sample Survey, 50th Round.*

Infrastructure: Road Density

Given the topographical structure of the State, roads are the only means for transport. An idea of the relative road infrastructure development of the State can be had from Table 3. It is seen from this table that the road density (length of the road per 1,000 sq.km.) in the State, as of 1994,[2] stands at 327 km which is far below the national average of 628 km. This lower density of roads in the state is accounted for mainly by the very low density of roads in the hill districts. Whereas the density of roads in the hill districts range from as low as 136 km/1000 sq.km. in Chandel to 383 km/1,000 sq.km. in Ukhrul, in all the valley districts of Manipur it is higher than the national average, viz., Imphal (1,188 km), Bishnupur (862 km) and Thoubal (1,345 km). *The road density figures give a direction that a road development strategy should take by emphasising the necessity of development in the hill areas of Manipur for a sustainable development in the State. Such a development would also act as a catalyst for emergence of horticulture and spices based activities in the outlying regions of the State. Further well-planned development of road networks can be expected to have far reaching effects on the land property rights system in the State. To begin with, such a development will definitely enhance the scope for private profits. This will in turn set into motion a move for institutionalizing the property rights system along modern lines.*

Economic profile

An aggregative of the economy of the State can be had from the State Domestic Product figures. Two series, one based on 1980-81 prices and another on 1993-94 prices, are given here. In Table 4, we give a picture based on the 1980-81 prices.[3] The reconciliation figures for the different series are not yet available for the State. It is evident from Table 4 that the Net State Domestic Product (NSDP) of the State rose from Rs.19,956 lakh in 1980-81 to Rs.1,75,521 lakh in 1997-98 at current prices. In other words, the NSDP of the State at current prices rose 8.8 times during the period from 1980-81 to 1997-98. At constant 1980-81 prices, the NSDP rose by 2.31 times during the same period.

Table 3 : Road Density by Districts, 1994 (length of road per 1,000 sq. km.)

District	Area (sq. km.)	Road Length (Km.)	Road Density
Valley Region:			
Imphal (East & West)	1,228	1,750	1,425
Bishnupur	496	443	894
Thoubal	514	726	1,412
Valley Total	**2,238**	**2,919**	**1,304**
Hill Region:			
Senapati	3,271	1,154	353
Ukhrul	4,544	1,827	402
Chandel	3,313	688	208
Churachandpur	4,570	1,024	224
Tamenglong	4,391	1,035	236
Hill Total	20,089	5,728	285
Manipur	**22,327**	**8,646**	**387**
All India 1992	**3,287,263**	**2,065,039**	**628**

Source: *Basic Roads Statistics, Manipur 1997 & Census of India 1991.*

As regards the per capita NSDP, it became Rs.8, 194 at current prices in 1997-98 as compared to Rs.1, 419 in 1980-81. In other words, the per capita NSDP rose 5.77 times in current prices and 1.52 times at constant prices during the period under discussion. Whatever the case, the rise in per capita NSDP has been lower than that of NSDP, implying thereby that the rise in income has not kept pace with the rise in population. The present sectoral shares of the NSDP are 52 per cent for services, 38 per cent primary and the remaining 10per cent manufacturing.

A picture with 1993-94 as the base year is provided in Table 5. The telling picture emerging from both the tables (Tables 4 and 5) is the weak expansion rate of the per capita income. This reinforces the weak basis for creation of agglomeration economies mentioned earlier.

The picture becomes more revealing if we compare the per capita SDP of the State with the national average. Such a comparison is provided in Table 6. As is evident from the table, the per capita income of the State is lower than the national average. Further, the distance between the national average and the State average has been widening over the years. In 1985-86, the per capita income of the State was about 82 per cent of the national average, but it has declined continuously to 79 per cent in 1990-91 and 77 per cent in 1996-97. This implies a relative slowdown of the economy.

Table 4 : Net State Domestic Product of Manipur, 1980-1998

Year	Net State Domestic Product				Per Capita NDSP			
	Current Prices (Rs. lakh)	Constant (1980-81) Prices (Rs. lakh)	Index with 1980-81 as Base		Current Prices (in Rs.)	Constant (1980-81 Prices (in Rs.)	Index with 1980-81 as Base	
			Current	Constant			Current	Constant
1980-81	19,956	19,956	100	100	1,419	1,419	100	100
1981-82	24,202	21,103	121	106	1,677	1,462	118	103
1982-83	25,635	21,445	129	108	1,729	1,447	122	102
1983-84	30,398	23,296	152	117	1,997	1,530	141	108
1984-85	34,444	24,257	173	122	2,205	1,553	155	109
1985-86	37,225	25,617	187	128	2,322	1,598	164	113
1986-87	42,604	26,125	214	131	2,590	1,588	183	112
1987-88	54,177	28,166	272	141	3,211	1,669	226	118
1988-89	60,583	29,526	304	148	3,502	1,707	247	120
1989-90	63,408	29,934	318	150	3,574	1,687	252	119
1990-91	72,301	31,622	362	159	3,976	1,739	280	123
1991-92	86,769	34,285	435	172	4,660	1,841	328	130
1992-93	95,711	35,939	480	180	5,023	1,886	354	133
1993-94	1,15,633	36,692	579	184	5,929	1,881	418	133
1994-95	1,30,579	39,584	654	198	6,542	1,983	461	140
1995-96	1,41,223	40,719	708	204	6,914	1,993	487	140
1996-97	1,57,065	43,406	787	218	7,510	2,075	529	146
1997-98	1,75,521	46,156	880	231	8,194	2,155	577	152

Source: Directorate of Economics and Statistics, Manipur.

Note: 1996-97 figures are quick estimates and 1997-98 ones are advanced estimates.

Table 5 : Net State Domestic Product of Manipur, 1993-2001

Year	Net State Domestic Product				Per Capita NDSP			
	Current Prices (Rs. lakh)	Constant (1980-81) Prices (Rs. lakh)	Index with 1980-81 as Base		Current Prices (in Rs.)	Constant (1980-81 Prices (in Rs.)	Index with 1980-81 as Base	
			Current	Constant			Current	Constant
1993-94	1,14,144	1,14,144	100	100	5,833	5,833	100	100
1994-95	1,22,269	1,11,518	107	97.70	6,102	5,565	104.61	95.41
1995-96	1,41,015	1,15,124	123.54	100.86	6,875	5,613	117.86	96.23
1996-97	1,67,116	1,32,899	146.41	116.43	7,961	6,331	136.48	108.52
1997-98	1,94,467	1,45,472	170.37	127.45	9,054	6,773	155.22	116.12
1998-99	2,31,107	1,54,095	202.47	135.00	10,520	7,014	180.35	120.25
1999-00 Q	2,55,430	1,62,445	223.78	142.32	11,370	7,231	194.93	123.97
2000-01 A	2,80,829	1,71,113	246.30	149.91	12,228	7,451	209.63	127.74

Source: *Directorate of Economics and Statistics, Manipur*.

Notes: Q: Quick estimates; A: Advanced estimates.

Table 6 : Per Capita Income in 1980-81 Prices, Manipur and India

Year	All India (Rs.)	Manipur (Rs.)	Manipur as a % of all-India
1985-86	1,944	1,588	81.69
1990-91	2,213	1,739	78.58
1996-97	2,698	2,075	76.91

Now this relative slowdown is to be seen in the background of the fact that in 1991 census there was a decline in the proportion of total workers in the total population to 41.51 per cent from 43.20 per cent in 1981. Further, the proportion of main workers declined from 40.35 per cent in 1981 to 37.36 per cent in 1991.

A picture of the distribution of usually working persons in the principal status is given in Table 7. The most revealing features of the table are the absolutely lower figure in the manufacturing sector in the urban areas and fairly high figure in the wholesale and retain trade services, and the very high figures for community services. It must be emphatically mentioned here that the manufacturing percentages given for the State are not due to development of industrial activities, but are accounted for by the high percentage of women reporting as engaged in the handloom sector.

Table 7 : Distribution of Usually Working Persons in the Principal Status by Industry, 1993-94 (Percentages)

Real	Rural		Urban	
	Manipur	All India	Manipur	All India
Agriculture	64.2	76.9	27.1	10.6
Mining and quarrying	0.1	0.7	-	2.2
Manufacturing	8.5	7.1	11.0	23.6
Electricity	0.3	0.2	1.2	1.1
Construction	3.2	2.6	3.0	6.6
Wholesale and retail trade	5.1	4.6	15.0	19.9
Transport, Storage, etc.	1.7	1.6	3.5	8.4
Financial, Insurance, etc.	1.0	0.3	2.0	3.5
Community services	15.8	5.9	37.0	25.1

Source: NSS 50th Round.

Sectoral Shares

What is of greater importance from the angle of Kuznets transformation are the sectoral shares. It would be interesting to review the evolution of the sectoral shares and compare this with the stylized facts from development history. In Table 8 we have a picture of the sectoral shares of Net State Domestic Product over the last two and half decades at constant prices. The figures from 1975 to 1979 are on the basis of 1970-71 prices, 1980 to 1992-93 on 1980-81 prices and the rest of 1993-94 prices. The pictures emerging from the table are revealing:

1. First, the scenario of Manipur is absolutely different from the Kuznets transformation. Whereas the stylized facts of Kuznets transformation are, *inter alia*, the increasing importance of the shifts from home work to employee status, increasing importance of formal education and the shift from agriculture to industry to services. The shift from agriculture to services bypassing industry seen in Manipur is not of the Kuznets variety.

Table 8 : Percentage Distribution of Net State Domestic Product at Constant Prices

Year	Primary Sector	Secondary Sector	Tertiary Sector
1975-76	58.21	8.62	35.17
1976-77	57.05	8.68	34.27
1977-78	58.65	8.55	32.80
1978-79	54.87	9.65	35.48
1980-81	49.10	7.65	43.25
1981-82	47.70	8.34	43.96
1982-83	45.86	8.42	45.72
1983-84	45.79	8.45	45.76
1984-85	44.96	8.80	46.24
1985-86	43.78	9.04	47.18
1986-87	41.85	8.80	49.35
1987-88	40.85	8.72	50.43
1988-89	38.79	9.76	51.45
1989-90	38.26	9.48	52.26
1990-91	38.02	10.20	51.78
1991-92	37.84	9.98	52.18
1992-93	35.64	10.28	54.08
1993-94	37.87	15.73	46.40
1994-95	36.92	15.43	47.65
1995-96	35.68	16.56	47.76
1996-97	32.76	18.66	48.58
1997-98	33.45	19.96	46.59
1998-99 P	32.36	24.99	42.65
1999-00 Q	32.10	26.29	41.61
2000-01	31.35	26.82	41.83

Note: P-Provisional estimates; Q - Quick estimates; A - Advanced estimates.
Source: Directorate of Economics and Statistics, Manipur.

2. Secondly, whatever shift being unfolded in Manipur has very little to do with raising the production capacity of the State. The educational services component of the services sector would of course have a positive impact on productive capacity in the long run, but the lion's share of the services sector are of hotels and restaurants[4] and petty traders and the administrative services.
3. The increasing share of the secondary sector being seen during the last decade is more of statistical jugglery than of real phenomenon. This is so because the NSS 50th Round rediscovered the real activity of people, and this forms the basis of the new series of domestic product data. In other words, it does not imply increasing scope of the secondary

sector in the State, but rather a better coverage of the activities people engaged in. As mentioned earlier, the major component of this turns out to be the traditional activities women engaged in, which were not properly covered earlier. The unregistered manufacturing and construction activities constitute around 99 per cent of the total secondary sector.

4. Further, the secondary and tertiary activities of the State, with their nature and composition explained above, are not externally creating activities, and *ipso facto*, do not create agglomeration economies.

Non-Agricultural Activity of the State: Public Sector Enterprises

It is already a common knowledge that of the few public sector enterprises the State has got, some have busted, some are incurring losses and some are absolutely non-functional. In any case there has been no value addition from these enterprises for quite many years. The technological and transaction cost of their revival are getting heavier by the day and uneconomical given the pace of technological changes in recent years. On hindsight, these enterprises seem to have suffered, besides the usual factors mentioned, from the following:

1. Any late starter in the industrialization process should possess a higher know-how capacity to either imitate or adapt the existing technology. These enterprises seem to have ignored this aspect in the beginning.
2. These enterprises could not adequately appreciate the aspect of geography as destiny. The geographical factors were not adequately factored-in while formulating the projects.
3. These enterprises started in a context of small market size, where the competition from outside would be particularly intense.
4. The administrative capability of the state to efficiently execute the projects was questionable at any time in the past and is still questionable.
5. The problem does not end with the administrative capability, but also extends to the political capital of the State. In fact, the political capital of the State is yet to be properly tuned to the requirements of industrialization.

Other non-Agricultural Activities

Given the industrial scenario explained above and in the absence of any fundamentally functioning industrial units in the State, it makes very little sense to talk of the industrial sector in the way we usually discuss. In fact, whatever secondary sector we basically observe in the State are non-agricultural activities of very low scales. Though there have been some diversification, these too are activities with little externalities and hence very little creation of agglomeration economies, if any.

The Economic Censuses being conducted since 1977 provide an idea of the non-agricultural activities being undertaken. There have been four such censuses since 1977. The 1977 Census covered only non-agricultural establishments employing at least one-hired worker on a regular basis. Since then, the scope of the Economic Censuses have been expanded to include even non-crop production agricultural activities and own account enterprises with no hired worker. That the non-agricultural activities in the State have remained more or less a household level of enterprises rather than evolving into a full-scale industrialization process is easily evident from the comparison of the number of persons employed per establishment. The number of usually employed workers per establishment was 5.63 in 1977 and in the Fourth Economic Census in 1998 it still remains around the same level at 5.79. The number of hired workers per establishment was 5.14 in 1977 and stands at 5.17 in 1998. This constancy in numbers indicates

a) the non-exploitation of economies of scale in the non-agricultural activities in the State; and
b) the absence of externalities in the non-agricultural activities of the State.

Economic Censuses

A picture emerging out of the Fourth Economic Census of 1998 is given in Table 9 as it relates to the non-agricultural activities. These activities have been classified into:

1. Mining and quarrying;
2. Manufacturing and repairing services;
3. Electricity, gas, water supply and sanitation;
4. Construction;
5. Wholesale and retail trade, restaurants and hotels;
6. Transport, storage and communication services;
7. Finance, insurance and real estate, and
8. Community, social and personal services.

Table 9 reveals that the 80,489 enterprises in the State give employment to 2,00,728 persons in the State at the rate of 2.49 persons per enterprise. This means, if we are to see the picture in totality the scale and externally dimensions are absolutely negligible. In other words, these in no case indicate a trend towards the Kuznets transformation.

This un-encouraging trend in the non-agricultural activity scenario becomes more revealing if we examine the growth trends of enterprises and employment as in Table 10. It is evident from Table 10 that the growth trends of enterprises during the last three Economic Censuses have far exceeded that of employment. This implies that the additional enterprises emerging are more of household one rather than in keeping with the stylized fact of growth. Further, there has been a slowdown in the growth rate indicating perhaps a point of saturation in this sector. This is so particularly because the slowdown is visible in both the own account enterprises and establishments in a very marked way.

Table 9 : Non-Agricultural Enterprises and Employment, 1998

Location	Number of all Enterprises			Number of Persons Usually Working in Enterprises		
	Own Account Enterprises	Establishments	Total	Own Account Enterprises	Establishments Hired Workers	Establishments Total
Rural	27,749 (51.01)	11,036 (55.42)	38,785	37,630 (51.88)	45,640 (44.35)	49,909 (43.28)
Urban	26,655 (48.99)	8,876 (44.58)	35,531	34,908 (48.12)	57,724 (55.65)	65,412 (56.72)

Note: Figures within brackets indicate percentages of the relevant total.

Source: Report on Fourth Economic Census, 2001.

Table 10 : Growth Trends of Enterprises, 1980-98 (Percentages)

Location	Enterprise		Employment	
	1980-90	1990-98	1980-90	1990-98
Rural	79.31	27.20	66.94	25.21
Urban	72.78	36.53	36.48	29.82
Combined	76.32	31.38	49.93	27.55

Source: Same as of Table 8.

The Bottom-Line

The picture emerging from the analysis of the non-agricultural sector can be summarized as follows:

i. The non-agricultural enterprises in the state are basically household based enterprises and absolutely small in size.
ii. They are neither labour nor capital intensive in their very nature.
iii. They are more of a nature with non or minimal externalities. So they do not generate agglomeration economies so important for growth in a regional context.
iv. They happen to be enterprises which would be there in any context rather than ones needed for Kuznets transformation.

Resources and Industrialization

The above scenario establishes that there has been no perceptible move towards the Kuznets transformation in the State of Manipur. The failure of all the public sector enterprises establishes beyond doubt the policy failure in the State. The increasing predominance of the own account enterprises indicates a reversal in the industrialization process. The lack of creation of externalities indicates absence of a conducive environment. The nature and scale of the activities imply lack cf any correlation with the resources.

In these circumstances we need a re-look at the concepts of resources and industrialization in the specific context of Manipur. By resources, we generally mean the elements of nature which we can convert into products. In the light of the experience of Manipur, it is felt that there is a need for redefining the concept of resource to include the market size, administrative capability, political capital, locational empirics and technological position. In fact, these are the most potent factors which might have pulled down the State in the race towards industrialization. As mentioned earlier, any industrial unit started in the State should be able to overcome the technological and topographical constraints and still be competitive, both in terms of price and quality, to the similar products from outside. This is a very tall order in any context, and more so in the case of Manipur.

Conclusion

The history of failure so far and the requirements for successful industrialization in the conventional sense raise the whole issue of what should be the orientation for industrialization in the State. The locational constraints have been a rather limiting factor to the State in so far as any product involving weight is concerned. The search should be for an industrialization strategy with much value-addition but very little weight, if any. This is the only way to make the products emanating from the State competitive. This points to the presence of high proportion of people with formal education, in which the technically qualified groups constitute a major portion, as the resource on which to build the future industrialization process of the State. This, in other words, means Manipur should rather be looking at the weightless way of industrialization rather than the conventional one involving transport of weighty materials across spaces.

Notes and References

1. The figures are of 1991 Census as the detailed 2001 figures are yet to be available. There is every possibility of higher concentration now particularly in the hill areas in the aftermath of the recent ethnic clash. The economic implication, however, is limited as the concentration might be mostly in the lower orders.
2. These figures would still be worse in real terms as we are to have the latest year figures as there has been very little maintenance during the last few years.
3. The reconciliation figures for the different series are not yet available for the state.
4. The hotels and restaurants in Manipur are mostly what we conceive of, but more of the road-side tea stalls.

4

Structural Change and Strategy of Development : Resource-Industry Linkages in Meghalaya

—Rajesh Dutta

Introduction

Structural change refers to the transition of a traditional inward looking agriculture-dominated economy into an outward looking industrial economy brought about by economic development. The transformation process brings about significant changes in attitudes and institutions. With increasing employment opportunities in the secondary and tertiary sectors accompanied by technological improvements, there is an increasing stock of capital; greater labour efficiency and superior exploitation and usage of natural resources. Such radical changes, however, can be brought about by sweeping changes in land reforms, enlargement of markets, new technologies in the production process, new and efficient credit institutions, etc. Since this pattern has not been observed in the State of Meghalaya this paper makes an attempt to investigate the probable reasons. In the course of doing so we analyze the nature of progress over the last 30 years. It also investigates into the nature and degree of structural transformation and the extent of resource-industry linkages with the intention of creating an awareness, to view and review, future policy options and programmes meant for the State. It must be mentioned here that there is a predicament when it comes to the availability and reliability of data. Different sources provide conflicting data and with this in mind the study has generously relied upon secondary data obtained from the State's Directorate of Economics and Statistics.

STRUCTURAL CHANGE

(a) Sectoral Origin of Output

Structural transformation requires the study of sectoral origin of aggregate output at constant prices as well as the occupational distribution of population. A study of the sectoral contribution to the Net State Domestic Product (NSDP) of Meghalaya (Table-1) reveals the following broad trends:

a) The share of the primary sector has gone down from 41.88 percent in 1980-81 to 35.14 percent in 1990-91 and further down to 28.75 percent in 1995-96. Estimates for 2000-01 and 2001-02 show a revival of this sector.

b) The share of the secondary sector of NSDP has decreased from 14.55 percent in 1980-81 to 10.65 percent in 1990-91. In 1995-96 there was a marginal increase and the estimates for 2000-01 and 2001-02 do not reflect a turn about performance of this sector.

c) The share of the tertiary sector improved from 43.56 percent in 1980-81 to 59.48 percent in 1995-96. However, estimates for 2000-01 and 2001-02 show a decline in this sector's share.

The overall trend in Meghalaya corresponds to the structural change in the national economy. However, the share of the primary sector at the national level is lower (around 26 %), while the share of the secondary sector is higher (around 22%) when compared to the State. A hasty look and one gets the impression that the State is keeping pace with the macro level trends. For instance, the primary sector's thinning percentage of contribution to the NSDP and a significantly contributing tertiary sector are definitely encouraging signs of an economy's growth and development. But then how long can these sectors' activities sustain themselves in the absence of a growth sustaining secondary sector. In fact the secondary sector of the State has remained virtually stagnant in the period under consideration. The dismal performance, as may be noted from table 1, of this sector necessitates a breakup and an examination of its sub-sectors. The break-up, exhibited in Table 2, discloses the following:

a) The share of manufacturing within the group is second to construction but with significant differences in contribution. This sub-sector's share, within the group, increased from 22.15 percent to 39 percent in 1980s. But, by 1995-96 its share fell to 35.64 percent and the estimates for 2001-02 puts the figure at 16.02 percent, a plunge of around 100 percent. Of the registered and unregistered units which comprise manufacturing, the share of the latter has remained greater than double. As a percent of NSDP, the contribution of manufacturing increased from 3.22 percent in 1980-81 to 4.2 percent in 1995-96, but within the next six years, its share fell to 2 percent.

Table 1: Contribution/Shares in NSDP of Meghalaya

Sector	Contribution (Rs. in lakhs)/Share (Percent in Bracket)					
	1980-81	**1985-86**	**1990-91**	**1995-96**	**2000-01(Q)**	**2001-02(ADV)**
Primary	7523 (41.88)	8405 (39.22)	10683 (35.14)	10506 (28.75)	67910 (32.59)	72393 (32.45)
Secondary	2614 (14.55)	2557 (11.93)	3236 (10.65)	4304 (11.78)	25543 (12.26)	27899 (12.51)
Tertiary	7825 (43.56)	10470 (48.85)	16480 (54.21)	21738 (59.48)	114909 (55.15)	122773 (55.04)
NSDP	**17962**	**21432**	**30399**	**36548**	**208362**	**223065**

Q = QUICK ESTIMATES, ADV = ADVANCE ESTIMATES

Note:Figures for 2000-01 and 2001-02 are at 1993-94 prices and for the others at 1980-81 prices.

Source: Directorate of Economics and Statistics, Meghalaya.

b) Construction, the largest constituent within the secondary sector, has made an average contribution of over 80 percent in the period under consideration. This is anticipated in a newly formed State because of the infrastructure required for administrative purposes. Rather the surprising aspect is the employment generated by this sub-sector as evident in the subsequent discussion. Its contribution to NSDP has oscillated and though its share declined from 11.67 percent in 1980-81 to 10.07 percent in 2001-02, it remains significant.

c) The final sub-sector viz., electricity and water supply has been subject to a negative rate of return (RoR) in the period 1980-81 to 1995-96. In fact in 1995-96, out of 17 State Electricity Boards (SEBs) all except those of Bihar, Assam and Meghalaya had a positive rate of return. In terms of section 59 of the Electricity (Supply) Act, 1948, SEBs are required to earn a minimum ROR of 3 percent of their net fixed assets in service, after providing for depreciation and interest charges (INDIA 1999). Though the new series of data gives a positive contribution of this sector, its contribution to NSDP has remained less than 1 percent.

Table 2: Contribution of Sub-Sectors to the Secondary Sector and NSDP (Rs. in lakhs)

Sub-Sector	1980-81	1985-86	1990-91	1995-96	2000-01(Q)	2001-02(ADV)
1) Manufacturing	579	709	1262	1534	4314	4469
	(22.15)	(27.73)	(39.00)	(35.64)	(16.89)	(16.02)
	[3.22]	[3.31]	[4.15]	[4.20]	[2.07]	[2.00]
(a) Registered	158	229	471	456	1435	1481
	(6.04)	(8.96)	(14.56)	(10.59)	(5.62)	(5.31)
(b) Unregistered	421	480	791	1078	2879	2988
	(16.11)	(18.77)	(24.44)	(25.05)	(11.07)	(10.71)
2) Construction	2096	2046	2572	3738	20273	22463
	(80.18)	(80.02)	(79.48)	(86.85)	(79.37)	(80.52)
	[11.67]	[9.55]	[8.46]	[10.23]	[9.73]	[10.07]
3) Electricity and	(-)61	(-)198	(-)598 R	(-) 968	956	967
Water Supply	(-2.33)	(-7.94)	(-18.48)	(-22.49)	(3.74)	(3.47)
					[0.46]	[0.43]
SECONDARY SECTOR TOTAL	2614	2557	3236	4304	25543	27899
NSDP	17962	21432	30399	36548	208362	223065

R = REVISED, Q = QUICK ESTIMATES, ADV = ADVANCE ESTIMATES
Note: (i)Figures within ( ) are percentages of Secondary Sector totals
(ii) Figures within [ ] are percentages of NSDP.
Source: Domestic Product of Meghalaya, State Income Division, Directorate of Economics and Statistics.

(b) Occupational Pattern in Meghalaya: An Analysis of Trend during 1971-2001

The occupational structure of the State also signals the degree of structural change. Table 3 provides an in-depth view of the population's occupational pattern. Despite the changes in the definition of 'worker' in various censuses, broad inferences on the trend of occupational distribution may be drawn.

Table 3: Economic Classification of Population

Category	1971	1981	1991	2001(P)
PRIMARY SECTOR				
i) Cultivators	308,978	363,010	395,804	457,195
	(69.15)	(62.56)	(55.31)	(61.55)
ii) Agricultural Labourers	44,131	57,899	89,492	172,975
	(9.88)	(9.98)	(12.51)	(23.29)
iii) Livestock, forestry, fishing,	11,885	37,898	45,735	
hunting, plantations, orchards	(2.66)	(6.53)	(6.39)	
and allied activities				
iv) Mining and Quarrying	669	3985	4266	
	(0.15)	(0.69)	(0.60)	
SECONDARY SECTOR				
v) Manufacturing, Processing,				
Servicing and Repairs				
a) Household Industry	4874	4862	2885	17,956
	(1.09)	(0.84)	(0.40)	(2.42)
b) Other than households	5645	9509	12,509	
	(1.26)	(1.64)	(1.75)	
vi) Construction	4240	10,131	11,349	
	(0.95)	(1.75)	(1.59)	
TERTIARY SECTOR				
vii) Trade & Commerce	13,323	20,410	37,617	
	(2.98)	(3.52)	(5.26)	
viii) Transport, Storage	5,603	7131	10,358	
and Communication	(1.25)	(1.23)	(1.45)	
ix) Other Services	47,480	65,385	105,572	
	(10.63)	(11.27)	(14.75)	
A. Main Workers (i-ix)	4,46,828	5,80,220	7,15,587	7,42,762*
	[44.17]	[43.44]	[40.32]	[32.21]
B. Marginal Workers	-	33,221	41,735	2,13,663
		[2.49]	[2.35]	[9.27]
Total Workers (A+B)	4,46,828	6,13,441	7,57,322	9,56,425
	[44.17]	[45.92]	[42.67]	[41.47]
C. Non Workers	5,64,871	7,22,378	10,17,456	13,49.644
	[55.83]	[54.08]	[57.33]	[58.53]
Total population (A+B+C)	1,011,699	1,355,819	1,774,778	2,306,069

P=PROVISIONAL; * INCLUDES (iii), (iv), v (b), (vi) to (ix)

Note: (i) Figures within ( ) are percentages of main workers

(ii) Figures within [ ] are percentages of total population

Source: Census of India 1971, 1981, 1991 and 2001 (PROVISIONAL)

The proportion of main workers engaged in the primary sector decreased from 82 percent to 75 percent in the period 1971-91. The 1990s saw a reversal of trend and the 2001 provisional census suggests a record percentage of main workers (more than 85 percent) engaged in the primary sector. The reasons maybe the following: (i) the availability of winter resistant seeds developed by the ICAR (Indian Council Of Agricultural Research) and (ii) the improvements in rural infrastructure(storehouses, connectivity, etc.) and (iii) the encouragement given to commercial crops because of the higher returns. An increase in the number of cultivators is however indicative of the sub-division/fragmentation of land and an increase in the number and percentage of agricultural labour points toward landlessness and poverty. An increasing percentage engaged in the primary sector also reveals the non-performance of the secondary and tertiary sectors in providing increasing and productive employment opportunities to the rapidly increasing population.

Less than 5 percent of main workers were engaged in the secondary sector in the period 1971-91. An increase in the employment in the household industry was witnessed in the 1990s after an absolute and percentage fall in the 1970s and 1980s. Even in the absence of detailed data for 2001, one can infer that the secondary sector continues to employ only an insignificant percentage of the total main workers.

Employment of main workers in the tertiary sector increased from around 15 percent to 21 percent within 1971-91. The present picture is of course different. The increasing percentage of main workers engaged in the primary sector means that the other 2 sectors provide for less than 15 percent of the main workers employment opportunities as per provisional census 2001. Therefore the combined share of employment in the secondary and tertiary sectors fell from around 25 percent in 1990-91 to less than 15 percent in 2001.

The analysis of the sectoral contributions to the NSDP and the occupational structure of the population show the retrogressive nature of developmental activities since the 1990s. What has led to this state of affairs? Apparently the non performance of the secondary sector is to fault. What then are the possible reasons for the non performance? The 'achievements' that one hears of and reads in the papers and statistical books seem mere rhetoric when people at large have not benefited. Meghalaya remains predominantly agricultural and rural (81%) with a vast majority living below the poverty line, 48.9 percent as per 1996-97 estimates, of which 54.5 percent is rural (10th Five Year Plan, Draft Proposals, Vol-1). Since this paper's focus is on resource-industry linkages, we can only comment on the apparent and provide some insights into the probable. Consequently, the negligence of other issues will raise numerous questions which will remain unanswered in this paper.

NEED FOR SECTORAL ADJUSTMENT IN THE STATE PLAN

The following section is an examination of the budget allocations across sectors over the planning period of the State. After national independence the areas of present Meghalaya were included in the State of Assam. The hilly areas remained largely inaccessible because of the Inner Line Permits which continued even after the colonial powers had left. However those who obtained licenses/permits exploited the resources of the simple minded tribals. But a rising class of indigenous elites armed with education, knowledge and foresight grouped together and pressurized the Union Government for greater autonomy. This led to a Constitutional Act and the establishment of Autonomous District Councils under the Sixth Schedule. Under these provisions though greater autonomy was granted to the minority

Table 4: Approved Outlays-Percentage Distribution by Sectors, Meghalaya

Sl. No.	Sector	4th Plan 1969-74	5th Plan 1974-79	6th Plan 1980-85	7th Plan 1985-90	Annual Plan 1990-91	Plan 1991-92	8th Plan 1992-97	9th Plan 1997-02 (P.O.)	10th 2002-07
1	Agriculture and Allied Activities	26.94	24.53	13.21	18.27	14.67	18.51	15.10	15.66	9.82
2	Irrigation & Food Control & Power	4.61*	18.34*	3.40	2.64	4.22	3.51	5.49	3.92	3.25
3	Industry and Minerals	6.78	6.10	4.04	4.33	4.90	3.44	4.57	4.08	4.80
4	Transport and Communications	33.95	21.04	21.28	18.18	18.71	18.67	24.30	19.24	18.02
5	Social & Community Services (including Education)	21.68	17.08	29.65	27.89	27.79	27.75	26.04	33.84	34.35
6	Economic Services		6.37	0.26	1.10	2.04	1.92	2.92	2.04	1.99
7	General Services		2.43	1.83	7.17	2.23	2.97	5.82	2.16	2.23
8	Unallocated/Others	3.92	4.10							
9	Energy			19.15	16.25	20.51	18.67	10.01	12.96	17.20
10	Science, Technology & Environment				0.39	0.23	0.35	0.34	0.29	0.26
11	Rural Development	0.79		2.94	2.75	3.51	3.63	3.90	5.34	6.58
12	Special Area Programmes (Border Area Development)	1.32		4.26	2.27	1.20	1.00	1.51	0.48	1.50
	Approved Outlays: Total (in Cr.)	38.00	89.53	235.00	440.00	175.00	210.00 (205 R)	1029.00	2500.62	3000.00
	Actual Expenditure: Total (in Cr.)	36.24	99.07	259.96	539.04	166.16	186.48	877.24(A)	1841.80(A)	

* = Includes Power, R=Revised, P.O. =Proposed Outlay; A= Anticipated

Source: (i) Draft Proposals of various Five-Year Plans; (ii) Pocket Statistical Handbook (various issues); (iii) Basic Statistics of North Eastern Region, 2000, N.E.C.

tribals of undivided Assam, the hill areas remained backward and underdeveloped. The feeling of alienation led to fresh demands for autonomy in the 1960s and when Meghalaya attained autonomy on 2nd April 1970 it was one of the most backward states in the country. The Fourth Plan of the State was carved out of the Hill Areas Plan of Assam without considering her special requirements. Given the socio-economic conditions the ad-hoc Fourth Plan sought to overcome numerous deficiencies.

The first self-governing Five-Year Plan for Meghalaya, i.e. the 5th Five-Year Plan Draft Proposal, was based entirely on adhoc estimates and broad objectives because of the absence of data. The emphasis was rightly on creating socio-economic overheads to speed up economic progress. The ambitious Draft Proposal was, however, short-lived as the proposed outlay was pruned by the Centre from Rs.203.62 crores to Rs.89.53 crores. This probably set the pace of development along with other factors.

Overall, the investment priorities have centered around four categories: (i) Agriculture and allied activities, (ii) Transport and Communications, (iii) Social and community services and (iv) Energy. It is expected that initially large investments were necessary for setting up administrative machinery. To achieve greater connectivity within the State the transport and communication sector has received a substantial share of every budget. The percentage share of this sector saw a sharp increase in the 8th plan and subsequently fell. Given the topography of the State the cost of laying roads is obviously higher than in the plain areas.

Agriculture and allied activities rightly received a significant proportion of the budgets in considering the fact that Meghalaya is largely rural with agriculture as the primary occupation. But the variations have been huge and the 10th Plan's proposed outlay for the sector is worrisome.

Energy, another priority area, received the initial attention it deserved. But the 8th and 9th Plans accorded low priority to this sector and clearly reflected the inability of the planners to gaze into the future. The State is in now in a power crisis in spite of its tremendous potential.

There's been little effort to develop industries based on the State's minerals. The meager investments and allotments to this sector have resulted in a stagnant and an underdeveloped secondary sector. On the other hand Social and community services (including education) have a high proportion of funds. While the percentage share in agriculture and transport and communication fell in the Tenth Plan, social and community services have received top priority. These sectoral changes in outlay are in conformity with changes in the National Plan. For instance, the Minimum Needs Programme (MNP) introduced in the Fifth Five-Year Plan was substituted by the Basic Minimum Services (BMS) during the last year of the Eighth Plan (1996-97). While the MNP laid emphasis on twelve items, viz. Rural Fuelwood and Fodder Development programme, Rural Electrification, Rural Health, Rural Sanitation, Rural Water Supply, Rural Housing, Rural Roads, Public Distribution System, Elementary Education and Adult Education, Environmental Improvement of Slums and Nutrition, the BMS has stressed on 7(seven) programmes viz., Universalisation of Primary Education, Health Care, Provision of potable water supply, village connectivity by roads, Housing facilities to the shelterless poor, Public Distribution System (PDS) and Nutrition/Mid Day Meal Programme.

The BMS was split up into 2(two) parts in 2000-01: (i) the Pradhan Mantri Gramodaya Yojana (PMGY) including universal primary education, primary health care, safe drinking water supply, housing for the shelterless and nutrition/mid day meal; and (ii) Pradhan

Mantri Gram Sadak Yojana (PMGSY) meant for road connectivity to unconnected villages.

In 2001-02, Rural Electrification was included in PMGY and P.D.S. removed. These changes have been initiated at both the Central and State level because the so-called 'trickle-down effect' of industrialization never materialized. Since the last year of the Eighth Plan efforts are being made at direct poverty alleviation.

In most cases, it has been found that in the formulation of the State's plan, the different aspects of the plan frame coincide with the national 5 Year Plans. Further, fund allocation by the Central Government based on the modified Gadgil Formula of criteria and weightage viz., (i) Population size (60%), (ii) Per-capita income (25%), (iii) Performance of the State (7.5%) and (iv) Special Problems (7.5%) has been repeatedly questioned and criticized. Since Meghalaya has its own set of special problems and requirements, the 'adopted' plan structure and fund alloca-tion becomes irrelevant to the indigenous requirements. As a consequence numerous goals and objectives have been only partially realized. The pace of development experienced due to the resource constraints and allocations led to unfulfilled aspirations and gradually fueled distrust and skepticism toward the Centre. There are even demands for sovereignty from certain quarters. To cite a few examples of the mismatch of funds: (i) the allocation of funds for industry and minerals has been meager and insufficient, even though the percentage share for Rural Development programmes under various plans have increased, it continues to remain inadequate for a state where more than 80 percent reside in the rural areas. Another sector requiring greater outlays is the Special Area Programmes involving Border Area Development. Border areas of Meghalaya account for 22 percent but the outlays have been insignificant.

Another aspect that requires immediate attention is the actual expenditures. Since 1990-91, actual expenditure has fallen short of approved outlays. This is primarily due to non-materialization of a large number of negotiated loans allocated under the plans, from L.I.C., G.I.C., and HUDCO etc. This has necessitated further sectoral adjustments and thus, only partial realization of goals. The sectoral allocations show that the State has not efficiently allotted its budgets on the basis of its inherent strengths and weaknesses.

Of late the State Government has been publicizing with great pride the notion of surplus budgets and the so called strong fiscal discipline of the State when the real picture is quite different. Allocated money that has been under-spent and returned to the Centre, when the State is in the doldrums, gives no reason for celebrations. Glorified achievements have little significance but only helps cover the failures and the under achievements. One also wonders as to the nature of these achievements. How many projects have finished in time? What is the nature of their functioning? What is their effective capacity utilization? What are the spill-over effects of the 'success' stories? Or, are the 'achievements' simply cosmetic? These and other questions could form the subject matter of another research project.

RESOURCE-BASE OF THE STATE

Natural resources consist of everything given by nature. It includes land, forests, water, minerals climate, rainfall, topography, fisheries and marine resources. They are available in varying varieties and quantities and have an influence on economic growth and thereby economic life and structure. The developments in science and technology have enlarged the resource-base and now there is a greater awareness of their role in the development process of an economy. However, an economy has to make prudent use of the non-renewable/exhaustible resources and at the same time, maintain the quality and quantity of the renewable resources.

LAND RESOURCES

The pattern of land utilization in Meghalaya for the period 1976-77 to 1998-99 is examined with the help of Table 5.

Table 5: Land Utilization Statistics of Meghalaya (in '000 hectares)

Particulars	1976-77 (Provisional)	1980-81	1990-91	1998-99
1. Geographical Area	2249	2243	2243	2243
2. Reporting Area				
(add Items 3 to 8)	2249	2249	2239**	2241
3. Forest Area	823	812	939	950
	(36.6)	(36.1)	(41.9)	(42.4)
4. Unavailable for Cultivation				
a. Under Non-Agricultural Use	80	85	84	
	(3.6)	(3.8)	(3.8)	
b. Barren and Uncultivable Land	229	231	142	220
	(10.2)	(10.3)	(6.3)	(9.8)
				(a+b)
5. Other Uncultivated				
Land Excluding Barren Land				
a. Permanent Pastures &	17	17	-	-
Other Grazing Land	(0.8)	(0.8)		
b. Cultivable Waste Land	453	454	493	466
	(20.1)	(20.2)	(22)	(20.8)
c. Others*	144	145	153	155
	(6.4)	(6.4)	(6.8)	(6.9)
6. Fallow Land				
a. Current Fallows	55	51	59	68
b. Other than Current Fallows	(2.4)	(2.3)	(2.6)	(3)
	274	261	167	164
	(12.2)	(11.6)	(7.5)	(7.3)
7. Net Area Sown	174	193	202	218
	(7.7)	(8.6)	(9)	(9.71)
8. Area Sown more than once	30	19	38	45
9. Total Cropped Area (7+8)	204	212	240	263

Note: * means land under miscellaneous trees, crops and groves, not included in net area sown.
** excludes area under Municipality and Town Committee
Figures in brackets are percentages of Reporting Area and corrected upto one decimal place.
Source: Compiled from (i)) Basis Statistics of North Eastern Region, 1980, 1990, 1995, North-Eastern Council (NEC), Shillong. (ii) Pocket Statistical Handbooks of Meghalaya, 1995, 1998, 2000.

Geographical Area

The geographical area of the State is 2243 thousand hectares (except for the 1976-77 provisional figures which was based on the Census of India 1971). The 1971 Census was on the basis of Police Station area in the United Khasi and Jaintia Hills District and Mouza area in the Garo Hills District. The Surveyor General changed the area to its present 2243 thousand hectares after the initiation of administrative changes and the subsequent creation of new districts in the new State of Meghalaya.

Forest Area

On the basis of available data the Forest Area appears to have increased from 36.6 percent in 1976-77 to 42.4 percent in 1998-99. The increase is however largely due to the clubbing of un-classed forest. In fact between 1985-86 and 1986-87, the area under un-classed forest increased by approximately 98 thousand hectares (see Table 6).

Land Unavailable for Cultivation

This category of land is subdivided into (i) under non-agricultural use, and (ii) barren and uncultivable land. Area under the former which includes all lands occupied by buildings, roads, rivers and canals and other lands put to non-agricultural uses has remained marginally below 4 percent for the entire period. On the other hand, the area under barren and uncultivable lands, which includes mountains and deserts and land which can be brought under cultivation but only at an exorbitant cost, has reduced to around 6 percent in 1998-99. It is not possible to say at this juncture whether such grades have been brought under cultivation and of what type (i.e. terrace or jhum). Another possibility could be that this type of land has been included along with forest area. Combining the two we find that the area under this category has reduced from 13.8 percent to 9.8 percent between 1976 and 1999. In fact, with an increase in population and urbanization one would expect to see the opposite trend, i.e. land unavailable for cultivation would increase over the years.

Other Uncultivated Land (Excluding Fallow Land)

The area of land under this category has remained sizeable (27 to 29 percent) and used to comprise 3 subclasses. While pastures and grazing lands (meadows and village common grazing land) have totally vanished, land under miscellaneous tree-crops and groves (classified as 'Others') increased by 11 thousand hectares between 1976 and 1999. Cultivable wasteland, one of the sub-categories, increased area-wise till 1990-91 and then declined. Such lands, though available for cultivation, have not been utilized during the previous 5 years or more and its share of reporting area has remained over 20 percent. This suggests that extensive jhumming areas are being kept fallow or that land covered with jungles and shrubs are not put into any use.

Fallow Land

The size of current fallows, i.e. cropped areas but kept fallow during the current season, has marginally increased to 3 percent in 1998-99 from 2.4 percent in 1976-77.

Land other than current fallows registered a secular and significant fall from 12.2 percent to 7.3 percent in the given period. While the decrease is encouraging, the reasons ascribed to keeping such lands fallows are eye-openers and require in-depth studies. Some of the factors are poverty, inadequate water supply, malarial climate and un-remunerative nature of farming.

Area Sown

Although the area under this class increased from 174 thousand hectares in 1976-77 to 218 thousand hectares in 1998-99 (an increase of 25.3 percent during the period), as a percent of reporting area it remains relatively low at 9.71 percent (in 1998-99). The total cropped area increased by 28.9 percent and the area sown more than once by 50 percent in the period under consideration. However, there needs to be greater effort to bring more area under cultivation by increasing the areas sown more than once. Given the limited scope for extensive cultivation in Meghalaya, intensive cultivation holds the key to achieving self-sufficiency in foodgrains.

B. FOREST RESOURCES

Of the total geographical area while the forest cover is 1566 thousand hectares (69.8 percent) the forest area occupies 950 thousand hectares (42.3 percent). In India forests are generally State owned (95 percent) but the situation is quite the opposite in Meghalaya. The State Forest Department in 1998-99 had control over only 10.7 percent or 99 thousand hectares of the total 950 thousand hectares (Table 6). The remaining forests are managed by the respective District Councils of Khasi Hills, Jaintia Hills and Garo Hills as per the provisions of the Sixth Schedule to the Constitution of India. The forests under the District Councils are of 3 types: (i) old un-classed forests which are directly under their control; (ii) forests owned by clans and communities and (iii) private forests over which the councils have little control except in the collection of royalty when timber is exported outside their own area.

Table 6: Area under Forest (in '000 Hectares)

Year	Reserve Forest	Protected Forest	National Park	Unclassed	Total
1	2	3	4	5	6
1971-72	74.00	13.00	-	602.00	689.00
1972-73	74.00	13.00	-	602.00	689.00
1973-74	74.00	13.00	-	653.00	740.00
1974-75	74.00	13.00	-	734.00	821.00
1975-76	71.00	1.17*	-	778.83	851.00
to 1977-78	Figures Reported are the same for each year				
1978-79	70.65	1.17*	-	779.18	851.00
to 1981-82	Figures Reported are the same for each year				
1982-83	71.07	1.17*	-	779.18	851.42
1983-84	71.07	1.17*	-	779.18	851.42
1984-85	71.07	1.13*	-	779.18	851.38
1985-86	71.07	1.13*	26.74	752.44	851.38
1986-87	71.07	1.49	26.74	850.30	949.60
1987-88	71.32	1.24	26.74	850.30	949.60
to 1996-97	Figures Reported are the same for each year				
1997-98	71.27	1.24	26.74	850.30	949.55
1998-99	71.27	1.24	26.74	850.30	949.55

Note:i) * Excludes Forests under District Councils

ii) Under the Government: Columns 2+3+4

Source: Pocket Statistical Handbook, Meghalaya, 2000

An interesting feature is the existence of pockets of undisturbed natural forests along the southern slopes of the Khasi and Jaintia Hills, at an altitude of around 1000 metres. Protected by the tribals and with an area of approximately 100 thousand hectares, these 'Sacred Groves' have evolved through ages and have remained virtually untouched because of the religious beliefs and myths attributed to them. These groves are a rich storehouse of vegetation wealth and provide numerous benefits such as soil protection, conservation of flora, fauna, water and genetic resources. They also help in the regeneration of the eco-system and act as windbreakers and shelterbelts.

Forests, which are an important renewable resource, confer many benefits to the State. The forests provide valuable timber trees like Teak, Sal, Titachap, Walnut, Mahogany, Khasi pine (*Pinus kesiya*) and other products like fuelwood, resin, tannin, gum, fiber, latex, essential oils, edible fruits, honey and numerous medicinal plants. The Bay leaves and cinnamon of Meghalaya are reputed for their quality. There are also a number of tree species which act as host plants for the rearing of silk worms for sericulture. Bamboo, reed and cane are other forms of forest wealth. The availability of such a variety of resources indicates the potentiality of industries based on forest resources.

The climate of Meghalaya (but undergoing serious changes) is responsible for its diverse and exotic flora and fauna. The 325 species of orchids available is second only to Arunachal Pradesh and of the 1000 species of butterflies in India, 25 percent are found in Meghalaya. The Blue Peacock, the Kaiser-e-hind, the Leaf Butterfly, the Dipper and the Bhutan Glory, to name a few, are world famous.

Table 7 : Area under Plantation/Afforestation (in Hectares)

Year	Teak	Sal	Plywood (Species)	Pine	Others	Total
1987-88	130	200	230	150	70	780
1988-89	140	78	260	145	121	744
1989-90	65	90	130	110	55	450
1990-91	140	140	190	175	164	809
1991-92	111	160	100	164	161	696
1992-93	57	60	90	55	155	417
1993-94	45	104	45	60	160	414
1994-95	20	10	50	30	115	225
1995-96	20	15	15	-	105	155
1996-97	55	70	40	-	155	320
1997-98	28	24	15	-	69	136
1998-99	56	77	30	-	154	317
Total	5463					

Source: Pocket Statistical Handbooks of Meghalaya, 1995 and 2000

Meghalaya has always been a timber surplus state because of the large-scale felling of trees, especially from the private forests. Most of the timber exits the State despite the restrictions imposed. *Jhum* cultivation, which is widely practiced, has caused further denudation and depletion of forest wealth. With the situation growing worse and at an alarming rate, afforestation and social programmes were taken up during the Seventh Five-Year Plan. Social forestry programmes were undertaken in community and private lands through grant-in-aid assistance to the District Councils. Schemes under afforestation included Teakwood, Salwood, Plywood, plantations of quick growing species and other miscellaneous plantation. The progresses under afforestation and forestry schemes are given in Tables 7 and 8, respectively. In this context it may be mentioned that the concept of Joint Forest Management is yet to be implemented in the State because of the nature of resource ownership. It is however known that certain villages are already involved with forest preservation.

In 1991, the Meghalaya Forest Authority Ordinance was promulgated to ensure joined involvement of the State Government and the District Councils for the effective implementation of Forest Protection Laws.

Table 8 : Progress under Forestry Schemes (in Hectares)

Year	Quick Growing Species Plantation	Economic Plantations	Social Forestry
1987-88	150	630	7311
1988-89	145	599	13168
1989-90	110	340	10173
1990-91	175	634	6658
1991-92	164	532	8871
1992-93	55	362	4585
1993-94	60	354	9999
1994-95	150	195	6825
1995-96	25	155	2375
1996-97	83	320	1943
1997-98	15	218	75
1998-99	57	317	100

Source: Pocket Statistical Handbooks of Meghalaya, 1995 and 2000.

C. WATER RESOURCES: Surface and Ground Water

Meghalaya has a distinction of being the highest rainfall area on the earth with Cherrapunjee and Mawsynram sharing the honours. The average annual rainfall in the State is about 2050 mm with 200 rainy days in a year. However, the physical features of the State assures high surface run-off of rainwater and there are regular problems of acute water scarcity. There are also several rivers but they are navigable only in the lower slopes. All the principal rivers flow into the Brahmaputra or its tributaries. Some of the important rivers of the State are the Simsang and Jingjiram in Garo Hills and Khri, Umiam, Umtrew, Kupli, Umïew,Umngot and Myntdu in the Khasi and Jaintia Hills. There are numerous waterfalls too, with a vast majority on the northern slope of the State. The State also has several lakes with some formed to generate electricity and provide irrigation water. In fact, after Arunachal Pradesh, Meghalaya has the highest hydro-electricity potential (1200 MW) in the North East. Of this, only 186.71 MW (15%) has been tapped so far. With per capita consumption being low (192.81 KWH in 1998-99 and 175 KWH in1999-2000) the surplus is sold to the neighbouring states (175.777 MKWH in 1998-99). Electricity generation in 1998-99 was 555.59 MKWH. The picture has rapidly changed. In the recent past there have been regular power cuts and the power generated is insufficient to meet the growing requirements of the people and the few industries that exist or being established in the State. The Table 9 shows the installed capacity of power projects in Meghalaya.

Table 9: Installed Capacity of Hydel Power Projects (M.W.) :1998-99

Projects	Installed Capacity (MW)
Umiam Hydel Projects:	
Stage 1	36.00
Stage 2	18.00
Stage 3	60.00
Stage 4	60.00
Umtrew Hydel Project	11.20
Sunapani Micro Hydel Project	1.51
Total	186.71

Source: Pocket Statistical Handbook, Meghalaya, 2000

Because of the high surface run-off of rainwater, the availability of water is basically restricted to waterfalls, springs and streams. Essentially these sources need to be harvested for domestic needs and irrigation purposes through structures like check dams, weirs etc. Springs, which are the major source of water supply and outlet for groundwater, numbering 200 have a discharge of 120 litres per minute (lpm). The scientific development of these springs can solve the problems of acute water scarcity and simultaneously provide safe drinking water to the rural population. In this connection, the Central Ground Water Board has carried out a number of ground water exploration and resource evaluation studies in all the districts of the State thereby completing 46 exploratory tube wells, 9 observation wells, 1 slin hole and 1 piezometer. The discharge of tube wells varies from 135 to 3705 lpm. There is also an artesian belt of 100 sq. km. in West Garo Hills where no energy is required to lift the groundwater. At present there are 31 Hydrograph Network Stations in Meghalaya which are monitored 4 times annually to determine the trend of ground water level. Table 10 which gives the groundwater resource potential in Meghalaya show that only 20.38 million cubic meters (MCM) or 4.1 percent of the total 495.06 MCM of the Utilizable Ground Water Resource has been drawn and limited to West Garo Hills alone.

Table 10: Ground Water Resource Potential

District	Gross Recharge (MCM)	For Drinking & Allied Purposes (15%) [MCM]	Utilizable Ground Water Resource (85%) [MCM]	Draft (MCM)	Ground Water Balance (MCM)	Unit Draft (MCM)	No. of Structures Feasible	Fund Required (Lakhs)
West Garo Hills	133.23	19.98	113.25	20.38	92.87	0.03	3095	1400
South Garo Hills	67.79	10.17	57.62	-	57.62	0.03	1887	850
East Garo Hills	64.34	9.65	54.69	-	54.69	0.03	1823	820
West Khasi Hills	101.26	15.19	86.07	-	86.07	0.005	14733	1100
East Khasi Hills	58.72	08.80	49.91	-	49.91	0.005	9982	750
Ri-Bhoi	36.72	5.51	31.21	-	31.21	0.005	6244	460
Jaintia Hills	120.36	18.05	102.31	-	102.31	0.005	20216	1500
Total	**582.42**	**87.35**	**495.06**	**20.38**	**474.68**	-	**57980**	**6880**

Notes : MCM = Million Cubic Metres
Source: Central Ground Water Board, Ministry of Water Resources, North-East Region, Guwahati, August 2002.

D. MINERAL RESOURCES

The State of Meghalaya is rich in mineral deposits and she occupies a significant position in the mineral map of India. The importance of mineral resources was realized and identified as one of the major resources to be exploited for industrial development way back in 1973 in the 5th Five-Year Plan Draft Proposals. Two agencies viz., Geological Survey of India (G.S.I.) and the Directorate of Mineral Resources (D.M.R.) have been involved in a continuous process of exploration involving geological mapping, core-drilling and exploratory mining for a proper assessment of geological and natural resources. Despite the availability of resources and the role of the Meghalaya Industrial Development Corporation (MIDC) in the implementation of various programmes, the State has remained industrially backward. A vast majority of the mining activities are carried out by private individuals on a small scale basis with the aid of only rudimentary tools and techniques. Further, the extracted minerals find their way outside the State and to other parts of the country and even abroad (Bangladesh) but without any value addition. The only exception is limestone which is used to some degree within the State as a raw material in cement industries.

A detailed account of the estimated mineral reserves along with their possible uses is presented in Table 11.

OTHER MINERAL DEPOSITS

Sillimanite

Not long ago it was acknowledged that in the Sonapahar region in West Khasi Hills there was the best variety of Sillimanite deposits in the world. However this mineral of great commercial value has depleted due to extensive exploitation.

Quartz and Feldspar

These minerals, which are components of the ceramic industry, have estimated reserves of 0.077 and 0.128 million tones respectively. Used in the pottery industries of Meghalaya and Assam, their deposits are found in Hahim, Mairang and Nongkhlaw in Khasi Hills and in Tura, Bonsgomgiri, Rombhangiri and Nengkhra in Garo Hills.

Granite

Dolerite or Black Granite suitable for making polished blocks and slabs are found in the eastern and northern part of West Garo Hills district with Jengjal and Hallidayganj as promising areas of dolerite deposits at present.

Reserves of about 45.00 million cubic metres of multi-coloured granite (Grey, pink and black) have been estimated in the areas around Nongpoh, Mylliem and Mawkyrwat, as well as in an area around Mendipathar-Songsak road.

Table 11: Estimated Mineral Reserves in Meghalaya

	Mineral and Location	Estimated Reserves (in Million Tonnes)	Possible Uses
1. LIMESTONE			
KHASI HILLS:	Cherrapunjee, Laitryngew, Mawlong, Ishamati, Komorrah, Shella, Borsora	2537.00	Cement, Paper Grade, Calcium Carbide and Chemical
JAINTIA HILLS:	Lumshnong, Sutnga, Syndai, Nongkhlieh, Lakadong, Nongtalang	1050.00	Industries
GARO HILLS:	Darrang-Ear-Aning, Chokpat, Siju-Artheka, Siju-Damugithim, Dapgiri	560.00	
	Total	**4147.00**	
2. COAL			
KHASI HILLS:	Laitryngew, Cherrapunjee, Laitduh, Mawbehlarkar, Mawsynram,	164.50	
	Lumdidom, Langrin, East Darrangiri, Pynursla, Lyngkyrdem, Mawlong-Shella-Ishamati and Borsora	40.00	Power Generation, Fertilizer Manufacturing, Smokeless Coke, Cement,
JAINTIA HILLS:	Bapung, Lakadong, Sutnga, Jarain, Musiang Lamare, Toksi, Khliehriat	359.00	Textile, Paper, Rubber, Brick and Pottery Industries.
GARO HILLS:	West-Darrangiri, Siju, Balpakram, Selsela, Pyndengrei		
	Total	**563.50**	
3. KAOLIN (CHINA CLAY)			
KHASI HILLS:	Mawkriah-Mawphlang, Smit, Laitlyngkot	1.30	
JAINTIA HILLS:	Thadlaskein, Shangpung, Mulieh, Mynsngat	1.94	White ware Industry
GARO HILLS:	Darungiri	1.20	
	Total	**4.44**	
4. CLAY KHASI HILLS:	Cherrapunjee, Kutmadan, Mahadek, Sohraram, Umsten	2.47	
JAINTIA HILLS:	Larnai, Tongseng		0.50
GARO HILLS:	Nangalbibra, Nengkrah, Dobu, Rewak, Damukgithim, Tura, Rangram, Khosal, Rongrenggiri-Khera, Songsak	78.00	White ware Industry
	Total	**80.97**	
5. GLASS SAND			
KHASI HILLS:	Laitryngew, Umstew, Kreit		
GARO HILLS:	Tura	2.40	
		0.14	Bottles or Sheet Glasses
	Total	**2.54**	

Source: (1) Technical Data on Minerals, Directorate of Mineral Resources, Meghalaya
(2) Quarterly Journal on North-Eastern States Economy - Vol.1. July 2002, North-Eastern Development Finance Corporation.

Uranium

Uranium and other radio-active minerals are found in various parts of the State with an estimated reserve of around 9.00 million tones. The uranium deposits at Domiasiat in West Khasi Hills District are of a higher grade vis-à-vis the deposits currently exploited in the country. Though exploratory mining of this strategic mineral started, not much progress has been made. Because of environmental and other concerns the Uranium Corporation of India Limited (UCIL) has come up against rigid resistance from various quarters. It has become a major issue of debate in the streets and seminars. The Corporation has been negotiating at various levels to ensure uninterrupted commercial exploitation of the 'yellow cake'. In recent news headlines (June 2003) even the State refused to co-operate until the parameters were explicitly laid out and beneficial to the State and the indigenous people. It is however apparent that the State will continue to remain exporting raw materials and a market for finished goods.

Phosphate

Deposits of phosphatic nodules of different sizes (range of pea to egg) are located in Rewak area of Garo Hills and Jaintia Hills. Chemical analyses of samples have however revealed low phosphate contents.

Gypsum

Gypsum, an important ingredient, in the cement industry, has been reported in Mohendraganj and Harigaon in West Garo Hills. No detailed work and no estimates of reserves have been made as the concentration of gypsum in the shale is very low (0.07%).

Iron-Ore

Iron-ore deposits are found in Aradonga area of Khasi Hills, Nishangram in Garo Hills and in Athiabari in Garo Hills. Having low iron-content, the estimated reserve is around 0.87 million tones.

Base Metal

Geological and geophysical investigations carried out by GSI from Tyrsad to Barapani in the Khasi Hills established the occurrence of copper, zinc, nickel and cobalt. At Umpyrtha in Khasi Hills there is a presence of copper, zinc along with traces of molybdenum and tungsten.

Gold

Occurrence of gold has been reported from Tyrsad in the Khasi Hills. However, the samples have revealed low gold content making it economically unviable for extraction.

Mineral Oil

Crude oil seepages (bubble discharge has been noticed in a number of places in the southern slope of the State. The Oil and Natural Gas Commission (ONGC) has applied for 'prospecting license' to explore the hydrocarbon deposits in the State.

Trends in Mineral Production

Annual official data on the various quantities of minerals extracted are calculated on the basis of royalties and cess that accrues to the State (the current royalties for coal and Limestone are Rs.120.00 and Rs.40.00 per tonne respectively). However, as the volume of unofficial trade is 3 to 4 times higher published data are grossly understated.

Official data (Table 12) is available only for the major minerals of the State viz. coal, limestone, sillimanite and clay.

Table 12 : Mineral Production in Meghalaya: Selected Years (in '000 tonnes)

Year	Coal	Limestone	Sillimanite	Clay
1975-76	59	164	5	6
1985-86	1265	236	4	0.2
1995-96	3248	440	NA	NA
1999-2000	4060	494	NA	NA

NA = Not available

Source: (i) Pocket Statistical Handbook, Meghalaya (various issues).
(ii)District Level Statistics, Meghalaya, 2002.

From the table 12 we see that the increase in coal production is far greater than that of limestone. The low ash content is the primary reason for the relatively greater demand for coal. Consequently though the extraction process has speeded up to meet the large demands from outside the State, the methods remain crude and unscientific. Perhaps many incidents of death and illness associated with surface mining remain unreported. But as things stand, most of the extracted coal is exported without any value-addition.

Between 1990-2000, as per official data, coal production was [illegible]3021 thousand tonnes and, if one were to add the volume of unofficial trade, which is estimated to be atleast 3 times higher [see, Dutta (2000)], the figure dramatically changes to over 99000 thousand tonnes. Using current official data of around 4200 thousand tonnes per annum the estimated coal reserves would last another 134 years. But when unofficial volumes are taken into consideration, the reserves would be exhausted within 45 years at the current rate of production.

In the case of limestone, only a portion is utilized within the State for manufacturing cement and lime making. The rest is exported with little or no value-addition. It appears to be the only mineral used in a major way within the State. At present there are 6 cement plants in Meghalaya with an installed capacity of 3, 58,050 tonnes per annum (tpa) with utilized capacity of around 51 percent (or 1,84,285 tpa) in 2000-01 ["Investment Opportunities in Meghalaya"-NEDFi].

Sillimanite, as mentioned earlier, has been exhausted due to extensive mining and current data on clay production are unpublished.

The minor minerals of the State are in the hands of the State Forest Department and the District Councils and the revenue generated and their mining trend is unknown in the absence of published data.

It may be noted that all mining activities in the unorganized sector are unscientific and in complete violation of the mining laws applicable in the rest of the country. For the extraction of major minerals a valid Mining Lease must be obtained from the EIA (Environmental Impact Analysis) and the EMA (Environ-mental Management Plan). Also, there is the presence of the Central Mine Planning and Design Institute (CMPDI) to develop mining along commercial lines, but it is still in the laboratory stage. The Coal India Limited (CIL) was initially interested but investments were discouraged because of the highly erratic seams of coal.

E. HUMAN RESOURCES

In economics, the concept of human capital defines people as capital assets. Such assets are formed by long-term and sustained investments in humans, i.e. through investments in 'education' and 'health-care services.' While education (general and technical) helps to improve one's mental capability and imparts skills, health-care services help improve the physical capability. Empirical evidences have exposed that the quality of human resource/capital have an important influence on the process of economic growth. It is logical to say that educated and healthy people, by and large, make rational choices. They are innovative and have a greater degree of geographical and social mobility.

Looking at figures that are indicative of the development of human resources, one finds that some advances have been made in the context of Meghalaya. The number of educational institutions increased from 3974 in 1974-75 to 5776 in 1997-98. The expansion has been at the primary, middle, high/higher secondary and college levels. But in the absence of engineering, medical and technological institutes (except 3 polytechnics) the stock of 'educated' manpower primarily consists of those from the general stream (traditional courses and subjects). The State annually sponsors a few students for higher studies in different streams in other States and universities against allotted quotas from the centre. Upon completion of their studies the State is unable to absorb them (engineers, medical students and diploma holders), Table 13, and yet it fears a shortage in the next 10 to 15 years. The fault lies not only on the Government for not creating adequate infrastructure in the rural areas but also with those who are asked to serve in remote and distant areas. Many prefer to commute to and fro either regularly or visit only on 'market days' in their posted areas.

As per the Provisional Census of 2001, the literacy rate in Meghalaya is 63.31 percent but remains below the national level of 65.38 percent. The census figures of 1971, 1981 and 1991 indicate some improvement in the literacy percent (29.4 percent, 34.08 percent and 49.10 percent respectively). While educational attainments serve as a proxy for skills and competence levels, it does not encompass other factors like the influence of experience and informal training. Further, the quality of human resources is determined by its mobility (geographical) and health. In this connection it may be mentioned that the road density (PWD Roads only) in Meghalaya was 32.67 km. /100 sq. km. (March 2001) and far lower than the national figure of 60 km. /100 sq. km. Also there is one Primary Health Centre / Heath care facility for a population of 21,643, one Sub-centre for 3070 people, one doctor for 5913 people and 109 beds per lakh population (10th Five Year Plan, Draft Proposals, Vol-1). Although 95 percent of the existing villages (5780) are provided with potable drinking water only 50 percent are connected with roads. Though improvements have taken place the infant mortality rate, death rate and total birth rate remain relatively high at 56 per 1000, 9.1 per 1000 and 28.7 per 1000 respectively as per provisional figures of 1999. Programmes for mass immunization and improving rural health and sanitation are being introduced by the State.

Table 13: Distribution of educated Applicants in the Live Register by Level of Education

Education Level	1995	1996	1997	1998
1) Matriculation	8892	9302	10909	9597
2) HSSLC/P.U./Intermediate	4108	6465	5487	5616
3) Graduates				
a) Engineering	96	90	16	141
b) Agriculture	3	19	34	24
c) Medical	-	4	-	12
d) Veterinary	-	-	3	-
e) Arts	1217	1292	1989	1862
f) Science	475	546	462	427
g) Commerce	303	327	392	482
h) Law	70	5	-	2
i) Education	-	109	4	113
j) Others	2	30	6	-
4) Post Graduates				
a) Engineering	-	-	-	9
b) Agriculture	23	40	5	7
c) Education	44	-	-	20
d) Arts	80	90	119	104
e) Science	159	67	92	101
f) Commerce	7	3	19	11
g) Law	-	-	19	-
h) Others	4	-	125	-
5) Diploma Holders	251	302	294	387
Total	**15734**	**18691**	**19975**	**18915**

Source: Pocket Statistical Handbook, 2000

INDUSTRIAL STRUCTURE OF THE STATE- RESOURCE INDUSTRY LINKAGES

This section is based entirely on official data obtained from various issues of Pocket Statistical Handbooks published by the Directorate of Economics and Statistics, Government of Meghalaya. Data is available under 3 categories: (i) Registered Factories, (ii) Small-Scale Industries (SSIs) registered with the Directorate of Industries (DOI) and (iii) Khadi and Village Industrial Units (KVIs) (Das: 2004).

(i) Registered Factories in Meghalaya (1974-75 to 1999-2000)

While the number of registered units increased from 45 units in 1974-75 to 72 units in 1999-2000 (Table 14) and registered a growth rate of 60 percent, employment in the same period increased by only 9.7 percent, i.e., from 2945 to 3232 employees. However, in the absence of a category-wise distribution of such units for all the years the trend in respect of industry-resource linkage cannot be examined.

Table 14: Registered Factories in Meghalaya

Year	Number of Units	Number of Employees
1974-75	45	2945
1980-81	55	3075
1985-86	56	3574
1990-91	58	3345
1995-96	58	2800
1999-2000	72	3232

Source: Pocket Statistical Handbook (Various Issues)

Table 15: Registered Factories by Type (1978-83)

Category	No. of Units	Percent of Total
A. Forest Based		
1. Plywood manufacture	2	
2. Saw Mills	10	26.3
3. Furniture & Fixture	3	
B. Agro-Horticulture		
4. Canning & Preservation	2	
5. Rice & Flour Milling	3	8.8
C. Demand Based		
6. Printing Press	7	
7. Motor Vehicle Repairs	11	31.6
D. Water Based		
8. Generation & Transmission of Electricity	6	10.5
9. Others*	13	22.8
Total	**57**	**100.00**

Note: * includes cement, beverage, motor assembling, pumping, cotton gunning, Mineral processing, etc.
Source: Pocket Statistical Handbook, Meghalaya, 1983.

An examination of the Category/Type wise distribution of this category of industries for the period 1978-83(Table 15) reveals the following features:

(i) 15 units or 26.3 percent are based on forest resources
(ii) 5 units or 8.8 percent are agro-horticulture based
(iii) 18 units or 31.6 percent are demand/need based
(iv) 6 units or 10.5 percent are based on water resources.
(v) As the cement and other mineral processing units are clubbed with "others", the relative strength of mineral based units could not be worked out.

(ii) Registered SSIs (1974-2000)

Industries under this category have grown at a phenomenal rate in the period 1974-

2000 (Table 16). The 1990s witnessed a prodigious growth rate. While the overall growth rate in respect of units has been 1301 percent in the period 1974-2000, employment too grew by 1121 percent in the same period.

Table 16: Growth of Registered SSIs in Meghalaya

Year	No. of Units	No. of Employees
1974-75	252	1645
1980-81	180	1440
1985-86	671	4240
1990-91	1558	9248
1995-96	2533	14791
1999-2000	3530	20086

Source: i) Pocket Statistical Handbook, Meghalaya (Various Issues)

ii) District Level Statistics, 2002, Directorate of Economics and Statistics.

A category-wise comparison of 1986-87 and 1998-99 data (Table 17) reveals:

i) The total number of industries increased from 802 to 3270 and registered a 308 percent growth rate in the time period.

ii) Forest based units grew by 315 percent but its relative share increased only marginally by 0.3 percent.

iii) Agro-based units (only Flour and Rice Mills) increased its share from 6 percent in 1986-87 to 7.4 percent in 1998-99.

Table 17: SSIs in Meghalaya by Type, 1986-87 and 1998-99

Sl. No.	Type of Industries	No. of Units in 1986-87	Relative Share of Group (%)	No. of Units in 1998-99	Relative Share of Group (%)	Absolute Change (Group)	Percent Change (Group)
1	**FOREST BASED**						
	a) Wooden Furniture	75		330			
	b) Cane and Bamboo	35		172	17.8		
	c) Saw Mills	30	17.5	79			
	Sub Total	**140**		**581**		**441**	**315**
	AGRO BASED						
	a) Flour and Rice Mills	48	6	242	7.4	194	404
	MINERAL BASED						
	a) Cement based industries	90		159			
	b) Stone Crushers and Sand-stone Chips	11	13.3	37	8.2		
	c) Lime making	6		73			
	Sub Total	**107**		**269**		**162**	**151**
	DEMAND BASED						
	(A) **SERVICE PROVIDERS**						

	a) Motor Repairing, Servicing	66		179			
	b) Tailoring	49	19.8	399	21.3		
	c) Tyre Retreading	17		70			
	d) Printing	27		49			
	Sub Total (A)	**159**		**697**		**538**	**338**
(B)	**GOODS PRODUCERS**						
	a) Weaving	12		164			
	b) Knitting & Embroidery	55		150			
	c) Bakery	90	24	249	23.3		
	d) Steel Based Industries	25		164			
	e) Leather Based Industries	10		36			
	Sub Total (B)	192		763		571	297
	Total (A) + (B)	351	43.8	1460	44.6	1109	316
6	**OTHERS**	156	19.4	718	22	562	360
	GRAND TOTAL	**802**	**100**	**3270**	**100**	**2468**	**308**

Source: Pocket Statistical Handbook, Meghalaya, 1987 and 2000.

iv) Though the number of mineral based industries increased, its relative share declined from 13.3 percent to 8.2 percent.

v) Demand based units increased their relative share from 43.8 percent to 44.6 percent. In the demand-based group the share of goods producers exceeds the share of service-providers in both the years. However, the relative share of service producers increased from 19.8 percent to 21.3 percent and that of the goods producers decreased from 24 percent to 23.3 percent.

vi) Industries clubbed under the category of "Others" have a relatively high share in the years 1986-87 and 1998-99, but since they are unspecified we cannot determine an exhaustive resource-industry linkage.

(iii) Khadi and Village Industries (KVIs)

The growth of KVIs (Table 18) for the period 1986 to 1998 is spectacular. Within 13 years the number of units increased dramatically from 344 units to 6224 units, an 18 fold increase or a growth rate of 1709 percent. Such impressive figures can also lead one to speculate on overlapping between SSIs and KVIs and the number of operational units.

Table 18: KVIs in Meghalaya (1986-99)

Year	No. of Units	No. of Employees
1986-87	344	4517
1995-96	5400	12520
1996-97	6224	14202
1997-98	6224 (14)	14202 (69)
1998-99	42	246

Note: (i) 1996-97 and 1997-98, figures remain constant due to non-availability of Funds (*Statistical Handbook 1998*)
(ii) Figures within brackets for 1997-98 (*Pocket Statistical Handbook, 2000*)

Source: *Pocket Statistical Handbooks of Meghalaya, 1987, 1998 and 2000.*

There is also discrepancy in data. While the Pocket Statistical Handbook of 1998 states no change in the number of units in 1997-98 as compared to 1996-97, the 2000 edition gives new figures of 14 units with 69 employees. The same source gives 42 units with 246 employees for 1998-99. Such figures suggest a negative growth rate and a miraculous disappearance of thousands of units. However, on seeking clarifications from the Meghalaya Khadi and Village Industries Board (MKVIB), it is now understood that the figures in the Pocket Statistical Handbook of 2000 refer to only those units which have been annually assisted (i.e. for establishment) under the new scheme of margin money. This then means that industries established prior to 1997, though in existence, have not been accounted for in the 2000 statistical handbook. Such lacuna in data can send the wrong signals.

A type/activity-wise distribution of KVIs (Table 19) for the year 1998-99 reveals the following:

(i) forest based units numbering 2863 units have a relative numerical strength of 45.6 percent;

(ii) agro-horticulture based units have a share of 30.3 percent (1905 units);

(iii) Need-based industries account for 14 percent (880 units).

(iv) mineral based industries, 10.1 percent (632 units), and

(v) Establishment of new units after 1990-91 (items 14 to 24) which are mostly need or demand-based.

Since 1997 the Meghalaya Khadi and Village Industries Board (MKVI) has been trying to generate rural employment through the Margin Money Scheme of KVIC. The period 1997-99 has witnessed few takers and limited success.

EXPLANATION FOR WEAK LINKAGES

The resource base of the State provides immense potentialities for a wide range/ variety of industries and manufacturing units and yet, the State remains industrially backward. Three decades of planning have led to some improvements in the basic physical, financial and social infrastructure of the State, but not adequate enough to transform the economy structurally. Physical achievements have more often fallen short of goals. Investments for industrial development have been almost non-existent and as a consequence, the secondary sector's contribution to the NSDP has remained virtually stagnant. The low credit-deposit ratios of Commercial Banks (15.67) and Regional Rural Banks (27.27) at the end of March 2000 indicate the existence of numerous self-financing and very small scale enterprises. In fact, out of the 56,497 enterprises (agricultural and non-agricultural) engaged in different economic activities other than crop production and plantation, 40,288 or 71 percent were self-financing (Report on the Fourth Economic Census of Meghalaya, 1998, Part I and II). The low credit-deposit ratios also reflect (i) low saving levels and (ii) unviable project proposals.

Market imperfections such as lack of information/inadequate information regarding the availability of products, available technologies, size of market, etc. has produced undesirable results. Ignorance has led to modes of production and behaviour contrary to what is necessary for rapid economic growth. In fact, it is a difficult task to explain the reality. Moneyed people prefer to 'invest' in landed property and shy away from risky ventures. Entrepreneurs are definitely a rare group of species in the State. However, one must also remember the peripheral location of the State, the terrain and inadequate infrastructure that has impeded extraction of resources and localization of industries.

Table 19 : Type wise Distribution of KVIs in Meghalaya, 1990-91 and 1998-99

Sl. No.	Type of Industries	Based on	1990-91	1998-99
1	Cane and Bamboo*	F	446	980
2	Carpentry and Black smithy*	F	1152	1883
3	Pottery*	M	269	342
4	Processing of Cereals and Pulses*	AH	741	1260
5	Lime industry*	M	117	290
6	Bee keeping	AH	185	381
7	Village oil	AH	49	58
8	Fiber Industry	AH	84	106
9	Leather	D	57	98
10	Soap	AH	3	4
11	Palm Gur	AH	30	60
12	Tailoring	D	166	539
13	Servicing	D	13	71
14	Textile*	D	-	136
15	Medicine	AH	-	16
16	Handmade Paper	D	-	3
17	Fruit Processing*	AH	-	20
18	Electronics*	D	-	15
19	F.V.P.*		-	9
20	Aluminium*	D	-	3
21	Tyre Rethreading*	D	-	3
22	Gold Smith*	D	-	1
23	Plastic Polymer*	D	-	1
24	Bone Crushing*	D	-	1
	Total		**3312**	**6280**

Note: (i) 1998-99 figures are obtained by adding figures of 1996-97 and new figures of 1997-98 and 1998-99.

(ii) *indicates the type of units receiving finance since 1997 under margin money scheme.

(iii) F=Forest; M=Minerals; AH=Agro-Horticulture; D=Demand.

(iv) In item (2) carpenters are given majority status.

Source: Pocket Statistical Handbook, Meghalaya, 1992, 1998 and 2000.

It is pointless to set up Industrial Estates and Export Promotion parks if the resources remain inaccessible in the absence of infrastructures. Such Industrial Areas tend to benefit only need-based units or by and large remain under-utilised.

Of the factors that determine/influence economic growth viz. Economic and Non-Economic factors, the former, which includes natural resources, capital accumulation, organization and technology etc. play an important role in the growth process. However, their lack or deficiency in neither an absolute handicap and nor does their abundance guarantee rapid economic progress. This then brings us to the domain of Non-economic factors, the underlying currents of growth. Social attitudes and values and institutions not only influence human behaviour but also direct them towards particular goals. The quality of human resource has a positive correlation with efficiency and productivity levels and a determined, stable and clean political and administrative set-up provides the stimulus to economic activity.

At this juncture, Table 20 can give us a better perspective of why things are the way they are in the State of Meghalaya.

Table 20 : Investment in Meghalaya: Objective and Perception Ranks

(I)	OBJECTIVE RANKS	Value	Rank in 1999
(A)	PHYSICAL INFRASTRUCTURE		
(i)	Power		
	Per capita consumption (Kwh)	135.00	21
	Villages electrified (%)	50.88	26
	Power Surplus/Deficit (%)	3.10	1
	Av. Industrial Tariff (P/Kwh)	184.70	9
(ii)	Telecom		
	Lines/100 persons	1.22	14
	No. of ISPs	0	17
	Population per cell phone	12,736	18
(iii)	Roads		
	Road length (per '000 sq.km.)	374.11	23
	Proportion of Surfaced Roads	47.03	17
	District Road Density	231.58	20
iv)	Railways	0.00	26
	Track length (per '000 sq.km.)		
(v)	Ports	N.A.	N.A.
(vi)	Airports	1	20
(vii)	Irrigation		
	Gross Irrigated Area (%)	18.91	18
(B)	QUALITY OF GOVERNMENT		
(i)	Infrastructure Management		
	Plant load factor (%)	N.A.	N.A.
	TUD losses (%)	16	3
	SEBs' RoR (Rate of Return) (%)	-51	17
(ii)	Fiscal Management		
	Fiscal Deficit/SDP (%)	N.A.	N.A.
	Revenue Deficit Growth (%)	29.54	11
	State Tax Revenue/Expenditure (%)	N.A.	N.A.
	Non-Dev. Rev. Exp./Rev. Receipt (%)	30.5	3
(C)	FINANCIAL INFRASTRUCTURE		
	Population per Bank Branch (in '000)	13	9
	Stock exchanges	0	16
	No. of NSE VSATS	0	21
(D)	LABOUR		
	Average Minimum Wage (Rs.)	35	8
	Average No. of Daily Workers	2	23

	Man-days Lost Due to Disputes	N.A.	N.A.
(E)	SOCIAL INFRASTRUCTURE		
	Literate Adults (%)	49.1	19
	Urban population (%)	18.6	18
	Hospital Beds (per '000 persons)	1.05	10
II. PERCEPTION RANKS		**Rank 1997)**	**Rank (1999)**
(A)	PHYSICAL INFRASTRUCTURE		
	Physical infrastructure	18	19
	Power Availability and Cost	14	15
	Quality of Power	18	16
	Proximity to Ports	17	15
	Presence of Industrial Zones/Belts	27	22
	Telecom and InfoTech Infrastructure	N.A.	24
	Extent of Ancillarisation	N.A.	24
	Office Infrastructure	N.A.	14
(B)	QUALITY OF GOVERNMENT		
	Quality of Local Administration	27	20
	State Government Support	15	18
	Law and Order	27	15
	Policy Implementation	15	20
	Flexibility of State Government Policies	14	16
	Political Stability	14	14
	SEB Privatisation	N.A.	12
	Presence of EPZs	N.A.	5
(C)	LABOUR		
	Work Culture of State	17	19
	Labour Relations	27	16
	Labour Availability	27	13
	Management Availability and Cost	N.A.	18
	Cost of Labour	20	15
(D)	SOCIAL INFRASTRUCTURE		
	Social Infrastructure	23	21
	Proximity to Markets	27	20
	Availability of Raw Materials	20	24
	Degree of Urbanisation	20	17

OBJECTIVE RANK-19, PERCEPTION RANK-19; THE RANK-20

INVESTMENT PROFILE

Total Investment	Rs.725 Cr.	
Electricity	67.4%	
Irrigation	2.2%	
Manufacturing		0.0%
Mining	0.0%	
Services	30.30%	
Under Implementation		Rs.539 Cr.
State's Share of FDI		0%
Government	100%	

Source: North East India Data Bank (NEDFI) Neidata-bank@hub.nic.in <mailto:Neidatabank@hub.nic.in> (based on Business Today, December 22nd 1999-January 6th 2000).

ROLE OF THE STATE

The State's role in promoting economic development has been intensely debated in development literature. While active state intervention was advocated after the Great Depression of the 1930s, of late, many economists have suggested a stronger orientation towards the market with less government intervention in certain areas, i.e. governments need to step in when market do not operate efficiently. Things seem to have come a full cycle because of the mixed experiences in many developing economies. The 1997 World Development Report says that the State is central to economic and social development as a partner, catalyst and facilitator but not as a direct provider of growth. In this respect, given the land relations and property rights in Meghalaya, the State Government has been acting in the manner as suggested by the World Bank economists since its formation in 1972.

The State of Meghalaya was created primarily to fulfill the unrealized aspirations of the natives and accelerate the process of development in the backward hill areas. The Commission on the Hill areas of Assam (Pataskar Commission) appointed by the Government of India made the following observations in 1965-66 regarding Meghalaya:

"Despite the progress already made, the economic difficulties continue to be particularly severe in the Hill Districts. It is not unnatural that because of the past neglect, a consider-able percentage of outlay in the hills, in the beginning, to be incurred on non-income generating (or less income generating) schemes. Due to sparse population and lack of the means of communication, the benefits that have accrued have also not yet found a satisfactory solution. In respect of some of their pressing needs, the progress too has been unsatisfactory". (*5TH Five Year Plan*, Draft Proposals Vol.1 and 2, 1973, p.7).

Similar observations were made by the Joint Centre-State Study Team in 1966 under the leadership of Shri Tarlok Singh, then Planning Commission member. When Meghalaya became an autonomous state on 2nd April 1970, the Fourth Plan of Meghalaya for the remaining years of the Plan was carved out of the Hill Areas Plan of the composite State of Assam, without considering the special requirements of Meghalaya. There were acute deficiencies, inadequate Plan allocation and also diversion of resources from development purposes to the extension of relief to the 7 lakh refugees from Bangladesh in 1971-72. There were also several other problems requiring immediate attention. They were:

a) problem of shifting cultivation in 75 percent of the cultivated area
b) underdeveloped border areas with Bangladesh
c) lack of central sector projects
d) inadequate assistance from Central Financing, Institutions and Nationalised Bank.
e) higher price levels due to insufficient facilities of transport and communication which depressed living standards, and
f) the lack of private investments due to the backward nature of the economy.

The indicators of economic development at that time suggested that Meghalaya was extremely backward. For instance, its per capita income was Rs.327.00 (all India - Rs.589.00); 82 percent of its population was dependent on agriculture with extremely low percentage of area sown more than once; a backward industrial sector with only one industry (Cherrapunjee Cement Factory); transport bottlenecks and extremely poor progress in rural electrification, public health and medical facilities.

Given this background and in the absence of data (because the Department of Economics and Statistics was being set up), the Draft of the 5th Five-Year Plan was prepared for the State. The Draft categorised the major resources into 3 groups for the purpose of industrial development: (a) mineral resources, (b) forest resources, and (c) resources based on agriculture including horticulture, livestock and sericulture. The Meghalaya Industrial Development Corporation (MIDC) was expected to play a vital role for the implementation of various programmes. Over the years the State Government has created some Industrial Estates and Areas with various facilities in different districts of the State. These Estates and Areas provide laid out land plots of different sizes with basic infrastructure like factory sheds, all season roads, sewerage and drainage, electricity, water, telecommuni-cation, weigh bridges, residential buildings on lease etc.

To promote export potential industries an Export Promotion Industrial Park (EPIP) was established at Byrnihat with an area of 250 acres, an Investment of Rs.14.50 crores, and operational since June 1998. Here too the Government has provided infrastructure like power, water, roads, etc. An area of 182 acres has been marked out at Mendipathar, East Garo Hills Districts, as a Growth Centre with the intention of promoting industrialization of backward areas and achieving balanced growth. The total outlay of Rs.18 crores on this growth center is on a cost-sharing basis between the Central Government, Industrial Development Department and the Government of Meghalaya. Along these lines, the State Government framed the Industrial Policy of 1997 specifying the objectives and identifying the thrust areas and declaring a package of schemes, incentives and assistance to the industries under "The Meghalaya Incentive Scheme, 1997". Besides, the MIDC has identified and prepared summary profiles of several resource based projects for potential investment with negotiable government participation.

Sectoral Measures in respect of forest resources involves the implementation of a project for the development of Forestry and Non-Timber Forest produce (*State Finances: A Study of Budgets of 2001-02*, RBI - January 2002, page 6).

In respect of agriculture, there is new emphasis on pulses, oilseeds and cash crops. For the marketing of agricultural produce, rural godowns have been built and Secondary Regulated Markets have been established. An autonomous board has been set up to promote plantation crops. The Agriculture Department has identified Tea as a promising plantation crop. Incentives like Cash subsidy of Rs.15, 000.00 per hectare, supply of plant protection materials like insecticides, weedicides, fungicides etc. at 50 percent subsidy and training programmes for the tea growers are being provided for raising micro sized tea plantations. There are at present 253 small tea gardens. Fruit processing is another promising industry because of the emphasis on the development of Horticultural crops where returns are higher per hectare. With this emphasis on horticulture, jhum cultivation can be curtailed. The 2(two) fruit processing factories at Shillong and Dainadubi in East Garo Hills have installed capacity of 60 M.T. and 40 M.T. respectively. They also serve as training centers for the local youth to create employment opportunities through establishment of cottage industries of agricultural produce.

The Minor Irrigation Wing of the Agriculture Department is engaged with identifying irrigation potentialities and installation of projects to facilitate cultivation around the year. So far 21,339 hectares have been brought under assured irrigation through 139 Minor Flow and Lift Irrigation projects.

The Meghalaya State Agricultural Marketing Board has been set up to ensure financial returns and remunerative prices for the farmers. At present there are 2(two) Secondary Regulated Market yards: (a) Mawïong (East Khasi Hills) - dealing with potatoes, ginger, broomstick, tezpatta, etc. and (b) Garobadha (West Garo Hills) - dealing with jute, mesta, cotton, mustard, pineapple etc.

Other secondary markets are to be set up at Williamnagar, Ampati, Dadenggiri, Romgram, Umsning, Lad Nongkrem, Dawki and Jowai.

Transport subsidy is being provided to co-operative organization for the organized procurement of fruits and vegetables from the interior areas and their disposal in urban areas. Equipment is also being provided at subsided rates to set up agro-based industries. There is also an AGMARK laboratory for monitoring the quality of certain agri-produce.

Role of the Centre

In view of the backward nature of the entire North Eastern Region (NER) the North-Eastern Council (NEC) was set up in Shillong by an Act of Parliament in 1971. The NEC was to act as an advisory body in respect of socio-economic development and ensure balanced development of the region. Since its functioning in 1972, the NEC has been involved in various capacities in the entire NER. However, the slow pace of industrialization necessitated the incorporation of the North East Development Finance Corporation Ltd. (NEDFi) in 1995 with the objectives of providing credit and other facilities for the promotion, expansion and modernization of industrial enterprises and infrastructure projects. In the Budget of 1998-99, the Government of India entrusted NEDFi to act as the nodal agency for the disbursement of central subsidies for the States in the NER. The Union Government's New Industrial Policy of 1997 provided various incentive packages for the setting up of new units. At the same time a Non-Lapsable Central Pool of Resources was created for the North East and Sikkim. Since it became operational in 1998-99, it has released Rs.1346.72 crores for various projects. Of this amount, Meghalaya has received only Rs.66.81 crores (the lowest) due to poor utilization of funds and lack of viable project proposals from the State government.

Role of the Market

Like the State, the Market too has a unique role to play. In an economy where resources are at the hands of private individuals, profit motive and self-interests guide production activities and, as Adam Smith argues, social benefits are automatically maximized. This is to say that market provides the incentives to economic growth. But it is a well-known fact that the market in developing economies is characterized by widespread imperfections. The lack of information and uncertainty go hand in hand. Production decisions based on inadequate information leads to inefficient allocation/distribution of resources and produce undesirable results. Such is the situation in Meghalaya. Inadequate information and a great deal of uncertainty have led to a distorted and small market size. The industrial structure of the State and the weak resource-industry linkage points out that the nature of market signals and planning efforts do not meet halfway but are indeed, poles apart. If such cases, the State/Government must definitely intervene to ensure changes in the crucial sectors of the economy.

PROBABLE POLICY OPTIONS

An overview of the State's economy clearly indicates that she is caught in a low level equilibrium trap and stagnating. The primary sector is overburdened, the secondary sector stagnant and the tertiary sector saturated. The vicious cycle of poverty is evidently in operation on both sides, i.e. demand and supply sides. The small market size has not only kept production levels low but has also operated as a disincentive to potential investors. A low level of capital formation because of small capacity to save and low inducement to invest have only led to low productivity levels, low income levels and poverty. The unscientific exploitation of natural resources and their exportation without any value addition has deprived the State of additional revenue and the essential forward and backward economic linkages. The present state of affairs is a paradoxical situation of poverty amidst plenty and policy options for such economies are far easier to prescribe than realize, unless of course, there are radical changes from within. Nonetheless, an attempt has been made in the following section keeping in mind the scarcity of capital, the inter-relationships between the various sectors of the economy and the time frame for different sets of policies. The probable possible options discussed here are generalized as specific solutions require context based studies. It is in this generalized framework that macro solutions have been discussed.

The immediate concern i.e. short run goals should be improvements in the rural set-up, which accounts for over 80 percent of the total population. An increasing number of agricultural labourers signify greater landlessness and poverty. As per 1996-97 estimates, 48.85 percent of the total population were below the poverty line and a breakup on the basis of rural and urban areas shows that the majority, i.e. 54.47 percent; were in the rural areas. The welfare of this section can be improved through need-based planning at the grass roots. Proper utilization of funds under Rural and Border Area Development programmes is called for in the short-run.

For long run benefits, a larger number of rural populace can be gainfully employed by encouraging and establishing Agro-Horticulture based units along co-operative lines. Community development schemes need greater thrust and must be context based for better implementation. Cultivators, too, need to be encouraged to take up cultivation of horticultural and other commercial crops where returns are higher and in which the State has surpluses. This needs to be supported by the Green Revolution package of better seeds, irrigation, fertilizers and better agricultural practices. Availability of finance, proper storage and efficient marketing networks will support and promote agriculture. In addition the frequency of awareness and demonstration camps must be increased to provide the necessary information about new trends in technologies and the nature of demand. An improvement in the welfare of the rural masses would generate demand for various goods and services and following a proper market survey, incentives may be provided for setting up specific need/demand based units.

Another thrust area is the promotion of Tourism through aggressive campaigns in different media. The natural beauty needs preservation and promotion to generate additional revenue for the State. This would necessitate and promote improvements in infrastructure like roads, transportation and communication. And to sustain the tourism industry, improved political and administrative policies will have to be pursued for solving her burning problems and removing all types of phobias from the minds of prospective tourists. Other benefits would be greater employment opportunities and a fillip to the Handloom and Handicraft sector of the State.

The water resources must be properly harnessed. So far only 15 percent of the potential power has been tapped. The difference between the potential (1200 M.W.) and the actual (186.71M.W.) can be reduced only by large scale investments. For this foreign firms with funds and technical expertise may be approached.

Since the state has remained industrially backward, the primary and tertiary sectors have had to bear the brunt of the population pressure. The agricultural sector has surplus manpower and the government is under tremendous pressure to provide more employment opportunities, i.e. white-collared jobs. A way out of this is to expand the secondary sector. Medium and long term policies would require that the State, either alone or through joint ventures, set up those basic and capital goods industries which have high linkage effects and considerable social benefits. This will set in motion the process of economic development and enlarge the market for other industries apart from creating employment opportunities. This, however, calls for an integration of economic planning, manpower planning and educational planning. In the short-run, the vast number of educated unemployed in the urban areas must be encouraged to initiate their own enterprises through the provision of loans at concessional rates. Since project proposals prepared by entrepreneurs need to be viable so as to secure loans under the available schemes, organizations like M.I.D.C. and N.E.D.Fi who offer various forms of assistance must play the roles of a catalyst.

On the issue of mineral extraction, local entrepreneurs involved in mining in the unorganized sector must be encouraged and motivated to move to the organized sector. Since resources are extracted in response to demand and exported without any value addition the income generated remains low. Short and medium term plans should encourage value addition and in the very short run, artificial scarcity may be resorted to, to fetch remunerative returns. In this context, it may be mentioned that the fixation of export price for minerals by the Centre is unjustified as this has promoted huge volumes of unofficial trade and incurred losses to the State exchequer in terms of royalty payments.

There is a need to tap other sources of funds outside the State. This would bring along technical expertise to kick-start new and dormant projects. Moreover with mounting state expenditure (because of the requirements of an ever increasing population, the jumbo sized State cabinets etc.) and paucity of funds (that to underutilized), numerous projects and programmes are either delayed, under-implemented or non-starters. Apart from creating a transparent, clean and efficient government, international financial institutions can be approa-ched for concessional loans for rural development purposes and infrastructural development projects. In the present era of liberalization and globalization the slow pace of progress would only be detrimental to the indigenous people. With the State gradually withdrawing the onus lies with the State to create the necessary environment so as to enable its people to not only participate and seek opportunities in a market oriented economy but also bear its onslaughts. Non Government Organizations (NGOs), voluntary associations and social workers can play a vital role in disseminating necessary information to the remotest areas of the State. And since these groups and individuals have greater ties with the people at the grass-roots they can be consulted before the implementation of various programmes. Finally, since indigenous tribals working outside the state pay income tax there definitely is a case, of bringing the elites and the affluent under the tax net of the State. This would increase the revenue of the State to a minute extent but more importantly check conspicuous consumption and inflationary tendencies on the price level. It may also inculcate in people a greater awareness towards expenditures (unwarranted, wasteful or developmental) of the State.

REFERENCES

Census of India: Meghalaya Series: 1971, 1981, 1991 and 2001(P).

Das, Gurudas, 2004, "The State of Manufacturing in Meghalaya: Resource -Industry Linkages", in Datta Ray, B and Gurudas Das, (eds), *Dimensions of Rural Development in North East India,* Akansha Publishing House, New Delhi

Dutta, Rajesh, 2000, "Coal Export from Meghalaya to Bangladesh: A Case Study of the Borsora Trade Route" in Das, Gurudas and R.K. Purkayastha (Eds.). *Border-Trade: North East India and Neighbouring Countries*, Akansha Publishing House, New Delhi.

Government of India: *India 1999*, Ministry of Information and Broadcasting, New Delhi.

Government of Meghalaya: "Area, Production and Yield of Principal Crops in Meghalaya, 1970-71 to 1986-87, Vol.1 and 1987-88 to 1998-99, Vol.II, Directorate of Economics and Statistics.

Government of Meghalaya: "Domestic Product of Meghalaya" 1980-81 to 1996-97 and 1993-94 to 2001-2002, Directorate of Economics and Statistics.

Government of Meghalaya: "Meghalaya: Investment Friendly"

Government of Meghalaya: "Meghalaya: Land and People" Vol.1, 1991, Directorate of Information and Public Relations.

Government of Meghalaya: "Minerals for Industrial Use" December 1973, Directorate of Mineral Resources.

Government of Meghalaya: "Report on Fourth Economic Census" Part I and II, 1998, Directorate of Economics and Statistics.

Government of Meghalaya: Directorate of Economics and Statistics, Pocket Statistical Handbooks, Various Issues and District Level Statistics, 2002.

Government of Meghalaya: Draft Proposals of Various Five Year Plans.

Government of Meghalaya: www. Meghalaya.nic.in

Jhingan, M.L., 1990, *The Economics of Development and Planning*, 23rd Edition, Konark Publishers, New Delhi.

Ministry of Water Resources: "Ground Water Resources of Meghalaya," August 2002, Central Ground Water Board, North Eastern Region, Guwahati.

Mishra, S.K. and V.K. Puri: *Economics of Development and Planning Theory and Practice*, 9th Edition, January 2001, Himalaya Publishing House, Mumbai.

NEDFi: "Quarterly Journal on North Eastern States Economy", Vol.I, July 2002.

North East India Data Bank (NEDFi): Neidatabank@hub.nic.in <mailto:Neidatabank@hub.nic.in>

North-Eastern Council: Basic Statistics of North Eastern Region, Various Issues.

North-Eastern Development Finance Corporation Ltd. (NEDFi): "Investment Opportunities in Meghalaya".

Reserve Bank of India: "State Finances: A Study of Budgets of 2001-2002", January 2002.

Supplementary Observation

Structure of Service Sector and Development Strategy for Meghalaya

—Nirankar Srivastav

Introduction

The economies of the world are passing through the different stages of the process of globalization. During this regime, a definite and distinguished pattern of structural transformation among these economies is being observed. One of the characteristic features displayed by these economies is better known as 'tertiarisation' of the economy. That means the share of service sector to the Gross Domestic Product is continuously rising. Mukhopadhyaya (2002) has shown on the basis of world development indicators that the economies of High Income countries like USA, Japan and France have been dominated by the service sector, as the share of this sector to GDP was well above 50% in these countries in 1980. Furthermore, these economies are depicting a rising trend and share of service sector has reached to above 60% in 1999.

This phenomenon is also being observed among the South Asian (relatively lower income) countries like India, Pakistan, Bangladesh, Sri Lanka and Nepal where the regional average of the share of service sector was 37% in 1980, which has increased to 47% in 1999. Specifically, in case of India this share has increased from 36% to 46% during this period. This clearly shows the growing importance of service sector during the era of globalization. The expansion of this sector expected to play a vital role in generating employment, trade and business opportunities in the most of the economies of future.

The present paper highlights some of the recent developments and trends in the service sector of a northeastern state of Meghalaya. We also analyse the structure of the service sector and the changes among the sub-sectors of the service sector from the period 1980-81 to 1993-94. This paper further deals with the possibility of the growth of service sector in and some of the possible suggestions for the developmental strategy for the state. The rest of the paper is organized in the following manner. The second section highlights some of the important socio-economic features of the state economy, sectoral economic structure and trends in past decades in Meghalaya are discussed in third section. Fourth section deals with some of the possible suggestions for the development strategy. Last section is devoted to concluding remarks.

Salient Features of the Economy of Meghalaya

Meghalaya is one of the states within northeastern region of India. This state has predominantly tribal population and rich in natural resources like land, water and forests resources of which, larger proportion is under utilized. Process of urbanization, which was initially slow before the independence, got momentum afterwards with the reorganization of administrative units. Under nodes became service centre and place for government jobs. Some industrial estates also developed in and around urban centres.

Economy of Meghalaya is predominantly agriculture based. There are places where still most primitive form of cultivation, i.e., slash and burn, is being practiced. Agriculture is the major economic sector, therefore, more than 65% rural population dependent for earning their livelihood from this sector. The variety in economic structure and distribution has significant impact on social settings, which is reflected in the behaviour pattern of the people of the state.

Industrial sector is not very much developed in Meghalaya. There were only a small number of large and medium scale industries. The distribution of small-scale industries (SSIs) was depicting a slow but rising rate of growth in past few years in Meghalaya. But as a whole economy of Meghalaya is yet to be industrially developed, 25 to 30% of the population earn their livelihood from tertiary sector.

The infrastructural sector is also less developed in the state than all India level. Per capita consumption of electricity is much below the national average. Similarly, percentage of surface road to total road length is lower and the per capita net state domestic product at current prices for the year 1993-94 is also lower than per capita net domestic product at the national level. These observations show that the economy of Meghalaya is less developed than the rest of India. This clearly shows that the state economy is trapped in the state of low equilibrium. This fact is further substantiated by the higher and increasing rates of unemployment in this state.

Structure of the Economy of Meghalaya

In the background of above discussed salient features, we now describe the structure of the economy of Meghalaya on the basis of sectoral share in NSDP. As shown in Table-1, Meghalaya was having highest share of non-manufacturing and service sector followed by agricultural sector in the year 1980-81. The manufacturing sector contributes around 3% share of NSDP. The share of agricultural sector has shown declining trend during the period 1980-81 to 1995-96. During the same period the share of manufacturing sector has shown a slower but increasing trend. But services sector have shown significant increase in their share of NSDP from 59% in 1980-81 to 74.4% in 1995-96.

Table-1 : Sectoral Shares in Percentage of NSDP at 1980-81 Prices for Meghalaya

State	Sector	1980-81	1985-86	1990-91	1995-96
MEGHALAYA	Agriculture	37.7	35.5	26.9	21.1
	Manufacture	3.2	3.3	4.1	4.5
	Non-manufacture & Service	59.0	61.2	68.9	74.4

Source: Table 29: National Accounts Statistics of India, EPW Research Foundation, Mumbai, October 1997.

These trends give the impression that all is well so far as the structural change follows the trend of other developed and developing economies of other states of India and abroad. But this may not be so proven when we do further deeper analysis of inter sectoral growth patterns for the economy of Meghalaya during this period.

We begin with analyzing the per capita NSDP, which was much below in Meghalaya than all India average in the year 1980-81. This should be kept in mind that Meghalaya has lower than national average of population density. That is to show that lower per capita NSDP in fact reflects the smaller size of the state economy. During the period 1980-81 to 1995-96 the all India per capita GDP have increased by 163%, while Meghalaya has shown increase in per capita NSDP lower than national average. This shows slower economic growth of the state economy and further supports the hypotheses that the state economy is trapped in the lower level equilibrium state. So, while preparing any development strategy for Meghalaya it is necessary to keep this fact in mind.

Table-2 shows sectoral composition of service sector on the basis of their percentage contribution to NSDP at factor cost by industry of origin for the year 1980-81 and 1993-94 respectively. First we look at the composition of service sector for the year 1980-81 where the highest share comes from public adminis-tration followed by construction. The share of banking and insurance and transport, storage and communication service sector was the lowest. Now, let us see whether this scenario has changed in 1993-94 (also, may be interpreted as post globalization era), where we find that percentage share of public administration in NSDP has in fact increased and the share of construction has declined. This clearly shows that major portion of growth in service sector shown in Table-2 is due to significant increase in public administration expenditure alone, which is mainly, state financed and sponsored. This implies that the state economy is yet to develop a self-sustaining and growth oriented service sector.

Table-2 : Sectoral Composition of Non-Manufacture & Service Sector, their Contribution (in percentage) to NSDP at Factor Cost by Industry of Origin and their Respective Rank Order for the Year 1980-81 and for the Year 1993-94 at 1980-81 Prices for Meghalaya

Non-manufacture & Service Sector	1980-81	Rank Order	1993-94	Rank Order
Construction	11.7	II	10.2	IV
Electricity, Gas and Water Supply	-0.3	VIII	1.9	VIII
Transport, Storage and Communication	2.3	VI	6.7	VI
Trade, Hotel and Restaurants	10.7	III	12.8	II
Banking and Insurance	1.7	VII	3.0	VII
Real Estate and Business Services	8.5	IV	7.7	V
Public Administration	12.0	I	16.9	I
Other Service	8.4	V	11.8	III
Net State Domestic Product	100.0		100.0	
NSDP (in Rs. Lakh)	**17962**		**32005**	

Source: National Accounts Statistics of India, EPW Research Foundation, Mumbai, October 1997.

Though the construction had large share (11.7%) in total NSDP in the year 1980-81 but it has declined to 10.2% in the year 1993-94. This should be seen in the light that construction sector is growing at faster rate in most of the states of India due to favourable policy measures taken by the central and state governments, like home credit at lower rate of interest and direct tax benefits. So, this has to be looked into as to why construction sector is not growing at a faster rate in Meghalaya.

Furthermore, the construction sector has to play a vital role in the economic development of the state, as Srivastav and Dubey (2001) has found in a study on rural non-farm employment that construction is one of the important sector that generates employment for low, middle and high wage earners simultaneously. So, this sector is highly labour intensive sector. Also, the proportion of construction workers has increased its share from 1.02% to 4.22% in the NE region from 1993-94 to 1999-2000.

The techniques of input-output analysis are helpful in quantifying the employment, output and income linkages of various economic sectors. But such information is not available for the NE states in general and Meghalaya in particular at disaggregated level. But in another study for the other parts of India (Srivastav, 1985), it has been shown that expenditure of public administration has lower employment and output linkages, whereas construction and trade, hotel and restaurant are the service sectors which have relatively higher employment and income generating capabilities. If the present trends continue then it can be said that the growth of service sector may not lead to generating additional employment and income opportunities. Thus, this type of development may not address the major economic problems such as growing unemployment.

Similarly, transport, storage and communication and banking and insurance have higher forward and backward linkages which in turn generates higher growth impulses, which facilitate the faster economic growth. Both of these service sectors are lopsided in Meghalaya. One of the possible reasons may be that these sectors have higher forward linkages with the industrial sector and when industrial sector is not fully developed the inter-dependent service sectors are also not developing within the state.

For the purpose of comparison, Table-2 also, demonstrates the ranking of sectoral composition of service sector on the basis of their contribution to NSDP for the year 1980-81 and 1993-94. Rank I denotes the highest and rank VIII denotes the lowest percentage share in the NSDP. It is evident by analyzing the trends that the ranking order of the various service sectors has not changed much during this period. This is implied that the basic structure of the service sector has not changed despite the significant growth in the share of service sector in the NSDP. It is evident, therefore that the post globalization situation and state incentives have not been able to generate sufficient push and pull to transform service sector which is required for more vibrant and growth oriented development for the state economy. In this context it is worthwhile to mention that on the basis of inter-state comparison of the structure of service sector of the NE states (including Meghalaya) with other states of India, Srivastav (2002) has shown that in relatively more economically developed states in India, the service sector is growing towards more growth, employment and income generating sectors such as trade, hotel and restaurants, construction, real estate and business and banking and insurance sector giving stimulus to economic growth. While Public administration has almost bottom rank among the services sector in these states.

Development Strategy for Meghalaya

Economic development of any region depends upon the availability of resource endowments, infrastructural support, evolution of right type of institutions, access to market and credit, supply of quality human resource including entrepreneurs and physical capital. These factors have so far been not favourable for the northeastern states of India in general and for Meghalaya in particular. Level of economic development is also determined by the socio-economic history and geographical location of any region. As these determine the initial level of economic development on which foundation could be laid down.

As a first step priorities have to clearly identify for the economy of Meghalaya and a mechanism has to be developed for the better participation of the people of the state in these priority sectors. While doing so we should take note of inherent features of the present economy and its past trends of economic growth. This process will help in developing an accountable and responsible system to ensure the more efficient use of available recourses and human capabilities.

Due emphasis should be paid to broaden and enhance the prevailing narrow economic base and the size of the state economy. This calls for to adopt those measures, which leads to higher economic growth. One of the possibilities is to encourage the 'deepening and widening' of the capital. This could be achieved by re-organising economic activities with better and appropriate technologies.

With the changing scenario of the national economy, it is not at all necessary and expected from the smaller states like Meghalaya to industrialize its economy by developing manufacturing sector, which will not ensure the comparative cost advantages and economic viability in the long run. But such economic sectors have to be identified in which state can specialize and at the same time could produce at the competitive prices.

More attention has to be paid to develop resource based industries and towards higher degree of value addition to the product instead of trading with raw materials as such. This will give higher economic returns distributed among the larger segment of local population by way of increasing employment and real income.

Resource based industries however have lower backward but higher forward linkages. But in most of the less developed economies the products are traded to relatively more advance regions as a result of which source economy is unable to absorb the advantages of higher forward linkages in the form of growth stimulus. This is also true in the case of Meghalaya at present. Enhancing developmental activities by the public sectors and the state could change this scenario.

One of the major difficulties for the state is the weak and under developed transport and communication links with the other northeastern states as well as with the rest of the country. This calls for more developed intra and inter regional integration within the nation. Possibilities should also be explored for the trade with neighbouring countries, especially between Mehalaya and Bangladesh.

Keeping in view of less developed economic infrastructure and peculiar socio-cultural situations, the state may not be the direct beneficiary of the regime of liberalization by way of foreign direct or private investment in any significant way at least in near future. Till then, the state apparatus has to continue to play the catalytic role for the rapid economic development.

REFERENCES

Economic and Political Weekly Research Foundation (1997): *National Accounts Statistics of India 1950-51 to 1995-96*, Mumbai, October.

Mukhopadhyaya, S. (2002): 'Globalisation and Indian Services Sector', Economic and Political Weekly, 38(40), October, p.4097-98.

Srivastav, N. (1985). "Sectoral Interdependency and Effects of Income Distribution in the Economy of Uttar Pradesh: A Study in Input-Output Framework', Ph.D. thesis (unpublished), IIT, Kanpur.

__________ (2002): "Development of Service Sector: Is There Any Hope for the Economies of North-Eastern India", Paper presented at the Seminar on "Globalisation, Employment, Migration and Trade: Relevance for the NER of India", NEHU, Shillong.

__________ and A. Dubey (2002): "Rural Non-Farm Employment in India: Spatial Variations and Temporal Change", *The Indian Journal of Labour Economics*, Vol.45, No.4, 745-755.

5

Economic Sustainability and Structural Transformation in Mizoram

—*Santanu Ray*

ntroduction

The concept of growth of an economy concerns the issues of generating income with ighest possible efficiency. The question of equity when added to the concept of growth we efer it as development. The scope of development economics, in recent days, has been videned enough to cover the issues not only related to the basic human needs. The income f an individual plays, of course, a crucial role to improve the level of living, which in turn as a positive impact on development. Altogether three basic universal values are commonly dentified as the primary goal of development economics (Rao: 1999): *Life Sustenance,)ignity of all individuals* in the society and most importantly *Freedom*. The first value in his regard covers the main objective of satisfying the basic human needs while second ne ensures the sense of worth or position of an individual to be recognized and respected s well. The third value, which is described, a freedom, in a way, echoes the words of abindranath *Where the mind is without fear* or Amartya Sen's discovery *Development as 'reedom*. This, in other way, implies the availability of choice or opportunities for etterment in broad sense covering every aspect of life. In recent studies, freedom of different ypes has been viewed as not only the primary ends of development, they are also described s one of its principal means (Sen: 2000).

Two pillars (Stern: 2002), which form the basis for the strategy for development, are lentified as *Investment Climate* to facilitate investment and growth and *empowering the oor* people to participate in that growth. The strategy for development, in this sense, has een definitely a strategy for *pro-poor growth*. The links between these two pillars of evelopmental goal aim at the ultimate object of poverty reduction.

The concept of sustainable development along with other normative aspects covers ne issues of resource stock recognition and resilience (Kadekori: 2002). It does not nclude only the environmental issues but also takes care the ability of future generations produce their needs of economic goods and services. The question of sustainability can e raised in terms of consumption, income, level of living, and use of natural resources of different categories. The conditions need to be fulfilled to maintain a sustainable development over time includes the proper use of different forces (human, man made, regenerative and non-generative natural resources) so that they do not decline over time. The increase in average income of an economy by any means, may lead to the people to a better level of living for time being provided the distribution of income is less skewed - but the goal of sustainable development remains unachieved. Therefore, the capital of all dimensions being used in the generation of income for present population should be maintained in such a way that the return will continue to flow at least at a non-declining capacity in future.

As income and well being of common people differ significantly, income, in recent days, is not considered as the sole indicator of development. Along with economic indicators the social and environmental indicators are also given equal importance in this regard. The economic indicators of sustainable development deal with the question whether the income level which is achieved today, could be sustained over a period of time. The social indications are framed with the consideration that quality of life is significantly associated with health, education and other social services. The environmental indicators suggest whether the use of natural capital is efficient. The stock of natural assets should sustain over time. We attempt to examine the development that has taken place in Mizoram, a small state in the North-East India, from the angle of various indicators to judge whether the development is sustainable.

Sustainability in Mizoram

In recent days, there has been a tendency to classify the developmental achievements of Mizoram, unlike the other northeastern states, as one of the rapidly developing states in the country. This is mainly due to the fact that a few established parameters of measuring developmental activities such as adult literacy rate, per capita incomes etc. happen to be high. The state of Mizoram has undoubtedly changed a lot during last few decades. The capital city of Aizawl with one fourth of state population has been emerging as one of the biggest urban settlements in the northeastern region. The study on number of private vehicles per capita could place the state in a higher ranking in the country. But the larger question to be addressed is whether these changes in the state are in expected direction of sustainable development. The spectacular achievements of the state, as being expressed in different levels, could be examined whether these will generate income for the future generations. Even though the question of equity is raised in occasions the larger question of sustainability has never been addressed. Here we attempt to examine the developmental achievements of the state through a set of indicators.

1. Economic Indicators

The performance of an economy is generally judged by its growth rates in GDP and NDP in per capita sense so that the standard of living of the people could be guessed. Of course, the per capita income can be a reasonable indicator of development only when the income inequality among people is reasonably low and other indicators of development such as adult literacy, infant mortality, and life expectancy are satisfactory. In addition, growth of all economic sectors must be maintained for a balanced development of the economy. The GSDP and NSDP (Table 1) in Mizoram during 1990's have grown at a moderate rate of 4.7percent and 4.85 percent respectively while NSDP per capita has grown at a very slower rate of 2.25 percent per annum. The rate of growth in NSDP is mainly due to increase in income in the secondary and tertiary sectors. The primary sector (Table 2) in which over 60 percent of the total work force of the state economy is engaged, has grown at an alarming rate of 0.54 percent, which is a matter of great concern. As Mizoram is one of the most urbanized state not only in the north-eastern region but also in the country as a whole with 49.50 percent of urban population, the slow growth in primary sector could be justified, if the participation rate in primary sector happened to be low. Agriculture, which has been the prime sub-sector of primary sector, is still a main source of livelihood of the state population. During 1991, about 65 percent of the state's main workers were engaged in agriculture either as cultivators (61.35 percent) or as agricultural labourers (3.28 percent) while during 2001 about 60percent of the state's workers were reported to be engaged in agriculture. Again in the last decade the percentage of agricultural labourers has increased from 3.28 percent to 5.86 percent of total workers indicating a growing level of unemployment in rural sector. The growth rate in agricultural income during 1990's is as low as 1.95 percent per annum while the share of agriculture in NSDP has dropped to 21.64 percent during 1999-2000 from 27.73 percent during 1993-94. Table 3 indicates that annual average growth of agricultural workers in last decade had been over 4 percent while the growth rate in agricultural income in the state was lesser than even 2 percent. The growth in non-agricultural work force in the state in last decade has been worked out at 6.29 percent per year while the growth in agricultural income is about 5.84 percent per annum. Therefore, both the agricultural and non-agricultural sectors of the economy have been suffering from the problem of over population. In both the sectors the growth in income is significantly reinforced by the high growth rate in labour participation resulting in low per capita income of the state economy as a whole.

The secondary sector (Table 2) of the state economy during the concerned years has grown at a rate as high as 6.90 percent per year. This may lead anybody to the conclusion that the industrialization process in the state economy has been satisfactory. The growth in this sector could be achieved due to the high growth rate of 10.07 percent per year in construction. The share of this sub-sector in NSDP has climbed to 11.53 percent during 1999-2000. The share of manufacturing has dropped to 1.22 percent with a negative growth rate (-12.61 percent per year), which could be described as the weakest part of the state economy. The claims made by the state government regarding the development of small-scale industries are not reflected at all in empirical realities. The history of industrial activities in the state had never been encouraging. After the promotion of the area as Union Territory in 1972 and as a full-fledged state in 1987, lack of comprehensive efforts of the state authority has further worsened the situation. The government, however, due to infrastructural and other problems always traces upon the development of small-scale industries (SSIs) in the state. The fourth economic census 1998 reports that about 5625 persons (including 2971 hired workers) in the state are engaged in manufacturing sector. In contrary the state industrial report informs that by the end of 31st March 2001 the total number of SSI units registered was 4600 with a total number of employment of 25974 persons. In addition, the total number of registered units under Mizoram Khadi and Village and Industries Board (MKVIB) had been 5772 with an employment of 15120 persons. A huge amount of monetary assistance has been provided to these units in forms

Table 1 : GSDP, NSDP and Per Capita NSDP in Mizoram during 1993-94 to 1999-2000

Year	Gross State Domestic Product (Rupees in Lakhs)				Net State Domestic Product (Rupees in Lakhs)				Per Capita Net State Domestic Product (in Rupees)			
	Current Prices	Constant Prices Base: 1993-94	Index Base: 1993-94		Current Prices	Constant Prices Base	Index Base 1993-1994		Current Prices	Constant Price Base 1993-94	Index Base 1993-94	
			Current	Constant			Current	Constant			Current	Constant
1993-94	71146	71146	100.00	100.00	61809	61809	100.00	100.00	8318	8318	100.00	100.00
1994-95	73877	64341	103.84	90.43	67178	62144	108.69	100.54	8793	8134	105.71	97.79
1995-96	93654	80939	131.64	113.77	85874	74215	138.94	120.07	10953	9466	131.68	113.80
1996-97	107234	92675	150.72	130.26	98293	84948	159.03	137.44	12210	10552	146.79	126.86
1997-98	112319	79417	157.87	111.63	102239	72290	165.41	116.96	12393	8763	148.99	105.35
1998-99	124590	82795	175.12	116.33	113896	75689	184.27	122.46	13479	8957	162.05	107.68
1999-00	140939	93072	198.10	130.82	128818	85068	208.41	137.63	14909	9846	179.24	118.37
Annual Growth Rate (percent)			4.70				4.85				2.25	

Source: Socio - Economic Review - Mizoram: 2000 - 01, Directorate of Economics & Statistics, Government of Mizoram.

of grant-in-aid, subsidy, loans, etc. for the over all development of manufacturing sector of the state. A sum of Rs.574.28 lakhs was reportedly released during 1999-2000 in different forms. However, the contribution of registered manufacturing sector in state income (NSDP) in the same fiscal year is reported at Rs.481 lakhs. This gives a clear picture of state adhocism in the name of the promotion of industries. A long-term sustainable industrial development through the optimum utilization of available natural and human resources and through the building up of physical infrastructure of the state has never been taken up in a planned manner.

Table : 2 : Income Growth of Sectors and Sub-sectors

During 1993-94 to 1999-2000 (At Constant 1993-94 Prices)

Sl. No.	Sector/Sub-sector	Exponential Annual Growth Rate ($\hat{g}$)	Coefficient of Determination (R^2)	Percent Share in NSDP (1999-2000)
I	**Primary**	**0.54**	**0.01**	**23.78**
a.	Agriculture	1.95	0.17	21.64
b.	Forestry	(–) 20.71	0.43	00.60
c.	Fishing	0.40	0.004	01.02
d.	Mining & Quarrying	18.49	0.33	00.52
II	**Secondary**	**6.90**	**0.35**	**13.46**
a.	Manufacturing	(–) 12.61	0.48	01.22
b.	Construction	10.07	0.58	11.53
c.	Electricity, Gas & Water Supply			00.71
III	**Tertiary Sector**	**6.65**	**0.77**	**62.76**
a.	Transport, Storage & Communication	9.58	0.78	01.37
b.	Trade, Hotels & Restaurants	(–) 0.76	0.02	10.50
c.	Banking & Insurance	11.93	0.95	01.48
d.	Real Estate & Business Services	8.59	0.87	14.28
e.	Public Administration	6.78	0.73	17.77
f.	Other Services	11.55	0.82	17.36
	NSDP	4.85	0.62	100.00

Source : Economics Review—Mizoram : 2000-01, Directorate of Economics & Statistics, Government of Mizoram.

The service sector (Table 2) in Mizoram economy makes up 62.76 percent of NSDP, which creates the confusion about the developmental performance of the state. Transport, Storage and Communication maintained a growth of 9.58 percent but accounts for 1.37 percent of NSDP during 1999-2000. Trade, Hotel and Restaurants grew at a negative rate but still contributes 10.50 percent of NSDP. Though the banking and insurance account for 1.48 percent with a growth rate of 11.93 percent per annum, the credit deposit ratio (27.28

percent during 2000-01) has been very low in the state. Real estate, ownership and business services, being one of the major contributor to NSDP, make-up 14.28 percent and grew at a rate of 8.59 percent per year. The public administration is the major sub-sector in the state economy, which contributes 17.77 percent of NSDP and grows at 6.78 percent per annum. The state government is the biggest employer providing employment of about 13 percent of total work force and the Central Government, Autonomous Councils, and Semi-Government Organizations provide another 2 percent employment during 1999-2000. The employment of 15 percent of the state working population in public sector is probably one of the highest in the country. The other services also grow at 11.55 percent and account for 17.36 percent of NSDP. The service sector as a whole grows at 6.65 percent per year mainly due the growth in income in public administration and other services. But the role, which the service sector should play to augment employment, income and the tax revenue of the state, has not been satisfactory. The high growth rate in few sub-sectors of the service sector is the clear reflection of huge public outlay flowing over the upper surface of the economy without efficiency, equity and transparency resulting in a dramatic hike in the level of living of a smaller section of population.

With a growth rate of 4.85 percent in NSDP the state could maintain a nominal annual growth rate of 2.25 percent in NSDP per capita in 1990's. The time series study of per capita income reveals that in early 1990's the state of Mizoram had been much ahead of national average while in late 1990's it is lagging behind. Therefore, to convert the growth of income in a fairly good growth of per capita income the control over the state population is very essential. The growth of population in the state in the last decade has been very high (2.59 percent per year) as compared to the national average (1.59 percent per year).

Table 3 : Agricultural and Non-Agricultural Activities of the State
(A comparative Study)

Sector	Annual Exponential Growth of Income during 1990's (at 1993-94 prices)	Annual Growth of Work Force During 1990's	Work Force Engaged in 2001
Agriculture	1.95% ($R^2 = 0.17$)	4.11%	59.81%
Non-Agriculture	5.84 % ($R^2 = 0.630$)	6.29%	4.19%

Source : 1.Economics Review— Mizoram : 2000-01, Directorate of Economics & Statistics, Government of Mizoram. 2. Provisional Data, Census, 2001.

Since the reduction of poverty is considered as one of the important elements of developmental goal, it is relevant here to mention the current poverty level. The level of poverty has never been estimated through scientific empirical studies. The figure shown by the state government has always been an over estimate. Block-wise statistics of the households living below poverty line shown in the state reports amount to 79,834 families as on March 2000. If this figure is converted into absolute number at least 50 percent of the state population is covered. Of course the official (state) figure is 56.60 percent, which appears to be unrealistic as compared to the values of other parameters like average life expectancy, malnutrition, percentage of working population, etc. The Economic Survey of India 2001-02, considering the poverty ratio of Assam as the base for all northeastern states, reports the poverty ration of Mizoram as low as 19.47 percent, which has reportedly reduced by 6 percent over the previous year. Even though the poverty ratio in the state is not clear enough, the income inequality and rural urban gap have been widening in Mizoram with the passage of time. The dualism that exists within the state economy has created a sharp distinction between capital city Aizawl and rest of the state in terms of income, level of living, employment opportunities, etc. In addition due the lack of planned vision a high degree of adhocism has developed in every sphere of state functioning. Open unemployment in the years of last decade seems to be a serious problem. The creation of employment is possible when there is a sustainable development approach in the economy over a long period.

2. Social Indicators

A number of human development indicators have been summed up in the form of a composite index, called Human Development Index (HDI). The index takes the status of purchasing power, health, education, etc. into account with proper weightage. A fairly good growth in income may not always refer to a high value of HDI. The Indian experience suggests that the national achievements in terms of per capita growth in income in independent years could not be translated into a fairly good value of HDI. In addition, Human Poverty Index (HPI) is a composite index capturing deprivation in the same aspects of human development.

The value of HDI of the country as a whole was calculated as 0.302 in 1981 and 0.381 in 1991. The index, however, has improved in 21st century to 0.472 in 2001, when estimates were made only in fifteen states and union territories. Mizoram scored a fairly high value of HDI, 0.411 in 1981 and 0.548 in 1991, which had been translated into an overall ranking of 8 in 1981, and 7 in 1991 among all 32 states and union territories of the country. The same for Mizoram is yet to be prepared for 2001. Considering a significant fall in per capita income in late 1990's, anxieties have already been expressed whether the tiny state could maintain its position in terms of HDI in the 21st century. On the contrary, the ranking as well as the value of HPI reveals an opposite scenario. The value of HPI in 1981 for the state (47.93) was very close to the national average (47.33) with an overall rank of 18. Further, in 1991 the rank rose to 14 with a value of 32.20 against the national average of 39.36.

The performance of the state in social sector has always been demonstrated as excellent in expanding the resources on human development. The birth rate during 1999-2000 is reported to increase from 20.08 to 21.38 percent. The increase in birth rate has been marked at both rural (17.97 percent) and urban (24.88 percent) Mizoram indicating the state has failed to change the attitude across the spectrum. The death rate has fallen significantly from 4.55 percent in 1999 to 4.02 percent in 2000. The infant mortality rate declined from 18.4 percent to 11.5 percent. However, the infant mortality rate in 1991 was reported to be very low at 53 percent for Mizoram as compared to the national average of 77 percent while the mortality rate was at 68 percent as against all India average of

94 percent. The fall in infant mortality rate during 1991 to 2000 is too significant to believe. However, the decline in death rate and infant mortality rate is much higher in rural areas as compared to urban areas. Since in the country as a whole and even in the developed states like Kerala, Tamil Nadu in particular the urban death rates are lesser than rural areas, the opposite scenario for Mizoram where a significant rural-urban gap can easily be marked needs to be checked. The fall in rural mortality rate by 11.58 percent within a year is not all understandable. In addition, the birth and death rates provided by the state authority cannot explain the high decadal growth in population. Apart from all these controversies, with wanted fall in death rates the control over the birth rate has been found essential.

Table 4 : Public Health Network in Mizoram ***(2000-01)***

Item	Hospital	Community Health Centre	Primary Health Centre	Subsidiary Health Centre	Sub-Centre
Number	7	9	45	13	351
Bed Capacity	688	286	450	130	–

Source : Economic Review—Mizoram : 2000-01, Directorate of Economics & Statistics, Government of Mizoram.

The health care system functioning all over the state is depicted in the Table 4. The rural and urban health is taken care of by seven hospitals with a bed capacity of 688; 9 community health centres with 286 beds; 45 primary health centres with 450 beds; 13 subsidiary health centres with 130 beds and 351 sub-centres. However, the number of beds per thousand population is computed as 1.74 while the number of medical personnel (doctors, nurses, health workers) per thousand population is 0.107.

The record of Mizoram in terms of access to school education is, in a word, brilliant which is well reflected in the high rate of literacy. The rate rose from 31.14 percent in 1951 to 88.48 percent in 2001. At present Mizoram stands second in terms of literacy rate in the country. The decadal fall in the number of illiterates in the state has been recorded as 13.35 percent as against the national average of 9.74 percent, which implies that out of 100 illiterates in the state in 1991 about 87 remain illiterate in 2001. Considering the high decadal growth rate in population it can be regarded as an achievement. However, the district level literacy rate reveals slightly different picture, at least in one district the rate is even much lower than national average which may be a constraint in reaching the target of fully literate state in future.

Since percentage of student enrolment in primary level is not provided the growth of student enrolment in different levels is presented in Table 5 with other information related to state educational system. Though decadal growth of population in the state is very high at 29.18 percent the growth of children of age group 0 - 6 happens to be comparatively lower at 10.34 percent. The high growth of enrolment especially at high school level gives an optimistic picture for a state where the glory of high literacy rate is seriously faded away by the high drop out rates at different levels of school education.

The important feature revealed from Table 5 is the average enrolment per school in primary, middle and high school level are surprisingly low - even lower than the level at which it could be economic. However, the student - teacher ratio at all levels is very low. The table also suggests that the bottlenecks in the goal of universal education are almost entirely on the side of demand - not supply. However, in other parts of the country the scenario is mostly opposite (Sen: 2002). Since almost in all urban schools in Mizoram enrolment per school and student - teacher ratio are found to be much higher than over all state average the inference can be drawn that there are many schools in Mizoram where the concerned ratios are much lower than the average. This in turn establishes that these schools are mostly running on teachers' strength. The opening of new school in Mizoram is primarily motivated to create employment rather than promoting school education. During 1999-2000, 17 percent of total revenue expenditure of the state, which constitute about 12 percent of NSDP, was spent on general and technical education. Out of the total expenditure on education the school education constitute about 80 percent in early 1990's. The state authority has always been successful to maintain these percentages in later years also. But the silence of the government regarding its failure in growing aspirations of the students to continue their school education clearly points out the seriousness of the problem.

Table 5 : School Education in Mizoram *(2000-01)*

Events	Primary (I-IV)	Middle (V-VII)	High School VIII-X)	Higher Secondary (XI-XII)
Number of schools	1280	770	377	30
Enrolment	102401	48441	37779	9089
No. of Students per School	80	63	100	303
Number of Teachers	4823	4896	2880	470
No. of Students per Teacher	21	10	13	19
No. of Schools per thousands population	1.436	0.864	0.423	0.034
Annual Growth Rate (%) in Enrollment during 1990's	1.57	1.93	4.59	41.99 (2000-01)

Source : Economic Review—Mizoram : 2000-01, Directorate of Economics & Statistics, Government of Mizoram.

The social sustainability does not only concern the issues related to health and education. There is no doubt that the condition of sustainability needs a healthy and literate society. But there are other indicators in this regard such as number of broken families, orphans living in the orphan houses, unmarried mothers, teen age pregnancy, number of drug addicts and HIV affected people, etc. which are always expected to be at minimum level. The state authority has always tried to hide these facts as if suppression is the best solution of these social problems.

3. Financial Indicators

The state of Mizoram is faced with a set of financial problems. They have raised a serious question mark against its financial sustainability. The fiscal deficit during 1999-2000 was as high as 5.6 percent of GSDP. The budget deficit has grown by over 40 percent during 1999-2000 to 2000-01. The revenue expenditure is growing at much faster rate than revenue receipts. Revenue expenditure forms about 81 percent of total expenditure. The low percentage of capital expenditure will definitely have a long-term effect on sustainability. Out of the total (own - source) revenue receipts in 2000-01, the share of non - tax revenue was about 73.6 percent (Thangchungnunga: 2002). The low tax receipt and GSDP ratio at about 0.005 during 1999-2000 indicates clearly the state efforts to increase the tax revenue were not adequate and flexible. Since the formula of determining the Central assistance, as an increasing function of state tax efforts was not applicable in the special category state, the state government had never been serious about the mobilization of tax revenue. This has pushed the state under a heavy burden of indebtedness. The ratio of total debt to GSDP has reached to its all time high at 0.88 in recent years. This is a clear indication of weakness in the financial sustainability of the state. Reforms in the state expenditure pattern, in the size of the government machinery as well as the tax efforts have become an urgent necessity for the state financial sustainability.

4. Environmental Indicators

The environmental sustainability of an economy refers to an efficient management of natural assets in which it is endowed. The natural capital - generally classified as physical, biotic and agro-mineral or from a different angle classified as re-generative and non-generative resources - has to be efficiently used so that it will continue to generate income for future generations at a non-declining rate. In addition, the issues related to environment are directly associated with the management of re-generative resources. The non-generative resources need to be managed properly for their rational exploitation. The use of certain unit on non-generative resources reduces the stock exactly by same units (Dasgupta: 1983).

Mizoram is not rich in natural resources. The state with no mineral deposit, however, is heavily endowed with forest resources. The land and water resources, if managed in a proper manner, will be of great importance.

4(a) Land Resources

The geographical structure of the state, in a word, is very complicated. About 2 - 3 percent of total geographical area falls under 0° - 8° slope which is suitable for permanent wet rice cultivation while about 7 percent of the area falls under moderate slope of 0° - 20° described as the maximum limit of sustainable crop cultivation. About 43 percent area has a slope of 20° - 50°, which is suitable for horticulture plants only. Remaining half of the total geographical area of the state is found with a slope of more than 50° distributed in different water shades and suitable for forests plants only. The high terrain derived mainly from young and immature rocks has a natural tendency to erode. The soil, in such a geographical area, is mostly formed from secondary rocks and classified as alluvium soil and residual soil. The soil, in general, is fertile and also tested as fertilizer - sensitive (Kumar: 1997). In such a hilly terrain the estimation of carrying capacity of the land resources defined, as the proportion of forest cover to be maintained to support one unit of sustainable cultivated land, is extremely essential. The estimation of carrying capacity is not only necessary for cultivation but also important for the issues related to urbanization. For example, the average density of population in Aizawl city has already crossed the figure of 2000 persons per square kilometre. Since the city outskirts have the density of even less than the half of the city average the central area of the city witnesses more than double of the average. The question can be raised in terms of sustainability whether this heavy concentration is within the maximum limit of sustainable carrying capacity in such a complicated immature hilly terrain.

4(b) Water Resources

Being endowed with numerous streams and moderate to heavy rainfall almost throughout the year the state has a significant potential in watershed management. The characteristic feature of the streams flowing through the state is that most of them originate in the central high land and show a natural tendency to flow either in the north or in the south direction. As ground water resources in hilly areas are uneconomic, the planned surface water management through the construction of water storage tanks, ponds etc. can solve the problem of drinking water in dry season, irrigation to the irrigable terraces. The major rivers in the state are found to be potential in generating hydroelectric power. A few hydel projects have been working in this direction. Table 6 depicts the estimated

Table 6 : Hydropower Potentials of Mizoram Rivers

SI. No.	River	Hydro-Power Potentials in MW
1	Tlawng	120
2	Tuirial	60
3	Tuivai	210
4	Chhimtuipui	60
	Total	450

Source : Lalrinthanga—2000

potential of total 450 MW from different rivers of the state. However, out of the total potential only 6 MW capacities had been exploited so far through ongoing Tuipang and Kau Tlabung Mini Hydel projects.

4(c) Forest Resources

Among all the natural resources available in the land of highlanders, the most important and multi-dimensional resource has been forest resource. Land use pattern of the state during 2000-01 reports that forests occupy about 77 percent of total geographical area. About 21 percent of total forest area of the state falls under the category of dense forest cover while remaining 79 percent under the category of state open forest. However, the Forest Survey of India (Anon: 1989) reported that Mizoram, with 86.20 percent forest cover, ranked third in the country after Andaman and Nicobar Island (91.96 percent) and Nagaland (86.80 percent). It is a known fact that due to practice of shifting cultivation and due to rapid growth of population with a very high degree of urbanization almost entire forest area of the state has been affected badly in recent years resulting in clearance of tree cover. Consequently there has been a serious degradation of land. The state with huge forest cover earns only about 0.6 percent of its NSDP from this sector (1999-2000), which may be viewed as an indication to the degradation of state forest. Reports of actual position of Mizoram forest cover have always been ambiguous. With the increase in population and urbanization the total forest cover is likely to decline. But the government, due to unknown reasons, is not ready to accept this fact. Studies made by the scholars (Lalramnghinglova and Jha: 1997) estimate that only 30 percent of the total state area have adequate tree cover. This estimate, interestingly, is just equivalent to the forest cover of the state under the status of notified forest area reported by the government agencies.

Forest types include Subtropical evergreen, Tropical evergreen, Tropical moist deciduous, Bamboo forest, Quercus, and *jhum* land. Under the *jhum* land category three different sub-categories are identified as current, old, and abandoned *jhum* land. All the forest types are richly endowed with different species and medicinal plants, orchids, canes, etc. The different species of Mizoram forest are depicted in Table 7. The conservation of forests in the state, with a very complicated geographical structure, is essential from both the angles of environmental degradation and economic sustainability.

Table : 7 : Forest Species of Mizoram

Forest Type	Description	Species Available
Sub-Tropical Evergreen	Dense forest in a high altitude of 1400 meters	Dipterocarpus turbinatus, Cinnamomum bejolghota, C. glaucecens, C. zeylanicum, Cannaricum neziniferum, Quercus spp., Phoebe goalparensis, Chiknasia tubularis, Daubanga gnandiflora, Michellia oblonga.
Tropical Evergreen	Most important & potential forest in a range below sub-tropical evergreen forest	Dipterocarpus turbinatus, Artocarpus Chaplasha, Terminalia mysiocarpa, Michellia Champaca, Amoora Wallichi, Chisocheton Paniculate, Callophyllum Polyanthum, Massua Ferrea, Toona Ciliata, Chikrasia tubularis, Anogeisus latifolia, Phoebe attenuata.
Tropical Moist Deciduous	Combination of deciduous & evergreen trees found below 1000 meters	Michellia Champaca, Toona Ciliata, Chikrasia tubularis, Schimawallichii, Sterculia villasa, S. Colarata, Podocarpus nerifolia, Adina cordifolia, Juglawsregia, Emblica officinalis, Macaranga indica, Bamboos.
Bamboo Forest	Spread all over the state	Arundinaria callosa, Melocalamus compadifloras, meloccana baccifera & about 20 species of bamoos.
Quercus Forest	Hill range below 900 meters	Different quercus species.

Source : Lalramnghinglova, J. H. and Jha, L. K.— 1997

Structural Transformation in Mizoram

It is obvious that the structure of the economy changes with the process of economic development. S. Kuznets and others have theorized this aspect of developing economy. They observe that in the initial stages the economic activity of a state/country is dominated by the primary sector as a whole and agriculture in particular - both in terms of income and workforce sharing. At least two conditions need to be fulfilled for the transformation of the economy from a traditional agro-based one to a modern industrial economy (Dasgupta: 2003)—generation of surplus in agricultural sector and a rapid industrialization in the economy. The agricultural surplus, defined as the excess of output after satisfying the needs of the people who are producing it, works well to enhance the purchasing power and can be used to initiate the process of industrialization. This again increases the purchasing power of the people, which creates demand for a certain goods and services in the economy. Subsequently a new sector, called tertiary sector emerges. In the later stages of development tertiary sector dominates the economy indicating simply that the surplus generated in the economy through the process of industrialization created certain demand, which cannot be satisfied by the production of primary and secondary sectors.

The stages of development are related in such a fashion that the emergence of tertiary sector depends positively on the performance of other two sectors. The surplus in agricultural sector, which is identified as the primary criteria for the structural transformation, can be generated in two ways: increasing the production and/or shifting gradually the work force engaged in primary sector to other sectors. The production in agriculture improves with better use of land, water, and other inputs like quality seeds, fertilizers, etc. There is also a need to change the agricultural pattern and its produces with the change in local and global market conditions. In the second phase, the industrialization is to be designed in such a way that ensures an optimum and efficient use of agricultural output as well as other local resources. The process of industrialization creates demand for the produce of primary sector and helps significantly to generate employment. In the later stages of development when both agriculture and industry generate sufficient surplus, the enhanced purchasing power of the people develops the tertiary sector. Once the economy reaches to this stage of development a negative association is observed to continue between income of the economy and occupation in primary sector. With the increase in income in per capita sense there is a likelihood of falling the labour force engaged in primary sector. On the contrary a positive association is established between income and labour force engaged in other sectors especially in service sector.

Therefore, sectoral contribution of economy can be used as a measure to understand the stage of development at which the economy belongs. The study of such changes helps the planners to identify the areas of the economy to be traced upon. In fact, this study determines the policy often called as strategy for development. The scenario of structural changes in Mizoram state economy is depicted in the Tables 8 and 9 from which the implications can be drawn:

- The primary sector during 1993-94 to 1999-2000 in the state economy has grown at an annual rate as low as 0.54 percent with a sharp decline of 9.45 percent in its relative share in NSDP. However the percentage of labour force engaged in the sector has fallen only by 3.57 percent during 1991 to 1998 indicating a clear picture of deterioration of the condition of the people engaged in primary sector. The share of agriculture in NSDP has fallen from 23.13 percent to 21.64 percent. Moreover, in a state where the level of urbanization is claimed to be 49.50 percent, a high rate of agricultural occupation (cultivators 53.91 percent and agricultural labourers 5.85 percent of the total work force: Census 2001) narrates a contradictory story. There is an urgent need to shift gradually the work force from agriculture to other occupations. The other sub-sectors in primary sectors - forestry and fishing have registered a sharp fall in the share in NSDP by 3.11 percent and 0.64 percent respectively. The only sub-sector, which has been able to increase its share by 0.39 percent, is mining and quarrying. It is noteworthy that the share of this sub-sector during 1999-2000 has been 0.52 percent of NSDP.

Table 8 : Sectoral Contribution : A Comparison

SI. No.	Sector/Sub-sector	Percent Share in NSDP		Change in Percent Share in NSDP (during 1990's)
		Early 1990's (1993-94)	Late 1990's (1999-2000)	
I	**Primary**	**33.23**	**23.78**	**(–) 9.45**
a.	Agriculture	27.73	21.64	(–) 6.09
b.	Forestry	3.71	0.60	(–) 3.11
c.	Fishing	1.66	1.02	(–) 0.64
d.	Mining & Quarrying	0.13	0.52	0.39
II	**Secondary**	**9.45**	**13.46**	**4.01**
a.	Manufacturing	2.74	1.22	(–) 1.52
b.	Construction	7.10	11.53	4.43
c.	Electricity, Gas & Water Supply	(–) 0.39	0.71	1.10
III	**Tertiary Sector**	**57.32**	**62.76**	**5.44**
a.	Transport, Storage & Communication	1.13	1.37	0.24
b.	Trade, Hotels & Restaurants	16.47	10.50	(–) 5.97
c.	Banking & Insurance	1.06	1.48	0.42
d.	Real Estate & Business Services	11.34	14.28	2.94
e.	Public Administration	15.22	17.77	2.55
f.	Other Services	12.10	17.36	5.26

Source : Economic Review—Mizoram : 2000-01, Directorate of Economics & Statistics, Government of Mizoram.

- In spite of the fact that Mizoram is categorized as 'No Industry Zone' in the country and even though the efforts towards the process of industrialization in the state has been limited to the declaration of First Industrial Policy 1989 and New Industrial Policy 2000, the secondary sector as a whole has maintained a growth rate as high as 6.90 percent per year. The share in NSDP has risen from 9.45 percent during 1993-94 to 13.46 percent during 1999-2000. This is mainly due to the rapid growth in construction sub-sector, which registers an increase of share by 4.43 percent - even higher than over all increase in secondary sector. The contribution of manufacturing in state income has declined by 1.52 percent, which to some extent indicates that the state with no heavy or medium industry has also been loosing its significance in small scale and cottage industries. The share of electricity, gas, and water supply moved from a negative figure to a positive one with a contribution of 0.71 percent during 1999-2000. The share of labour force in secondary sector as a whole has risen from 5.07 percent in 1991 to 6.50 percent in 1998 indicating a clear scope of shifting the state agricultural labour force to this sector.

- The performance of tertiary sector in terms of income share is often considered as a measure of the stage of development at which the economy belongs. Its share in NSDP has increased from 57.32 percent to 62.76 percent with a promising growth rate of 6.65 percent per annum during 1990's. The high value of coefficient of determination (R^2 = 0.77) of the estimated growth function indicates significantly less fluctuation in its contribution over time. All the sub-sectors except trade, hotel and restaurants have improved their relative share in NSDP during 1990's. Public Administration and other services together contribute 35.13 percent of NSDP during 1999-2000 with an improvement of income share by 7.81 percent during the post-reform years. However, the sector could increase its labour force sharing only by 2.14 percent of the total work force of the state during 1991 to 1998.

Table 9 : Structural Transformation in Mizoram

(Figures are in percentage)

	Early 1990's		Late 1990's		Structural Transformation	
Sector	Share of NSDP in 1993-94	Share of Main Work Force (1991)	Share of NSDP in 1999-00	Share of Main Work Force (1998)	In terms of Share in NSDP	In terms of Share in Main Work Force
Primary	33.23	65.99	23.78	62.42	(–) 9.45	(–) 3.57
Secondary	9.45	5.07	13.46	6.50	4.01	1.43
Tertiary	57.32	28.94	62.76	31.08	5.44	2.14

Source : 1. Census 1991, Series 17, Part II-B. 2. Economic Census of Mizoram, 1998.

The nature of structural changes that have taken place in Mizoram during a span of seven years apparently indicate that the economy hardly fits into Kuznets transformation. The shift of labour force from primary sector to other rapidly growing sectors of the economy has been nominal and observed to be little biased towards service sector (2.14 percent) as compared to the secondary sector (1.43 percent). One should recall here that the concept of stages of development is based on fulfillment of certain conditions: creation of surplus in agriculture and rapid industrialization. In case of Mizoram economy both the conditions, to move forward, remain unfulfilled. The loss of share of primary sector in Kuznets transformation does not mean at all fall in output and low growth in the sector. The surprisingly low growth along with high rate of labour participation in agriculture rules out the possibility of surplus generation. Again, a significant fall in manufacturing with a nominal contribution of 1.22 percent in NSDP clearly explains that the state has also miserably failed to fulfill the second condition of Kuznets transformation i.e., rapid industrialisation. The spectacular growth in tertiary sector does not indicate the rise in purchasing power of the people engaged in other two sectors. However, this can be explained as the result of huge public outlay concentrated mostly on tertiary sector. Therefore, the scenario of structural change in a small state points out clearly that the situation has been definitely different from Kuznets transformation. The low production in agriculture and fall in industrial income cannot be termed as Kuznets transformation.

Conclusion

The scenario of structural transformation in Mizoram clearly describes that there is no perceptible shift towards Kuznets transformation. The loss of income share of primary sector is compensated by other two sectors with a significant fall in agricultural per capita income and with a serious decline in income from manufacturing. The over all dominance of tertiary sector in the state economy during 1990's could be explained by the huge public outlay which had worked well to destroy the market mechanism and also by the serious failure of Government policies in expanding the state resources on sustainable income generation. Since the period of declaration of Union Territory in 1972 the total public outlay in absolute term grew at exceptionally high rate and reached to its maximum level in 1995-96 when per capita revenue receipts was Rs.8399/- as against the national average of Rs.1494/-. In that fiscal year the per capita income in current prices had been Rs.10,953/ as against the national average of Rs.10160/-.

An unprecedented developmental fund was made available for Mizoram, which had been in isolation for years together and was highly disturbed by armed revolution at least for two decades. The long period of lawlessness in a strife-torn society and pumping in plenty of money have had a dire consequence on the social morality resulting in widening the gap between rich and poor, privileged and deprived within a so called classless tribal society. A group of urban elite has emerged in the state with a mindset of 'get-rich-at-any-price' (Thangchungnunga: 2002). Due to lack of clear vision and entrepreneurship the income of this small group is being invested only in private construction, which is heavily reflected in high growth of constructional income in 1990's. A positive association is observed also between the income of tertiary sector and that of construction and quarrying as well. The exceptional growth in construction, however, threatens the environmental sustainability of Aizawl city, which falls, in Zone-V described as highly seismic zone. Again, in the absence of local self-governmental bodies (municipal corporation etc.) the contractors of multistoried buildings in a small area of Aizawl city hardly bothers about the environmental norms. On the other hand, a simple study can establish that the huge investment in private construction, which has been taken as the most important indicator of measuring development in post statehood era, has an uneconomic return even lower than the nominal interest offered by the commercial banks. The growth in construction is primarily motivated by the ethnic pride and secondly, by the lack of investment alternatives.

The threat to sustainability of the state economy has been found very acute in terms of infrastructure. The central assistance of any amount takes hardly few hours to flow out. The velocity of circulation, which can multiply the value of cash assets by rolling the same within the economy, could not be developed at all. All most all the items of consumption and infrastructural goods are being procured from outside the state. Even after the three decades of planned developmental efforts the state has not been able to identify specific items, which could be grown and produced in opulence in the state. The macroeconomic condition also does not favour the production at large scale. As the visible hand of central divisible pool has been playing a crucial role in increasing the aggregate demand and setting the prices at exorbitant, high level the cost function in the state is also uneconomic. Import of goods and labour services from neighbouring states has been found profitable in short term. And obviously, in the race of earning quick money within a short period the long term sustainability finds little consideration.

To promote economic development the state authority should take care of its financial management, which has a deep connection with all other economic problems. With the stimulus provided by the central government, the state could have achieved success in attaining a sustainable development. The proper planning, which could have led the state to a resource based industrial economy, was never adopted. The major bottleneck in fixing and implementing the state objectives with a normative outlook is the absence of meaningful political leadership in the state with a powerful command on the bureaucracy. Instead of adopting the policy of adhocism, a long-term sustainable developmental plan should be immediately adopted.

At least two important researches (Swaminathan and Tata Economic Consultancy: 1998) have been conducted by the professionals to identify the potential areas of the state. Both suggest almost same finding for sustainable agricultural and rural development with an emphasis on the promotion of agro-based, forest-based industries as well as on sericulture, horticulture, etc. In this field, tea and coffee industry with a primary objective of providing an alternative cash crop and settling the farmers in permanent cultivation; rubber and tung plantation as most potential tree based occupation to the rural *jhumias*; culture of orchid and rural nurseries with an aim of increasing employment opportunities to the educated youth; etc. could be developed keeping the socio-economic, climatic, topographical, and human ability related factors under consideration. The production and commercialization of horticulture and sericulture can be promoted through the improvisation of marketing system and simultaneously small to medium scale industries should be established in a planned manner so that growing open and disguised unemployment can be controlled. A planned effort of resource-based industrialization in Mizoram will definitely create an investment alternative for the local elites, which in turn will help to build up an *investment climate* identified as one of the two pillars of the strategy for development. A favourable *investment climate* in the state economy through improvisation of the present system and through mass participation of the poor people in that developmental activities can generate a *pro-poor growth* which will sustain over time.

Finally, the development is a process, which cannot be imposed on a society through an exogenously designed model. In addition, the issues related to the development of tribal community with certain unique features and practices are very sensitive. The balancing between two components identified as protection and development is a compromise of certain degrees with one for another. The state of absolute protection leads to isolation, which in turn threatens national integrity while the rapid change in the name of development breaks down the tribal value system resulting in an acute identity crisis. Few questions always remain unanswered in this regard. How long the tribal community will keep themselves isolated to preserve their culture at the cost of level of living? What exactly is the opportunity cost of sacrificing the traditional tribal values in the process of modernization? What should be the choice tune for evening melody - whether following a subsistence dinner it would be *Laldanga ...Awi ...Awi* or in a voluptuous pizza corner it would be M - TV?

Notes

As data in Mizoram have always been a constraint, in some cases the comparison between two periods exactly on the same figures could not be made. In such a situation *non-availability of exact data should not stop the research* endeavours. For example, in table: B.1.2, due to non-availability of main workers' break-up for the year 1999-2000, the same of 1998 has been compared with the percent share of NSDP in 1999-2000.

The data used in this paper have been mostly reported by the Directorate of Economics & Statistics, Government of Mizoram. Since they provide figures only on current prices and since price index of any kind has never been prepared in Mizoram, the conversion of current prices into constant prices be possible. However, on the basis of few selected items (24 commodities) a rough behaviour of prices has been worked out and reported by the Directorate. This information is used to prepare a WORKABLE PRICE INDEX for Mizoram and accordingly, current prices have been converted into constant prices taking 1993-94 as the base year.

The calculations of per capita figures (NSDP & GSDP) by the state authority have always been an over estimate as these have been computed on the basis of projected population figures which are lower than actual. The actual average growth of population during 1990's in the state was 2.59 percent per year while the aforesaid figures of per capita income were computed with a growth rate of about 2.55 percent per year. For convenience, this paper uses the per capita figures provided by the Directorate.

The growth curves and growth rates are always estimated in this paper using a multiplicative true relationship between the variables concerned. And the method of linear least-square is applied on its logarithmic transformation. For example,

$Z_t = A\ B_t\ v_t$ —— true relationship

$Y_t = \hat{a}o + \hat{a}_1 t$ ——estimated relationship

Where,

$Yt = \log Z_t$

$ao = \log A$

$a_1 = \log B = \log(1 + g)$,

g stands for annual estimated growth rate

REFERENCES

Agarwal, A. K. (1988) : *North-Eastern Economy—Problems & Prospects*, Mittal Publications, New Delhi.

Appasamy Paul P (2002) : 'Sustainable Development of Tamil Nadu : A Critique', in V. Pandit, *et. al.*, edited *Data, Models and Policies*, Proceedings of the 38th Annual Conference of the Indian Econometric Society.

Chelliah, R. J. & K. R. Shammugam (2002) : 'Some Aspects of Inter-District Disparities in Tamil Nadu', in V. Pandit, *et. al.*, edited, Data Models and Policies' Proceedings of the 38th Annual Conference of the Indian Econometric Society.

Colney Rualkhuma (1997) : *Small Scale and Cottage Industries—Mizoram,* L. B. Associates, Aizawl.

Dasgupta, P. (1983) : *The Control of Resources,* Oxford University Press, Delhi.

Kadekodi, Gopal K. (2002) : 'Environment and Development', in R. N. Bhattacharjee, edited *Environmental Economics—An Indian Perspective,* Oxford University Press, Delhi.

Kumar, G (1997) : 'Resource Bases of Mizoram', in L. K. Jha, edited, *Natural*

Resource Management, Ashish publication, New Delhi.

Kumar, G. (2001) : 'Environment and Development in Mizoram', in R. K. Rai, *et. al*, edited, *Environment, Resources and Development*, The Geographical Society of North-East Region, NEHU, Shillong.

Lalramnghinglova, J. H. & L. K. Jha (1997) 'Forest Resources—An Overview', in L. K. Jha, edited, *Natural Resource Management*, Ashish Publication, New Delhi.

Lalrinthanga (2000) : 'Comparative Economics of Jhum and Settled Cultivation,' Unpublished research work.

Lianzela (1997) : 'Status of Agriculture in Mizoram,' in L. K. Jha, edited *Natural Resource Management*, Ashish Publication, New Delhi.

Meier, G. M. & James E. Rauch (2000) : *Leading Issues in Economic Development,* 17th edition, Oxford University Press, New York.

Rao, B. Sarveshwara (1999) : 'Ethical Dimensions of India' Development—Some Reflections,' The Indian Economic Journal, Vol. 47, October-December 1999-2000, No. 2.

Ray Santanu (1995) : Impact of Dismantling of Policy—Distortions on Hill Agro-forestry in North-East India (Focus—Mizoram), Unpublished Seminar Paper.

Sen Amartya (2000) : *Development as Freedom,* Oxford University Press, Delhi.

Sen Amartya (2002) : Introduction—*The Pratichi Education Report*, No. 1, Pratichi (India) Trust.

Stern Nicholas (2002) : 'Keynote address—A Strategy for Development', Annual World Bank Conference on Development Economics, 2001 /2002; edited by Boris Pleskovic and Nicholas Stern, World Bank and Oxford University Press.

Swaminathan M. S. : A Blue Print of Sustainable Agriculture and Rural Development (Agenda-21, For the State of Mizoram), by the M. S. Swaminathan Research Foundation, Chennai.

Thangchungnunga (2002) : 'Fiscal Management in Mizoram,' Dialogue, Vol. 4, No. 1, July-September 2002, Astha Bharati, New Delhi.

Tata Economic Consultancy (1998) : Perspective/Visionary Plan—For the State of Mizoram, Formulated by Tata Economic Consultancy Services, Mumbai.

Supplementary Observation

Structural Change and Resource-Industry Linkages in Mizoram: Some Issues to Ponder

—Gorky Chakraborty

The ending of poverty and ignorance and disease and inequality of opportunity[1] has been the cornerstone of our 'tryst with destiny'. Nation building was sought to be achieved through economic planning, the roots of which were firmly entrenched in our long freedom struggle. Although there were three different plan proposals, each differing from one another according to their ideological stand points[2] yet in all the proposals economic planning was considered to be the best viable option for the welfare of the masses at large. Our plan proposals intended for an 'autonomous' path of development where the state was proposed to play the important role of investor, employer and facilitator as well as act as protector of labour and indigenous capital against the onslaught of 'metropolitan' capital. The proposals were undoubtedly pious but contradictions emerged once these plan proposals were implemented through the mechanism of five year plans where the class character of the state acted as the biggest deterrent in implementing the wishful plan proposals. So absentee landlordism was abolished yet land ownership remained highly skewed in rural India and on the industrial front although some monopolistic practices were checked yet indigenous capital was able to increase its asset concentration with the tacit support of the state apparatus. The biggest casualty in this process has been the limited expansion of the market for mass consumption goods in India as skewed asset and income pattern narrowed the purchasing power of the Indian masses. This has been dealt with from time to time initially with 'internal stimulants' and later only relying upon 'external stimulants'. The state here had to fulfill two different yet incompatible roles[3] — one of expansion of the domestic market through investment and employment opportunities for the masses (actually a section of it in reality) at large and on the other protecting the interest of those groups which has monopolistic asset concentration in their hand. The state exchequer under such circumstances acted as the disbursement tool where doses of disbursement (read doles) and the beneficiaries were determined by political expediency.

Thus as the state has been unable or unwilling to address and rectify these contradictions between its plan formulation and its implementation neither during the period of state led capitalist growth (read planning for socialistic pattern of society) nor the recent surge of liberalization, privatization and neo-liberal globalization has been able to usher in an era of balanced and sustainable development as has been dreamt during our 'tryst with destiny'.

II

The contradictions mentioned in the earlier section regarding intention and implementation of Indian development model are equally manifested in India mainland as well as in its peripheries. In other words, it is widely felt that the existential reality of the Indian peripheries are often, if not always, misinterpreted and misunderstood by our development planners, which adds further contradictions other than those mentioned above. In case of India's north east the situation became more intriguing for Indian planners as they confront with various issues, e.g., different relations of production, tribal-feudal continuum, hill plain divide, different customary laws, ethnic aspirations and their identity assertions through various constitutional and extra constitutional means which are not so prominent in mainland India. Moreover the nation builders often deal with the people of north east in a historical plane keeping aside their legacy of a proud history and the subsequent colonial history under the Britishers. This lack of understanding of the mindset of the people of north east in general and imposition of development model with the yardstick of mainland India has more than often resulted in schism, strife and discord which has again been quelled by stern force and ammunition. The ultimate exasperation on the part of people has always resulted in flaming frontiers which has hampered the overall peace, security and development of the nation at large.

Various part of north east came under colonial administration at different points of time. The degree of colonial penetration also varied accordingly among the hills and plains. Over a period of seven decades the whole of north east was subjugated by the Britishers. Assam plains came under British rule in 1826. Cachar plains in 1830, Kashi Hills 1833, Jaintia Hills 1835, Karbi Anglong in 1838, North Cachar in 1854, Naga Hills during 1866-1904, Garo Hills 1872-73 and Lushai Hills in 1890.[4] The time of colonial subjugation, the period of colonial rule and the adaptation and reaction of the indigenous people against the colonial rule has been an important bench mark in understanding the aspirations of different ethnic groups which somehow has missed the attention of the scholars. So a historical frame of analysis, a lack of understanding of the relations of production of the tribes, misinterpretation of the aspirations of people of north east has always given rise to various contradictions which has either been dealt by disbursing doles in the name of welfare or by creating a 'class for itself' through a development model which is alien to the culture of India's north east.

III

Mizoram is inhabited by Mizos, which is a generic term representing several major tribes and sub-tribes of the area belonging to the Mongoloid stock. There are five major tribes and eleven different sub-tribes in Mizoram. Now initiating a dialogue on resource industry linkage, the first aspect which needs elaboration is what constitute resources? Moreover do the term resource has the same meaning and significance for all group of people who have different relations of production?

The term resource[5] has been interpreted variously, e.g., that which can be drawn upon as a means of help or support; natural advantages, especially of country, as forest, oil deposits; available wealth or property; skill or ingenuity in meeting any situation; any way or method of coping with a difficult situation etc. There are other interpretation and classification of resources but in each and every interpretation great emphasis is laid upon the situational aspect which determines the necessity for using a particular resource. In other words, without being a historical determinist it can be argued that the use of particular resource is determined by its historical necessity and normatively speaking the necessity should emerge from within the ethnic group or nationality under whose jurisdiction the resource is available. Again, it should also be clarified that for whom the resource belongs - the state or the people. In an indigenous society the resource is always the peoples' resource. This aspect should be kept in mind before elaborating upon the concept of resource-industry linkage.

Now dealing with the issue of historical necessity as mentioned above it can be argued that whether there has been such a historical necessity to identify resources in case of Mizoram which could usher in an era of industrialization in the state? Or the issue of industrialization is thrust upon them by 'others' in order to stimulate their own markets? Citing the case of bamboo it can be said that the presence of this shrub has been there since time immemorial. Various consultancy and research studies have forwarded the case for setting up paper industry in neighbouring state(s)/areas where these bamboo can be utilized properly. Now in that case, how does Mizoram benefit from it? Neither employment scope nor income opportunities will be enhanced for the local Mizos if industries are set up outside Mizoram. Moreover, the state government will also be unable to impose any tax, cess or levy over these industries located outside its jurisdiction. So the issue of location of industries has to be settled first, i.e., where should they be located: near the market (i.e. neighbouring states) or near the source of raw material (i.e., Mizoram). Similarly, it should also be understood whether a cultural symbol (bamboo) can also be treated as an economic resource by the same people.

Considering the resource base of Mizoram the classical industrialization programme with resource industry linkage seems to be wishful thinking at present. Although Mizoram certainly has a base and scope for village and cottage industries, yet it should be understood that no region has reached the stage of industrialization relying only on village and cottage industries. Under these circumstances the clichés of rapid industrialization, industrial expansion etc. seem to be an attempt to understand the peripheries with yardsticks of mainland India.

Similarly in case of *jhumming* the perception since the inception of our planning process has been such that as if *jhum* will automatically be replaced by terrace cultivation once the tribals are made to believe that *jhum* cultivation is harmful for environment and secondly, the yield of *jhum* is lower than that of permanent wet rice cultivation. Now while preaching their diatribes against *jhum* cultivation they forgot that generation of large quantity of marketable surplus is alien to the production process as well as thought process of the tribals. Whatever was/is produced as *jhum* crops were/are more or less equitably distributed among the participants. Moreover lower levels of production also did not allow the creation of a lazy class who could enjoy the benefits of production without actually participating in it.[6] So alluring the *jhumias* (among whom some may even have limited monetized activities) from *jhum* cultivation to that of settled cultivation with the argument of marketable surplus and increasing yields have not been able to achieve desired success.

The question of deforestation in the hills is related more with National Forest Policy than with *jhum* cultivation. The national policy prescribes that one third of the geographical area should remain under forest cover, but there are not much forest left in the plain areas. The plainsmen seem to be reluctant to grow forest in one third of the territory under their possession, and thereby benefit from the alternative use of land. Under such a situation the tribals are asked to sacrifice their living for forest areas, and thus make up losses incurred in the plains.[7] Further, there is scarcity of convincing proof that the rate of soil erosion is much higher in north east *jhum* areas than the rate of soil formation.[8] Moreover construction of terraces are difficult in certain regions with loose soil. Again settled cultivation is mono-crop where as *jhum* is multi-crop in nature. All these factors along with few others make the replacement of *jhumming* with terrace cultivation difficult.

Considering the above mentioned arguments, it is not difficult to understand why the area under *jhum* has gone up over the years despite our best efforts to contain it. Of course, there has been a rise in productivity of *jhum* crops yet it should be understood that there is an optimum limit beyond which raising productivity is not feasible. Thus the age old system of *jhum* cultivation would continue in future also, the wholesale transformation of the tribal economy to abandon it is not possible in near future. Hence the solution of the problem has to be sought in the village itself without great deal of dislocation in the tribal family life. Efforts should be made for better utilization and management of *jhum* land to lessen the possible damages.[9] This statement was made some 15 years back and today it seems that it still remains prophetic.

IV

Similarly certain re-thinking is also necessary when one interprets the special category status of a state like Mizoram. Why does the Indian state confer the north eastern states with special category status? Is it that the Indian state love, adore, care and respect a Mizo more than a Malayalee, Bengali or Marathi? The answer is perhaps no and the reality is some what else. The Mizos along with other tribes of India's north east guard those areas which are international boundaries of the nation-state but ethnic boundaries for the tribes concerned. These tribes are the sentinels of the nation's frontiers. The geographical or locational position of the areas which are inhabited by these tribes forces the Indian state to consider the special category status for them. From the security point of view maintaining the international border is a matter of utmost significance for the state and therefore the people guarding those areas has to be treated in special way than those residing in mainland India. It is simply not that the Indian state sympathises with the tribes of north east and therefore treats these areas under special category status.

It is a different matter as to how the benefits from the special category status are to be utilized i.e., whether the special category status creates a microscopic minority to further the cause of a skewed state structure or the benefits are utilized in an egalitarian way keeping in mind the ethos of tribal culture. In Mizoram and in other north eastern areas, due to the class character of the state it has chosen the former route instead of the latter due to which the benefits of the special category status flow to only a handful of the population in and around the Aizawl region of Mizoram. It is due to this reason that both special category status and welfare character of the state are grounded in the ideas of charity, benevolence and paternalism instead of mutual respect and social justice.

Thus while dealing with the issues of development it is imperative that the resources of a state like Mizoram are to be identified with the proper participation of the people and also properly understanding the mindset of the people on the part of the plan formulators. The resource base and its utilization among all variable alternatives should emerge from within the tribal societies and ultimately the fruits of utilization of those resources should reach the tribal masses for whose benefit the structural change is proposed to be brought about.

Notes and References

1. Jawaharlal Nehru's speech at Constituent Assembly, New Delhi, on 14th August 1947.
2. National Planning Committee set up towards the end of 1938 by the Indian National Congress had members drawn from a broad spectrum of Indian society including capitalist, trade unionist as well as intellectuals. Later on many well-known capitalist of NPC (1938) went on to frame the Bombay Plan of 1944. Another plan document named Peoples' Plan authored by M.N. Roy representing a Left Position and 'Gandhi Plan' authored by Shriman Narain visualized a self-sufficient village economy. For a detailed analysis see Patnaik, Prabhat, 'Some Indian Debates on Planning', in Byres, Terence J. (ed.), *The Indian Economy: Major Debates since Independence* (New Delhi: Oxford University Press, 2000).
3. For further analysis see Patnaik, Prabhat and C.P. Chandrasekhar, 'Indian Economy under Structural Adjustment; *Economic and Political Weekly*, Vol.30,No.47, 1995 and Chandrasekhar, C.P. and Jayati Ghosh, *The Market that Failed: A Decade of Neo-Liberal Economic Reforms in India* (New Delhi: Left Word, 2002).
4. Datta, P.S.(ed.), *Ethnic Movements in Poly Cultural Assam* (New Delhi: Vikas, 1990).
5. *The New International Webster's Pocket Dictionary* (New Delhi: CBS Publishers and Distributors, 2001).
6. Dutta, P.S., *India's North East in Transition* (New Delhi: Vikas, 1992).
7. Mishra, Bani Prasanna, 'A Positive Approach to the Problems of Shifting Cultivation in Eastern India and a Few Suggestions to the Policy Makers' in *Shifting Cultivation in North East India* (Shillong: NEICSSR, 1976).
8. Dutta, P.S., 1992, *op. cit.*
9. Goswami, P.C. 'Control of Shifting Cultivation in North East India: Certain Basic Issues', in *Review and Reappraisal Seminar on Shifting Cultivation in North East India* (Shillong: NEICSSR, 1985).

6

Structural Change in Nagaland Economy : Resource-Industry Linkages and Strategies for Development

—*B. Kilangla Jamir*

INTRODUCTION

Structural change is not only a useful vintage point for analyzing the growth of economy at large, it also elucidates some of the key factors that govern the speed and direction of economic development (Johnson and Kilby: 1975) and facilitates policy makers to devise appropriate strategies for future economic development.

The process of economic development in Nagaland has started in real sense only after its statehood in 1963. During that time, the state economy was purely agrarian in nature with more than 89 percent of its working population directly dependent on agriculture. The technique of production was more or less pre-Newtonian type with very low productivity and income. The levels of urbanization and infrastructural development were also very low and industrialization was virtually non existent.

During the last four decades of economic planning, the process of sectoral transformation has been initiated in the state with building up of social overheads and infrastructure for economic and human development. However, the economy has failed to move towards the right direction which could have ensured sustainability and self sufficiency in the state.

The present study attempts to analyze the pattern of structural transformations that have taken place in the state and the extent of resource industry linkages that has developed in the state. Secondly, it attempts to take stock of the potential resources which could be used for industrial development in the state. Finally, policy options have been suggested based on the observed conditions in the state.

STRUCTURAL CHANGES IN NAGALAND

The structural change in modern economic growth implies the process of transformation of the economy from traditional agricultural society to industrial economy.

The process works through the transfer of population from primary sector to secondary sector, and subsequently to tertiary employment. Consequently the share of primary sector in net and gross national product declines and the shares of secondary and tertiary sectors increase. Decline in the share of primary sector does not mean a fall in its output; rather the agricultural productivity and output must increase in absolute terms with improvement in technique of production to meet the growing needs of the population and also to support the raw materials needs of industries (Clark: 1991). The structural change is usually followed by social transformations which may be gauged from the level of urbanization. As such, economic progress is associated with certain predictable changes in occupational structure, which in turn, brings changes in net domestic product. The structural transformation in Nagaland may therefore be observed through changes in sectoral employment structure and sectoral shares in net state domestic product.

Pattern of changes in occupational structure in Nagaland (1961-91)

Generally, economic growth is initiated by a progressive shift in investment from primary to secondary sector, providing gainful employment opportunities to both skilled and unskilled workforce, and subsequently tertiary sector starts to progress.

Table 1: Occupational pattern in Nagaland

Year	Primary sector	% share	Secondary sector	% share	Tertiary sector	% share	Total worker	% growth rate	% to total population
1961	196402	89.55	2326	1.06	20483	9.34	219211		59.40
1971	207147	78.95	2778	1.05	52471	19.66	262396	19.64	50.80
1981	269220	72.03	5461	1.46	99073	26.51	373754	42.43	48.23
1991	378829	73.01	7324	1.41	132667	25.57	518820	36.65	42.89

Source:Statistical Hand Books; 1966, 1973, 1981, 2000. Directorate of Economics and Statistics: Government of Nagaland. Kohima.

The labour distribution among the categories of employment thus progresses in a similar pattern. The changing pattern of occupational structure in Nagaland, however, presents a very different picture, where almost three-fourth of its working population is still engaged in primary sector and the employment in secondary sector remains almost stagnant at a very low level while the share of workforce in tertiary sector had witnessed growth till the1980's but declined thereafter. The trend of sectoral employment beyond 1991 could not be portrayed due to paucity of secondary data. The details of the shift in occupational structure are indicated in table 1.

Table 1 indicates the following facts about the occupational pattern in the state:

The share of primary sector in the total workforce declined from 89.51% in 1961 to 73% in 1991. The absolute number of working population in this sector had however increased progressively by 5.47%, 29.96% and 40.71% during 1961-71, 1971-81 and 1981-91 respectively.

The share of Secondary sector has remained almost static at around 1 percent while tertiary sector has shown a significant shift from 9.34% to 19.66% and 26.51% during 1961, 1971 and 1981 respectively. Thereafter, it has declined to 25.57 percent in 1991, as the initial momentum could not be maintained since the tertiary sector is mainly dominated by public and government administrative institutions, in which, the absorption capacity is limited and thus has reached a saturated point.

The proportion of workforce to total population has declined consistently from 59.50% in 1961 to 42.89% in 1991. This implies an increase in the dependency ratio.

The growth of Net State Domestic Product in Nagaland (1971-98)

The resultant change in the composition of sectoral shares in Net State Domestic Product (NSDP) and per capita income is indicated in table 2.

Table 2 : Net State Domestic Product 1970-71 to1997-98 in Nagaland (at current prices)

Year	Rupees in Lakhs								Per Capita Income	
	Primary sector	% share	Secondary sector	% share	Tertiary Sector	% share	Total NSDP	% growth	Rs.	% growth
1970-71	1199	48.09	263	10.54	1032	41.37	2494		489	
1980-81	4635	42.68	1607	14.86	4570	42.26	10812	33.35	1426	191.61
1990-91	19267	29.07	8047	12.14	38942	58.77	66256	51.28	5638	295.37
1997-98	58932	27.59	43557	20.38	111193	52.03	213682	222.50	13052	109.38

Source:Statistical hand Books: 1986-87, 1990-91, 1995-96 and 1999-2000, Nagaland Directorate of Economics and Statistics. Government of Nagaland, Kohima.

Table 2 reveals that the sectoral share in NSDP have followed a similar growth pattern as the changes in occupational structure. Accordingly, the share of primary sector declined from 48.09% in 1971 to 27.59% in 1998, while the tertiary sector had assumed a prominent position in the NSDP with an increase from 41.37% in 1971 to 58.77% in 1991 and thereafter declined to 52.03% in 1998. However, the secondary sector had remained almost static till 1991, and then increased to 20.38 percent in 1998. The fluctuation in sectoral shares in NSDP may be probably attributed to the changes in the employment structures. It may also be noted from the given data that the NSDP had increased significantly during the observed period. A similar increase in the per capita income of the State can also be seen.

An analysis of the sub-sector may give a more comprehensive idea about the pattern of change in the economy, as is shown in table 3.

The analysis of the shares of sub-sectors in NSDP during the last decade reveals the following observations:

Agriculture, with an average share of 82.75%, has been the major contributor to the primary sector during the last decade, followed by forestry and logging. However, this share had declined following the Supreme Court Order (1997) banning logging activities in the region. The contribution of fishery, although trivial, has increased.

Among the sub-sectors in the Secondary Sector, construction has been the major contributor with an average share of 64% (with the exception in the years 1992-93 and 1993-94, when percentage shares were exceptionally high, i.e., 77.89 and 78.62 percents respectively). This was followed by manufacturing sector which had fluctuated between 26 to 39 percents. Gas and Water together had given negative impact till 1993-94. But from then on; its contribution to NSDP became positive, though very marginal.

Table 3 : NSDP at factor cost by industry of origin at current prices 1990-91 to 1997-98 (% of sub sectors to sub-total)

	1990-91	1991-92	1992-93	1993-94	1994-95	1995-96	1996-97	1997-98
Primary Sub Sectors	***29.07**	***30.85**	***27.85**	***29.70**	***27.58**	***23.82**	***25.44**	***27.87**
Agriculture	79.41	81.13	89.65	85.74	81.41	80.25	80.10	85.14
Forestry& Logging	19.27	17.77	13.09	12.71	17.07	17.55	17.20	12.27
Fishery	1.32	1.09	1.43	1.53	1.51	2.18	2.68	2.51
Secondary Sub sectors	***12.18**	***11.25**	***13.36**	***12.72**	***12.62**	***18.05**	***18.65**	***20.38**
Manufacturing	35.26	39.73	28.33	29.38	26.02	30.67	33.80	29.53
Construction	65.66	61.62	77.89	78.62	66.53	61.27	61.27	65.76
Electricity, gas & water	-0.93	-1.63	-6.33	-8.01	7.44	7.44	6.68	4.69
Tertiary Sub Sector	***58.77**	***57.88**	***58.77**	***57.57**	***59.59**	***58.12**	***55.89**	***52.06**
Transport, storage & communication	8.45	8.74	9.28	8.97	26.95	24.83	25.34	23.97
Trade, Hotels & Restaurants	12.51	13.43	11.96	11.73	9.66	10.05	11.05	11.62
Banking & Insurance	3.34	3.78	3.43	3.86	1.94	1.93	2.45	2.27
Real estate, ownership of Dwellings and Business services.	18.86	19.71	23.40	23.90	20.20	20.37	20.54	21.01
Public Adm. & other service	56.81	58.10	55.34	55.37	41.19	42.78	40.59	41.11

Source:Statistical hand Books: 1995-96, 1999-2000. Nagaland Directorate of Economics and Statistics. Government of Nagaland, Kohima.
*% to total

Public administration and other community services has been the main sub-sector in the Tertiary Sector. However, its percentage share has witnessed a decline from 56.81% in 1990 to 41.11% in 1997, this may be due to increase in the share of Transport and Communication from 1994-95 onwards. The remaining sub-sector such as hotel and restaurant, banking and insurance and real estate have shown mild variations.

The decline in the role of primary sector both in employment and in NSDP is not due to technological innovation in agricultural sector. The primary sector is still dominated by traditional system and technique of cultivation (jhum). In Nagaland, about 76 percent of the net area sown is still under jhum cultivation and the level of productivity is very low with 1.49 tonnes/hectare and the level of utilization of fertilizer, high yielding seeds and machineries etc. are equally low. These facts reflect the underdeveloped nature of the agricultural sector. Further, high concentration of labour force with low productivity in this sector reveals the poor economic condition of the rural population. This limits their purchasing power and in turn, lowers market demands and consequently hampers the process of economic growth.

The present analysis reveals that the industrial development policies and actions of the State government have not made much impact on the state's economy, as such, the secondary sector remained almost static (both Employment and NSDP). A few medium industries that were started through public investment have been de-industrialized and therefore, displaced workforce from these units. Eventually this has caused great economic adversity to the displaced workers and their families. The initial shift in the tertiary sector was mainly due to expansion of government sectors, but this sector has been saturated already. Ultimately, educated unemployment is increasing at an annual rate of 6.80 percent during the last decade.

In underdeveloped countries the tertiary activities are labour intensive requiring low capital investment like small scale trade in retail and whole sales dealing in consumable goods and services that tend to attract a large number of work force due to lack of employment opportunities in Secondary sector (Bouer and Yamey: 1951). Hence, the dominance of Tertiary sector in NSDP in Nagaland may be considered as an indication that the economy is underdeveloped.

Sectoral Plan Outlays (1974-97)

The sectoral shares in the state plan outlay indicate the sectors of priority. This is shown in table 4.

Table 4 : Sector-wise Percentage Distribution of Plan Outlays in Nagaland (1974-1997)

Sectors	5th plan 1974-75	6th plan 1980-86	7th plan 1985-90	1990-91	1995-96	1996-97
Primary Sector	**33.59**	**36.00**	**34.98**	**37.20**	**36.75**	**31.21**
Agril.& allied	26.62	23.6	22.18	27.77	24.17	21.63
Irrigation, Flood & power	1.58	0.6	0.6	9.43	12.58	9.58
Secondary sector	**8.38**	**6.6**	**7.05**	**5.93**	**3.55**	**3.10**
Industry & Manufacturing	8.38	6.6	7.05	5.93	3.55	3.10
Tertiary sector	**58.09**	**57.4**	**57.96**	**56.85**	**59.66**	**65.65**
Transport & Communication.	26.34	23.00	24.64	16.27	7.72	9.92
Social services & Edu.	31.07	28.8	26.36	27.53	28.77	37.05
Econ.Services & sc.& tech.	0.53	0.4	1.92	7.81	17.12	15.59
General services	-	5.2	2.86	5.24	6.05	3.09
Unallocated	0.15	-	2.2	-	-	-

Source: Basic Statistics-2000. NEC, Shillong.

Table 4 reveals that the State Government has given maximum priority to tertiary sector in its plan outlays. The tertiary sector has received more than half of the plan outlay. Among the sub-sectors, social and community service including education had received maximum attention, the combined share of which rose from 31 percent during 5th plan to 37 percent in 1997. Transport and communication was the second priority sub-sector till the 7th plan period. Since then, its share has declined drastically while the shares of economic services and science and technology have increased.

Primary sector was the second main concern in State's plan outlay. Its share has fluctuated between 31 to 37 percents during the observed period. Secondary sector was given the least importance, with its share dropping from 8 to 3 percent during the observed period.

This reveals that the sectoral allocations in the state plan outlay do affect the pattern of the sectoral development, economic growth, and economic performances in the state.

NEED FOR SECTORAL ADJUSTMENT

The overall economic development scenario shows a skewed pattern of development. The tertiary sector has increased considerably as a result of investment made by the state government. This sector developed mainly to meet the needs of the administration and other community services. The secondary and primary sectors were not given due importance in the plan outlay and, therefore, they lagged behind. This imbalanced sectoral growth will have long term adverse effect on the economic growth of the State. The readjustment in the state plan outlay is, therefore, essential. The secondary and primary sector should be given priority as they form the backbone in the process of economic development.

In Nagaland, it is also important to modernize the traditional agricultural sector through improvement in technology, so that, a net flow of surplus capital and raw material supplies from this sector will contribute significantly to the growth of non farm sector, besides meeting the food requirements of the people.

Reasons for Weak Linkages and Underdevelopment

The weak linkage between agriculture and other sectors is due to the fact that the entire production is destined for domestic consumption. Moreover, shortage of agricultural products has emerged as a serious constrain that restricts investment in other sectors, because a large proportion of budget is spent on importing basic food items from outside. Unless productivity and income in this sector increase sufficiently and rapidly, the market for industrial goods and raw material supplies will remain inadequate and this will hamper developmental process. Thus the neglect of agricultural sector could be suicidal for the state.

Nagaland lags behind the rest of the country in industrial and infrastructural development. The recent development in service sector like transport has created job opportunities and started to contribute significantly in NSDP. However, these services are still not fully developed.

Moreover, most of the business enterprises are run by non local merchants in the state, who do not usually reinvest their capital within the state. Many private entrepreneurs, in collaboration with non locals, have invested in wood processing. However, the revenue from these activities did not lead to an increase in the productive capacity of the state. Resources were moved out from the state to meet the demands from the larger economy and revenues earned were backwashed through market operation. It is also observed that the developmental programmes have benefited only a handful of people. But these people do not reinvest the accumulated fund but spent on conspicuous consumptions.

Recent socio-political situation has shaken the confidence of the private investment within the state. Bidding up prices to recover the losses inflicted upon the business owners through extortion has weakened the market competitiveness. All these facts have resulted in the flight of capital from the state rather than attracting them.

Besides physical drawbacks like geographical remoteness, lack of infrastructure and institutions, the State also lacks good governance; entrepreneurial skill, politically conducive atmosphere, right attitude towards work etc, have all combined together to result in a weak linkage between resources and industries in the state. Under the present economic condition, we agree with the view put forward by Nurkse (1953) that "sustained and cumulative development requires not only physical capital but also development in human capital, attitude, effective and incorrupt administrative setup, conducive political atmosphere and historical incidence" (Nurkse: 1953). Absence of these prerequisite conditions in the state has resulted in stagnation of economic progress, regardless of huge fund flow from the center for development. To formulate strategies for economic and industrial development in Nagaland requires a careful examination of existing production capacity, institutions and resource potentials in the state.

INDUSTRIAL STRUCTURE IN NAGALAND

Despite its vast endowments of natural resource, Nagaland could not make much progress in industrial development. The state is considered as one of the most industrially backward state in the country. The extent of industrialization and supporting institutions in the state may be gauged from the following discussion.

Industrial structure of Nagaland may be classified, based on resource uses, into the following categories:

- *Agro-based industries* include Sugar mill, Tea & rubber, grain mill (rice and flour), food processing, canning, sericulture, fishery, animal husbandry and citronella oil etc.
- *Mineral based industries* include oil, coal, cement, stone crushing, tiles, brick, pottery etc.
- *Forest based industries* include ply wood, saw mill, paper and pulp mill, match making, furniture, bamboo, wood carving and caned based and cottage industries.
- *Other industries* include beverages, printing, hand loom, transport and related service industries, hotels and restaurant, repairing etc.

Growth of Medium Scale Industries in Nagaland

There were virtually no industries in the state during the 60's. Handicraft and handloom production only met domestic needs. From 1970 onwards a few medium scale local resource based industries have come into existence (Government of Nagaland: 1993-2000), viz.

1. Wazeho Mini Cement Plant with a capacity of 50 TPD located at Wazeho in Phek district was salvage from near closure in the mid 1990's and commercial operation has started from February 1999 onwards.
2. Nagaland Sugar Mill at Dimapur and its distillery unit were commissioned during 1973-74 at a cost of Rs. 37 corers with installed capacity of 100 MT sugarcane per day. This mill was closed down in September 2001. The factory workers were forced to avail voluntary retirement scheme, causing great economic hardship to their families.
3. Paper Mill at Tuli in Mokokchung district. Commissioned in 1983 with a crushing capacity of 100MT of bamboo per day, it was a joint venture of the State government and Hindustan Paper Corporation. The production has been suspended since early 1990's mainly due to power shortage and other infrastructural bottlenecks.
4. Nagaland Mechanized Brick Plant has been started with a proposed capacity of 100000 bricks per day with a total cost of Rs.12 crores during 1980's. Yet this project is not fully completed due to technical problems.

5. As per the State government report, 13 Ply Wood mills were running under trial during 1999-2000. Tizit Ply Wood mill is leased out to a private entrepreneur.
6. Fruit and Vegetable Processing cum Cold Storage unit at Dimapur with an investment of Rs.4.50 corers was commissioned in August 1995. This unit produces squash, bamboo shoots etc. This project also has its own problems.

Growth of Small Scale Industries

In Nagaland the small scale industries began to emerge since 1970's, based on loca resources, like food and fruit processing, wood processing, furniture, handloom, handicraft bee keeping, citronella oil etc, and other demand based industries like plastic based, iroi based, laundry, soap and servicing industries etc. The growth of small scale industries ir Nagaland is highlighted in table 5.

Table 5: Registered SSIs in Nagaland (1981-2000)

Year	SSI Units	% in NER
1981	345	3.5
1985	395	2.9
1988	509	2.5
1991	615	2.3
1995	731	2.0
1996	749	1.8
2000	1850	-

Source: Basic Statistics NER 2000, 1995 NEC Shillong; State Industrial Policy, Government. of Nagaland, Directorate of Industries, Nagaland, Kohima.

Table 5 reveals that the number of small scale industries has increased at an annua growth rate of 21 percent; however its percentage share in the region had declined consistently. The growth rate alone does not illuminate the workings of these units Therefore, data concerning workings, capacities etc. are shown in table 6.

Table 6: Workings of SSIs in Nagaland, 1998

	SSI working units	Employ-ment (numbers)	Fixed Invest-ment Rs.in Lakhs	Fixed invest. plant in (Rs. Lakhs)	Working capital in (Rs.	Production value in Rs. Lakh.
Nagaland	183	3059	729	489	649	11247
NER	9330	68593	16628	8241	11943	103881

Source: Basic Statistic 2000. NEC, Shillong

Although Nagaland accounts for the lowest percentage of working SSI units in the region (2.00 percent) in 1998, it shows the highest per unit investment in terms of botl fixed (Rs.3.90 lakh) and plant (Rs.3.54 Lakh). As such, per unit production value wa

Rs.3.69 lakhs against Rs.1.51 lakh for the region. Out of the total working SSI units, 53% is manufacturing/assembling units, 26.78% processing, 6.26% servicing/ repairing and 14% in different combinations of activities.

Handloom and Handicraft Industries in Nagaland

Handloom and Handicraft industries are resource-based industries having great importance to the rural population and generate employment and income next only to agriculture. These industries have great export potentials. The policy for the promotion of these industries must, therefore, not only be to preserve the traditional richness of the handloom and crafts but also to improve upon the hereditary skills of the weavers and craftsmen to suit modern demands and requirements. Special emphasis should also be given for the expansion of market infrastructures along with technical support and training facilities so as to improve their skills and upgrade the quality and designs of the products.

Handloom

As per the handloom census of 1995, Ministry of Textile, Government of India, there were 42,224 weaver households and 1159 non-household (cooperative) weavers in the state. Majority of the weavers are full time professionals, while the others worked part time to supplement their income from agriculture. However, most of them use traditional looms and their products are not cost effective because of its high labour inputs. This industry thus, needs technical support such as modern looms, good quality raw materials, timely and adequate flows of capital.

Keeping in view the constraints, the state government is taking suitable measures with the help of the Ministry of Textiles, Government of India, by giving financial and infrastructural assistances to make the products compatible with other loom products.

The schemes that have been taken up during 1992-2002 for the promotion of handloom units are training on the use of fly-shuttle loom, loans and grants were provided to cooperative societies as working capital, as well as, build work sheds cum housing and health care for the members of the society.

During 1993-2002, the state government received Rs.56.98 crores from the central government to provide loans to 691 handloom cooperative societies.

Table 7: Handlooms in Nagaland 1988 and 1998

Sl.No.	Particulars	1988	1998
1	Domestic handlooms	1400	1750
2	Commercial handlooms	100	2170
3	Yarn consumed ('000 kgs.)	231.60	NA
4	Cloth production ('000 mts.)	1852.80	NA

Source: NEDFI Ltd., Guwahati; NEC Basic Statistics, 1995, 2000.

From Table 7 it may be observed that both, domestic and commercial handloom units have increased, yet the increase in the latter has been staggeringly higher which may be, due to the incentive policy of the government that comes in the form of subsidies and loans and also recent changes in market conditions. However, the high figures given in the government statistics needs to be verified in order to determine the actual position of these units.

Sericulture

Nagaland has potential for development of sericulture industry as climatic and soil conditions favour the growth of natural food plants for muga, eri, tasar and mulberry silk. The state Government and the cooperative societies may establish fully mechanized silkworm rearing centres at strategic points, so as to improve the quality of silk. The small farmers may sell mulberry and other leaves to those silk worm farms at remunerative prices.

In the light of its advantages, sincere efforts are being made to promote sericulture by the state government, giving subsidies, financial support and opening centres for development of sericulture. The physical achievements made by the department of sericulture during the last ten years (1992-2002) are highlighted here:

1. A Silk Yarn Reeling and Twisting units at Dimapur and Ambar Charka Eri Silk Spinning Centre at Dhansiripar under Dimapur district were established during the Eighth Plan period.
2. Eri Cocoon Production cum Demonstration farms were established at strategic centers at Hakchan and Niam under Tuensang District, Tizit in Mon district and Longjang under Mokokchung district.
3. Mulberry farms were established at Wokha village under Wokha district, Kuzukichika under Zunheboto district, Yajang and Saring under Mokokchung district.
4. During 1999-2000, a total number of 1200 persons were provided self-employment through different sericulture activities.

Table 8 indicates the different sericulture activities in the state during the last decade.

Table 8: Seri Culture Activities in Nagaland 1990-91 to 1999-00

Sl. No	Year	Land Area under Mulberry (Hectare)	Production of Mulberry Reeling Cocoon (Mt.)	Production of Oak Tsar Reeling Cocoon (Lakh/Nos.)	Production of Eri Cut Cocoon (Mt.)	Production of Muga Cocoon (Lakh/Nos.)
1	1990-91	112	0.159	4.90	0.276	1.25
2	1992-93	431	7.20	2.54	23.00	0.12
3	1995-96	510	5.55	1.70	28.00	1.14
4	1996-97	497	3.75	1.70	28.00	NA
5	1999-00	NA	7.80	7.80	38.00	2.60

Source: Statistical Hand Book Nagaland, Directorate of Economics and Statistics; 1996, 2000, Kohima, Nagaland.

Handicrafts in Nagaland

Handicraft constitutes as one of the major economic activities among the Naga people from time immemorial. Major handicraft activities in the state are basketry of bamboo and cane, wood works like furniture and decorative pieces, artistic textile, toys and dolls terracotta, pottery, brass and bell metal, stone carving, wood carving, embroidery, musical instruments spear and bow, arrow, dao, etc. making.

The number of craftsmen and the value of handicrafts products during 1992 is indicated in Table 9. However the details of the other years could not be produced here due to paucity of secondary data.

Table 9 : Number of craftsmen and value of product in Nagaland, 1992

Sl. No.	Particulars	Numbers of Artesian	Value in Rupees (lakhs)
1	Cane and Bamboo	152	140.00
2	Wood Work	100	100.00
3	Artistic Textile	452	560.00
4	Toys & Dolls	15	01.00
5	Terracotta/Pottery	21	08.00
6	Brass & Bell Metal	15	01.00
7	Stone Carving	18	00.08
8	Embroidery	36	03.01
9	Head gear	17	12.00
10	Spear	35	01.06
11	Bow & Arrow	20	01.02
	TOTAL	881	827.17

Source: Statistical hand book 1995-96. Directorate of Statistics and Economics. Nagaland, Kohima.

The total umber of artisans had increased from 200 to 881 during1988 to 1992 and further increased remarkably to 1.26 lakh person in 1999. The value of the products was Rs.827.17 lakhs that constituted around 4% of the total product of the region in 1992. This sector has potential to accommodate a large proportion of rural labour and generate value added products with unique designs, having export potential that will directly help the rural population.

The facilities created for handicraft development during the last decades are as follows:

1. Nagaland Handloom and Handicraft Development cooperative Ltd. at Dimapur is responsible for production and market promotion of handloom and handicraft in the state.
2. 5 (five) cottage industry training cum production centres were set up at Dimapur, Mokokchung, Tuensang, Zunheboto and Aghunato. Besides there are 9 (nine) rural artesian programme training centres in the state.
3. A Branch Office for the Development Commissioner (handicrafts) Ministry of Textiles was established at Kohima.
4. Marketing infrastructures were created both within and outside the state.

Khadi and Village Industries

Cottage and village industries fall under this category. The Khadi and Village industry Commission (KVIC) promotes and imparts training to the local entrepreneurs and artisans.

Table 10 : Performances of Khadi and Village Industries (Rs. in Lakhs)

Years	Production	Sales	Employment in lakhs	
1998-99	1816.92	2008.03	0.19	956.00
1992-93	315.00	359.00	0.10	176.00
1988-89	163.90	180.00	0.04	67.20
1982-83	19.00	38.00	NA	12.00

Source: NEC, Basic Statistics, 1999. Shillong.

INSTITUTIONAL INFRASTRUCTURE FOR INDUSTRIES

The major institutions for industrial development in Nagaland are as follows (Deka 1999).

1. Nagaland Handloom and Handicraft Development Corporation (NHHDC) was established in 1977 and has been playing an important role for promotion of handloom and handicrafts industries. It supplies raw materials and advances capital and also takes up responsibility for market promotion of the products at home and abroad as well.
2. District Industrial Centers were set up during 1978-79 as nodal agencies to provide support services and other needs to the entrepreneurs.
3. Nagaland Khadi and Village Industries Board have started functioning since 1978. Its main objective is to promote socio-economic condition of the rural population through self-employment. It imparts training to the rural population.
4. A medium sized Industrial Estate at Dimapur and 2 (two) mini estates at Kiphire and Tizit (with 6 sheds each) were constructed to provide infrastructure needs to the entrepreneurs at concession rates. However, these estates are apparently having problems.
5. Five Emporiums have been set up, three within the state and one each at Delhi and Calcutta as outlets for cottage and small-scale products.
6. Financial Institutions:

(i) *National Cooperative Development Corporation (NCDC)* has been funding various small-scale units in Nagaland such as Tapioca Starch Manufacturing Unit under Mankolemba sub-division during 1998-99 with a total cost of Rs.95 lakhs and a Power Loom unit under Handloom Development Scheme during 2000-01 with a total cost of Rs.141.30 lakhs at Baghty in Wokha district.

(ii) *Nagaland Industrial Development Corporation (NIDC),* an IDBI authorized state financial corporation, was set up in 1971 at Dimapur and its branches spread over the state to assist and execute industrial development in the state. The major projects undertaken since its inception are Sugar mill at Dimapur and its distillery unit which, was handed over to Nagaland Sugar Mill Ltd., Nagaland Hotel Ltd., Industrial Estate at Dimapur and Citronella distillation unit at Yaongyimsen under Mokokchung district. Besides, the corporation has implemented a number of schemes under medium and small-scale industrial units.

Training Centers

1. *Training Small Industries Service Institution (SISI)* at Dimapur
2. *Cottage Industries Training Centers* at Aghunato, Dimapur, Mokokchung, Tuensang and Zunheboto.
3. *Carpet Weaving Training Center* at Dimapur.

4. *Weaving Training Centres* at Pfutsero under Phek district, Wackching under Mon district.
5. *Rural Artisian Centres* at Kohima-2, Dimapur-2, Tuensang-2, Zunheboto-2, Wokha-1 and Phek-1.

Proposed and Ongoing Infrastructural Development

- *Industrial Growth Centre:* A centrally sponsored project with a total cost of Rs.17.0 crores at Ganishnagar in Dhansiripar under Dimapur district was inaugurated in 1998 with an objective to provide infrastructures to the educated unemployed youths.
- *Indo-Myanmar Export Promotion Border Trade Centers* at Longwa, Pangsa, Nimi, Molhe and Avangkhu are identified and declared as export promotion centers and the preliminary works have already been initiated, a joint venture of state and central governments.
- *Industrial Zone* have been demarcated during the current year under different districts and legislative measures have been enacted to facilitate mortgage of land, excise duties and income tax exemption on certain industries set up within the zone.
- *Cold Storage* facility is being proposed at Mokokchung and Kohima.
- *Government Industrial policy:* The promotion of medium scale industries was the State priority sector during the IV and V Plan period. But this could not succeed, mainly due to lack of infrastructures and ongoing socio-political problems in the state. There is apparently a shift in the current State industrial policy, towards promotion of small-scale industries, tourism and information technology.

RESOURCE-INDUSTRY LINKAGES: THE POTENTIALS

This section of the paper attempts to map out the resource availability and its potential for industrial development. The suggested potential put forward in the following section has been made in a very broad manner; therefore, the state may settle on those industries having maximum forward and backward linkages with due consideration to existing market conditions, infrastructures and other feasibility aspects.

Agro-Based Industries

Nagaland has a total land area of 16579 sq.km and the altitude varies between 194 meters to 3048 meters above sea level. The topography is very severe, full of high ranges that break into wide chaos of spurs and ridges. This facilitates a wide variety of climatic condition that ranges from cool temperate climate (12° c to 20° c) over the hills to sub tropic climate in the foothills (12° c to 37° c). The annual average rainfall is between 200 cm and 250 cm, occurring over 7 (seven) months from April to October. These natural conditions influence the vegetations and crops of the state.

Agriculture is the main occupation of the majority of the people in the state. Nevertheless, it is still under subsistence level, dominated by traditional jhum cultivation. Rice is the main crop that occupies about 60% of the cropped area, followed by Maize and Pulses. However, Oilseeds is gaining ground in respect of cropped land in the state.

Among the agro-based activities, rice milling is the most common activity. Its by-product rice-bran is used as animal fodder. It can also be used for the production of bran oil, wax etc. The husk can be used to produce hard board, soft board, waterproof boards, packing material etc. The straw can be used for making a variety of straw boards and packing materials.

Maize grows well as both kharif and rabi crop. Besides meeting the daily consumption requirement it can be extensively used for small scale and medium scale industries such as making starch, maize breakfast cereal etc.

Pulses like beans, soya bean, arhar, gram, peas and others grow well in the state. These crops may be processed into value added products like different nutritional drinks, sauces etc.

Tea and rubber plantation is gaining popularity in the state. Based on these plants a variety of by-products and auxiliary industries may be set up.

Horticulture Based Potentials

Horticultural activities includes fruits, vegetable and flower production. Nagaland is ideal for growing different kinds of temperate and tropical fruits. Sub-tropical fruits commonly grown are orange, grapes, lime lemon, passion fruit etc.; temperate fruits are apple, plum, pears, apricot, wild apple, walnut etc. and in lower altitude with warmer climate fruits like banana, mango, papaya, guava, pine apple, jack fruit, litchi, coconut, arecanut are grown.

In 1999-2000, a total land area of 31,820 hectares was put under horticultural crops (10,980 under fruits, 17,655 hectares under vegetables and 3,185 hectares under spices), which were increased from 9,751 hectares in 1990-91 against a total potential area of 40.5 thousand hectares. The increase in cropped area was followed by increase in production; however, the productivity does not show any significant improvements.

The identified potential areas for horticultural production are Chungtia, Aliba, Kiniunger, Changki, Longnak, Longjang, Longpha, Tuli, Chuchuyimlang under Mokokchung district; Medziphema belt in Dimapur district and Baghty belt under Wokha district and Pfotsero in Phek district.

The potential horticulture-based industries are canning, slice, squash, jam, pickle, jelly, candy, alcoholic beverages, essential oil from peels and seeds of orange and lemon, powder from peels of oranges etc.

The production of vegetables and tuber crops has increased by 36 percent and land area by 34 percent during 1992 to 2000. The productivity has shown only a minor increase from 10 mt/ha to 11.34 mt/ha during the corresponding period. This implies that the increase in production was due to increase in acreage rather than yield.

The potential vegetable based industries are: wafers, starch, canned products, flake from potatoes; sago, starch, liquid glucose, dextrin, animal feeds from tapioca, sweet potatoes may be used for canned, flour, cake, biscuits, starch, vine for animal feeds etc, Tomatoes may be processed for canned, juice, sauce, ketchup soup etc.

Castor, linseeds, sunflower, mustard seeds may be used for setting up oilseeds based industries.

Spice crops like ginger, turmeric, chillies, garlic, black and green pepper, cardamoms grow well in the state. Based on these spice crops items like pickles, essential oil, vinegar and other food items may be produce.

Floriculture and mushroom cultivation have been gaining importance commercially among housewives in the urban areas, which has wide market potentials.

Agricultural and horticultural crops are highly perishable in nature. As such, large quantities are lost during various stages of the operation. Moreover, transportation of these bulky crops to far-flung market centers is not economically viable. Thus, small scale processing and semi processing units for these products at the strategic points appears to be the most relevant and appropriate solution for a hilly state like Nagaland. This will minimize the transport costs and other losses at various stages and, it will provide the small farmers a good market opportunity at their doorsteps. It will also ensure the farmers a maximum returns as they will be producing value added products. Moreover, by constructing cold storage facilities at each district head quarter may protect the farmers against losses and enhance their marketed surpluses.

Live stock Based Industries

Animal rearing has always been a part of socio-economic life of the Nagas. Animal products form an important source of protein and also supplement the income of the households. In every Naga household, at least, one or two animals are being reared mainly for domestic consumptions. The animal of preference is pig in both the rural and the urban areas.

Commercial livestock farming is a recent phenomenon in the state. Cattle and poultry farming are gaining importance as these products commands a higher market value. And the waste product like manure is also marketed to vegetable growers and florists.

The local breeds are inferior in quality and smaller in size and, therefore, they are less productive. But so far, the farmers especially in the rural areas have not made any significant attempt to improve them. The production from the state is, thus, too meager to meet the increasing market demands. Accordingly, a large quantity of livestock and their products are imported from other parts of the country to meet the daily demands in the state.

The mountain eco-system provides great opportunity for livestock based integrated land use system of low-cost watershed farming, having scope for growing concentrated food crops and perennial fodder for animals and birds. The other potential livestock farming is silvi-pastoral farming. These methods of live stock based farming will ensure soil and water conservation, besides, meeting food demand of the people.

As per the Report on land use in Nagaland, by Remote Sensing Division Dehra Dun (1978) 23.7 thousand hectares of land may be utilized under pasture for live stock production in the State. However, the past land use pattern in the state indicates that no land area had been utilized for pastoral development despite its vast potentials.

1. Inputs Based potential industries are: fodder, breeding, feed meal, livestock and dairy formulation farms.
2. Service based industries are: mechanized slaughter-house, transportation, farm implements, packaging etc.
3. Processing based activities are meat processing, meat canning, milk processing, ghee, butter, milk powder, soft drinks etc.
4. Market based activities are transportation, cold storage, packaging, sale counter, container making etc.
5. Waste based industries are casing from hides, skin, bone meal, blood meal, semi mechanized tannery etc.

Forest-Based Industries

Forest is the home for more than 80 percent of the rural population, who directly depend on forest resources for their survival. The urban population also indirectly depends on forest. In Nagaland, forest occupies 8, 62,930 hectares of land that constitutes about 52 percent of total geographical area of the state. Out of the total forestland, 88.30 percent is under private forest, owned by the clans, village communities and individuals. Under this privately owned forest area, about 32% falls under degraded category. Government forest area constitutes only 11.70 percent of the total forest area. They are being utilized as reserved, protected forest and wild life sanctuary.

During the 1950's, the forest resource utilization pattern in the state has represented a pre-capitalist and pre-commercia-lized stage of forest economy. The resources were exploited mainly to meet the local needs within a non-market framework. The first stage of commercialization of forest resource was initiated since 1966, with the setting up of furniture making units and the supply of hard wood mainly for the construction of railway sleepers. The degree of forest exploitation was slow with simple tools. The second stage of commercialization began in the 1970's; with the setting up of highly sophisticated forest based industries like paper mill and plywood mills. The demands have then shifted from hard woods to soft woods and bamboos to meet the raw material needs of the growing industries. Since then, the forestbased industries have become more diversified, with setting up of match making, pulp industries etc. Subsequently, the forest based institutions and organizational set-ups too have undergone changes to fit into the modern method of production and operations.

Potential forest based industries:

1. Plywood and hard board industries,
2. Paper and Pulp industry,
3. Bamboo and Cane industry,
4. Match making industry
5. Handicraft based on forest resources.
6. Resin production based on pine forest
7. Exotic flowers, indigenous medicinal plants and herbs from the forest having worldwide demand may be exploited commercially.
8. Eco-tourism may be promoted rapidly and extensively. For which, government may develop Botanical and zoological gardens and recreational parks.

In the past years large forest area has been turned into bushes, due to mindless commercial exploitation of forest resources like logging and the faulty agricultural practices. The process of forest exploitation has not been followed by investment for regeneration until very recently.

The forest-based industrial development must be taken up with due consideration for conservation of natural flora and fauna. This will ensure sustainable forest resource development in the state. To achieve the dual objectives of forest resource conservation and economic growth, the State must pursue a policy of exploitation followed by regeneration action plan without any gap.

Mineral Resources in Nagaland

Nagaland is fairly endowed with mineral resources. However, they are not fully explored and exploited for the benefit of the people in the state. The status of mineral resource deposits, so far identified by the Geological Survey, is indicated as follows:

Table 11: Mineral Resources in Nagaland

Mineral Deposit	Inferred Reserve (MT)	Proved Reserve (MT)	Places
Petroleum & Natural Gas in foothill region	600.00	26.77	Champang Oil Field
Magnetite with nickel cobalt & chromium with ophiolites	Not fully explored	5.00	Phek and Tuensang district
Limestone & marble 1000.00	More than	1000.00 district	Phek (wazcho) and Tuensang (Nimi)
Coal	50.00	10.00	Foot hill areas of Mon, Mokokchung, Wokha and Tuensang districts
Dimensional & Decorative stones marble, Spilite, Basalt, sand stone	Not fully explored	Substantial reserves	Mainly found in Tuensang and Phek district
Metals like zinc, molybdenum and gold and platinum group	Not explored		Phek & Tuensang district

Source: Nagaland (1995-2002) Directorate of Information & Public Relations. Govt. of Nagaland, Kohima.

Mineral Resource Utilization

1. A 50 TPD Mini Cement plant project, a Government undertaking, at Wazeho .
2. Two decorative and dimensional stone units have been commissioned recently, one each at Chumukedima and Wazeho with production capacities of 200 sq ft. of polished stone slabs per day, have been established under NEC sponsorship during 2000-01.
3. The Government of Nagaland has installed a semi-mechanized brick plant at Chumukedima with a capacity of producing 1, 00,000 bricks per day based on the low-grade clay deposits in Chumukedima and around. However, the project is now under suspension due to technical problems.

Potentials for mineral based industries in Nagaland

1. Slate and Decorative/ Dimensional Stones: The department of geology and mining had completed the detailed assessment of the slates deposits in Nagaland and the viability for small scale commercial productions were identified at Rotomi area under Zunheboto District and Tseminyu area under Kohima District.
2. A 1200 TPD cement plant at Longpotrop in Tuensang district may be developed based on the high-grade limestone/marble deposits of around 10 million tonnes in the Longpotrop Block. An overall potential reserve of 1000 million tones is estimated in the entire belt from Khongka to Thannamier may be used to feed the plant's raw material demand.

3. The Government of Nagaland has proposed to install a 50 TPD Hydrated Lime plant at Longpotrop to manufacture paper grade lime at a capital cost of Rs. 4 crores. The estimated consumption of coke breeze is 5000 tonnes annually, which is imported from outside the state and requires subsidy for transportation.
4. Integrated Plant for the production of 20 TPD calcium carbide, 18 hydrated limes and 1TPD bleaching powder near Dimapur may be installed depending on the local availability of raw materials.
5. Coal deposits at Chanki belt at Mokokchung, Borjan and Koya at Mon and Tuensang districts may be fully exploited for small scale mining to feed the other industries in the state.

Potential for Development of Tourism Industry

The rich natural picturesque view, the diverse flora and fauna, and the unique socio-cultural heritage, offer Nagaland as an unexplored interesting destination for tourists. This industry will become a constant source of revenue for the state, if only the infrastructures are fully developed and also if the socio-political environment becomes normal. This industry alone can provide profitable employment opportunity to thousands of people. The state Government has now recognized this potential. As such, Tourism as an industry has been given importance in the recent state industrial policy. The state has adopted 'Nagaland tourism policy' in 2000.

The following measures have been taken up by the government, with a view to promote tourism:

1. Nagaland Registration of Tourist trade Act 2000.
2. The major impediment for tourism in the state has been the Protected Area Permit, which was issued by the Ministry of Home Affairs. Recently there has been some relaxation as the All India Mission Board and all the Foreigners Registration office in the Metropolis are now authorized to issue the entry permits.
3. The District headquarters have been provided with basic accommodation facilities for tourists and other facilities were upgraded.
4. Training programmes have been conducted by the state government for the personnel involved with the trade during 1999-2000.
5. Traditional festivals of different Naga tribes and Hornbill festivals of Nagaland are being promoted as annual tourist events to exhibit the diversity of the Naga culture and traditions.
6. Special attention is being given to the development of adventure tourism, like trekking in the Dzukou valley. Additional spots like Kohima Lake, the Shuizeezie Lake at Kohima and Amoklushi Lake under Mokokchung district were beautified (Government of Nagaland: 1993-2000).

Water Resources

The major river catchment areas in Nagaland are shown in Table 12:

Table 12: Major Water Catchments in Nagaland

Sl.No.	Name of Water Catchments	Area in sq. km.	Length of flow in K.M.
1	Tijab	550	30
2	Dikhu	3951	100
3	Jhanji	920	50
4	Disai	670	-
5	Doyang	3480	150
6	Dhansiri	1740	86
7	Upper Barak	820	-
8	Tizu	4390	-

Source: Soil Survey and land use Planning of Nagaland, Prepared by Soil Survey Division. National Remote Sensing Agency. Dehra Dun. 1978.

Along these water catchments, activities like terrace cultivation, vegetables cultivation and fishery may be developed. The underground water resources may supplement the requirement of water for irrigation. But this source is not being fully exploited in the state. This will, no doubt, involve huge investments and efforts. Nevertheless, it will ensure food self sufficiency and sustainable development in the agricultural sector.

Hydro-power potentials

The hydro power potentials in the state are indicated in Table 13.

Table 13: Hydro power potential in Nagaland (M.W)

Sl. No.	Name of the project	Power Potentials
1.	Doyang	75
2.	Likimro	24
3.	Drura	1.5
4.	Duilmuroi	.5
5.	Kithuri	.2
6.	Tsutha	.7
7.	Horangki	.5
8.	Dikhu	1
9.	Khekau	1
	TOTAL	104

Source: Annual Administrative report. Department of Power, 1995-96.

Despite the vast potential, the power generated within the state is quite insignificant. According to the Annual administrative report of the department of Power, the total power generation was 3.21 (MU) and the total purchase was 230 (MU) in 2000-01. Thus, the state could generate only 1.39% of the total power requirements. The state mainly purchases power from NEEPCO, NHPC and PGCI.

The state government's new programmes for augmenting power supply in near future are: (i) Telangsao MHEP (3X200 KV) in Mon. (ii). Tehak (1MW), Shilloi (6MW), Lang (1 MW) and (iii) Likimro Hydro Electric Project (Basic Facts 2001, Nagaland).

Fishery Development

Fishery is a water resource based industry, having vast market potential in the state. In Nagaland fishes are being imported from outside to supplement the local supply.

The fish production and the area put under fishery in Nagaland are indicated in Table 14.

Table 14: Fishery Activities in Nagaland

Year	Number of fishery ponds	Value of fingerlings (Rs. lakhs)	Production of fishes	area	Total water (hectares)
			M/T	Value in Rs. in lakhs	
1995-96	702	80	3000	810	N.A
1996-97	951	79.91	3500	813.6	3735.03
1997-98	1310	87	3700	859	3988.7
1999-2000	1430	94	4500	1090	3700

Source: Statistical Hand Book 2000. Directorate of Statistic and Economics, Kohima.

During the last decade, about 3700 hectares of water area have been developed under fishery and has benefited about 895 fish farmers. The fish production was about 4500 metric tonnes and the fish seeds production was about 50 millions, worth Rs. 94 lakhs.

During the last five year plan period, the government has taken up the following schemes:

1. **Conservation of rivers/ streams** for protection of natural flora and fauna, so as, to maintain ecological balance was one of the thrust area of the state government.
2. **Reservoir fishery development:** Doyang Hydro project has a total capacity of holding about 6000 hectares of land under water; efforts are therefore being made to utilize this body of water for commercial fish production.

Integrated Fish-Paddy Farming

Paddy cum fish culture is an integrated form of farming which is being practiced from time immemorial in a few areas of eastern Nagaland, especially in Kohima and Phek districts. In the terrace field, paddy is cultivated along with fish which is locally known as "Zabu". Also it is worth mentioning that in Phek district, Khikruma villagers have devised an indigenous method of integrated farming, where run-off rain water is harvested in artificial ponds, which is locally known as "Ruza". The impounded water is then used for fish-cum-paddy production. There is ample scope for increasing the size of these ponds, for which, the government should give financial help and technical assistance. This indigenous method of farming may be adopted in other parts of the hilly areas too, where the natural water source for farming is scarce.

It is reported that around 1000 hectares of paddy fields are being utilized for fish culture with paddy cultivation and the production is about 600 to 700 kg per hectares of water area during 2000.

Potential for Fishery Development

An attempt has been made to estimate the gap between the demand for and supply of fishes in Nagaland with an assumption that the minimum norm of consumption requirement is at a rate of 11 kg per person annually. The present demand for fish in Nagaland is estimated at 21, 874 tonnes. The gap between supply of and demand for fishes is thus, estimated to be 17,374.99 tonnes per annum. The deficit in local production in relation to demand indicates that there is market potential for fishery development in the state.

The following action plans may be taken up by the state government for promotion of fish production:

1. Government may encourage and give technical training to the local fish farmers to construct small tanks wherever terrain permits.
2. The Government may intensify their ongoing programmes of fish breeding by opening more centres at district level, which would supply the fingerlings to the farmers at a reasonable rate.

Human Resources

Nagaland had witnessed a significant decline in the proportion of working population to total population. About 48.23 percent of the total population has been classified as workers in 1991, which has been declined to 42.68 in 1999. It has also been witnessed that the total employment in organized sector has increased from 66 thousands to 71.6 thousands during 1991 and 1999 respectively, giving an annual percentage growth rate of 1.06 percent. The workforce composition is, 96 percent employed in public sector and 4 percent under private establishments in 1991. However, in absolute terms the additional employed labour in public sector was increased by 5 thousands and in the private sector by 7 hundreds. This gives an annual growth rate of 0.97 percent for public sector and 4 percent under private sector during the last decade.

The potential human resources for industrial development are mainly comprised by the educated unemployed labours. But due to the lack of industrial development, the unemployment problem is becoming critical in the state. The number of unemployed persons according to the live register is summarized in Table 15.

Table 15: Educated unemployed in Nagaland, 1981-1999

Year	Number (in '000)	Annual Growth (in %)
1981	8.50	
1991	19.40	12.82
1999	35.4	10.30
2000	37.09	4.77

Statistical Hand Books 1981, 1995, 2000, Nagaland.

It is revealed in Table 15 that the level of unemployment has been increasing at a declining rate of 12.82 percent during the 1980's, 10.30 percent in the 1990's and 04.77 percent in 1999-2000. The employment in organized sector has increased by 1.06 percent, while the number of job seekers has been increasing at the rate of 10.30 percent per annum during 1988 to 1999 according to the NEC data. Therefore, the gap between employment and job seekers is estimated to be growing at a rate of 9 percent per annum.

If we consider that the demand for and the supply of educated manpower increase by the above mentioned rates in the future years, then, it is expected that the state will have an excess supply of educated manpower of around 57 thousands by 2005 and 75 thousands by 2010. However, these figures do not indicate the details of skilled/ qualification-wise manpower demand and supply conditions. As per the information of the state employment exchange for the period 1991-99; it has been revealed that the unemployed postgraduate youths has been increasing at an annual growth rate of 43 percent. During the same period, only 0.91 percent could be employed through employment exchange. The scenario of graduate unemployment is not much better; the growth rate during the period was 18 percent per annum, while only 0.73 percent could be employed through employment exchange.

From the above discussion it follows that the graduates and above represent about 50 per cent of the total unemployed persons. This group can play a decisive role in the field of industrial development, if proper training for skill formation is provided. The remaining 50 percent of the unemployed undergraduates, and below too can play a vital role. They can either develop their own enterprises or supply manpower required to do less skilled work in the industries.

Population Growth and Economic Development

Among the states in India, Nagaland shares the highest population growth rates during the last two decades with 5.6 and 6.4 percents per annum during 1981-91 and 1991-01 respectively. As such the population has increased from 12,09,546 in 1991 to 19,88,636 in 2001. The density of population has shown a corresponding increase from 73 to 120 persons per sq.km.

A growing population with increasing resources need not cause alarm, as long as, the production and income increase at a higher rate. However, the present economic scenario in Nagaland reveals that the level of production is very low, which could hardly meet peoples' requirements. Therefore, the most appropriate strategy may be to increase the productive capacity of its labour force through improvement in health, education, technology and skills. So this may raise the level of income and living standard of the people in the state. Once the productive activities speed up, the large number of population will turn out to be a great asset for the state. As peoples' purchasing power increases, it will offer a steady market for the industries.

The population cycle in the various developed countries has proved that with a substantial rise in the standard of living, the rate of population growth is bound to slow down (Higgins: 1999). Therefore, in Nagaland the strategy of raising the standard of living is an indirect measure to control population growth.

Conclusion

The economic progress involves a significant decline in the proportion of population engaged in agriculture and an increase in the secondary sector like manufacturing units followed by increase in commerce, transport and services of all kinds. Subsequently, an increase in productivities in all sectors and improvement in the living conditions of the people follow. The rate of population growth and unemployment decline. However, this did not ensue in the state economy.

After forty years of economic development, the state economy is at a critical stage with resources remained underdeveloped and a larger section of the population is under poverty, with discontentment towards the long operation of an unsound political and economic system. Primary sector (traditional agriculture) still dominates the economic structure while the secondary sector remaining underdeveloped. The initial momentum of development seems to have dissipated, as the force of development was not firmly rooted within the domestic economy. Thus, the large amount of valuable capital inflow from the centre for economic development has been squandered away mainly due to mismanagement.

The task ahead for the present generation, especially the policy makers for economic development must focus on improving the rural economic condition by diversifying agricultural and other primary activities with improvement in technologies, so that the rural sector may be able to contribute significantly in the process of economic development. Simultaneously, appropriate measures and policy actions should be taken up for development of secondary sector, based on the local conditions and resources, which will be followed automatically by progress in tertiary sector.

STRATEGIES FOR DEVELOPMENT IN NAGALAND

On the basis of the forgone analysis, the following strategies may be considered for industrial development in the state:

1. In the past, it has been experienced that the shortage of infrastructure was one of the major drawbacks for the industrial backwardness in the state. Therefore, development of infrastructures like power supply, transport and communication, banking institution, water supplies, health etc. must be given top priority.
2. Sincere efforts should be made to resolve the ongoing political problem in the state, so as to restore conducive atmosphere for economic development in the state.
3. In response to the needs of the time, our educational system needs to be restructured. The importance of research, training and teaching and the diffusion of knowledge must be recognized.
4. Agricultural sector must be given importance in the state plan outlay. As this sector becomes modernized, its productivity will increase. Development of this sector will contribute to overall economic development and will bring about structural transformation in a significant pattern, with transfer of factors of production to manufacturing sector. Increase in rural purchasing power will become synchronized with the growing importance of commodity flow of raw materials and food out of our agricultural sector. In return, a return flow of consumer goods from the manufacturing sector will take place. The tertiary activities like transport, marketing, financial institutions and other services will expand to meet the growing needs of the various sectors. These will facilitate a strong linkage between the sectors.
5. The cottage and small scale industrial development in rural areas should be given priority in the state plan outlay as they create employment opportunities both full and part time and provide subsidiary income to the rural communities. These will mobilize capital and labour resources, which will otherwise, remain unutilized. Moreover, their production techniques do not represent sharp departure from the traditional mode of production and organization. Steps should also be taken to foster the advances in productivity through

innovation upon the existing technology and diffusion of new knowledge. These will make the industries rooted in the rural areas and simultaneously industrial centre will sprout around rural areas as was experienced in Taiwan during the 1950s-60s.

6. Nagaland must focus on industrial development based on local resources.
7. Export potential goods must be identified and promoted, taking advantages of the geographical location bordering Myanmar. These earnings may be utilized for development of physical infrastructure in the state.
8. Public health and sanitation, family planning and nutritional programmes need to be revamped especially in the rural areas. Further, women education need special attention in view of controlling the present rapid population growth, if not, it will drag on economic growth of the state.
9. Reduction in the role of government intervention in the process of development may affect positively on resource allocation and management. Thus, it may bring about a change in the economy, empowering community in general.

REFERENCES

Bouer, B.T & Yamey, B.S, (1951), *The Economics of Underdeveloped Countries*, Cambridge University Press.

Clark, Colin, (1991), *The Condition of Economic Progress*, London, Macmillan & Co.

Deka, Phani, (1999), *Planning Approaches to Different Resources Based Industries; Industrial Development (Resources & Opportunities),* Omsons Publications , New Delhi.

Government of Nagaland, (1993-2000), *A Decade of Stability, Progress and Development*, Directorate of Information and Public Relations.

Government of Nagaland, (1995), *State Industrial Policy*, Directorate of Industries, Nagaland, Kohima.

Government of Nagaland, *Statistical Handbook*, Kohima.

Higgins, Benjamin, (1999), *Economic Development: Problems, Principles and Policies*, Universal Book Stall, New Delhi.

Jamir, B. Kilangla, (2002), Structural Change in the Nagaland Economy, in Thomas, C. Joshua and Gurudas Das (eds.) *Dimensions of Development in Nagaland*, Regency Publications, New Delhi.

Johnson, Bruce F. & Kilby, Peter, (1975), *Agriculture & Structural Transformation*, Oxford University Press, New York.

Mali D.D & Deka. P (1987) *Industrial Development In North East India*, Omsons Pub., New Delhi.

NEC, Basic Statistics, NEC, Shillong (1995, 2000)

Nurkse, Ragnar, (1953), *Problems of Capital Formation in Underdeveloped Industries*, Oxford Basil Blackwell & Mott Ltd.

Singh, Ghanshyam, N., (1994), *Structural Change in India*, Some Dimensions, Har-Anand Publications.

Comment

—E. Bijoykumar Singh

This background paper is concerned with the appropriateness or otherwise of the development strategy in Nagaland. The terms of the discourse has been clearly spelt out to concretize the development strategy for the state. I must congratulate the author for providing the basic inputs for discussion. I have chosen to focus my comments on the areas that I believe deserve further reflection.

The key idea of development is the enhancement of individuals' abilities to shape their own lives. The attack on poverty, a global challenge, involves in large measure empowering poor people to shape their own lives - through opportunities to obtain education and health care, through risk reduction and mitigation and through participation in the decisions that affect them and their families. The eradication of poverty along with its correlates should be the prime consideration when the appropriateness or otherwise of a development strategy is discussed.

The issue of structural change needs to be studied, beyond the conventional trio of primary, secondary and tertiary sector, in terms of more disaggregated sub-sectors. The available time series on such sectors and sub-sectors would enable us to make inferences on the growth rates and the nature of change in growth rates. While studying any time series in the Indian context, it has become imperative to conduct sub-period analysis at least for the 90's, being the decade of economic reforms. Though Nagaland's economic policy may not have undergone any radical change in the 90's, the impact of momentous changes at the national level cannot be ignored. In short, the neglect of more disaggregated sub-sectors and sub-periods is a glaring omission.

The author's sweeping comment "However the analysis of the structure of different sectors of the economy reveals that the state economy could not take the right direction which ensures self-sustaining and sustainable economy" is too early. Nagaland's experience is also not unique. The question of self-sustainability of a small state's economy is a tricky one. At the sub-national level it implies an unnecessarily restrictive policy space. Small states have to go for plans, big for their own resources. The issue of 'right direction' is also value loaded. 'Right' in terms of development based on using only known and available resources optimally for known ends is essentially a static outlook.

It will be interesting to study the linkage, if any, between the commodity producing sector and the service sector. Growth of service sector based on the growth of commodity production in the state is quite different from one based on the growth of mainland commodity production.

Output measures in money terms are best measured in constant prices. The association between growth rates of tertiary sector in net domestic product and the per capita income may be investigated using constant price series and regression analysis. The degree of association will be useful for policy.

On the section "Need for Sectoral Adjustment" more light should be thrown on the emerging sectoral allocation in the state plan to substantiate any nexus between the emerging pattern of development and sectoral plan allocation. Though empirical literature has so far yielded mixed results on the effects of government expenditure and its composition on economic growth, the level and type of spending undertaken by government do matter for economic performance. A study of the lead-lag structure of the relationship between sectoral plan allocations on the one hand and NSDP on the other in the regression framework will be equally illuminating.

The author has rightly pointed out the flight of capital in the hands of corrupt bureaucrats, political leaders and non-local merchants outside the state. A lot is generally said about corruption without doing little about it. Nor has its effects been clearly spelt out. Corruption, to be meaningful for policy, may be divided into corrupt public practices and private corruption. Since much of public corruption can be traced to government intervention in the economy, policies aimed at liberalization, stabilization, deregulation and privatization can sharply reduce the opportunities for public corruption. Bigger the role a government plays in economic development, the larger is the scope for public corruption. Empirical evidence suggests that corruption lowers investment and retards economic growth to a significant extent. Some other consequences of public corruption are misallocation of talent, loss of tax revenue, adverse budgetary consequences, lower quality of infrastructure and public services, distorted composition of public expenditure, etc. Thus the effects of corruption are much intense in a state like Nagaland where the government does practically every thing.

"Deindustrialization" has been used uncritically and its reference is incomplete. Decline in employment in manufacturing as a share of total employment need not always be a negative phenomenon. Even advances in the service sector rather than in the manufacturing sector are likely to encourage the growth of living standards in the future. Besides in most north-eastern states private investment is yet to play any significant role in industrialization. Comments like "lack of enthusiasm to work among the people, lack of entrepreneurial skills" etc. need more objective probing. The fall in the proportion of workers in total population definitely implies that a larger proportion of population are dependent. It may be due to the fact that the youth now are spending more time in schools and colleges. Human capital formation is now considered a key to economic development. It can be confirmed from the age profile of workers using NSS data. Regarding unemployment, employment exchanges data should be supplemented with NSS data.

Regarding "Government Industrial Policies in Nagaland", government incentive policies should be assessed vis-à-vis constraints as identified by entrepreneurs. Pre-conceived views may render the incentive matrix meaningless. Entrepreneurs operate in a complex environment and confront a diverse array of constraints.

Some such broad constraints to be examined are lack of access to finance, regulatory constraints, constraints on access to non-financial inputs and cost constraints. Learning which constraints bind entrepreneur is only a first step in setting priorities for reform to promote small and medium enterprises.

Throughout the paper there is an unmistakable vision of an economy able to stand its own deriving its growth impulses from state specific resources. A more comprehensive picture will emerge if the determinants of growth of the economy both on the aggregate and sectoral level are examined using regression analysis.

Resources base of the state has been adequately presented. The potential for tourism industry along with tourism-promoting measures has been spelt out. It may not be out of context to point out that the neighbouring state of Manipur also claims Dzuko valley as part of Manipur. The issue of resource-industry linkages needs to be studied in more detail.

There is no reason why one should have only industries for which resource are locally available. Industries can also be demand based. Industrialization is an area where a small state can capitalize on the advantage of being a part of a big country. Trade based on comparative advantage can take care of the issue of sustainability. Nagaland's resources should be put to best use over time. Immediate exploitation may be inoptimal.

Industrial backwardness in Nagaland needs to be seen in the context of the 'regional' problem in the country. The growth in net domestic product in the manufacturing sector, in registered manufacturing, in unregistered manufacturing, in the total tertiary sector, in agriculture and NSDP for Nagaland vis-à-vis some highly industrialized states like Maharashtra, some industrially backward states like Bihar would be highly illuminating. Are they unrelated with the national level? Which of the 3 basic organizational groups (i) household unit; (ii) factory units; (iii) non-factory non-household units dominate the structure of manufacturing in Nagaland? One can use Annual Survey of Industries data to see whether the overall poor performance of the industries in terms of employment and value added in Nagaland is confined to a few industries or a group of industries. One can have a decomposition exercise to assess structural vs. regional factors. By regional factor we mean availability of entrepreneurs, natural resources endowment, public investment, land prices, wage rates, etc. It is possible to examine the divergence of the growth rate between a region and a nation into a part that emerges out of the differences in the industrial structure of the region vis-à-vis that of the nation and the other which arises out of differing growth rates given the same industrial structure.

7

Resource–Industry Linkages in Sikkim : Strategy of Development in the Context of Structural Change

—Anil Bhuimali & Kanak Kanti Bagchi

INTRODUCTION

Sikkim is a state of mountains and valleys. It has an area of 7,299 square kilometers. Its altitude is 12,000 feet and is dominated by Kanchanjunga. The capital is Gangtok, Sikkim's only town, in the south-eastern quarter of the state. Its modern history began in 1642 A.D. *Lepchas* are the aboriginal inhabitants of Sikkim who came from the foothills of Assam and Upper Burmah (now Myanmar) (White, 1971). They are very simple and calm and they behave mildly. Most of the *Lepchas* live in the hilly forest areas leading a very plain way of living. They are nature lovers and so fond of animals, insects and plants and they have their own names for each of them. Agriculture is the main source of their livelihood. Originally they were the worshipers of mountains, rivers and forests but in course of time they have become the worshipers of Lord Buddha. After the *Lepchas*, the *Bhutias* came to Sikkim long before (before 1642 A.D) the accession of the Sikkim Kings. The *Bhutias* are of the Tibetan origin. Professionally they are traders and herdsmen although some of them engage themselves in agriculture. They are followers of either Buddhism or Lamaism. The third group of people who constitute the largest number of total population in Sikkim are the *Paharias* who have migrated from Nepal. They are Hindus and within them caste system prevails. A few people are of Indian origin like *Marwaris* and some other business communities who came and settled in Sikkim since 1888 under the protection of the British *Raj*.

British supremacy over Sikkim lapsed when India attained her freedom in 1947. In 1947 India assumed control of Sikkim's external affairs, defence and communication while Sikkim has the autonomy in her internal affairs. As per a treaty between the Maharaja of Sikkim and the President of India signed on December 5, 1950, the old colonial relations that existed between the British India and Sikkim were scrapped. Since then Sikkim could enjoy every internal autonomy leaving the defence and the external matters to Indian Government. The Government of India for the running of a good administration and economic development of the state did agree to pay a sum of Rs. 300,000 annually.

On September 4, 1975 Sikkim became the 22nd associate state of India. The present article intends to explain, in brief, the resource-industry linkages in the hilly economy of Sikkim and in this context discuses the strategy of development in the context of structural change.

INDUSTRIAL STRUCTURE

Apart from the cottage and tiny industries, there are only fourteen state public sector industries. All the state undertaking enterprises excepting Sikkim Time Corporation are making losses. One serious drawback in the way of setting up of new enterprises in Sikkim is that the Indian Companies Act does not apply in the state of Sikkim. Similarly the Industrial Disputes Act is not applicable in Sikkim. Industries in Sikkim are registered under Registration of Companies Act, Sikkim, 1960. According to this Act any type of industries in Sikkim cannot raise equity from the domestic capital markets.

Table 1 presents a picture of small-scale units, employment created and investment made in these industries in the state of Sikkim.

Table 1 : Small-scale Units, Employment Created and Investment Made in Sikkim (1975-76 to 1998- 1999)

Year	Number of Units	Investment made (Rs. Lakhs)	Employment Created (Nos.)
1975-76	11	9.64	104
1976-77	Nil	Nil	Nil
1977-78	1	0.52	12
1978-79	4	26.87	77
1979-80	Nil	Nil	Nil
1980-81	6	61.92	51
1981-82	2	.86	4
1982-83	3	858.49	330
1983-84	1	.68	3
1984-85	Nil	NIL	Nil
1985-86	8	4.47	44
1986-87	8	29.10	59
1987-88	18	68.49	232
1988-89	16	9.91	180
1989-90	31	190.04	445
1990-91	28	86.49	197
1991-92	20	224.96	209
1992-93	18	12.28	90
1993-94	29	135.35	204
1994-95	19	18.21	152
1995-96	33	34.76	143
1996-97	23	107.84	179
1997-98	13	12.45	55
1998-99	9	61.09	69
Total	**301**	**1954.42**	**2835**

Source: Directorate of Industries, Sikkim

In Sikkim there are four districts comprising eight towns and 447 villages. The districts are East, West, North and South. Of the four districts only one district, viz, the East district is relatively industrially developed. Table 2 shows district wise positions of small-scale units, employment and investment in them.

Table 2 : Districtwise Distribution of Small-scale Units, Employment and Investment in Sikkim (1998)

Districts	Number of Small-scale Units	Number of persons	Investment (in Lakhs of Rs.)
East	219	1933	1521.43
West	28	127	35.47
North	4	8	.94
South	50	767	396.58
Total	301	2835	1954.42

Source: Directorate of Industries, Sikkim.

Table 3 shows typewise distribution of SSIs in the districts of Sikkim.

Table 3 : Typewise and Districtwise Distribution of Small-scale Units in Sikkim in 1998-99

Industry	Districts				
	East Dist. (No.of units)	West Dist. (No.)	North Dist. (No.)	South Dist. (No.)	Total
1. Carpet and *Lepcha* weaving	7	4	1	2	14
2. Handicraft Units	4	1	Nil	3	8
3. Printing Press	31	Nil	Nil	2	33
4. Wooden Product & Furniture	13	1	Nil	1	15
5. Tyre retreating	3	Nil	Nil	1	4
6. Bakery & Confectionery	23	2	Nil	9	34
7. Paddy de-husking mills	28	14	1	6	49
8. Engineering products an allied works	25	Nil	Nil	8	33
9. Garments	23	4	Nil	3	30
10. Candies	4	Nil	Nil	2	6
11. Leather Products	7	1	Nil	Nil	8
12. Watch assembly units	3	Nil	Nil	1	4
13. Automobile repairs of motor vehicles	6	1	1	1	9
14. Photo Studio	4	Nil	Nil	2	6
15. Mazda	3	Nil	Nil	2	5
16. Data processing	6	Nil	Nil	Nil	6
17. Photo Copying	3	Nil	Nil	Nil	3
18. Tea Packing	2	Nil	Nil	Nil	2
19. Food Processing	2	Nil	Nil	Nil	2
20. Thank	2	Nil	Nil	Nil	2
21. Herbal Products	2	Nil	Nil	Nil	2
22. Chemicals	2	Nil	Nil	Nil	2
23. Bottle	Nil	Nil	Nil	1	1
24. Misc.	16	Nil	1	6	23
Total	219	28	4	50	301

Source: Directorate of Industries, Sikkim

From Table 3 it is clear that small-scale units in Sikkim are not spread out evenly in all the four districts. There is heavy concentration of the small-scale units in the East district. Out of 301 units, 219 units are in this district. The second largest concentration occurs in the South district where the total numbers of units are 50. In the West District there are only 28 small units. In the East district there are thirty-one paper and printing presses and twenty-eight paddy de-husking mills. There are 25 units dealing with engineering and allied works. There are twenty bakery and confectionary units and the total number of garments units are twenty-three. In the West district the major small-scale industry is the paddy de-husking mill. There are fourteen paddy de-husking mills in this district. There are only four units each in carpet and *Lepcha* weaving and garments industries. The most backward district in terms of small-scale units is the North district where there are only four industries (carpet and *Lepcha* weaving 1, paddy de-husking mill 1, automobile repairs 1, bottle 1). The Industry wise positions of the small-scale units, employment created in these units and the capital-labour ratio are presented in Table 4.

Table: 4 : Industry-wise Investment, Employment and Capital-labour Ratio (1998-99)

Units	No. of Units	Investment (Rs. in Lakhs)	Employment (No.of Persons)	Capital Labour Ratio
Carpet and *Lepcha* Wearing	14	9.67	116	.08
Handicraft Units	8	4.88	149	.03
Paper & Printing Press	33	102.65	191	.54
Wooden Products & Furniture	15	61.92	111	.56
Tyre Retreating	4	6.03	15	.40
Bakery and Confectionery	34	170.28	454	.38
Paddy de-husking and Mills	49	128.7	173	.74
Engineering product & Allied Works	32	142.3	232	.61
Garments	30	35.49	285	.12
Candles	6	6.41	27	.24
Leather Products	8	8.84	56	.16
Watch assembly units	4	857.81	329	2.61
Automobiles repairs	9	5.95	91	.07
Photo Studio	6	20.23	28	.72
Masala	4	12.37	34	.36
Data Processing	6	19.14	38	.50
Photo Copying	3	4.5	5	.90
Tea Packaging	2	1.15	10	.12
Food Processing	2	80.55	23	3.50
Thanka	2	.27	12	.02
Herbal Products	2	13.1	48	.27
Chemicals	2	.66	31	.49
Bottle	1	137.49	210	.65
Miscellaneous	25	109.59	167	.66

Source: Directorate of Industries, Sikkim.

STRUCTURAL CHANGE IN THE ECONOMY

We present below in tables 5 to 10 the sector-wise gross state domestic product (GSDP) in current and constant prices as well as the per capita gross state domestic product at constant and current prices. We also present the data of gross and net state domestic products and per capita income of Sikkim at current and constant prices.

Table 5 : Sector-wise Gross State Domestic Product (GSDP) in Sikkim At 1980-81 Prices (Rs. in lakhs)

Year	Agriculture and Allied Activities	Industry	Services	Total
1980-81	2535	1089	1583	5207
1981-82	2812	1125	1630	5567
1982-83	3249	1240	1782	6271
1983-84	3231	1360	1868	6459
1984-85	3709	1444	2241	7394
1985-86	3638	1738	2717	8093
1986-87	3744	2605	3220	9569
1987-88	5458	2478	3395	11331
1988-89	5657	2635	4251	12543
1989-90	5932	3102	4811	13845
1990-91	6179	2744	6224	15147
1991-92	6256	2878	6527	15661

Source: Central Statistical Organization, Government of India.

The above table shows a sector-wise increase in GSDP in Sikkim at 1980-81 prices. The increase of GSDP in service sector was remarkable during 1990 and 1991-92 (Rs. 6224 lakhs and Rs. 6527 lakhs respectively). Both the agriculture and allied sector and industry grew. But the rate of growth of both these sectors are not comparable with that of the service sector. This is due to the traditional method of cultivation in the primary sector and in industrial underdevelopment. We find the same picture of sector-wise GSDP at current prices as shown in Table-6 below.

The dynamics of unbalanced sectoral growth of the state economy may be explained as follows. In course of our analysis we have already identified and elucidated the causes of industrial backwardness in the state. As far as the growth of agricultural sector is concerned, it may be noted that though the growth of agricultural sector lags behind that of the service sector, the growth of the former is impressive in terms of area under High Yielding Variety crops (Table 13). However, the main causes of agricultural backwardness are the lack of irrigation facilities (only 11% of cultivated area are irrigated), low level of fertilizer consumption and low level of credit facilities available to the farmers.

Table 6 : Sector-wise Gross State Domestic Product (GSDP) in Sikkim at Current Prices (Rs. in lakh)

Year	Agriculture and Allied Activities	Industry	Services	Total
1980-81	2,535	1,089	1,583	5,207
1981-82	2,881	1,204	1,814	5,899
1982-83	3,486	1,342	2,141	6,969
1983-84	3,853	1,557	2,603	8,013
1984-85	4,824	2,153	3,213	10,190
1985-86	5,788	2,396	4,028	12,212
1986-87	6,676	3,022	4,822	14,520
1987-88	7,818	3,326	5,580	16,724
1988-89	8,157	3,496	6,812	18,465
1989-90	9,191	3,588	7,622	20,401
1990-91	9,974	3,448	9,972	23,394
1991-92	10,670	4,065	11,211	25,946
1992-93	9,661	4,105	12,948	26,714
1992-94	16,379	5,387	14,389	36,155
1994-95	22,886	5,406	14,737	43,029
1995-96	23,218	7,079	17,100	47,397

Source: Central Statistical Organization, Government of India.

The agricultural sector, in addition to the reasons stated above, has limits to growth due to non-availability of adequate amount of cultivable land as the terrain of the state is entirely hilly. Under these circumstances, the State Government has no alternative but to deliberately favour and promote the service sector, which is responding positively with relatively higher rate of growth than the other two sectors of the economy.

Table: 7 : Gross State Domestic Product and Per Capita Income at Current Prices

Year	Gross state domestic product (Rs. in lakh)	Per capita Gross state domestic product (in Rs.)	Percentage change over the previous year: Gross state domestic product	Percentage change over the previous year: Per capita gross state domestic product.
1993-94	37743	8457	-	-
1994-95	40277	8714	6.17	3.04
1995-96	48130	10056	19.5	15.4
1996-97	55262	11141	14.82	10.79
1997-98	65106	12644	17.82	13.49
1998-99(p)	75463	14142	15.91	11.85
1999-2000(q)	81695	14816	8.25	4.17

Source: Central Statistical Organization, Govt. of India.

Table 7 presents the GSDP and per capita GSDP of Sikkim at current prices. According to the above table in 1993-94 the estimates of GSDP was Rs. 37743 lakhs. The table shows that the GSDP is increasing overtime. The percentage change of GSDP and per capita GSDP over the previous year in 1994-95 were 6.17 percent and 3.04 percent respectively.

Table 8 : Gross State Domestic Product and Per Capita Income of Sikkim at Constant Prices

Year	GSDP (Rs. in lakh)	Per capita GSDP (in Rs.)	Percentage change over previous year	
			GSDP	Per capita GSDP
1993-94	3773	8457	(-)	(-)
1994-95	37183	8045	1.48	4.87
1995-96	41122	8590	10.59	6.80
1996-97	45630	9200	10.96	7.08
1997-98	52002	10099	13.96	9.77
1998-99(Q)	55915	10479	7.53	3.76
1999-2000(Q)	60015	10884	7.33	3.86

Source: Central Statistical Organization, Government of India.

These were highest in 1995-96. In 1995-96 the percentage change of GSDP and per capita GSDP over the previous year were 19.5 and 15.4 respectively. These show that maximum growth occurred in 1995-96.

The estimates of GSDP and per capita income of Sikkim at constant prices have been shown in table-8.

The above figures show that in 1994-95 the GSDP in real terms (1993-94 prices) decreased from Rs. 37743 lakhs to Rs. 37183 lakhs. This shows a negative growth of -1.48 percent over the previous year. After 1994-95 there had been an upward trend of GSDP. It was highest in 1997-98, which was 13.96 percent over 1996-97.

The net state domestic product (NSDP) and per capita income of Sikkim at current prices have been shown in table-9 :

Table 9 : NSDP and Per Capita Income at Current Prices

Year	NSDP (Rs. in lakhs)	Per capita NSDP (in Rs.)	Percentage change over previous year	
			NSDP	Per Capita NSDP
1993-94	33694	7550		
1994-95	35570	7669	5.57	1.93
1995-96	42619	8905	19.82	15.71
1996-97	49111	9901	15.23	11.18
1997-98	58368	11324	18.73	14.37
1998-99(P)	67475	12645	15.72	11.67
1999-2000(Q)	73644	13356	9.14	5.62

Source: Central Statistical Organization, Government of India.

Table 9 shows that there has been an upward trend of both NSDP and per capita NSDP at current prices. The table also shows that the maximum level of increase in per capita income was 19.82 in 1995-96 over the year 1994-95. The per capita NSDP was the maximum in 1995-96.

The net state domestic product and per capita income at constant prices in the state of Sikkim are shown in table-10.

Table 10 : Net state Domestic Product and Per Capita Income (NSDP) of Sikkim at Constant Prices

Year	*NSDP (Rs. in lakh)*	*Per capita NSDP (in Rs.)*	*Percentage change over previous*	
			NSDP Income	*Per Capita*
1993-94	33694	7550		
1994-95	32874	7113	-2.43	-5.79
1995-96	36533	7633	11.13	7.31
1996-97	40851	8286	11.82	7.90
1997-98	46984	9125	15.01	10.79
1998-1999(Q)	50371	9440	7.21	3.45
1999-2000(Q)	54126	9816	7.45	3.98

Source: Central Statistical Organization, Government of India.

Table 10 shows that there has been a decrease of NSDP from Rs. 33694 lakhs to Rs. 32874 lakhs from 1993-94 to 1994-95. Since then there has been a continuous upward trend of NSDP. It is highest in 1999- 2000 when the NSDP is Rs. 54126 lakhs. The per capita income in real terms has decreased from Rs. 7550 in 1993-94 to Rs. 7113 in 1994-95. This shows a negative growth (-5.79 percent). After that there has been an upward trend of NSDP in percentage term up to 1997-98. The percentage change of NSDP in 1998-98 over the previous year becomes 7.21. This slightly rises to 7.45 in 1999-2000. The per capita income in percentage term becomes negative (-5.79) in 1994-95 over the previous year. After that there has been a positive trend of per capita income in percentage term. It is highest in 1997-98 (10.79 percent).

Table 10 reveals a mixed trend of growth of both net state domestic product and per capita income. It may be noted here that due to the lack of a comprehensive industrial policy the resource-industry linkages were weak in the state economy of Sikkim. However, as stated in the later part of this paper, in 1996, a comprehensive Industrial Policy Statement has been made by the State Government. It is believed and expected that after this latest Industrial Policy Statement, the desired linkages will be strengthened. At present, the time period is too short to assess the impact of this Policy. In the subsequent studies the results of this Policy may be tested. It is, however alleged that, whatever facilities are promised by the Government to the private entrepreneurs, through Industrial Policy or otherwise, are not actually made available to the latter.

RESOURCE BASE OF THE STATE

Land

The major land-use statistics of the state as revealed by the Indian Remote Sensing Satellite - IA in November 1988 are as follows:

Table 11 : Land-use Pattern in Sikkim

Land-Use	Total Area (sq.kms.)	% of the Total Geographical Area
Total Tree Cover	2857.31	40.27
Snow	1231.87	17.36
Alpine Scrub/Pastures	1071.48	15.09
Alpine Barren	818.15	11.53
Crop Land	760.56	10.72
Forest Blanks/Scrubs	192.43	2.71
Lakes/Streams	137.90	1.94
Miscellaneous	13.23	0.19
Major Land Slides	10.53	0.15
Township	3.54	0.05

Source: Technology Information, Forecasting & Assessment Council (TIFAC) (1997): A Vision for Sikkim: Technology Perspectives & Business Opportunities.

It is evident from Table 11 that 760.56 Sq. Kms. or only 10.72% of the total geographical area is under crop land. However, it has a huge area with tree cover which is 40.27% of the total geographical area. Alpine scrub/pastures together with forest blanks/scrubs comprise as large an area as 1263.91 Sq. Kms. or 17.80% of the total geographical area. The existence of this latter area implies that there is perhaps an ample scope of raising of live stock and development of dairy industry in the state. Water resources of the state are also in a noteworthy position. It can be seen from the table that lakes and streams comprise about 138 Sq. Kms. of geographical area of the state.

Since the economy of Sikkim is mainly based on agriculture and animal husbandry, let us look at the relative share of different crops in total food production (1980-1998) and the coverage of HYV seeds under different crops in the state (1980-81 - 1996-97). It can be seen from Table 12 that maize is the principal food crop in the state in terms of production along with all the coarse varieties of food grains comprised nearly 60% of the total food production in 1997-98. Rice, wheat and pulses occupy the second, third and forth position respectively.

Table 12 : Share (Percent) of Different Crops in Total Food Production (1980-98)

Crops	1980-81	1985-86	1990-91	1995-96	1996-97	1997-98
Maize	47.76	48.25	44.07	52.51	0.00	0.00
Rice	17.18	16.94	18.96	20.31	20.89	20.70
Wheat	21.51	16.63	16.19	14.20	13.99	13.73
Barley	0.74	1.44	2.14	1.46	0.00	0.00
Buck Wheat	2.23	2.05	1.90	1.62	*59.45	*59.86
Finger Millet	6.21	4.41	5.48	4.41	0.00	0.00
Pulses	5.37	10.28	11.26	5.50	5.67	5.71

Note: * this includes all the coarse varieties of food grains including maize.
Source: Sikkim Human Development Report 2001, p.47.

Improvement of income of the farmers would depend upon the increase in productivity of different crops that in turn depends upon the rate of adoption of HYV technology, i.e., water-seed-fertilizer technology. Since the increased income partly indicates additional demand for industrial goods which may be an important factor helping industrialization of the state, therefore, spread of the use of HYV seeds assumes a lot of significance. Table 13 below exhibits the coverage of HYV seeds in the state over the years 1975-76 to 1996-97.

Table 13 shows that there has been a steady progress towards the coverage of HYV seeds for Rice, Wheat and Maize in Sikkim over the years 1975-76 to 1996-97. But the progress is not satisfactory for all crops. Though the area coverage is the highest for Maize, the adoption of HYV seeds for this crop is the lowest (39.36%). In the case of Rice also though the area coverage is the second highest, the adoption of HYV seeds is only 40.95%

Table 13 : Coverage of HYV Seeds in Sikkim (1975-76 to 1996-97)

Year	Crop	Area Coverage (Ha)	HYV Coverage (Ha)	Percentage of Coverage
1975-76	Rice	11,400	800	7.01
	Wheat	150	120	80.00
	Maize	28,500	4,000	14.03
1980-81	Rice	14,800	2,000	13.51
	Wheat	6,850	6,500	94.89
	Maize	30,200	7,000	23.17
1985-86	Rice	15,900	3,400	21.38
	Wheat	7,200	6,800	94.44
	Maize	38,100	8,600	22.57
1990-91	Rice	18,610	5,400	29.01
	Wheat	7,950	7,500	94.33
	Maize	40,780	14,000	34.33
1995-96	Rice	15,940	6,778	45.52
	Wheat	8,240	8,200	97.38
	Maize	39,400	16,720	42.43
1996-97	Rice	15,870	6,500	40.95
	Wheat	7,940	7,800	98.23
	Maize	39,380	15,500	39.36

Source: Sikkim Human Development Report 2001, pp. 49-50.

which is not-up to the mark. Therefore, there is enough scope and necessity of spreading HYV technology in agriculture in Sikkim in order to increase the income of farmers. This in turn necessitates the provision of supportive inputs like irrigation, fertilizer, credit etc. at a subsidized rate by the government.

It has been rightly observed, "With the employment in the government sectors practically saturated and not much scope available to absorb the manpower in industry due to constraints of power and raw material, a large section of the population will have to be absorbed in agriculture. Higher employment in agriculture with limitation of the land is only possible by increasing the use of HYV seeds, fertilizer and pesticides along with irrigation. If the present rate of use of agricultural inputs are not increased by several times, the possibility of finding more employment in agriculture does not seem feasible." (www.sikkim.nic.in/sw/home.eco.htm)

Forest

Forest is one of the richest natural resources of Sikkim. In 1997, forest area constituted 44.9 percent of the total area of Sikkim, as compared to 19.4 percent for the country as a whole (Lama, 2001). Three distinct types of forests have been recorded in Sikkim: i) the *Sal* forests, which occupy an area of 8,500 acres extending from an altitude of 700 feet to about 3,000 feet in the Tista, Rangit and Rishi Valleys; ii) the broad leaved forests comprising the middle and upper hill forests; and iii) the coniferous forests, which extend over 45,000 acres along the valleys of Lachen, Lachung and Dombang. While in the eastern and western Sikkim deciduous and evergreen forests are more commonly found, there is the predominance of coniferous forests in northern Sikkim (Debnath, 1974).

Sikkim has a unique bio-diversity. More than 5,000 species of angiosperms are found in the State - nearly one third of the total species of angiosperm found in the country. The state houses over 4,000 species of flowering plants, 300 species of ferns and its allies, 450 to 500 species of orchids, 40 species of oaks, 8 species of tree ferns, 40 species of primulas and 20 species of bamboos, 144 species of mammals, 600 species of birds, over 400 species of butterflies and moths and many species of reptiles (Government of Sikkim, 1999). Several species of medicinal plants and herbs are found throughout the state.

Forests are an important source of livelihood for the Sikkimese people. In addition to wood, forests are also sources of medicinal herbs and plants. This is a potential growth area for Sikkim. The commercial cultivation of medicinal herbs like Ipecac, Rauwoulfia serpentina and lycopodium, could be an important source of revenue to the Government.

Thus the forests of Sikkim provide wood, fuel, fodder and medicine. Bamboo of different species is an important raw material for craftwork. Medicinal plants and herbs have potentialities of various industrial uses. Different types of timber available in these forests is suitable for a number of wood based industries like tea chest baton, wooden boxes, match boxes, match splints, pencil, sophisticated furniture, activated carbon etc. (Tarafdar, 2002).

Minerals

The state of Sikkim is endowed with some geological resources. The department of mines and geology has been responsible for exploration and extraction of mineral resources. Among the minerals available in the state, the most important are copper, coal, limestone and graphite and the less important minerals are dolomite, garnet, quartzite, zinc, lead, talc etc. However, the state is not so rich in mineral resources and not much viable and exploitable mineral deposits have so far been discovered.

RESOURCE-INDUSTRY LINKAGES

We may now bring out the possible resource-industry linkages in Sikkim on the basis of the resources some of which we have mentioned above as well as resources that we will mention now. Let us first of all take up the case of tourism industry in Sikkim.

Tourism

Tourism is considered as the backbone of Sikkim's economy. It has brought economic prosperity in Sikkim. With the salubrious climate, the natural beauty and the fine cultural heritage of Sikkim, the growth of tourism has immense possibilities. There are large number of places of tourist attraction particularly the snow land mountains, the lakes and unspoiled forest areas and valleys of flowers. The advantage of having very fine monasteries in Sikkim can also be taken to attract Buddhist tourists from countries like Japan and the Southeast Asian countries.

A 15-year perspective plan on tourism has been started in 1998. Implementation of this plan has started yielding results. This is evident from Table 14 below:

Table 14 : Growth of Tourism in Sikkim

No. of Tourists	1987	1998	1999	2000	2001
Domestic	2,958	1,20,103	1,35,273	1,40,151	1,44,203
Foreign	1,883	8,985	9,821	11,320	7,757

Sources: i) Government of Sikkim (2001); *Sikkim at a Glance*; ii) Ganguly, Tapash (2002).

From Table 14, it is clear that there has been a steady increase in the number of tourists in the state over the 13-year period from 1987 to 2001. Between these two years the number of domestic tourists have increased by nearly 49 times and 4 times respectively. With all its grandeur and scenic beauty, Sikkim has a far more untapped potential for attracting both domestic and foreign tourists.

The government is trying its best to sell Sikkim as a tourist hot spot. Roads have been constructed on a war footing by the Border Roads organization. Tourist lodges, guesthouses and hotels have come up in many places. Transportation has improved a lot. The government is operating mountain flights using helicopters. The efforts have started paying off. Apart from the increased inflow of tourists, the state has also bagged an award from the Union tourism ministry for being the best performing state in the north-east.

We may note here that Sikkim has all the natural advantages over many other regions of India to promote adventure tourism, eco-tourism and religious tourism in addition to the traditional tourism in the beautiful hill resorts of Sikkim with its snow-clad magnificent Kanchenjungha and rich flora, fauna, orchids and flowers. It is believed that each of the former categories of tourism has its committed groups of rich and wealthy practitioners both in India and abroad. The State is taking steps in the right direction by according topmost priority to the promotion of tourism as the most viable industry in Sikkim with the great potential of its backward and forward linkages with other sectors of the economy. In this sector, invitation to domestic private entrepreneurs and Multi-National Corporations may be another welcome step on the part of the State Government.

FOREST BASED INDUSTRIES

Medicinal Herbs

Sikkim is a versatile storehouse for a multitude of medicinal plants. As many as 91 medicinal plant species have been notified until now and many remain yet to be exploited. For the important medicinal herbs germaplasm conservation, gene analysis, patenting, quality analysis, crude drug preparations, extraction of active principles for domestic consumption, development of new formulations and dosage forms for various ailments etc. are urgently needed. The medicinal plants have, therefore, huge potential for industrial use.

Floriculture and Orchids

Sikkim is renowned for its orchids and rhododendrons. There are 40 species of rhododendrons available in temperate to sub-alpine zones in Sikkim. Of about 1100 species of orchids found in the country, Sikkim alone accounts for almost 450 species of exotic orchids. Right from the warm humid tropical foothills through temperate forests till the alpine meadows orchids form a dominant flora of these hills. They are attractive as they have beautiful foliage and are highly colourful, fragrant and long lasting. Sikkim is known to be a paradise for flowers. Beside rhododendron, gladioli, anthuriums, lilliums, primulas and many other floral species thrive there.

Unfortunately the natural orchid populations in the state are on the decline due to excessive collection by botanists and over harvesting by the traders. Many orchids are becoming endangered or threatened on account of deforestation and habitat destruction. Several measures are needed to be taken, such as conservation of certain endangered species, adoption of plant protection measures, development of high yielding fragrant varieties, fertilizer and soil management, adopting scientific post harvest technologies, processing and packaging. Flower and orchids can be used to produce perfumes and other cosmetic products, natural dyes and colour. These can be exerted to earn valuable foreign exchange. There is an immense potential for developing floriculture on a commercial basis here.

HORTICULTURE

Horticulture is one of the major economic activities of the people of Sikkim. The principal cash crops and commercial horticultural crops in the state of Sikkim are large cardamom, ginger, turmeric etc. in spices and oranges, lemon, guava, banana etc. are the principal fruits grown in the state. Sikkim is the largest producer of cardamom and also boasts to utilize largest area for its cultivation.

Horticultural production, including fruits, vegetables, potatoes, other tubers, cardamom, ginger and turmeric has increased by nearly six times between 1975-76 and 1995-96 as shown in table 15 below:

Table 15 : Horticultural Production (in Tonnes) from 1975-76 to 1995-96

Crops	1975-76	1980-81	1985-86	1990-91	1995-96
Fruits	4700	6350	8200	10500	12000
Vegetables	2000	3400	13900	15000	28000
Potato	5000	6646	16400	18000	24000
L. Cardamom	2300	3500	3900	2600	3600
Other Tubers	100	200	400	600	1000
Turmeric				90	100
Ginger	2000	3200	109000	16000	24000
Total	16100	23296	151800	62790	92700

Source: Lama (2001), p. 51

There is an immense scope for setting up of package programmes to increase per unit area yield through the use of better varieties, judicious use of fertilizers, soil correctives, adequate plant protection measures, adoption of scientific post harvest technologies etc. Fruits have the potential of industrial extraction of juice, making of concentrates, powder etc. and exports. Spices can also be used as industrial raw materials to produce concentrates value added products such as spice oils, oleoresins etc. can also be exported.

Sikkim is a suitable place for the extension of acreage under oranges with its favourable topography and climate. But due to overage of major part of the orange orchards and low rate of re-plantation, production is said to be falling rapidly and there is an urgent need for necessary policy intervention (Lama, 2001).

Proper marketing is absolutely essential for the promotion of horticulture. This is weak in Sikkim. Transport costs are high. Information on markets and farmers' access to markets is limited. Wide dispersal and small quantity of production of individual producers do not allow farmers to realize economies of scale in marketing. If marketing infrastructure is strengthened, then Sikkim has tremendous potential for the development of horticulture and floriculture.

ANIMAL HUSBANDRY AND DAIRY

The congenial temperate climate and its vegetation existing in the Himalayas are highly favourable for exotic high breed livestock. Moreover, the highlanders like *Lachungpas*, *Lachenpas*, *Gurungs* and *Sherpas* have a traditional pastoral economy which has been handed over from generation to generation with their typical kinds of livestock such as yaks, sheep, mountain goats, pigs and poultry.

In a predominantly rural economy like Sikkim, animal husbandry forms an extremely important component in an attempt to bring about substantial improvements in living standards. The overall area available for agricultural operation is limited to about 15% of the geographical area of the state. With the increasing population, per capita land availability has been consistently declining. It is, therefore, essential that supplementary sources of income should be developed in order to provide not only the much needed support to the rural families but also to make available in increasing quantity of protein rich items such as milk, egg and meat and organic manure for crop production.

The present rural livelihood system is said to be well balanced from ecological point of view. However, with the increase in population and the limited availability of land there is already great pressure on the cultivable land and forest on the environment as well. Many farmers are complaining about the change in environment and decline in soil fertility. In such a situation livestock farming which requires minimal use of land, labour and capital would be an ideal sustainable model for development. Moreover, since almost 70% of the farmers rear their livestock under stall fed condition, it has drastically reduced pressure on land due to overgrazing. The grass and legumes planted on topsoil not only provide nutrition but also protect the land from erosion and add nitrogen to the soil.

Therefore, there are good prospects for setting up dairy and animal husbandry units on a commercial basis. Milk production offers opportunities for developing processed food products like cheese, butter etc. The population being predominantly non-vegetarian, meat processing and packaging units offer promise in the state.

For the promotion of animal husbandry and dairy the Department of Animal Husbandry and Veterinary Services has already taken certain measures. The overall efforts are a combination of providing necessary infrastructure for animal health through a network of veterinary Hospital, Veterinary Dispensaries and stockman centres. Side by side, the up-gradation of indigenous live stock breed with the exotic breed to increase their production and productivity was taken up. The introduction of genetically superior poultry birds, pigs, angora rabbits and other livestock has been initiated. Necessary facilities have been provided for training the progressive farmers and overall support required for marketing facilities for livestock products especially milk and meat. The measures are expected to yield good results in the near future.

From the above delineation of agro-horticultural resource base of the state economy, it appears that there is a wide scope of setting up and development of agro and food-processing industries in Sikkim including fruits, spices and vegetables processing and thereby making substantial value addition to the forest and agro-horticultural products. This would provide supplementary sources of income and employment to the population.

INDUSTRIAL POLICY 1996

Before laying down a policy agenda for Sikkim for its industrial development at the desired rate and level we may have a quick look at the latest industrial policy of Sikkim which has been effective since April 1996. The central objectives of this policy, it may be noted, were speedy industrial development and generation of adequate employment opportunities through self-employment.

The policy envisaged the following objectives:

i) Creation of an atmosphere conducive to industrial growth, taking into consideration the available natural resources and the local socio-economic environment.
ii) Maintenance of the Green State image while promoting industrial activities.
iii) Rehabilitation of sick industries with comprehensive assistance and guidance from the Department of Industry and privatization of select State Public Sector Undertakings.
iv) Enrichment of the agriculture sector through the establishment of appropriate linkage between agriculture and agro-based industries.
v) Ensuring balanced regional development through promotion of *khadi*, village, cottage, tiny, small and ancillary industries.
vi) Promotion of traditional handloom, handicrafts and artisan sector by providing adequate support in the form of common facilities like service centers, cheap raw materials, technical inputs, marketing networks, skill development etc.
vii) Development of tourism as an industry.
viii) Development of Sikkim as a major centre for manufacture and marketing of tea.
ix) Productive participation of all concerned Government agencies to facilitate industrial growth.
x) Rapid development of basic infrastructure so that industrial growth is facilitated.
xi) Encouraging self-employment and identification of avenues for the same.
xii) Human resource development through appropriate skill and entrepreneurship development programmes, behavioral training etc. at district, subdivision and block levels, to meet the emergent skill requirements of the state within a stipulated time frame.
xiii) Encouraging joint ventures between local entrepreneurs and industrialists from outside the state.

xiv) Simplification of procedures and opening up of Sikkim with a view to attract both internal and external investors with respect to projects whose long-term viability is carefully evaluated.

The 1996 industrial policy has provided some concessions and incentives, to attract investors (Government of Sikkim, 1996). Some of the incentives are:

i) Provision of state capital investment subsidy: This is provided on a graded level. It depends on the scales of operation, to both new and old units carrying out modernization and expansion activities. For the thrust areas, investment varies from 10-20 per cent and for the non-thrust areas from 5-15 percent of total capital investment in plant and machinery.

ii) Provision of interest subsidy on working capital: This is provided for five years for interest in excess of 14 percent of the interest payable by industrial units on the working capital loan obtained from banks. Depending on the scale of operation, the amount varies from Rs. 15,000 to Rs. 1,10,000 or actual difference in interest whichever is less in thrust areas and Rs. 10,000 to Rs. 100,000 in non-thrust areas.

iii) Exemption from State and Central Sales Tax: This is provided for 7 years from the date of actual commercial production.

iv) Price preference: This is 10-15 percent over the rates quoted on same quality of product from outside Sikkim to industrial undertakings established in Sikkim on the purchase made by various State Government departments and organizations.

v) Provision of subsidy on captive power generating sets: This is provided to the thrust area industries to the extent of 30 percent (maximum Rs. 1,25,000) and 25 percent (maximum Rs. 1,00,000).

vi) Subsidy on power consumption: This is provided to the extent of total reimbursement of the first Rs. 50,000 power consumption per annum of the unit and then on *pro-rata* basis. The thrust area industries receive a subsidy of 30 percent in power tariff.

But it has been observed that there has not been any visible impact of these provisions on the industrial proposals and actual setting up of industries (Lama, 2001). The reasons have been identified to be as follows:

i) Severe budgetary constraints have made it difficult to implement the incentives meaningfully.

ii) Many key departments are not actually complying with the provisions of this scheme thereby making the newer approaches redundant.

iii) The entrepreneurs from outside the state find it very difficult to furnish documents like domicile residential certificates.

iv) Land laws do not permit alienation of land to outsiders.

v) The inadequacy and delay in getting working capital, many a times leading to the closure of the units and increase in non-performing assets.

vi) Poor social and industrial infrastructure, especially power.

vii) Lack of a mechanism within the Government to monitor and evaluate the implementation of policies. As a result, most of the incentives have remained on paper.

POLICY AGENDA

On the basis of the analysis of the current status and prospects of industrial development in Sikkim with its resource base and pronouncements laid down in the Industrial Policy, 1996 and the experiences of its fall out in the subsequent years we may now outline the following broad policy agenda for industrial development in Sikkim.

1. **Revitalization of the agricultural sector:** Since agriculture is the livelihood of majority of the population, development and revitalization of this sector is absolutely necessary for an industrial take off of the state. Purchasing power of the people engaged in this sector can only be increased through modernization and development of this sector. Moreover, as Sikkim has a huge potential for development of agro-based industries like dairy, spices, medicinal products from plants and herbs, forest based industry etc., therefore, improvement of this sector should get priority. This is important for creating self-employment opportunities too.

2. **Identification of thrust areas and effective promotion of industries in these areas:** From our earlier discussion it follows that certain key areas are to be identified where there is a great potential for development. These thrust areas may be: a) agro-processing industries including fruit, vegetable and spice processing, b) animal husbandry and dairy products, c) minor forest based products, d) handloom, handicrafts and village industries, e) tourism, f) precision oriented, high value, low volume products and g) hydroelectric power.

3. **Adoption of investor-friendly policy:** The policy for the investors has to be very clear and investor-friendly. To generate an entrepreneurial spirit and encourage investments in industry, there should be an attractive package of incentives and facilities, keeping in mind the increase in competition among different states. These incentives may be in addition to the already existing incentives provided by the central Government. By taking more market-friendly approach, by combining the virtues of both the public sector and the private sector, the State can be a great facilitator of economic development as exemplified by the experiences of the highly successful South-East Asian countries. Such a step has been all the more necessary in the context of present milieu of liberalization, privatization and globalization. Thus, it appears that Sikkim, like any other state of India, does have no other alternative but only to adopt more and more investor-friendly measures for rapid development of the state.

4) **Special promotional measures for rural and traditional industries:** Rural industries comprise enterprises owned by rural entrepreneurs in agriculture and semi-urban areas and are sub-sectors of small scale enterprises and micro enterprises. Special promotional measures ought to be undertaken by the state government to strengthen these sectors. For example, a yarn bank may be set up to provide woolen and cotton yarn to the weavers at a reasonable price, which will encourage self-employment among trained carpet weavers. There is a need for encouraging traditional cottage, handlooms, handicrafts and *khadi* industries from the point of view of generation of income and employment.

5) **Rehabilitation package for sick industries:** In Sikkim there are large number of sick industries. The Government should introduce specific schemes for their rehabilitation. After studying the viability of each unit it is to be decided whether the units should be run by the original promoters, new management, as joint ventures with the Government or shut down.

6) **Revamping of public sector undertakings:** Since Sikkim is a state which has just embarked upon the journey of industrialization, it is expected that it will shoulder the responsibility of promoting this at least for some time in future. Therefore, the existing state public sector undertakings are to be revamped and revitalized by infusing additional funds if required and by all other possible ways. More central public sector undertakings are also to be set up in viable lines of production or service. However, the Government

should undertake business ventures only in the core sectors and keeping with the policies of the central Government, some of the public sector undertakings may be privatized.

7) **Improvement of industrial and social infrastruc-ture:** To attract new industrial units by industrialists from outside the state as well as non-resident Indians upgradation of industrial and social infrastructure is necessary. Gearing up of the commercial banks is required to make the much needed adequate and timely working capital available to the industrial units. Upgradation of Bagdogra airport as a national and international airport for both tourists and transportation of high value, low volume goods are necessary. There should be improvement of roads. A prospective investor should get all his requirements and information relating to setting up of any trade or business cleared through a single authority. The single window concept will facilitate expediting of all necessary clearances from various departments like Pollution Control Board, Power Department, Urban Development and Housing Department, Public Health Engineering Department etc. The land laws of Sikkim need to be relaxed in order to enable entrepreneurs to acquire land to set up industrial units.

8) **Development of marketing support systems**: The Government should create adequate marketing facilities for goods and services produced in the state. The activities of the existing marketing organizations like the State Trading Corporation of Sikkim and Sikkim Industrial Marketing Federation are to be strengthened. These organizations should also take up marketing of the hitherto neglected products.

9) **Development of appropriate training and education facilities:** For accelerating the rate of industrial development training in various technical fields through training institutes like ITI, Polytechniques etc. is crucial. Skill development is the key to the improvement of quality and productivity and the means to make avenues of employment available to the local people. Upgrading and modernization of the existing industrial training institutes and other training institutes is necessary. It is also necessary to open up new training centers to provide training as per the present and future requirements of the industries in the state. Setting up of engineering, medical and business management schools and colleges under private and semi/government management is required for the development of human resources which will in turn help the development of industries. The Government should introduce training programmes for peoples to develop skills in forestry, food processing, floriculture, horticulture and other fields.

We may conclude this paper with a note of optimism that Sikkim's trade possibilities are becoming brighter with the reopening of border trade with China. The trading route will be through the Nathu La Pass of Sikkim. In order to accelerate the pace of trade in this hilly state it is necessary to revamp and re-christen the State Industries Department and provide it with a wider array of responsibilities. The Government of Sikkim has already chosen the Department of Industries as the "Nodal Agency" for all trading activities with China through Nathu La route. The name of the "Industries Department" has been changed to the "Department of Industries and Commerce". Within a very short period of time the state government has been flooded with so many queries from potential investors and organizations that are interested in the opening of this route for trade with China.

Sikkim's trade prospects would depend heavily on the Central Government's attitude towards northeastern border management. Instead of looking at these borders as impregnable fences to restrict external influences and natural flow of trade, we should treat them as natural extensions of the Indian market.

REFERENCES

Agarwal, A.K. (1987): *Economic Problem and Planning in North East India*, Starling Publishers Pvt. Ltd., New Delhi.

Bardoloi, G and A.K. Neog (1986): *Economy of North Eastern India: A Statewise Analysis*, Vol.-I, LBS Publication, Guwahati.

Basnet, L.B. (1974): *Sikkim: A Short Political History*, S. Chand and Co., New Delhi.

Bhasin, M.K. and Veena Bhasin (1995): *Sikkim Himalayas: Ecology and Resource Development*, Ramala-Raj Enterprises, Delhi.

Bhattacharyya P.K. (1984): *Aspect of Cultural History of Sikkim: Studies in Coinage*, K.P. Bagchi & Company

Bhattacharyya, Sibnath (1980): *Rural Industrialisation in India (Its Nature and Problems)*, B.R. Publishing Corporation, Delhi.

Chand, M and Vinay Kumar Puri (1997): *Regional Planning in India*, Allied Publishers Ltd.

Coronation Souvenir Book Committee, Gangtok, Sikkim (1994): *Sikkim Coronation*, The Statesman Press.

Das, G. (1992) : "Structural Change in the Economy of Arunachal Pradesh", *Journal of North-East India Council for Social Science Research*, Vol. 16, No. 2 October.

Das, Gurudas (1995): *Tribes of Arunachal Pradesh in Transition*, Vikas Publishing House Pvt. Ltd., New Delhi.

Dasgupta, Manas (1992): *Sikkim: Problem and Prospects of Development*, Indus Publishing Co., New Delhi.

Datta, Amal (1991) : *Sikkim Since Independence*, Mittal Publications, New Delhi.

Deb, Sharmila (2000): *Role of Infrastructure in the Developmental Process in Sikkim*, M.Phil thesis submitted to the Centre for Himalayan Studies, University of North Bengal.

Debnath, J.C. (1974): *Development of the Sikkimese Economy Under Planning*, Ph.D. Thesis (unpublished) submitted to the Calcutta University.

Debnath, Subrata (1998): *Human Development in Sikkim: An Evolution*, Ph.D. thesis submitted to the Centre for Himalayan Studies, University of North Bengal.

Desai, Vasant (1983), *Problems and Prospects of Small-scale Industries in India*, Himalayan Publishing House, Bombay

Dhamala, R.R. (1998): 'Panchayati Raj Institution in Sikkim - As an Instrument of Development' Paper presented at the *Seminar on Problems and Strategies of Development in the Eastern Himalayas*, March 18-19, at Centre for Himalayan Studies, University of North Bengal.

Dhamala, R.R. (ed.) (1993): *Problems and Strategies of Development in the Eastern Himalaya*, Gyan Publishing House, New Delhi.

Dhobal, G.L. (1987): *Development of Hill Areas*, Concept Publishing Company, New Delhi.

Ghosh, Bappa (1999): *Development of Roads and Transport of the Sikkim Himalayas with Particular Reference to Landslide Problem*, M.Phil thesis submitted to the Centre for Himalayan Studies, University of North Bengal.

Government of Sikkim (1983, 1985, 1987, 1989, 1995, 1997): *Sikkim at a Glance*, Bureau of Economics and Statistics, Gangtok.

——————— (1996):Industrial Policy of Sikkim, Department of Industries, *Sikkim Government Gazette*, No.GO/2/DI/96-97 dated 18.12.96.

Gupta, S.P. 91989): *Planning and Development in India*, Allied Publishers Private Ltd.

Lahiri, A.K., Saumen Chattopadhyay and Anuradha Bhasin (2001): *Sikkim: The People's Vision*, Government of Sikkim.

Lama, Mahendra, P. (2001): *Sikkim Human Development Report*, Government of Sikkim, Social Science Press, New Delhi.

Meir, G.M. and James E. Rauch (2000): *Leading Issues in Economic Development*, Oxford University Press.

Panda, S.C. (1996), *Entrepreneurship Development in Small-Scale Industries*, Anmol Publication Pvt. Ltd., New Delhi.

Patnaik, S.C. (1988): *Industrial Developments in a Backward Region: Dynamics of Policy*, Ashis Publishing House, New Delhi.

Raina, J.L. (ed.) (1992): *Himalayan Environment: Man and the Economic Activities*, Pointer Publishers, Jaipur.

Roy, S.C. (1990): *Himalayan Environment and Culture*, Indus Publishing Company, New Delhi.

Rustomji, N. (1987): *Sikkim : A Himalayan Tragedy*, Allied Publishers Pvt. Ltd.

Sen, A.K. (1960): *Choice of Techniques: An Aspectt of the Theory of Economic Development*, Basil Blackwell.

Sharma, S.K. & Usha Sharma (1998): *History, Geography and Travels of Sikkim and Bhutan*, Anmol Publications.

Shukla, S.R. (1976): *Sikkim: the Story of Integration*, S. Chanda & Co. (Pvt.) Ltd.

Sinha, N.K.P. and M.B. Singh (1993): *Perspectives on Industrial Development in India*, Rawat Publications, New Delhi.

Subba, T.B. (1989): 'Agrarian Social Structure and Change in Sikkim', *Social Change*, Vol. 19, No. 1

Suri, K.B. (ed.) (1988): *Small-Scale Enterprises in Industrial Development*, Sage Publication, New Delhi.

Tarafdar, A. (2002): *The Small Scale Industries in Sikkim: Problems and Prospects*, M.Phil Dissertation submitted to Centre for Himalayan Studies, University of North Bengal.

The Hindu (2002): *India Book of the Year 2002,* Encyclopaedia Britinnica (India) Pvt. Ltd. and The Handy

While, J.C. (1971): *Sikkim and Bhutan: Twenty-one Years On the North-East Frontier 1887-1908*, Vivek Publishing House.

8

Structural Change and Strategy of Development: Resource-Industry Linkages in Tripura

—K.S. Chakraborty

INTRODUCTION

The north-eastern region of our country is nature's veritable arcadia but its hilly terrain and certain complexities (relating to socio-culture life, traditional knowledge, technology, infrastructure etc.) have made it lag behind the other states of the country. The region has a combined potential of becoming the richest segments of the country yet it remains under-developed. Independence saw the north-east as a war ravaged, economically unstable, politically weak but ethnically potent area and ideal for development with a huge natural resource base but apathetic treatment by economic policy makers has been culpable for non-development. Being a geographical conglomerate of seven states of this region Tripura is no exception.

A tiny and hilly state Tripura, formerly a feudal state, physiographically represents the western fringe of the typical 'ridge and valley' province commonly known as Indo-Burma Ranges. Like the other north-eastern states, its topography too is undulating and characterised by numerous hillocks, plains, valleys, lungas, rivers, etc. other than the forest cover. About 83 percent of its population live in rural areas. The economy of the state is basically dominated by the primary sector. As far as industrialisation is concerned, the state is yet to emerge out of industrial backwardness. This is reflected by the fact that the Central Government has declared the entire state as 'A' category backward area for the purpose of giving central investment subsidy. The overall backwardness of the state is evident from the Composite Infrastructure Index evolved by the Centre for Monitoring Indian Economy (CMIE) based on the availability of power, irrigation, road, railways, post office, education, health and banking. As per the CMIE index, Tripura is the second most backward state in the country. Therefore, it is not an exaggeration to assume that the state requires a composite strategy for development.

The impetus for State planning was mostly contributed by rapid urbanisation and increasing regional disparities in rural, urban and industrial development (Agarwal 1988). Till date various studies have been made at both theoretical as well as empirical level, to understand and explain the problem of regional development. Economic growth does not take place at a nation-wide scale, specific State or Region provides a specific incubator function for specific new activities (Hoover and Vernon, 1959). A pertinent question here is the identification of favourable locational conditions that act as motivators of new activities. In this framework, a State or Region profile analysis may be useful and appropriate analytical tool in order to identify by means of strength-weakness analysis which state are favourable for stimulating the rise of promising enterprises, given the locational requirement of new firms. For example, the regional entrepreneurial vitality, the industrial diversity, the available infrastructure and so on. It is worthwhile to mention that the locational behavior of many enterprise exhibits a certain bias towards areas in which the entrepreneurs live, but new locations will only become a success if they are realised in favourable regions. Thus the successful State development policy is increasingly focusing attention on the revitalisation of indigenous regional resources which may trigger off the creation of new activities (Keeble and Wever,1986).

In this situation research studies to assess the development potential of a state is perhaps the most important task. This is particularly true in case of a predominantly rural state like Tripura.

The Present Study

Structure of an economy can be described mainly by the way of analysing a) changes in the sectoral composition of income b) changes in the occupational pattern. The other indicators of structural change are : (i) changes in the organisational structure (ii) urbanization and urban growth (iii) diversification of exportable items (iv) modernisation of industrial sector, and (v) reforms in agricultural sector.

In this backdrop, a study to formulate the strategy for development of Tripura by analysing structural changes in the economy of the state is proposed and planned. Thus the main object of the present study is to find out the gap if any, between the state's resource base and industrial base through the analysis of economic facts specially after independence and to suggest the strategy for further development. To achieve this objective the following component objectives are also analysed in the discourse :

i) Growth and development of agricultural resources.

ii) Growth and development of other resources of the state.

iii) Industrial growth of the state.

iv) Urbanisation and urban growth of the state, and

v) Infrastructure of the state.

Methodology and Data

Perhaps it requires no mention that the present discourse is an analytical work. Dealing with the above issues naturally entails a thorough study of the economy of the state, development of agriculture, resources of the state, economic policy, industrial policy, infrastructure of the state and so on.

Therefore, in the process of analysing the issues, basic statistics of the state are mainly collected from the Statistical Abstract (Government of Tripura publication) and Economic Review (Government of Tripura publication). Other Government publications, documents and notifications, administrative reports and, published and unpublished documents relating to the study, besides a number of text and reference books on the related topics are also consulted for observation. Data have also been collected from the various Government departments, organisations, and institutions. While discussing the trends, a period of 50 years, 1951-2001 is considered for discussion. But due to non-availability of data relating to any information the study deals only with the available data during the said period.

It may be stated here that the present study has been chalked out in a nutshell. Due to the limited scope of the work certain areas had to be left out in the course of discussion. Apart from that certain other limitations which were confronted during the study has been referred to as an when it was found necessary.

Structural Change in the Economy of Tripura

Each economic system has a complex internal structure and its performance can be assured by the mutual relationship between its different component parts (Banerjee and Mazumdar: 2001). Therefore, structural change in an economy highlights the changing pattern of economic activities in various parts of the economy. The present section discusses the structural change in the economy of Tripura.

State Domestic Product (SDP) is the sum total of goods and services produced by different sectors of a state during any particular year. The analysis of SDP data of Tripura highlights important structural changes during the period 1960-61 to 2000-01, such as increasing role of tertiary or secondary sector, etc. The share of different sectors in the SDP of Tripura during the period 1960-61 to 2000-2001 are shown in Table 1. The data reveal that the contribution of the primary sector was 62.72 percent in 1960-61, while the contributions of the secondary and tertiary sectors were only 5.71 percent and 31.57 percent respectively. The share of the primary sector in SDP were highest during the period 1960-61 to 1980-81. However, share of the primary sector has declined gradually over the plan periods specially after 1980-81. In 1990-91 the share of the primary sector in SDP declined to 43.21 percent. On the other hand, the contribution of the secondary sector reached to 6.98 percent, with variation over the years. But the interesting feature is that the contribution of tertiary sector has increased from 31.57 percent in 1960-61 to 49.81 percent in 1990-91. According to a quick estimate it is expected that the contribution of tertiary sector has further increased to 55.25 percent in 2000-2001. In 1998-99, the sector's contribution was 55.19 percent. The contribution of secondary sector over this period has increased to 13.93 percent in 2000-2001. And the contribution of primary sector has declined to 30.82 percent in 2000-01. Thus it appears that the economy of the state dominated by primary sector was continued till eighties and after that tertiary sector continues to dominate the SDP. In this connection it is, however, to be noted that "mining and quarrying" has been considered in secondary sector and "construction" has been included in service sector. Many economists opine that "mining and quarrying" should be treated as primary activities and "construction" as secondary activity.

Table 1 : Share of different sectors in the State Domestic Product of Tripura During 1960-61 to 2000-2001 (in percent)

Sector	1960-61	1970-71	1980-81	1990-91	2000-01(Q)
Primary Sector	62.72	70.02	60.22	43.21	30.82
Secondary Sector	05.71	07.01	08.55	06.98	13.93
Tertiary Sector	31.57	22.97	31.28	49.81	55.25
Total - (SDP)	100.00	100.00	100.00	100.00	100.00

Q = Quick Estimate.

Source :- Directorate of Economics & Statistics.

Note :- Share of all sectors in the above table have been expressed as a percent of SDP at factor cost (at 1960-61 price for 1960-61 to 1980-81 and other at 1993-94 prices).

Share of different sectors in the SDP of Tripura by industry of origin during the period 1960-61 to 1999-2000 are shown in Table 2. From the table and the detailed data gathered from the Directorate of Economics and Statistics, it reveals that in the primary sector, agriculture alone contributes nearly 85-95 percent of the total contribution of the primary sector to SDP. Others like forestry and logging, fishing, mining and quarrying etc. contribute the rest. It is noteworthy to mention that the contribution of mining and quarrying has increased from Rs. 987 lakhs in 1993-94 to Rs. 4779 lakh in 2000-01. The share of manufacturing has decreased from 5.71 percent in 1960-61 to 0.94 percent in 1999-2000. It implies that the decrease in the share of primary sector to total SDP is not compensated by an increase in the share of the secondary sector rather it is tertiary sector which has increased substantially. According to available data the share of electricity, gas, water supply etc. was negative due to heavy losses in the public sector units. But the contribution of construction sector has increased significantly. Thus the contribution of sector consisting of construction, electricity, gas, water supply etc. has increased from 4.28 percent in 1970-71 to 12.29 percent in 1999-2000. The share of transport, storage, communication, trade, hotel, banking etc. has increased from 17.51 percent in 1960-61 to 25.91 percent in 1999-2000. This depicts a lopsided economy heavily dependent on service providing activities. The share of public administration has also increased remarkably from 7.61 percent to 15.55 percent during the period.

It is needless to mention that a corresponding change in the occupational classification of the work force is expected. Data on occupational classification of the population are not maintained and published annually. These are available only at decennial intervals through census data. Therefore the census data of 1951,1961, 1971,1981 and 1991 on occupational structure are considered for the analysis. However the occupational data of these censuses are not comparable in their original form. Because the occupational categories and their definitions have undergone changes from one census to another. The 1951 census did not distinguish between working and non-working population. It classified livelihood category as agricultural and non- agricultural class. The 1961 census classified the population into two broad categories of workers and non-workers. The 1971 census concentrated only on the main activity of the person enumerated. Hence the census data left out a large number of workers, mostly the female population who were employed in agricultural work or some house-hold economic activity.

Table 2 : Share of different sectors in the State Domestic Product of Tripura by Industry of Origin

(Rs. In Lakhs).

Sector	1960-61	1970-71	1980-81	1987-88	1993-94	1998-99	1999-00
1. Agricultural &	1780	2614	3659	4524	61555	75218	77709
Allied sectors.	(62.72)	(70.02)	(60.22)	(52.22)	(38.01)	(32.24)	(31.52)
2. Manufacturing	162	102	231	332	5289	2479	2324
	(5.71)	(2.73)	(3.80)	(3.82)	(3.27)	(1.06)	(0.94)
3. Construction	--	160	286	92	7976	26829	30302
Electricity, Gas,							
& Water Supply							
4. Transport,	497	499	923	1788	41918	60419	63871
Storage,	(17.51)	(13.36)	(15.20)	(20.60)	(25.89)	(25.90)	(25.91)
communication,							
Trade, Hotel							
5. Public	216	152	543	817	20854	35763	38355
Administration	(7.61)	(4.07)	(8.94)	(9.41)	(12.88)	(15.33)	(15.55)
6. Other service	183	207	434	1119	24335	32566	33990
	(6.45)	(5.54)	(7.14)	(12.89)	(15.03)	(13.96)	(13.79)
Total	2838	3734	6076	8682	161927	233274	246531
	(100)	(100)	(100)	(100)	(100)	(100)	(100)

1) 1999-2000 data are provisional.
2) Percentage in bracket.
3) Share of all sectors have been expressed as a percent of SDP at factor cost (at 1960-61 prices for 1960-61 to 1980-81 and at 1993-94 prices for 1993-94 to 1999-2000).
Source - Directorate of Economics & Statistics, Govt. of Tripura.

This made the figure of workers not comparable with either the 1961 or the 1951 data. Both the census 1981 and 1991 distinguish between main workers, marginal worker, non-workers. Moreover these census classified the main workers into four simple categories. Thus these two census are comparable. Changes in the occupational structure of the state are shown in Tables 3, 4, and 5. Table 3 shows the livelihood categories of Tripura's population according to the census of 1951. Table 4 depicts the occupational classification of total population according to 1961, 1971, 1981 and 1991. Occupational classification of Tribals in Tripura are shown in Table 5 during the above mentioned census years.

Table 3 : Livelihood Categories of Tripura's Population (1951 Census)

Livelihood Category	Population	Percent
I. Agricultural Class.	486,881	75.4
(a) Cultivators of land wholly or mainly owned and their dependents.	384.147	59.5
(b) Cultivators of land wholly or mainly unowned and their dependents.	57.930	9.0
(c) Cultivating labourers and their dependents.		
(d) Non-cultivating owners of land, agricultural	31,886	4.9
rent- receivers and their dependents.	12,918	2.0
II. Non-Agricultural Class -	158,826	24.6
(a) Production other than Cultivation.	38,395	5.9
(b) Commerce	40,838	6.4
(c) Transport	3,314	0.5
(d) Other Services and misc. resources.	76,279	11.8
	645,707	100

Source - NCAER (1961), Techno-Economics Summary of Tripura, New Delhi, P-120.

During the 1951 census (Table 3), it is seen that the agricultural class comprised the lions share of the occupational categories i.e. 75.4 percent. Of these, those owning the land was 59.5 percent and only 9 percent did not own any land, 4.9 percent were cultivating labourers and only 2 percent were rent receivers or non-cultivating owner of land. The rest of the population (24.6 percent) were engaged in non-agricultural jobs like commerce 6.4%, production 5.9%, transport 0.5% and other services (11.8%).

The census of 1961-1991 (Table 4) shows that cultivation, as a means of livelihood kept on declining even as population increased. It was 64.24 percent in 1961 and though the numbers increased, the percentage decreased to 38.09 percent in 1991. While the agricultural labourers have increased from 7.53 percent in 1961 to 24 percent 1981 with a slight fall to 23.38 percent in 1991. Those engaged in livestock, fishing etc., did not show any worthy change. Even the share of production other than cultivation (household or others) have declined from 8.23 percent in 1961 to 4.9 percent in 1991. Trade and commerce have taken up another small space in the occupational structure. While total number of workers have doubled within the 4 decades (4,37,229 to 8,02,063) the non-workers have gone up by 2.5 times more i.e. 7,04,776 to 18,98,688.

Table 4 : Occupational Classification of Total Population of Tripura.

No. of Persons.

Occupation	1961	1971	1981	1991
1. Cultivation.	2,80,881	2,35,252	2,63,427	3,05,523
	(64.24)	(54.41)	(43.28)	(38.09)
2. Agricultural labourer.	32,912	86,340	1,46,089	1,87,538
	(7.53)	(19.96)	(24.00)	(23.38)
3. Livestock, fishing, Forestry,	12,193	9,570	16,563	18,591
Hunting and Plantation etc.	(2.79)	(2.21)	(2.72)	(2.32)
4. Mining	*	*	1,082	2,236
			(0.18)	(0.29)
5. Manufacturing, Processing,	35,992	15,229	33,192	39,327
Repairing etc. (Both household and other than household)	(8.23)	(3.52)	(5.45)	(4.90)
6. Construction	4,100	3,138	11,892	11,752
	(0.94)	(0.73)	(1.95)	(1.47)
7. Trade & commerce	18,521	24,437	37,796	61,621
	(4.24)	(5.65)	(6.21)	(7.68)
8. Transport, Storage &	4,779	6,194	13,137	22,193
Communication	(1.09)	(1.43)	(2.16)	(2.77)
9. Other services.	47,851	52,263	85,411	1,52,892
	(10.94)	(12.08)	(14.03)	(19.06)
A. Total Workers.	4,37,229	4,32,463	6,08,463	8,02,063
	(100)	(100)	(100)	(100)
B. Marginal workers.	...	...	53,860	56,454
C. Non-workers	7,04,776	11,23,889	13,90,609	18,98,688
Total Populaton (A+B+C)	11,42,005	15,56,342	20,53,038	27,57,205

Source - Census Reports, Govt. of India.
• Includes in item no.3 under heading livestock, finishing etc.

Even if we limit our scanning of occupational structure to tribal population of the state the picture is not quite promising (Table 5). 85.68 percent of the tribal people took up cultivation in 1961 which declined to 57.34 percent in 1991 while agricultural labourers increased about 5 times during the decades, 5.04 percent in 1961 to 29.92 percent in 1981. Even those engaged in livestock. fishing, etc. is increasing though marginally. Construction, trade and commerce, transport etc. too have quite a few tribal workers. It needs to be mentioned here that though the total workers have increased since 1961 sizeably, the non-workers have out numbered this category.

A brief analysis of the Tables 3, 4 and 5 reveals that though Tripura is primarily an agricultural state, the occupational structure has become varied with too much pressure on land. Although cultivation is still the mainstay but land has other utilisation too in this tiny border state with the population bursting at the seams. It may be noted that as cultivators decline, agricultural labourers shoot up. If there were industries, such uneconomic labour force could have been engaged but with a weak infrastructure that probability is ruled out. Trade and commerce, transport could have absorbed a sizeable population of this category but being a border state, almost landlocked, except for that narrow strip through Assam, trade does not get due importance. Hence this explains the huge and rising number of non-workers over the decades.

Table 5 : Occupational Classification of Tribal Population of Tripura.

	No. of Persons.			
Year Occupation	1961	1971	1981	1991
1. Cultivation.	80,000 (85.68)	1,07,122 (75.37)	1,35,151 (64.04)	1,57,825 (57.34)
2. Agricultural labourer.	4,710 (5.04)	28,626 (20.14)	60,616 (28.72)	82,343 (29.92)
3. Livestock, fishing, Forestry, Hunting and Plantation etc.	147 (0.16)	1,749 (1.23)	3,197 (1.51)	5,106 (1.86)
4. Mining	--	--	92 (0.04)	467 (0.17)
5. Manufacturing, Processing, Repairing etc.	(0.21)	(0.40)	(1.09)	(1.09)
6. Construction	62 (0.07)	46 (0.03)	483 (0.23)	533 (0.19)
7. Trade & commerce	224 (0.24)	261 (0.18)	721 (0.34)	2,134 (0.78)
8. Transport, Storage & Communication	--	215 (0.15)	443 (0.21)	1,134 (0.41)
9. Other services.	2,397 (2.57)	3,538 (2.49)	8,054 (3.82)	22,702 (8.25)
10. Household Industry	5,628 (6.03)	--	--	--
A. Total Workers	93,366 (100)	1,42,134 (100)	2,11,055 (100)	2,75,252 (100)
Total Population (A+B+C).	3,60,070	4,50,544	5,83,920	5,47,809

Source - Census Reports, Govt. of India.

Includes in item no.3 under heading livestock, finishing etc.

It is noted earlier that the contribution of primary sector to SDP of Tripura has declined to a noticeable extent and the contribution of tertiary sector has been increased on the other hand. But in spite of a continuous decline in the contribution of primary sector, the occupational structure has not changed to that extent. Thus the main feature of the structural change is the failure of the occupational structure to coincide with the sectoral changes in SDP. The maximum portion of the working people still depend on the primary activities for their livelihood. In 1961 about 74.56 percent of the work-force were engaged in the primary sector consisting of agriculture, forestry, fishery etc. Although this figure declined to 64.08 percent in 1991, this sector still houses the largest portion of the work force in the state. While the primary sector contributed 62.72 percent of SDP in 1960-61 and only 43.21 percent in 1990-91. So it can be concluded that although a greater portion of the work force in the state engaged in primary sector , its contribution to SDP has declined significantly and does not coincide with each other. The aspect of structural change showing a substantial decline of primary sector in SDP, no doubt, is the sign of development. But the other aspect, i.e., decline of work force in primary sector has not been to the expected proportion. This is because of failure of other sectors to absorb not only the growing number of workforce from new entrants but also to divert a substantial portion of work force from primary sectors. Another significant feature within the occupational pattern in primary sector is that increasing number of agricultural labourers in the state. It was 7.53 percent in 1961 and increased to 23.38 percent in 1991. This implies the growing problem of landlessness of the rural people of Tripura. (Bhattacharjee, P.R. 1993,p.86).

As regards structural change in the distribution of SDP between commodity and non-commodity, it is observed that the non-commodity has been growing much than the commodity sector. The changing share of the modern sector in SDP is also one of the indicators of structural change in the state economy. This can be perceived by the increasing role of trade, transport, communication, etc. in the economy. The share of transport, storage, communication, hotel, trade etc. has increased from 17.51 percent in 1960-61 to 25.91 percent in 1999-2000.

It is observed that the tertiary sector in Tripura has developed before the development of the secondary sector. With the expansion of transport, trade & commerce, the contribution of the tertiary sector has also been increasing in the state. However increase in this sector may not be taken as an indicator of growth in real output of the State.

State Plans

Table 6 reveals an outstanding fact at the very first glance, there is a giant leap forward between the First and the Second plan so far as Planned investment is concerned. Tripura had not attained statehood in the First Plan Period, hence the total plan outlay was Rs.197.86 crores with transport and communication getting the maximum benefit: 37.40 percent followed by social and community welfare: 34.16 percent, cooperation got only 14.30 percent while agriculture was allotted only 8.46 percent. Second Plan (1956-61) allotted Rs.896.10 crores of which infrastructure building took up quite a sizeable amount, road network was completed by the 2nd Plan period hence further investment needed for transport and communication (40.45). As can be seen from Table 6, social and community services also received priority during the entire Plan Period hovering around 34-35 percent. Due emphasis was given to refugee rehabilitation programme, tribal welfare, jhumia settlements. Education and medical services also required much. However, agriculture, power and irrigation were not among top priorities during the first and second plans. Tribal economy basically was jhum based which had already started posing ecological problems as well as low productivity and sustaining capacity. Wet-rice cultivation was just gaining grounds without the advent of the immigrants from East Pakistan, there was ample scope for increasing agricultural production.

The Third Plan also showed similar variations, except for the fact that spending on transport & communication was lowered (27.52percent) perhaps because the road network was completed by the end of 2nd Plan period. Agriculture received a spurt this time, the allotted sum was 22.45 percent of the total outlay. Social service (37.97 percent) too increased while economic (1.13) and general services (0.24) were gaining a foothold in sum allocation. However, power and irrigation, industries & mineral still lagged behind 4.23percent and 4.62 percent respectively. After the Third Plan, the Fourth five year Plan could not be started. Thus three annual plans were formulated by the Govt. of India- 1966-67, 1967-68, 1968-69 aiming at bridging the gap in the planning process. In Tripura's case it was found that a huge amount of outlay was made in the Fourth Plan (1969-74) i.e. Rs 35.41crores and this further increased manifold henceforth. In the Fourth Plan, a rise in the allotment was seen in the power & irrigation sector (28.86 percent) at least a six times increase since the Third Plan. Agriculture allotment was reduced (18.19 percent) while the same happened in transport & communication though marginally.

Table 6 : Sector-wise plan expenditure in Tripura. (in percent) (1st, 2nd, 3rd, 4th, 5th & 6th plan)

Name of the Sector	First Plan (1951-56)	Second Plan (1956-61)	Third Plan (1961-66)	Fourth Plan (1969-74)	Fifth Plan (1974-78)	Sixth Plan (1980-85)
1. Agriculture & Allied Servicing	8.46	14.51	22.45	18.19	24.12	24.89
2. Co-operation	14.30	1.78	1.86	1.38	1.59	1.98
3. Irrigation power	2.70	3.76	4.23	28.86	30.45	24.68
4. Industries & Minerals	2.98	4.76	4.62	1.83	6.99	4.12
5. Transport & Communication	37.40	40.45	27.52	24.43	14.18	12.73
6. Social Community	34.16	34.70	37.94	24.74	22.32	30.31
7. Economic Service	--	0.04	1.13	0.07	0.17	0.15
8. General Service	--	--	0.24	0.50	0.18	1.14

Source: Directorate of Economics & Statistics, Govt. of Tripura

During the Fifth Plan the most outstanding fact was that more than 30 percent of plan expenditure was made on power & irrigation. It should also be mentioned that agriculture too received 24.12 percent of the total expenditure as well as industries and minerals received 6.99 percent. A jute mill, a sugar mill, paper and pulp mill were set up, this is an achievement undoubtedly as only 1.83 percent was laid aside during the last plan. Transport and communication could not boast of huge fund allocation (14.18) as all essential construction of roads, bridges were completed except for railways and telecommunications. Social & community services still received high priority in the matter of fund allocation (22.34 percent).

Once again 2 years of Rolling plan (1978-80) had to be initiated. The allocation pattern of Plan fund during the Sixth Plan period showed another giant leap in terms of total outlay, Rs 292.71 crores. Expenditure went up enormously, but the allocation procedure almost resembled the Fifth Plan.

In the Seventh Plan (1985-90) there was a total re structuring of the heads of development. Economic services meant agriculture and allied services, rural development, special programmes, industry etc., as shown in Table 7. Under social services were categorised education, sports, medical, welfare etc. Rest came under general services. Agriculture got the top priority in the Seventh Plan, 16.35 percent, followed by energy, 11.63 percent, while transport received 11.08 percent. Irrigation & flood control received 8.37 percent while social service still maintained a high of 31.34 percent. The heads, which got due importance during the Seventh Plan, was rural development sector (7.16 percent) and Special Area Programme (7.45 percent). These catered to the Tripura Tribal Areas Autonomous District Council linked to tribal areas development. It is also remarkable that opening of schools, medical facilities received priority during this plan period as well as provision of basic civic amenities (housing, water supply) so necessary for the growing urbanisation. The Eighth Plan once again showed similar characteristics of plan expenditure. The heads, which were stressed upon, were similar to the last plan. However transport sector dwindled in its fund allocation structure from 11.08 to 9.29 percent. A new need was added perhaps to cope up with environmental pollution that is forestry and wild life where 2.30 percent of plan expenditure was allocated. The Ninth Plan, however, shows varied changes, agriculture allotment reduced to below half, i.e. 6.53 percent, while rural development gained immensely, 13.84 percent. Irrigation and flood control received higher allocation, 7.53 percent while transport once again received more funds, 14.25 percent. Significantly, expenditure allocated for energy purpose dwindled to 6.80 percent and even industry and mineral allocation (3.08 percent) social service continued to get higher allocation i.e. 40 percent of the total outlay, forestry fund was almost halved i.e. 1.06 percent.

Table 7 : Sector-wise plan expenditure in Tripura (7th, 8th & 9th plan)

(in percentage of total expenditure)

Name of Sector	Seventh plan	Eighth plan	Nineth plan
A. Economic Service -			
1. Agriculture & Allied Activities	16.35	18.00	6.53
2. Rural Development	7.16	6.52	13.84
3. Special area programme	7.45	8.00	5.44
4. Irrigation & Flood Control	8.37	6.63	7.53
5. Energy	11.63	10.73	6.80
6. Industry & Mineral	4.63	5.72	3.08
7. Transport	11.08	9.29	14.25
8. Communication	0.00	0.00	0.04
9. Science, Tech. & Env.	0.46	0.31	0.12
10. Gen. Economic Service	0.43	0.63	0.47
B. Social Service	31.34	30.97	40.00
C. General Service.	1.36	0.87	0.93
D. Forestry & Wild life.	--	2.30	1.06
	100	100	100

Source: Directorate of Economics & Statistics, Govt. of Tripura

The analysis of plan expenditure gives both qualitative and quantitative aspects during plan period. Obviously Tripura witnessed a spurt in the economic activities with the government stressing upon infrastructure requirement. Quite a lump sum was later allocated for development and modernisation of agriculture as also industrial base, it is another story that this dream could not be realised owing to other reasons. Throughout the period the government's concern with social and community services (education, medical facilities, welfare of the weaker sections etc.) was predominant.

So far as the growth of SDP is concerned it has risen from Rs 28.38 lakhs in 1960-61 to Rs 86.82 lakhs in 1987-88 at constant price (1960-61). The per capita income during the same period has also increased from Rs 248.53 to Rs. 321.56. At constant price of 1980-81 the SDP has grown from Rs 26261 lakhs in 1980-81 to Rs 48969 lakhs in 1992-93.The per capita income during this period has also increased from Rs. 1297 to Rs. 1713. Excessive population growth owing to mass scale immigration in the state is one of the main reasons for low rate of growth in per capita income. However the SDP at constant price (1993-94) has increased from Rs. 161927 lakhs in 1993-94 to Rs. 246531 lakhs in 1999-2000 and Rs. 260739 in 2000-01 (quick estimate). On the other hand per capita income during this period has increased from Rs. 5350 to Rs.6604 and Rs. 6813 respectively.

To accelerate the development of the scheduled tribes in Tripura, a special strategy was adopted from the Fifth Five Year Plan. This is known as 'Tribal Sub-Plan' (TSP). TSP strategy is a mechanism under which each development departments of the State Government is required to qualify and set aside an amount of their plan budget provision for implementation of schemes exclusively for the welfare of schedule tribes. Such fund should not be less than the percentage of schedule tribe population in the state. According to an estimate an amount of Rs. 14716.71 lakhs was spent on TSP in the year 2000-01.

Similarly the Special Component Plan (SCP) strategy for the welfare of schedule castes was introduced during the Sixth Plan period. It is a mechanism under which various State Government departments are required to quantify and set aside an amount of their own plan budget provision for various welfare activities of the schedule caste population in the state. The quantified amount should not be less than the percentage of schedule caste population in the state. To implement the programme under SCP, the state government has identified 298 gram panchayet villages having SC concentration. The SCP outlay for the year 2000-01 was Rs. 66.10 crores as against a total state plan outlay of Rs. 4815 cores. This is 13.62 percent of the total state plan outlay and 20.69 percent of the divisible state plan outlay.

Resource Base of Tripura

The Encyclopedia of Social Sciences defines 'Resources' as 'those aspects of man's environment that render possible or facilitate the satisfaction of human wants and the attainment of social objectives.' Hence, resource does not mean an object or substance but its functionality. Anything. which has an utility and functionality can be considered as resource. The changing concept of resource is that resources have not been created naturally but human being with their wisdom, knowledge and technology have created the same. As man's intellect advances, resource too increases. Earlier, anything obtained from Mother Nature was thought to be a resource but now we know that something is not a resource until, there is a demand for it to satisfy man's need. Those that are not necessary for man, either to satisfy his hunger or ambition or even which he cannot utilise easily are not resources. We can say, mineral oil or gas are not resources by themselves - it is their functionality that makes them resources. The functionality of resources is dynamic and keeps on changing with development of science and technology.

A brief profile of a few important resources, both natural as well as cultural, of the state are taken up for discussion here. This section, however, deals only with agricultural resources, forest resources, mineral resources and human resources. Industrial resources of the state is dealt separately.

Agricultural Resources

The variation in the land utilisation pattern is an important indicator of change in the primary sector of an economy. Table 8 gives a comparative picture of proportions of land put under various uses in 1952-53, 1990-91 and 1999-2000. Forest land as can be seen from Table-8 constituted 59.73 percent of the total reported area in 1952-53 and 57.78 percent in 1990-91 as well as in 1999-2000. So it may be said a major portion of the total reported area in Tripura is categorised as forest and it also appears that much has not changed within a span of almost 50 years regarding this forest cover of the state. However, here forest is defined only in a legal way without actually referring to vegetative cover. It is noticeable that land not available for cultivation has increased from 2.28 percent in 1952- 53 to 12.65 in 1990-91 and 12.82 percent in 1999-2000. It is also significant that cultivable waste land, fallow and current fallow have also reduced to nominal figures. The net area sown through the period indicated a sharp increase from 18.45 percent in 1952-53 to 26.42 in 1990-91 and 26.59 percent in 1999-2000. This means there has been agricultural development taking place through the years and there is hardly any scope of bringing more areas under agricultural use.

Table 8 : Land utilisation pattern in Tripura **Area in '000 ha.**

Particulars of Land use	1952-53	1990-91	1999-2000
1. Foreset	636.83 (59.73)	606.168 (57.79)	606.168 (57.79)
2. Land not available for cultivation. (Non-agri. use + barren + uncultivable land)	24.29 (2.28)	132.700 (12.65)	134.500 (12.82)
3. Parmanent pastures and land under Mire, tree crop.	180.09 (16.89)	27.000 (2.57)	27.151 (2.59)
4. Cultivable waste land	10.93 (1.03)	0.660 (0.063)	0.600 (0.057)
5. Fallow land other then current fallow.	9.31 (0.87)	0.700 (0.067)	0.700 (0.067)
6. Current fallow	8.09 (0.75)	4.747 (0.45)	0.050 (0.100)
7. Net area sown.	196.68 (18.45)	277.200 (26.42)	279.000 (26.59)
Total	**1066.22**	**1049.169**	**1049.169**

Source: Directorate of Economics and Statistics, Govt. of Tripura

Among the production of the crops in Tripura, rice constitutes the main crop. It increased from 135 thousand matric tonnes in 1950-51 to 513.40 thousand matric tonnes in 2000 -2001. Increase is also evident in the production of pulses, oil seeds and very significantly in potato. However production of wheat, jute, and cotton crops shows a sharp downward trend though it had risen earlier. Rise in productivity is particularly spectacular in the case of potato 3.16 M.T. in 1950-51 to 104.8 M.T. in 2000-2001. (Statistical Abstract, Govt. of Tripura). It is also observed that area under rice production has increased noticeably from 158 thousand ha. in 1950-51 to 247.17 thousand ha. in 2000-01. The area under jute cultivation shows a general decline over the period. Area under pulses, oil seeds though has increased over the years these crops do not occupy any important place in the state's agriculture. Sugarcane production is suffering from stagnation while production of cotton has reduced to insignificance. An explanation can be sought for the decrease of important cash crops. During the pre - independence period cash crops like cotton and oilseeds produced under jhum cultivation in the hills played a very important role in the rural economy of Tripura. Now potato seems to take the place as both the area and the production of this crop have increased manifold.

About the yield of the main crops it can be said that there is an increase in crop intensity, yield per hectare and hence we can see a rise in the yield through the decades.

Table 9 : Requirement and Production of Foodgrains in Tripura.

(in '000 M.T.)

Year Food grains	Total requirement of Food grains	Total production of	Gap.
1950-51 (Pre-plan period)	145.38	135.00	(-) 10.38
1955-56 (End of 1st plan)	217.51	138.03	(-) 79.48
1960-61 (End of 2nd plan)	257.40	159.12	(-) 98.28
1965-66 (End of 3rd plan)	308.80	205.05	(-) 103.75
1973-74 (End of 4th plan)	385.66	364.04	(-) 21.62
1977-78 (End of 5th plan)	443.36	375.35	(-) 68.01
1984-85 (End of 6th plan)	522.96	379.38	(-) 143.58
1989-90 (End of 7th plan)	603.40	473.27	(-) 130.13
1996-97 (End of 8th plan)	723.53	674.37 (T)	(-) 49.16

T- proposed Target

Source : Development in Agriculture in Tripura, Dr. T.K.Paul in Tripura in the 21st century, Tripura State Council for Sciences and Technology, Agartala

Though primitive agriculture persists in some areas, a mild wave of modernisation has taken place overhauling the production of agricultural crops. It is worthwhile to state that in spite of application of modern technique, self sufficiency in foodgrains is still a far cry. It is evident from Table 9 that according to an estimate at the end of 8th plan period, the total production of foodgrains in Tripura was 49.16 thousand MT less than the requirement. This gap was 10.38 thousand MT in the year 1950.51.

The hilly terrains of the state delimit plough cultivation as well as cultivation of other field crops. These slopes are more suitable for horticulture and plantation crops. Pineapples and oranges are two traditional crops of Tripura that are gaining much commercial importance at present. Lichi, banana, lemon, mango etc. also have good prospects of development (Chakraborty: 2000). Horticulture was not paid much attention earlier and so commercial production of these fruits are yet to give better results, as they have the potentiality for that undoubtedly, the production of these crops has increased considerably over the decades yet it needs to be added that there is still ample scope for their expansion. Plantation crops, e.g. coconut, arecanut, cashewnut and rubber have taken a significant place in the economy of Tripura. Though not exploited optimally, crops like coconut and cashewnut surely have the potential to create a niche for themselves in the export market.

Rubber plantation was introduced to this state in the early sixties and the quality was found to be excellent, ranking almost as the premier brand in the country. This has led to the increase in areas under rubber plantation rapidly. The ecologically viable ones can act as an alternative to shifting cultivation and also generate a stable economic base for the poorer sections, both tribal and non-tribals. They can boost up the state's economic growth and offer excellent opportunity for expanding agro-industrial base of Tripura.

Tea plantation can be traced back to the 1930s although it has not been able to act as an impetus to the economic growth. The area has remained almost stagnant, rather there are cases of opening up of the gardens to other use, yield per hectare has increased only marginally hence, this plantation has not been able to play an important role in providing employment and relieving excessive pressure on agriculture. Perhaps lack of skilled enterprise, leadership, fluctuation in tea prices, increasing sickness of industries and inability of capturing the market are the reasons which have held back tea production. Though the data on tea plantation of the state show a considerable hike in terms of area, production and total employment - the figures are not encouraging as mainly the landless flock in to work in the gardens hence there is a continuous in-flow and out-flow of labourers.

Regarding the number of operational holdings of different size groups in the state (Table-10) it may be stated that the marginal holdings (i.e.below1.0 ha) has remained almost constant comprising the major portion of the holding showing around 67.7 and 69.5 percent of total holdings. These are increasing continuously throughout the period under study. However the area has not registered any conspicuous increase, rather it has decreased from 33.6 percent to 28.2 percent during 1985-86 and 1990-91. Even the small and semi-medium holdings, i.e., between 1 and 4 ha. is also increasing. However, it needs to be mentioned that though the small, marginal holdings (1-2 ha.) has increased abnormally 18.8 percent to 22.6 percent during 1970-71 and 1985-86, the semi-medium holdings (2-4 ha.) has remained almost constant i.e., 8.9 percent and 8.8 percent, respectively. Yet the medium holdings (4-10 ha) seemed to have decreased over the years i.e. from 6452 holdings in 1970-71 to 2803 in 1985-86 and rose only to 3571 in 1990-91. One is astonished to find that the large holdings i.e. above 10 ha. is also steadily declining from 625 to 137 during 1970-71 and 1985-86 and increased slightly in 1990-91, i.e., 166. Thus one can easily find

Table 10 : Number of operational holding of different size groups and area of holding in Tripura According to Agricultural Census report.

Category	1970-71 Number	1985-86 Area (Ha.)	1990-91 Number	Area (Ha.)	Number	Area (Ha.)
Marginal	1,73,790	70,170	211,302	106,835	216,826	87093
(below 1.0 ha.)	(69.5)	(27.6)	(67.7)	(33.6)	(68.1)	(28.2)
Small	47,049	66.167	70.442	1,14,127	69,217	106150
(2-4 ha)	(18.8)	(26.1)	(22.6)	(35.9)	(21.8)	(34.4)
Semi-medium	22,218	59.866	27,396	74.253	28,432	76597
(2-4 ha.)	(8.9)	(23.6)	(8.8)	(23.4)	(—)	(24.8)
Medium	6,452	35,667	2,803	14,253	3,571	18356
(4-10 ha.)	(2.6)	(14.0)	(0.9)	(4.5)	(8.9)	(6.00)
Large	625	22,207	137	8,128	166	20180
(10 ha.and above	(0.2)	(8.7)	(Neg.)	(2.6)	(Neg)	(6.50)
	250,134	**254,077**	**312,080**	**317,596**	**318.212**	**308.376**
	(100)	**(100)**	**(100)**	**(100)**	**(100)**	**(100)**

* Neg. = Negligible
Source: Agricultural Census - 1970-71,1985-86, 1990-91, Govt. of Tripura.

the abysmal nature of uneconomic holdings in the state which act as a great hindrance to the agricultural development of the state. Tripura is a land of small and marginal farmers. The proportion of marginal holdings has not changed much but the semi-medium and medium holdings have fallen drastically and that of the large holdings have become negligible. The growing fragmentation of holdings prove that legislative or administrative steps, alternative non-agricultural employment and increase of crop intensity are required to remove poverty. Tiny holdings are bound to be uneconomical and cannot be put to proper use.

Forest resources

Almost 2/3 of Tripura was densely covered with forests in the yesteryears. With population pressure this forest cover has been subjected to unending destruction. The jhum cultivation too has taken its toll on the forests. The forests were 'opened up' to create rehabilitation area for the jhumias as well as refugees from erstwhile East Pakistan. This is reflected in the downward trend of the total value of out-turn of forest products during the 60s (Table-11). However after that it started increasing gradually and during 1990-91 it shot up to a huge sum Rs.453.39 lakhs. This may be attributed to aforestation programs and regenera-tion of forest.

Table 11 : Out Turn Forest Producers in Tripura

Year	Major Produce	Minor Produce	Total
1956-57	68.38	25.76	94.14
1960-61	138.63	8.97	147.60
1970-71	18.71	4.04	22.75
1980-81	95.03	38.11	133.14
1990-91	453.39	19.74	473.13
2000-01	55.37	82.28	137.65

As is evident from Table-11 that total value of the forest products rose to a considerable sum during 1956-57 and 1960-61 i.e. Rs.94.14 lakh to Rs. 147.60 lakhs. The major contributors were timber, plumb wood and match wood, round wood and firewood, which are categorised under major forest produce (from Rs. 68.38 to Rs. 138.63 lakhs). While the values of minor forest produce i.e. bamboo and cane, fodder, tonning etc. actually fell from Rs.25.76 lakh to Rs.8.97 lakhs during the same period. However, interestingly in the later years i.e. 1960-61 and 1970-71 there was a dismal drop in the value of Major produces from Rs. 138.63 lakhs to Rs.18.71 lakhs. And though it rose gradually to Rs. 453.39 lakhs during 1990-91 in 2000-01 the value of the produces dwindled to Rs. 55.37 lakhs. Interestingly, during 1990-91 and 2000-01 the value of minor produces showed a mighty upward trend i.e. from Rs.19.74 lakhs to Rs.82.28 lakhs totaling upto Rs. 137.65 lakhs where the major produces value was only Rs. 55.37 lakhs. Perhaps dwindling cover of the forests vegetation responsible for the decline in the major produces value. Meanwhile increasing demand of Tripura's cane and bamboo products in and outside the state have raised the value of minor forest produces. This is a positive indication of the growing industrial base with indigenous products.

Mineral Resources

Apart from minor minerals like plastic clay, silica sand, limestone and hard rock, no major mineral resource is available in Tripura.

Plastic clay, quite a good quality, occurs in the quaternary sediments in the form of flat bodies. These sediments contain gray plastic clay at depths of 1 to 2m restricted to the broad valley portions flanked by gently raising hills/hill ranges to the flood plains of major rivers. There is a presence of partly decomposed vegetable material with this clay which represent the rock Duptilla/Tipam sediments or even older rocks deposited under stagnant water condition. Clay in the state is siliceous with a very high iron content. Those showing aluminum content of more than 20% displace moderate to high plasticity. These are mostly used to making of sewer pipe, mineral tiles floor tiles and terracotta items and ceramic industries. Geological survey has found the occurrence of clay at Khowai, Ampi, Teliamura, Udaipur, Santirbazar, Chesrimail and Tulamura.

Sand deposits belonging to Dupitilla formations have been reworked by present day rivers and re-deposited in Holocene flood plains. These are mostly composed of quartz with subordinate mica, vegetable material, various quantities of clay and ferrugenous materials. These silica sands are suitable for manufacturing glassware and sheet glass. They are treated in the bank of Bijainadi (Bishramganj), East Champamura Dukli, Maheshkhala, Banks of Howrah river, Mohanpur, Dasarambari area. Lime stone occurs within Bhuban formations of Surma group near Manpui and the surrounding areas of Jampui Hills. It may be used along with clay in mini lime puzzalana mix plants.

Hard rock are sand stone silt stone dark gray calcareous sand stone and shell lime stone occurring within the Bhuban formation of Surma group and sand stone with subordinate siltstone unit occurring within Boabil group. Rocks suitable for bitumen, tararpet roads macadam roads for asphaltizing concrete roads are found at several places in the state. These occur around Monpui , Kanchanpur, Phuldangsei Jampui Hills, Gola, Gogra, streams of Longtarai range, Atheramura range, Kebanshi tilla area etc. Small and thin bands pyrite forms, noncoking character lignite are reported from Ujan-Tangang, Hirachera Tea estate, Detricherra, etc. These are over lain by thick cover of rocks with no economic significance.

ONGC has a gas production potential of about 1.95 MMSCMD from the three fields viz. Baramura, Agartala Dome and Rokhia. Additional gas resource can be generated in Tripura through new discoveries in the existing fields or adjoining areas.

Human Resource

Tripura has always maintained a high population growth rate which is shown in Table 12 where the growth of population is compared to the regional and country as a whole. The table reveals that the growth rate of the North Eastern Region is always higher than the all India average of which Tripura contributes quite a huge number. This rising population trends during this century may be attributed to slow falling birth rate and declining death rate but most important is the fact that a majority is contributed by influx of displaced people from neighboring countries. This unabated growth of population contributed to the rising trends in the state's GDP in the initial stage and thus helped to achieve high rate of economic growth. But the abnormal growth rate of population hampered the capital formation in the state (Ganguly: 1983).

This alarming rate of population growth pull down the pace of development in the state, it cannot absorb the population in the labour. There are no dearth of natural resources but the development prospect of the state shows no sign of picking up. Thus such abnormal growth rate in the state, obviously led to much adversities (Chakraborty 1998). Human are both the means and end of development. If the size of population is more than what can be absorbed, it leads to a number of problems. The only way to overcome this hindrance in Tripura is to formulate a policy which over the years will induce a decline in the birth rate , put a check on influx and simultaneously induce an increase in the rate of economic development .

Table 12 : Decadal growth of population in Tripura

Year	Tripura	North East	India
1901-1911	32.48	18.40	5.73
1911-1921	32.59	18.60	0.30
1921-1931	25.63	19.40	11.00
1931-1941	34.14	20.10	14.23
1941-1951	25.86	19.10	13.31
1951-1961	78.71	41.20	21.64
1961-1971	36.28	35.00	24.80
1971-1981	31.92	35.90	25.06
1981-1991	34.30	—	23.05
1991-2001	15.74	—	21.34

Source: Census Report, Various issues.

According to census - 2001, the provisional population of Tripura is 31,91,168 with a decadal growth of 15.74 percent. The density of population in the state is 304 per sq. km. and literacy rate is 73.66 percent. Nearly 83 percent of its population lives in rural areas. The estimated birth rate is 17 per thousand which is much lower than all India figure of 20.7 per thousand population. The prevailing death rate and infant mortality rate are also much lower than all India level. It is worthwhile to mention that state's literacy rate and sex ratio are much higher than all India averages.

Industrial Structure of Tripura

The necessity of industrialisation as a means of achieving rapid growth and prosperity has long been recognised in the strategy of development of any region and Tripura is no exception. But it is unfortunate to mention that even after 50 years of independence, the state is yet to emerge out of industrial backwardness. It is mentioned earlier that the Central Government has declared the entire state as 'A' category backward area for the purpose of giving central investment subsidy.

The process of setting up large and medium scale industries in the state is not satisfactory due to several constraints like limited size of market, lack of skilled and semi-skilled manpower, inadequate infrastructure, undulating topography, low level of per capita income, insurgency & extremist problems and so on (Chakraborty and Das, 2002). At present there are only two large and medium scale industrial units in the state. Development of small-scale industrial sector (SSI) therefore, is the only alternative to the problem that needs immediate solutions, i.e. unemployment. Importance of SSI in removing economic backwardness of a state lies in its significance for generation of employment with low capital cost. Moreover small-scale industries are adaptable to rural and semi-urban areas where infrastructure has not been fully developed.

In spite of vast scope, the development of SSI in Tripura still remains at a very nascent stage, although as a result of a few policy measures taken and support provided like financial and technical, the SSI sector has grown considerably in the recent years. Yet it is not satisfactory in the context of regional or national growth rate.

Table 13 : Principal Characteristics of Industries in Tripura. (1955-56 and 1965-66)

	1955-56	1965-66
Number of Industries	25	49
Number of Industrial Units	5133	3695
Number of Workers Engaged	10,438	13,626
Fixed Capital (Rs.)	24,06,565	95,13,000
Working Capital (Rs.)	6,60,122	48,38,000
Fixed Capital Per Unit (Rs.)	468,84	2574.56
Working Capital Per Unit (Rs.)	130.36	1309.34
Employment per Industrial Unit	2.03	3.69

Sources: 1. Techno-Economic Survey of Tripura, NCAER, New Delhi, 1961.
2. Report of the Fact-Finding Survey of Tripura, UBI, Calcutta-1970.

Principal characteristics of industries during early plan periods in Tripura are depicted in Table 13. The information on 1955-56 is based on Techno-Economic Survey of Tripura, NCAER, New Delhi. 1965-66 data relate to Report of the Fact - Finding Survey of Tripura, UBI, Calcutta. The table reveals that there were 25 industries in 1955-56 which increased to 49 in 1965-66. Number of workers engaged has also been increased from 10,438 to 13,626 during the period. These two reports indicate the diversification and modernisation of industrial structure of Tripura. The reports also indicate that inspite of modernization, traditional industries of the state constitute the lions share.

Principal characteristics of Registered Small Scale Indus-tries (as on 31.03.1998) based on Second All India Census of Registered SSI, Tripura are shown in Table 14. According to that census report there were 809 reporting units with employment of 10,069 persons. The numbers of units engaged in manufacturing activities were 438 and the numbers of units engaged in processing activities were 130 as on that date. Another interesting feature is that there were 17 exporting units in the state.

Table 14 : Principal characteristics of Registered small Scale Industries in Tripura (as on 31.03.1988)

Number of registered working units	-	812
Number of reporting units	-	809
Employment (Nos.)	-	10,069
Fixed Investment (Rs.Lakh)	-	1,473
Gross value of production in 1987-88 (Rs. Lakh)	-	2,957
Units located in rural area	-	365
Units located in urban area	-	444
Units registered under Factories Act	-	190
Number of proprietary units	-	716
Number of partnership units	-	68
Number of units engaged in manufacturing Activities.	-	438
Number of units engaged in processing Activities.	-	130
Number of units not consumed energy	-	125
Number of exporting units.	-	17

Source: Directorate of Industries, Government of Tripura. The Second All India Census of Registered Small Scale Industries, Tripura State.

Various types of SSI industries in Tripura (1971-72 and 1987-88) are shown in Table 15. It is evident from the table that the metal products have the highest number of units followed by wood products, food products, chemical products etc. during the year 1971-72.

Table 15 : Small Scale Industries in Tripura (1971-72 and 1987-88)

Industry	Number of Units		Employment (Number)	
	1971-72	1987-88	1971-72	1987-88
Wood products	41	99	314	799
Metal Products	51	62	250	464
Repair Services	26	86	129	394
Rubber & Plastic Products	21	95	60	298
Paper products & printing	1	51	11	267
Chemical Products	6	18	154	158
Metal products (Basic metal & Alloy)	3	5	19	110
Machinery and parts.	17	23	127	56
Electrical machinery.	5	19	16	51
Hosiery & Garments	3	5	10	28

contd.

Misc. manufacturing Industries.	5	6	9	20
Transport. Equipment.	-	4	-	18
Leather products	2	5	11	17
Other services.	-	3	-	15
Beverage & Tobacco	-	3	-	9
Non-metallic mineral products.	8	78	256	4998
Food products.	37	247	323	2367
Total	246	809	1698	10069

Source: (1) Directorate of Industries, Govt. of Tripura, The 2nd All India Census of Registered Small Scale Industries, Tripura State.
(2) Basic statistics of the North Eastern Region, NEC, Shillong, 1977 and 1982.

Table 16 : Registered Small scale Industries in Tripura (1997-98 to 200-01)

(Rs. in Lakh)

Name of	1997-98	1998-99	1999-2000	2000-2001				
District	Unit	Investment	Unit	Investment	Unit	Investment	Unit	Investment
West	1704	398.5	1747	323.4	1785	272.8	1804	389.1
North	421	301.8	435	150.8	445	71.31	454	406.6
South	292	10.7	295	32.3	309	45.04	310	6.00
Dhalai	7	64.6	11	43.1	11	43.1	14	5.05
Total -	2424	774.6	2488	549.6	2547	432.2	2582	806.75

Source:Economic Review, 2000-01, Directorate of Economics & Statistics, Government of Tripura.

Table 17 : Numbers of Registered Factories In Tripura

Year	**Under Sec. 2000 (i)**	**Under Sec. 2000 (ii)**	**Under Sec. 25**	**Total Factories**
1981	97	77	44	218
1990	173	244	593	1010
1991	163	172	647	982
1992	174	167	751	1092
1993	193	169	766	1128
1994	201	150	800	1151
1995	208	136	829	1173
1996	226	125	860	1211
1997	223	111	895	1229
1998	244	119	935	1298
1999	250	121	960	1331
2000	252	130	967	1349

Source: Factories & Boilers Organisation, Government of Tripura.

While food products have the highest number of units followed by wood products, rubber and plastic, non- metallic, mineral products etc. during the period 1987-88. There were 1698 person employed in 1971-72 and 10, 069 people in 1987- 88 in these SSI units. The numbers of units and their investment during 1997-98 and 2000-2001 have been depicted in Table 16. During this period the number of units have increased from 2424 to 2582 units. Investments in SSI have also increased from 775.8 lakhs to 806.7 lakhs. West district of Tripura has the highest number of SSI units followed by North, South and Dhalai. The number of registered factories in Tripura during the period 1981 to 2000 is presented in Table 17. During this period the number of factories have increased from 218 to 1349.

In the face of acute poverty and rising unemployment in the state the pressing need for rapid economic development has led the state government to spell out its policies and programmes in favour of industrialisation. In the process of achieving such rapid industrialisation, the growth of sickness in SSI units is causing a severe strain on the economy of the state. The phenomenon of sickness not only tended to aggravate the problem of unemployment, but also rendered infractuous capital investment and consequently created an adverse climate for further industrial growth.

Table 18 : Working and Closed Units in North-Eastern Region

(As on 31-03-1998)

States	Working Unit	Closed Unit	Total Unit	% of Closed Unit
Arunachal Pradesh	326	36	362	9.94
Assam	4430	1732	6162	28.10
Manipur	2078	169	2247	7.52
Meghalaya	587	136	723	18.81
Mizoram	917	306	1223	25.02
Nagaland	183	83	266	31.20
Tripura	809	603	1412	42.70
N.E.Region	9330	3065	12395	24.72

Source: 1) Basic Statistics of North Eastern Region, 2000. NEC, Shillong.

2) Government of Tripura, Directorate of Industries

The magnitude of the problem is evident from the fact that 42.7 percent of the total units in the state are closed which is fairly high compared to many other states of the North East Region (Chakraborty and Pramanik: 1999). There are some more working units which are either sick or on the verge of getting so. According to an estimate 20-25 percent of reported working SSI units in the state are sick (Tripura Industrial Development Corporation, Agartala). It is shown in the Table 18 that Tripura has the highest percentage of closed units followed by Nagaland (31.20%). So far as the number of closed units are concerned Assam has the highest (1732) followed by Tripura (603) and Mizoram (306) respectively. According to an estimate, out of total number of sick units in the state, there are only 26 potentially viable sick units and rest are non-viable sick units (Directorate of Industries, Govt. of Tripura and Indian Institute of Entrepreneurship, Guwahati).

In the process of development of SSI sector, the increasing incidence of sickness in the SSI units in Tripura is a woeful phenomenon which is causing a severe strain on the banks and financial institutions. It is therefore necessary to diagnose this malady. Sickness in an industrial unit, however, cannot be attributed to a single factor alone. It is a cumulative effect of many factors, which may be interrelated, or independent of each other. It would, therefore, be difficult to recognize a particular factor responsible for a particular sick unit. The factors responsible for unhealthy situation in the small scale sector of Tripura have been perceived by many experts, committees and study groups (UBI, 1970, Debnath, 1990, Chakraborty, 2002 NECON, 1995,etc.).

Some of the identified factors are as follows :

(i) Frequent changes in the policies, rules and regulations of state government, banks and other financial institutions towards SSI units.
(ii) Absence of adequate railway facilities (only 45 km.) and high transportation costs in comparison to other states.
(iii) CMIE evolved composite infrastructure index of Tripura shows the infrastructure backwardness of the state, resulting in longer gestation period and weakness of the supporting services.
(iv) Absence of attractive incentive schemes
(v) Unattractive sale tax regulation
(vi) Shortage of power supplies in the state. During the year 1998-99 there was 25 MW shortage of power, which was highest among the North-East States. Per capita consumption of power in the state is also low in comparison to the other states of the North-East.
(vii) Shortage of skill workers, efficient managers and above all motivated entrepreneurs
(viii) In comparison to other parts of India, working capital requirement in SSI units of Tripura is more due to infrastructure and geographical barrier resulting in inadequate working capital finance by the funding agencies as they abide by uniform rules.
(ix) Frequent blockades of the Assam - Agartala road (lifeline of Tripura) causing uncertainties and shortage of essential raw materials and construction materials.
(x) Outdated and inferior techniques of production resulting in higher cost of production.
(xi) Limited market support by the government in the from of unplanned purchases at the end of financial year by the government departments and organisations.
(xii) Inadequate modern marketing facilities.
xiii) Disturbed socio-political conditions of the state.

At present there are 6 industrial estates / areas in the state providing 76 industrial sheds, out of which 38 units are working (Govt. of Tripura, IDBI, 2001). Few more industrial estates are coming up with Central Government assistance. A review of working of various industrial estates in North-Eastern region (status paper on industrial estates by SIET, Guwahati) shows that the primary cause of non-working of many industrial units in industrial estates is the location of the estates. Bodhjungnagar Growth Center in West District and Dewanpara Integrated Infrastructure Development Center in North District are such examples. Therefore, the industrial estate should be located in places where other infrastructure facilities (social and economic) are available. And selection of site should be made on the basis of techno- economic consideration rather than on political consideration. Level of productivity of SSI units in the state has also to be improved. This is possible only if the entrepreneurs aim at production of quality goods with local resources at the lowest cost (NECON,1995).

Many small units of the state have difficulties in marketing their products because they can not afford the expenses involved in an elaborate marketing set up. Very few SSI units of the state are fortunate to have a committed market close by. It is, thus, necessary to have some organisation to look after the marketing of products manufactured by small units. The state government can encourage the setting up of industry wise marketing organisation in the co-operative or government sector. At present various incentive schemes are available to the SSI units of the state. Central and State government's package of incentives includes mainly capital investment subsidy, sales tax exemption (5 yrs.), interest subsidy, transport subsidy, and income tax exemption (10 yrs.) (IDBI, 2001and Department of Industries, Government of Tripura, 1995). These subsidies are grossly inadequate and their provisions are also not encouraging (Chakraborty, 2002). Therefore, these need to be enhanced as also some other type of subsidy introduced for accelerating industrial growth.

Entrepreneurs have a severe limitation in terms of their time and expertise. They are to perform various statutory requirements with Industry Department, Labour Department, Sales Tax, Income Tax, ESI, Provident fund, Factories, Banks, Financial Institutions etc. There should be a single agency, which can help the entrepreneur in dealing with the various government bodies. Such an agency will free the entrepreneurs to concentrate on the critical areas of business. There should also be another agency in the state which can co-ordinate the various activities pertaining to SSI, namely, promotion of new industries, identification and training of entrepreneurs, preparation of feasibility reports, arrangement of loans from financial institutions, providing consultancy services, monitoring the activities of the units and so on. The above task of 'Single Window' system may be entrusted to the Tripura Industrial Development Corporation Ltd. or any other similar organisations like SISI.

Revival of potential sick units is perhaps the foremost task. But uniform guidelines or parameters for revival of sick units, delay in decision making particularly by banks and TIDC in rehabilitation cases, absence of standard documentation of rehabilitation facilities etc. act as impediments in the process of revival of sick units. The main impediment to development of SSI is perhaps the non-viability of many units, which are started without much consideration to the resource endowments in the state and eventually turn sick. It is mentioned earlier that 99 percent of total sick units are non viable in the state. Therefore, potential areas for development of SSI should be identified.

Economic growth of a region depends upon the level of infrastructure. In Tripura, the infrastructure facility is not favourable in terms of quantity and quality compared to either the nation as a whole or other North Eastern States. The overall backwardness of the state is evident from the Composite Infrastructures Index evolved by the Centre for Monitoring Indian Economy.

Electricity

Electric power in Tripura in the form of generation by diesel engines came into existence as early as 1910. The state has two sources of power generation - Hydro and Thermal. The state also has natural gas, which can be used for thermal power generation. Out of the two major sources of power generation, thermal power accounts for more than 77 % while the remaining is generated from Gomati Power Project (hydro). Due to increase in demand for electricity, the state is experiencing persistent power shortage and hence frequent power cuts are enforced upon. During 2000 - 2001 the total installed capacity was 85.35 MW and total power generated was 318.38 MU, total purchase of power was 268.00 MU in 2000 - 2001 which is 8.85 MU higher than that purchase in 1999 - 2000

(Table 19). The total unit sold to ultimate consumers in 2000-2001 was 388 MU, maximum was taken up by irrigation/public water/sewage/ domestic consumption (103.75 MU), industries (74.69 MU) and for commercial purposes (46.52 MU).

Table 19 : Generation and Consumption of Electricity in Tripura

(In M.U)

Year	Installed capacity	Power Generated	Power purchased	Power consumption	No. of village (1971 Census) Electrified	Rural Electrification % of village electrification
1	2	3	4	5	6	7
1994-95	53.35	171.69	106.07	193.70	3578	75.69
1995-96	69.35	194.01	130.00	223.66	3640	77.00
1996-97	65.72	246.05	128.12	270.00	3700	78.27
1997-98	85.35	302.82	147.68	315.88	3720	78.69
1998-99	85.35	337.68	228.89	363.12	3751	79.00
1999-00	85.35	314.18	259.15	362.43	3775	79.8
2000-01	85.35	318.38	268.00	388.00	—	—

Source:Office of the Chief Engineer Electrical, Tripura and Statistical Abstract of Tripura, 2001 Govt. of Tripura

As can be seen from the available data that power consumption is steadily, on the rise in the last decade. Of all the heads, irrigation and public works gets the lions share while the tea gardens requirement seems to dwindle after 1997-98. Public lighting consumed a sizeable amount of power which almost halved after 1998-99. With population growth the demand for domestic supply has risen too. Moreover industries being a negligible entity has attracted a meagre amount compared to irrigation and public water, yet the demand is rising continuously.

Therefore, despite commendable successes, the position in relation to needs remains highly unsatisfactory. The per capita power consumption is meagre. Power being an essential ingredient of economic development is required both for commercial and non-commercial use. It is observed that demand by commercial sector has risen considerably over the last decade. It is obvious that a large expansion of this source of energy is required. As such about 79.80 percent of the villages and 100 percent towns are electrified which raises both the income and the expenditure of the department. But it is found that expenditure far exceeds the income (almost 3-4 times). Kutir Jyoti, a centrally sponsored scheme to give assistance to the people living below poverty line is providing electricity, free of cost. Till 1997-98, there were 6217 connections under this scheme which rose to 15,688 in 1998-99 and to 37,979 in 2000-2001.

Irrigation

Tripura's only source of water is rainfall, 90 percent of which is confined to 4-5 months. This water cannot be stored by constructing dams, due to lack of suitable foundation. Farmers dig canals from streams (chheras) and construct 'bonds' (seasonal). Other modes e.g. tank irrigation is uncertain as there is always a possibility of inadequate rainfall. Wells cannot be dug due to loose and porous soil condition, wells have to be sunk very deep and has to be operated by power which again involves high cost. Three medium irrigation projects - Gumti, Khowai, Manu feed the entire cultivable land.

Tripura has a total cultivable land of 2,79,000 ha and irrigation potential of 1,17,000 ha. in 1999-2000. Out of this 79,000 ha can be brought under assured irrigation through surface water and 38,000 ha by ground water resources (Economic Review, 2000 - 2001). The net potential utilization up to March 2001 was 57,183 ha. Ground surveys have shown harnessing of ground water is under progress through boring of shallow tube wells, deep tube wells and artesian wells. Artesian wells are ideal for the state as the soil is free from rocky substratum.

The state's data show that a meagre percentage of total cropped area is being irrigated though the gross cropped area is increasing steadily. A wide difference can be seen between the potential created and actual irrigated area in different regions of the state. Perhaps inefficient and unsatisfactory management and maintenance of irrigation works and improper drainage system is to be blamed. Ground water resources are being improperly used due to lack of drainage system, financial handicaps of the farmers, non-availability of power.

Transport and Communication

Tripura is narrowly connected with the mainland of the country by a strip of land in Assam. There is a narrow railway link of 45 km. from Kumarghat (N. District) via Dharmanagar to Badarpur and Lumding (Assam) by metre gauge. Agartala is connected by Airlines with Calcutta and Guwahati. Since independence the road network is expanding and improving. After merger (1949) the P.W.D. had undertaken construction of the 'life-line', i.e., Assam-Agartala Road known as National Highway-44. Now this highway is extended till Sabroom, the remotest southern tip for facilitating direct communication. A total of 15,177 km. road length of which 3523 km. of black topped road, 2589 km. brick soled road and remaining 9065 km. roads are earthen. It is evident from the 'Statistical Abstract' (Govt. of Tripura) that the length of national highway is 333 km, village road (RD/ADC) 7912 km, village roads (PWD) 4491 km and major district road 454 km. The number of registered motor vehicles in the state was 37,893 in 1997-98 that rose to 45,199 in 1999-2000 and in 2000-2001 it stood at 50,139.

Table 20 : Bank wise Branches in Tripura (as on 31.3.2000)

Sl. No.	Type of Bank	Rural	Semi-urban	Urban	Total
1	State Bank of India	17	8	7	32
2	Commercial Bank/ Nationalised Bank	32	9	19	60
3	Regional Rural Bank	71	11	5	87
4	Agartala Co-operative	-	-	1	1
5	Tripura Co- operative Land Dev. Bank	-	4	1	5
6	Tripura State Co-operative Bank	18	10	8	36
	Total	138	42	41	221

Source: Statistical Abstract, Government of India, 2001

Allied to the transport system is the communication system comprising of postal services, telegraph services, telephone services etc. These facilities in the state have been growing steadily in recent years. As can be made out from the postal information, the number of post offices have increased during the decade but the increase is only marginal Interestingly number of telephone connection have increased tremendously, from 5391 in 1990-91 to 44,834 in 1999-2000, the increase is mostly in the West District. These trends obviously point towards the spreading of communication network throughout the state which facilitates development.

Banking

There is a close interaction between financial infrastructure and economic development. Banks have expanded their network extensively particularly during last two to three decades in Tripura. In 1969 there were 5 commercial bank branches which served an average population of 2,76,000 per branch. Till December 2000 there were 221 bank branches in the state comprising of Nationalised Banks, Regional Rural Bank and Co-operative Banks. 138 branches are in the rural areas, 42 in semi- urban areas and 41 in urban areas.

Development Focus

Foregoing analysis prompt us to conclude that the basic problem of Tripura's economy is the problem of economic development, i.e., providing minimum needs to its fast growing population. A large part of this population lives below the poverty line. Ruralised economy of the state, inadequate infrastructure, industrial backwardness, undulating topography, low level of resource mobilisation, low level of per cepita income, high rate of population growth etc., have made the state as one of the most backward states in our country. The overall backwardness of the state is also evident from the data prepared by CMIE. In this situation any strategy for development should concentrate to uplift the socio economic condition of the people of the state. Observations emerged from the foregoing discussion and a few suggestions in the form of strategy for development are in order.

Conventional development strategies have been rationalized on the grounds that poor people cannot save and that large-scale production is more efficient. As a result of these two assumptions, there is little reason for the section of poor people to participate in the development process because the majority of the population in less developed countries or underdeveloped countries is poor and the major part of their productive activities is carried on in small-scale production. This is particularly true in case of a backward state like Tripura. Majority of its population is poor, live in rural areas and they have small land holdings, small farms and small business units. In Alternative Development Strategies, however, these assumptions do not apply. The assumptions instead are that poor people can save and that small- scale production is more efficient, particularly from the point of view of investment needs.

Thus it is becoming increasingly clear that conventional development strategies, which emphasize the growth of GDP or per capita income, without inquiring into the pattern of growth, which determines its fruits, do not always alleviate mass poverty and unemployment. As the past patterns of development in Tripura have not yielded the desired results, there is clearly a need of current development strategies to be reoriented towards the elimination of poverty and the unemployment and the fulfillment of basic needs. These three elements are all interrelated. Unemployment and underemployment prevent the majority of the population in the state from having access to minimum personal consumption needs. Thus the strategy for development in Tripura should aim to meet the requirement of the small farmers, small-scale industries and the informal sector producers.

According to the Fourth Economic Census (1998) of the State, the numbers of employment in agricultural enterprises are 4751. Out of which 3820 are rural and 921 are urban. There are 2,63,506 number of employments in non-agricultural enterprises (rural-163,840 and urban-99,666). Thus the number of employments in agricultural enterprises had increased from 4977 in 1980 to 5,242 in 1990, but declined to 4751 in 1998. However the number of employments in non-agricultural enterprises has increased from 129,411 in 1980 to 21,5346 in 1990 and 263506 in 1998. It indicates the growth of non-agricultural sector in the state.

So far as government employees are concerned the number of employees have increased from 7173 in 1954 to 9863 in 1960 to 34,288 in 1974, to 76,714 in 1962 and to 1,11,026 in 1998. This indicates the increasing involvement of Government in the overall developmental activities of the state.

It is observed that the occupational structure has changed very little and agriculture is still the mainstay of majority population. The changing share of the modern sector in SDP has also been observed in the state economy. It is one of the indicators of changes in the organisational structure of an economy. It is seen that the share of traditional sector in SDP has declined marginally. Although sectoral composition of SDP has changed in favour of non-agricultural sector, the persisting dominance of primary sector to generate adequate employment opportunities in the state continued.

A serious move to improve the economic conditions of the state started with the launching of the First Five Year Plan. Since then we have completed five decades of state planning during which period a number of significant changes have taken place in the state economy. Plan expenditure has increased significantly, SDP and per capita income of the state have also increased. But the economic condition of the majority of the population of the state has changed little. One of the main causes for this is the high rate of population growth.

It is worthwhile to mention that the state government has identified seven priority sectors for overall development of the state. These include, agriculture and irrigation; drinking water; housing; communication; education, rural electrification and health. It is mentioned that under the 'Gramodoya' scheme, these priority sectors are adequately emphasized while formulating developmental plans for villages, blocks and districts.

Agriculture is the backbone of the state's economy. Land productivity and total agricultural production can be raised substantially through the inputs of improved seeds and ferti-lizers. But these inputs become more effective and their potential better utilised if adequate energy and power are made available to the farmers. In the agricultural field of Tripura HYV seeds are used for crop production, but are limited only to a fewer food crops. In 1999-2000, 86 percent of land for rice and 100 percent of land for wheat had been brought under HYV seeds. Over a period of two decades or so, the use of HYV seeds has widely spread in Tripura. The numbers of agricultural implement and machinery have also increased. But such increase is insignificant. For example, there are only 360 power tillers or 342 tractors available to the farmers of the state at the end of 1997. Consumption of chemical fertilizers in Tripura, however, has increased significantly. In 2000-2001, the total consumption of the state is 11,315 tones while it was 8,995 tones in the year 1990-91.

The marketing margin between the cultivator and consumer may be taken as an index of the soundness of the marketing set up of any produce (Gopalaswamy, 1997). A number of studies stand to confirm that a large number of middlemen function at various stages of agricultural marketing in our country and they reduce the share of the producer in consumer's price (Krishnaswamy, Hari Narayan and Vijoy Kumar, 1968). The price spread in agricultural market of Tripura is also considerable and the cultivators' share in the consumer's rupee is very small (Chakraborty, 2001). These highlight the high marketing cost and indicate the inefficient market pattern. Therefore, effective agricultural marketing in the state is essential for overall development of the people of Tripura. Unless adequate care in agricultural marketing is taken, it is very difficult to think in terms of development of rural population in the state which accords more than 80 percent of state's population.

Decline in the per capita holding has led to low productivity and widespread poverty. This decline of land holding under the possession of the peasants is a new phenomenon, termed as land alienation. Keeping in mind the undulating terrains where 80 percent of the total land is mountainous and 55 percent of arable land laying in the hills, the mounting population pressure has led to this land alienation. Two kinds of tenures exists: one in the hills and the other in the plains, whereas communal ownership persists in the hills, land is privately owned in the plains. As tenants were large in numbers and quite eager to cultivate land at inferior right and a higher rent, thus, started sub-infeudation, and whenever the rents could not be paid land was usurped by the owner. Tenancy legislations existed but very few peasants actually resorted to litigation. Gradually forest borders, low hillocks, swamps were used up which drove away the autochthons to the remote hills as well as altered the configuration of the land completely along with inheritance, partition, purchases etc. To bring some relief, the Tripura Land Revenue and Land Reform Act was passed in 1960 aiming at abolishing intermediaries as well as imposing land ceiling but did not serve its purpose. The Act was further amended (1974) which reduced the ceiling limit, an increase in the number of holdings was noticed but at the same time the size of large land holdings increased which pointed out further alienation. Land alienation, thus seems to be more of a symptom than a disease, a symptom of a general depression in the economy leading to a loss of economic independence of a particular class and gain of socio-economic power of another. The root cause perhaps lies in the nature of economy, indebtedness, government's apathy, loopholes in the legislations etc. Therefore, land question of the state are to be settled immediately for overall economic development of the state.

It is not an exaggeration to say that SSI should be assigned a pivotal role in the scheme of industrialization and economic development of the state. Inspite of various measures taken by the state government, there has not been any significant improvement in the scenario. Various study groups and experts have identified the basic constraints for the development of SSI units in Tripura. A strategy should therefore be framed to remove all such constraints. Any attempt in this respect be viewed at a wider perspective involving the state and central governments, commercial banks, promotional organisations, financial institutions and entrepreneurs. As the state is endowed with abundant resources, entrepreneurs should be induced to set up industries based on these resources. For this, a detailed up-to-date inventory of available resources of the state will have to be made along with industry wise potential survey of the state. It is also necessary to have a data bank as a source of information accessible to entrepreneurs, which can guide them in decision making when selecting a new project or for expansion and diversification.

Survey of industrial potential in the state was first made by the National Council of Applied Economic Research (NCAER). It classified the potential industries of Tripura into (a) processing industries, b) engineering industries, c) wood based industries, and (d) leather industries. Another similar survey was conducted in the year 1970 by a Joint Institutional Study Team consisting of the representatives of the RBI, IDBI, ICICI and the IFC. The Plan Evaluation Organisation of the Government of Tripura also made a survey of the SSI units in two industrial estates located at Agartala (Arundhutinagar) and Udaipur in 1975. Thereafter Entrepreneurship Development Institute of India (Project Opportunities in Tripura, 1992), North Eastern Industrial Consultants Ltd. (Report on Prospects and Possibilities of Setting up Industrial Estates in Manipur, Mizoram and Tripura,1995) and Tripura Industrial Development corporation (Industrial Potential Survey in Tripura, 1998-99) have made the industrial surveys in the state.

The natural resources, favourable agro-climatic conditions and manpower available in the state may be used for setting up of SSI units (EDII, 1992). The Shivaraman committee suggested that in the north-eastern region, small scale industries based on locally available natural resources and industries capable of meeting growing local needs might be promoted. Considering the marketability and manpower ability, demand pattern and the existing constraints the most appropriate areas for small scale industries may be identified as follows : i) forest based, ii) agro based, iii) livestock based, iv) gas based, and v) service sector based. Therefore the state government needs to revamp its industrial policy and concentrate more on setting up industries based upon these.

Tripura is endowed with dense forests, occupying an area of about 606168 hect. and accounting for more than 58 percent of the total geographical area. Out of the total forest resources in the state, only 30.22 percent is in actual use, leaving large areas potentially exploitable. Value of outturn of forest product in Tripura was Rs. 137,65000 in the year 2000-2001. The forests are rich in timber, bamboo, cane, agar-wood, grasses and medicinal herbs. Thus the forests may provide raw materials to a number of small scale industries based on these resources.

Agriculture, in the state, also can play an important role in industrial development. It provides raw materials to a number of small scale and cottage industries. Cash crops and spices with commercial potentiality like sugarcane, jute, mesta, cotton etc. are being successfully cultivated in the state. Citronella, an aromatic crop has emerged as an important crop with industrial potentials. Production of essential oils from various species of herbs grown in the state may lead to development of industries like cosmetic, perfumery and pharmaceutical products. The state also produces a variety of fruits. The marketable surplus of these is enough for opening up more fruit processing industries in the state as revealed by a study conducted by North-Eastern Council. Production of high value, low volume items like pepin from papaya or pectin from citrus peel is pertinent for horticulture based SSI units in the state. SSI units for preparation of common rubber goods have ample scope for development, as the region is famous for quality rubber production.

Cashewnut, arecanut and coconut are widely produced in Tripura. Small industry has scope to develop based on these cash crops particularly coconut which is abundantly grown in the state (3183 MT in 2000-2001) in an area of 8370 hectares. Processing of coconut may give rise to many industries like coir, rope, mat, carpet, oil etc. The industries based on coconut is highly employment oriented also.

Handloom and handicrafts are other potential areas for SSI units. At present handloom is the largest industry in Tripura. There are about 1.25 lakh handlooms employing about one lakh weavers in the state. Unfortunately only 9000 handlooms are in commercial operation which cannot meet the requirements of the state. Therefore, there is wide scope to develop handloom industries in the small-scale sector. Inspite of locally available resources and manpower the handicrafts industry of Tripura is not up to the expectation due to several problems. At present there are about 5000 craftsman engaged in producing different varieties of handicrafts. However as the state has long been known for its traditional skill in bamboo and cane work, the handicrafts industry has wide scope for development including export to other countries.

Tripura also has immense potential for livestock, poultry and fishery. The state not only has the required agro climatic conditions but also all the resources necessary for increased animal production. According to various livestock census there are adequate number of live- stock and poultry in the state. These may cater to develop SSI units in the related areas.

Finally development strategy for backward state requires simultaneous action on various fronts for increasing employment opportunities, production and productivity. Agriculture, needless to mention, being the largest single source of income and employment in Tripura, takes precedence over other activities in the state. Development of agriculture, however, is, to a limited extent, dependent upon the development of the infrastructure, tertiary sector and rural industries. Cottage and village industries in Tripura have traditionally provided substantial employment opportunities to rural people of the state. These are traditional occupation of various artisan classes in the village of the state. Cane & bamboo, village pottery, village oil gur and khandeswary , bee keeping, processing of cereal & pulses, etc. are a few of those available in rural areas of the state. These industries having forward linkage with agriculture, provide considerable scope for increased production and employment. Therefore, strategy should be formulated to modernise these industries with an aim to make them more economically viable for competition.

REFERENCES

Agarwal, A.K. (1988): *North Eastern Economy : Problems and Prospects*, Mittal Publications, New Delhi.

Banerjee, A. and D. Mazumder (2001): *Fundamentals of Economic Principles and Problems,* ABS Publishing House, Calcutta.

Bhattacherjee, P.R. (1993): *Economic Transition in Tripura*, Vikas Publishing, New Delhi.

Chakraborty, K.S. (2001) : *Marketing of Agricultural Produce in Tripura,* Agricultural Marketing, Ministry of Agriculture, Govt. of India, Vol.XLIV, No.1

Chakraborty, K.S. (2000) : 'Rural Market and Marketing of Agricultural Produces in Tribal Areas - A Study with reference to a few tribal dominated rural markets of Tripura', TUI, A quarterly research journal of Tribal Research Institute, Govt. of Tripura, Vol. VIII, Sl. No. 30

Chakraborty, K.S. (2002): 'Sickness in Small Scale Industries of Tripura', Vidyasagar University Journal of Commerce, vol.7, Midnapur

Chakraborty, K.S. and B.C. Das (2002): 'An insight into the development of SSI in Tripura', Southern Economist, Vol-41, No-8, Bangalore..

Chakraborty, K.S. & Pramanik A.K. (1999): 'Sickness in Small Scale Industries of North-Eastern Region', Southern Economist, November 1

Debnath, P. (1990): Industrilisation in Tripura, Unpublished Ph.D. Dissertation, Ranchi University.

Entrepreneurship Development Institute of India (1992): Project Opportunities in Tripura, Gujrat.

Gopalaswamy, T.P. (1997): *Rural Marketing-Environment, Problems and Strategy*, Wheeler Publishing, New Delhi

Govt. of India; Census Report, Various Issues.

Government of Tripura, Directorate of Economics and Statistics: Economic Review, Various Issues.

Government of Tripura, Directorate of Economics and Statistics: Statistical Abstract, Various Issues.

Government of Tripura, Evaluation Organisation (1975): Evaluation Report on Industrial Estates in Tripura.

Government of Tripura, Directorate of Industries: The Second All India Census of Registered Small Scale Industries.

Government of Tripura, Directorate of Industries: Tripura Incentive Scheme, 1995.

Government of Tripura, Tripura Industrial Development Corporation (1998-99): Industrial Potential Survey in Tripura Prepared by TCS.

Government of Tripura, Tripura Industrial Development Corporation (2001): Investment Opportunities and Industrial Infrastructure in Tripura.

Hoover and Vernon (1959): *Anatomy of a Metropolis*, Havard University Press, U.K.

Keeble and Weaver (1986): *New Firms and Regional Development in Europe*, Croom, Helv London.

Krishnamurthy, J (1984) Changes in the Indian Workforces, EPW, vol.XIX, No.50.

Krishnaswamy, Hari Narayan and Vijoy Kumar (1968) : A Study on Price Spreads of wheat in Rajasthan, Agricultural Situation in India. Vol. XXII, no.7, July.

Mali, D.D. and Deka, P. (1987): *Industrial Development in North-East India*, Omson Publications, Guwahati.

Mitra, Ashok (1980): *Population and Area of Cities and Towns and Urban Agglomerations,* 1872-1971, Allied.

NISIET: Small Industry Development in India. Policy : Programmes and Institutional Support, Hyderabad.

National Council of Applied Economic Research (1961): *Techno Economic Survey of Tripura*, New Delhi.

North Eastern Council: Basic Statistics of North Eastern Region, 2002, Shillong.

North Eastern Industrial Consultants Ltd. (1995): Report on Prospects and Possibilities of Setting up Industrial Estates in Manipur, Nagaland, Mizoram and Tripura for IDBI, Agartala.

Uma Kapila (Ed.) (1998): *Indian Economy Since Independence*, Academic Foundation, New Delhi.

United Bank Of India (1970): *Report of the Fact-finding Survey of Tripura*, Calcutta.

9

Structural Change and Resource-Industry Linkages in North East India

—*Utpal Kumar De*

Introduction

The North-Eastern region of India, in spite of being rich in biological and natural resources, has remained economically backward for a long time. The region has received much national and international attention during the past few decades for the escalating insurgency problem. Even over three decades after the formation of North Eastern Council, it could not accelerate the pace of development significantly. Whatever development has taken place during the last few years is purely skewed towards the tertiary sector. The secondary sector, whose contribution to national income and employment normally increases with the progress of an economy, continued to remain in a fragile stage.

The present paper attempts to throw some light on the status of industrial progress in relation to the availability of resources in the region. The plan of the paper is as follows. First we shall describe the nature of structural change in the region's economy and then assess the status of industrial progress in the region. Finally, the basic reasons behind the observed pattern of industrial development and its relation with the existing resource base will be discussed.

Structural Transformation of the Economy of North-Eastern Region

The progress of any economy is always associated with some kind of structural transformation, where the non-agricultural sectors normally found to become relatively more and more important compared to their agricultural counterparts. Thus with the advancement of an economy, people are found to be increasingly engaged in the secondary and tertiary sectors. In other words, with the progress and rising per capita income, percentage of main workers engaged in the primary sector decreases and that of secondary and tertiary sector increases (Clark, 1940). With the increase in total or per capita gross and net domestic product, relative contribution of primary sector in the employment of workforce and to GDP decreases, while those of secondary and tertiary sector increases.

Majority of people in the region lives in rural areas and earns their livelihood primarily from the agriculture and allied activities. Here also notable changes in the contribution of different sectors to the GDP have been observed during the last few decades. There has been a significant progress made in terms of the growth of the tertiary sector and in terms of its contribution to the national and state domestic products. Though the percentage contribution of primary sector to net state domestic product has decreased, it still has the predominance in the employment and income of the people. On the other hand, the secondary sector has remained very weak. The pattern of change however varies noticeably across different states of the region. An inter-state comparison would be much useful to know the pattern of structural change of the states of North-East India and that will help to identify the areas that need more attention.

Needless to say that the per capita income, which is one of the indicators of economic development, has experienced a slow progress over the years compared to the states of other region. Just the data of last few years (as shown in Table-1) exhibit the slow growth of per capita income, which is even negative in the states of Mizoram and Nagaland.

Compound growth rate of per-capita income, during 1993-94 to 1999-00, is the highest in Tripura among all the North-Eastern states and lowest in Mizoram. The rate of all the North-Eastern states are much lower than the national average. It is because of the slow growth of net state domestic product and significantly higher rate of growth of population. Moreover, though agriculture remained the main economic activity, its productivity remains very low due to the persistence of traditional technique of cultivation. Though governments have taken some steps and allocated more funds for the development of this sector, the adoption of modern technology is very limited. In addition to that, during last few decades, population growth was much rapid, which put much stress on land and forest, leading to a fall in productivity of land and forest, despite the Green Revolution in the country.

Table-1 : Compound Growth Rate of Per Capita Income of the North-Eastern States of India during 1993-94 to 1999-00

State	Per Capita Income at 1993-94 prices (Rs.)		Compound Average
	1993-94	1999-2000	Rate of Growth
Arunachal Pradesh	8579	9170	1.12
Assam	5715	5978	0.75
Manipur	5833	7231	3.65
Meghalaya	6703	7826	2.62
Mizoram	8158	8109	-0.10
Nagaland	9129	9118*	-0.024
Tripura	5350	6813	4.11
India	7690	10067	4.59

Source: Basic Statistics of North-Eastern Region.

Note: * indicates that it corresponds to the year 1998-99 for Nagaland.

If we look at the percentage contribution of different sectors to state domestic product, we observe a high increase in the contribution of tertiary sector in Arunachal Pradesh during 1993-94 to 1999-00. It decreases in Manipur and Mizoram. Anyway, though the contribution of primary sector has decreased, it remains the dominant sector (Table-2). Its contribution has however increased in Nagaland and marginally in Meghalaya. The contribution of secondary sector to state domestic product remains very low in all the North Eastern states.

Table-2 : Contribution of Different Sector to State Domestic Product of North-Eastern States in Different Years (in percentage)

	Arunachal Pradesh	Assam	Manipur	Meghalaya	Mizoram	Nagaland	Tripura
1993-94							
Primary	49.70	48.04	37.87	31.87	33.23	25.85	38.01
Secondary	21.37	13.36	15.73	11.92	9.45	12.24	8.19
Tertiary	28.93	38.59	46.40	56.21	57.32	61.91	53.79
Total	100	100	100	100	100	100	100
1999-00							
Primary	35.28	45.21	32.10	32.01	26.89	29.09	31.52
Secondary	21.88	15.65	26.29	11.45	13.41	14.57	13.23
Tertiary	42.84	39.14	41.61	56.54	59.69	56.33	55.24
Total	100	100	100	100	100	100	100
% Change							
Primary	-29.01	-5.89	-15.24	0.44	-19.08	12.53	-17.07
Secondary	2.39	17.14	67.13	-3.94	41.90	19.03	61.54
Tertiary	48.08	1.43	-10.32	0.59	4.13	-9.01	2.70

Source: (i) NEDFi Databank, July, 2002
(ii) Basic Statistics of NER, various issues, North Eastern Council

The Resource-Base and Industrial Development

The scope and pace of Industrial development in any region basically depend on the following conditions:

(i) First, industries are set up in a place on the basis of availability of resources.
(ii) Second, it depends on the availability of water and energy at the reasonable price in the respective industrial growth centres.
(iii) Third, the location of industrial development depends on the access to market.
(iv) Fourth, policy-induced industrialisation may take place for the generation of employment and opportunities as well as development of areas.
(v) Lastly, sometimes industries are also set up in areas without having much resources or inputs if there is sizeable local demand for those particular industrial products. In that case, those commodities can be produced by importing the material inputs from outside, if sufficient human resources are locally available and there is competitive price support to run those industries at their optimum scale/capacity.

To study the pattern and depth of resource industry linkages in North-East India, we need to first, study the potential availability of basic natural resources and the possibility of accessing those resources at a reasonable cost in that region. It is also required to have a close look at the existing industrial set up and their categories in the concerned region as well as the level of material and other resources used by those industries, which are available either in their neighbourhood or imported from other regions. Finally, the level and potential availability and generation of human resources and their utilisation along with the technological progress are also to be considered. By doing so one can find out the divergence between the industries that could be grown out of the potential use of those resources and the actual industrial growth. Thereafter, it would be much easier to analyse the basic reasons for the particular relation (may be strong or weak) between resource position and the industrial situation of any region.

The linkage between resource use pattern and the level of industrial development of any region depends primarily on the level of technological, social, economic, institutional and infrastructure development of that region vis-à-vis the other neighbouring regions. If the neighbouring areas are found to have already achieved some progress or maturity in the production and productivity of some industrial products, then as a late starter it is very difficult for the other region to compete with the comparatively more matured industries located in the neighbouring region for the competitive advantage that they have already achieved, due to their long working experience. However, if special thrust is given for the manpower development and policy induced technological advancement takes place, then it may be possible to achieve the desired progress in the desired direction.

Another point to reckon with is that the development of industries is also to some extent, contingent upon the ownership pattern of the basic resources (material inputs) and the attitude of industrial entrepreneurs. If the inputs like minerals are owned privately by some one, who is lacking entrepreneurship skill and earn sufficiently high amount just only from mining, she/he will have very little interest to invest in industrial set up based on those inputs. Rather she/he will invest more on profitable mining and sell those minerals to the existing industries located in the other region from which, she/he can earn more. This is a common feature across the North-Eastern states of India.

The Resource Base of North-East India

The rate of development of any region depends mostly on the rate of industrial progress, as the growth of agricultural sector is constrained by the supply of land resources, which is the primary input of agricultural activities. The technological progress cannot go on raising the agricultural productivity continuously at an accelerated pace unless there is a continuous shift of technology. Moreover, there is a trade-off between the current rate of growth of agricultural productivity (by intensive use of land) and the future productive capacity of land. Therefore, without judicious and sustainable use of land the agricultural production is bound to come to a halt. So the other alternative for development of any region is the growth of industries, which in turn depends primarily on the availability and use of the resource base of that region.

Usually by resources we mean the material resources and therefore when we talk of the exploitation of resources, we mean the resources, which the people of any region need, directly or indirectly, for their socio-economic development. Of course, it is already mentioned that if any region possesses high quality human resources and even though the region is not gifted with much of natural material resources or faces geographical and locational disadvantages; the improvement of its economic condition may be possible by using the potential human brain/resources (through improved technology) and importing material inputs from other regions. An important example of it is the case of Japan, which could become one of the most industrially developed countries in the World, even without having much natural resource base. Human resource in this case plays an important role, as an alternative to material resource. However there is no denying of the fact that the rate of industrial progress would be more rapid, if the natural resource base of an area is stronger.

In many cases, natural resources (renewable as well as non-renewable) are being overexploited to meet the growing need of rising population and causing future availability of those resources uncertain. Whereas, the existence of a balanced natural resource base like forest is always essential for leading a good and healthy life not only by the present generation but also by the generations to come. Hence the question of intergenerational equity of distribution of natural resource arises (Becker, R. A., 1982). Moreover a critical amount of natural resource is essential for the sustainable development of any region (Hanley et al 1997, p. 428). Thus balanced use of resources is essential for maintaining continuous growth of the economy.

Like any other region, the resources available in the North-East India can be divided into two broad categories. These are material resources and human resources. The material resources can also be divided into two categories: one is man made and the other is the natural resource. But the man made resources are also dependent on the availability of natural resources and human resources. Therefore, natural resources along with human resources are the main source of development of any region. Natural resources again can be divided into two broad categories: renewable and non-renewable resources. Forest, flora, and fauna, water, solar energy, and fishery are some prominent examples of renewable resources. Whereas, the minerals like coal, petroleum etc. are major non-renewable resources.

All the North-Eastern states possess a variety of diverse natural resources. The agro-climatic condition also gives the region a unique feature for the development of particular land use pattern and life style of the people. The techno-economic report of National Council of Applied Economic Research (NCAER) (1967) has recognised the forests and hydropower as two important resources of the region that have great potential for the region's development. The survey team however felt that the whole of region is not well endowed with mineral resources that can be effectively utilised for any worthwhile industrialisation programme in the region (Datta, 1991). Not only that, in most cases the extraction cost is very high compared to its economic value and hence many of the mineral extraction projects have not been undertaken because of non-viability as well as high environmental cost associated with them.

Major Mineral Resources of the Region

First we consider the major mineral resources of North-East India. Geological investigation in Northeast India has been in progress since 1825. Still it has not been possible to fully explore the total mineral position of the region. Extensive survey has been made so far in Assam, Meghalaya and Tripura while the shooters of survey is very poor in other North-Eastern states like Arunachal Pradesh, Manipur, Mizoram and Nagaland because of remoteness and inaccessibility. GSI and mining department of the respective states are engaged in investigating the mineral reserves of those states. Also ONGC and Oil India Ltd (OIL) have been carrying out extensive survey of the oil reserves of the region. The investigations revealed so far the deposits of mineral oil, coal, natural gas, limestone, dolomite, sillimonite, clay, fuller earth, feldspar, quartz, marble, asbestos, rock phosphate, iron, copper etc. in the region. Deposits of estimated 100 million tonnes of uranium has also been discovered a few years back and mining has also been started in Meghalaya.

When we talk of mineral resources, the name of petroleum comes first, for which, the state of Assam occupies an important place in the country for a long period of time. India's first oil reserve was found in Assam and mining started at Digboi and then its neighbouring areas. Major portion of India's mineral oil is found in Assam and some in Nagaland. Limited oil reserves have also been found in Arunachal Pradesh a few years back. Among others, coal of different varieties is abundant in Meghalaya and Assam. Some amount of coal is also found in Arunachal Pradesh and Nagaland. Huge amount of natural gas deposit is found in Tripura and explored every year for domestic and industrial purposes. Total reserves of major minerals across the North-East are given in table-3.

Table-3 : Estimated Major Mineral Reserves in the North-East India

Mineral	State	Reserve (million tonnes)
Crude Oil	Assam	70.46
Natural Gas	Assam	23000.00 (million cubic metres)
	Tripura	25000.00 (million cubic metres)
	Total	**48000.00 (million cubic metres)**
Coal	Assam	371.00
	Meghalaya	564.00
	Arunachal Pradesh	91.000
	Nagaland	17.200
	Total	**1043.20**
Lime Stone	Assam	463.00
	Meghalaya	4147.00
	Arunachal Pradesh	350.00
	Manipur East	6.40
	Nagaland	357.00
	Total	**5323.40**
Kaoline	**Meghalaya**	**5.24**
Clay	Meghalaya	28.00
	Tripura	0.5
	Total	**28.5**
Dolomite	**Arunachal Pradesh**	**247.00**
Graphite	**Arunachal Pradesh**	**85.00**
Quartzite	Arunachal Pradesh	3.00
	Assam	17.00
	Total	**20.00**
Sillimonite	**Assam**	**50.00**
White Clay (Fuller's Earth)	**Assam**	**20.00**

Source: NEDFi Databank Quarterly, July 2002.

Notes: The data are compiled from Basic Statistics of NER, 1990 and updated with NEDFi databank, 2002.

Total amount of oil reserves of Assam was estimated to be 70.46 million tonnes from which, around 5000 thousand tonnes of crude oil was explored every year (Ministry of Steel and Mines, Department of Mines, Indian Bureau of Mines, Mining & Mineral Statistics Division). Nagaland is also producing some amount of crude oil each year. Total production of crude oil in Assam and Nagaland has increased from around 3367 thousand tonnes in 1970-71 to 5111 thousand tonnes in 1997-98, which is 51 per cent higher than the production of 1970-71. Arunachal Pradesh has started exploring crude oil in 1980-81 on a small scale (around 2 thousand tonnes per year) and in 1997-98 its production increased to over 35 thousand tonnes.

Total gas reserves estimated in Assam and Tripura is 48000 million cubic metres, of which, 23000 million cubic metres was found in Assam and 28000 million cubic metres in Tripura. The data for other states are not available. Total production of natural gas in Assam, Nagaland and Arunachal Pradesh was around 980 million cubic metres per day in 1970-71 and increased to 2191 million cubic metres per day in 1997-98. However present production potential of Tripura is about 2.03 MMSCMD (NEDFi databank, July 2002). Now a part of daily gas production is used for electricity generation as well as to meet the domestic and some industrial demand.

Out of country's total estimated coal reserves of 186.04 bn. tonnes, only 0.98 bn. tonnes are found in North-Eastern part of India (Deka, 1998). It is occurred in several small deposits in Assam, Meghalaya, Nagaland and Arunachal Pradesh and mostly owned by the private individuals. Occurrence of coal in Upper Assam was known since the beginning of 19th Century but quarrying was first started in 1828. Systematic and commercial mining was initiated by Assam Railway and Trading Company (AR & T Co.) in 1882. At that time, only Makum coalfield was explored and others were not accessible due to the complex geographical structure and lack of demand for coal. Even the domestic fuel requirements were met by using the forest resources. The local tea planters, railways and other local industries mostly used coal produced by that time. Production of coal was taking place at a very low scale. The level of annual production was only 0.49 million tonnes in 1974-75 and after nationalisation it rose to about 0.83 million tonnes during 1989-90 and now it has further increased to 1.4 million tonnes in 1994-95. However, the character of coal available in North-East India is unique by virtue of low ash content, high sulphur and strong caking characteristics in some of the coalfields. Coals with high carbon and hydrogen content indicate a sub-bituminous to bituminous rank. The caking index of the coal available here, is over 20 and coke type is of G/G2. Also coal with low rank properties is available in the region, which is used for blending with prime coking coals for making coke without affecting the quality of the coke. However major portion of coal can be used for cement industry, coal gasification etc besides domestic use and other minor industries. This coal has already found place in the industries like cement, generating energy and in steel plants, where coal is accepted as a blend for coke-making and hence it has a great potential in shaping industrial progress in the region.

In the region, total coal deposits were estimated to be around 1043.2 million tonnes, most of which are found in Meghalaya (Table 3). The coalfields occurred in the Gondwana belt along the thrust sheets of outer Himalayas, Arunachal Pradesh and the Gondwana outcrops in Singrimari in Assam and Meghalaya. The coal deposits are also in the platform area of Garo Hills, West Khasi Hills, Jaintia Hills, Mikir Hills and in small amount in Eastern Khasi Hills. The Tertiary-Oligocene coalfields are located in Makum, Assam which is the largest coalfield of North-Eastern region and the others are Dilli-Jeypore coal-field, Namchik-Namphuk coal-field, Borjan coal-field and small occurrences in Nagaland and Jhanzi Disai Valley. A part of Makum coalfield is extended over to Tirap District of Arunachal Pradesh.

The Makum coalfield contributes about 95 per cent of total coal production of North-East. Active mining has been in progress there for about ten decades. The annual production was about 0.97 million tonne in 1999-2000, where as the figure was about 1.15 million tonne in 1994-95. The demand in 1999-2000 was however assessed to be about 1.20 million tonne.

Limestone is another important mineral abundant in North-Eastern India. The total deposit is estimated to be 5323.4 million tonnes of which 4147 million tonnes are in Meghalaya, 463 million tonnes in Assam and 350 million tonnes are found in Arunachal Pradesh. This limestone has good potential for use in cement, paper grade lime, calcium carbide, and chemical industries.

In addition to those, substantial amount of clay, white clay, kaoline, dolomite, graphite, quartzite, sillimonite, uranium, and other minerals are explored in different states of North-Eastern India.

Land Resource

Let us consider the other important resource that is land resource. This is one of the important primary factors of production. Though land has very limited connection with the growth of industries, it is the primary factor for the agriculture, the sector, which can supply inputs to agro-based industries and therefore the pattern of land utilisation for the generation of different agricultural products may create conditions for the agro-based industries. The agricultural and forest products, besides meeting food and fodder requirements also supply inputs for the growth of agro and forest based industries.

Table-4 shows that per capita availability of land for utilisation has decreased drastically in all the North-Eastern states during 1971 to 1991. Most part of North-Eastern India is hilly and thus naturally a large part is unavailable for cultivation. Moreover, there has been a rapid growth of population (because of high natural growth as well as net immigration). The population in 1991 was 1.61 times to that of 1971 and in 2001 it was (3.85 crores) more than double to that of 1971. Hence one can imagine how availability of land for cultivation has been decreased. This is in spite of reclamation of many uncultivable wastelands that led to rise in net area sown across the states. Moreover there is the soil erosion due to destruction of forest as well as following of traditional jhum (shifting) cultivation. Report of Forest Survey of India has shown that only in two years from 1995 to 1997, net 175 sq. km. of forest has been degraded due to shifting cultivation, most of which has occurred in Assam, Manipur, Nagaland, Meghalaya and Arunachal Pradesh (Forest Survey of India, Dehradun). Till now around 4.5 lakhs families are practising shifting cultivation.

Because of very low population density, per-capita availability of land is the highest in Arunachal Pradesh among all the North-Eastern states. It is the lowest in Assam, which is the most populated state in the region and followed by Tripura, the second most populated state. Over the years because of rising population, increasing need for urbanisation, degradation of soil, desertification, per capita availability of land for agricultural purposes has fallen substantially. Moreover the slash and burn technique of

Table-4 : Population and the Per Capita Availability of Land in Different North-Eastern States during 1971 to 1991

	1971			1981			1991		
	Reporting Area for utilisation (000' Hectares)	Population (Thousand)	Per Capita Land (Sq. Km.)	Reporting Area for utilisation (000' Hectares)	Population (Thousand)	Per Capita Land (Sq. Km.)	Reporting Area for utilisation (000' Hectares)	Population (Thousand)	Per Capita Land (Sq. Km.)
Arunachal Pradesh	5643	467.5	12.07	5486	631.8	8.68	5495	864.6	6.36
Assam	7852	14625.2	0.54	7852	19896.8	0.39	7850	22414.3	0.35
Manipur	2211	1072.8	2.06	2211	1420.95	1.56	2211	1837.1	1.2
Meghalaya	2249	1011.7	2.22	2249	1335.8	1.68	2241	1774.8	1.26
Mizoram	2102	322.4	6.52	2102	493.8	4.26	2088	689.8	3.03
Nagaland	1653	516.4	3.20	1388	774.9	1.79	1546	1209.5	1.28
Tripura	1048	1556.3	0.67	1048	2053.1	0.51	1049	2757.2	0.38
NER	22758	19582.3	1.16	22336	26607.2	0.84	22480	31547.3	0.71
India	304043	547949.8	0.55	—	685184.7	—	304863	846302.7	0.36

Source: Basic Statistics of North-Eastern Region, various issues.

cultivation followed by many families in the north-east and drastic fall in fallow period (due to increasing requirement of food and fodder for growing population) has left land prone to over use and more degradation. In addition to that, there is the disintegration of joint family system and gradual transformation from community ownership to individual ownership that causes fragmentation and reduction in the size of land holding. Therefore the state governments have been trying to implement modern methods of shifting cultivation as well as to bring more and more farmers, wherever possible, under settled cultivation without hampering the productivity of land.

Thus it seems that with the rapid population growth and reduction in per capita availability of land for cultivation it became harder notwithstanding the significant rise in productivity of agriculture to maintain per capita food supply from indigenous production. Per capita food production in North-Eastern region in 1990-91 was 154.78 kg (considering 1991 population) and decreased to 142.16 kg in 1997-98. Production of rice per capita, which is the staple food crop of the region, has decreased from 143.53 kg in 1990-91 to 131.04 kg in 1997-98. For all India average, production of foodgrain per capita has decreased from 208.23 kg in 1990-91 to 194.77 kg in 1997-98 and per capita production of rice has fallen from 88.13 kg to 83.30 kg during the same period. In both cases for estimating per capita production of foodgrains and rice in 1997-98, interpolated population of North-Eastern Region and India as a whole in 1998, calculated by the author have been used.

Forest Resources

Forest is an important source of renewable natural resources, which may also provide basic raw materials for the growth of some industries. Despite meeting the direct biological needs (food, fodder fuel etc.) of the people, and the source of flora and fauna for the entertainment and cosmetic needs of the people, forest supplies huge resources of high economic value and helps growing associated industries. In addition to that, it helps protecting other natural resources like soil. Especially in hilly areas, existence of forests prevents soil erosion and thus preserving the productivity of soil. Thus National Forest Policy 1986 recommended maintaining at least 33 per cent of geographical area of the country under forest cover and at least 60 per cent of land in hilly region under the forest cover. The proportion is maintained in the North-Eastern states by the existing forest area, which is around 64 per cent of the total geographical area. But if we consider the actual tree cover (crown density) the actual level is far away from the desired level.

Forest in the region, accounts for more than a quarter (around 26 per cent) of India's total forest cover, is also subject to rampant exploitation. It has a great importance not only for its market value and other uses but also because of the existence of rich bio-diversity. For its great biological diversity the region has been identified as one of the eighteen hotspots in the World.

Growing need of the people for forest products has led to the indiscriminate destruction of forest. Hence degradation of forest took place across all the North-Eastern states. This is mainly because of the commonness of the North-Eastern forests or the absence of property rights (De. 2002). A large part of forest in North-East India especially, in Meghalaya and Nagaland is under private or community ownership or controlled by district council (table-5). But there is lack of proper planning in the utilisation of those forests. Finally high concentration of poverty is another important reason for the degradation of natural forest in the region. Majority of poor people of North-East India lives in rural areas and depends highly on the natural resources, mainly on forest for their sustenance. They used to collect fuel-wood, leaves, fodder, fruits, timber for daily consumption, making dwelling cottages, grazing their cattle and collecting other means of livelihood in exchange of timber and other materials collected from the forest.

Major products based on forest resources of North-East India are round wood, fuel wood, industrial round wood, pulpwood, sawn wood, wood based panels, veneer sheets, plywood, particle board, fibre board, wood pulp, newsprint, printing and writing paper. In addition to that North-East India is famous for producing various sophisticated craft items based on bamboo and cane that is the source of employment of a large number of population of the region. A number of saw mills and plywood and handicraft industries have been running on the basis of those raw materials, collected from the forests. According to the Times of India Publication report, in 1986, over 540.7 lakh sq. metre plywood was produced in North-East India and most of the production came from Assam and Arunachal Pradesh. Total capacity of the plywood industries of the region was 823.87 lakh metre (Data Bank, 1987, Times of India Publication). Annually over 70 lakh tonnes of bamboo and around 8 lakh cubic metres saw timber used to be produced in mid-1970s (Basic Statistics of NER, 1980). So there is a great potential of forest resource base industrial development in the North-Eastern region. However, rampant felling of trees and deforestation appears to be a great concern because of its environmental and long-term economic consequences. However, the Supreme Court order of 1997 banning cutting of trees has led to the closure of several saw mills and plywood industries in the region.

Table-5 : Proportion of Area under Forest Cover, Dense Forest & Open Forest in North-Eastern States during 1989-99 (in Percentage)

State\Year	1989			1999		
	FA	DF	OF	FA	DF	OF
Arunachal Pradesh	82.27	78.93	21.07	82.21	83.89	16.11
Assam	33.19	60.20	35.96	30.20	61.28	38.72
Manipur	79.99	28.29	71.71	77.86	34.15	65.85
Meghalaya	69.76	21.84	78.16	69.70	37.90	62.10
Mizoram	86.19	21.36	78.64	86.99	20.65	79.35
Nagaland	86.85	32.27	67.73	85.43	36.27	63.73
Tripura	50.81	22.80	77.20	54.79	38.78	61.22
All-India	19.47	58.97	40.21	19.38	59.22	40.02

Note: FA means percentage of total geographical area under forest,

DF means percentage of dense forest area to total forest area (havimg >40 per cent crown density)

OF means percentage of open forest area to total forest area (havimg 10-40 per cent crown density)

Source: Forest Survey of India, Ministry of Environment and Forest, Government of India, New Delhi.

Table-5 shows that during 1989-1999 the percentage of geographical area under forest has decreased in almost all the North-Eastern states except Mizoram and Tripura, though the figures are still higher than the national average. Whereas the percentage of forest cover under dense forest has increased in all North-Eastern states except Mizoram. However if the area under open forest and area with less than 10 per cent crown density is considered, we observe considerable degradation of forest land during the same period, in all North-Eastern states except Assam and Mizoram.

The average annual compound rate of degradation was highest (-8.57 per cent) in Arunachal Pradesh and the lowest in Manipur (-0.90 per cent). It increased by .08 and .75 per cent respectively in Mizoram and Assam (table-6) comparing with the states of other regions of India, the degradation was found to be on the higher rate in the North-Eastern states, which may be due to the practice of traditional *jhum (shifting)* cultivation (Reddy et al., 2001).

Table-6 : Extent of Degraded Forest in North-Eastern States during 1989-99

State\Year	Compound Growth Rate per annum (Percentage)
Arunachal Pradesh	- 8.57
Assam	0.75
Manipur	- 0.90
Meghalaya	- 3.48
Mizoram	0.08
Nagalend	- 1.33
Tripura	- 2.18
All-India	0.20

Source: Government of India, Ministry of Environment and Forests, *Forest Survey of India*, New Delhi

The classification of forest in North-East India is presented in Table 7. It shows that almost one-third of North-East Indian forest is reserved forest and a very few area is under protected forest, which also increased from 5.49 per cent in 1980 to 9.23 per cent of total forest area. More than fifty percent of the forest is either unclassified or owned by community or private individual or managed by district council.

Table-7 : Forests in North-East India According to Ownership (in thousand Sq. Km.)

	Total Forest		Reserved Forests		Protected Forests		Others	
State	1980	1997	1980	1997	1980	1997	1980	1997
Arunachal Pradesh	51540	51540	11131	15321	1	8	40408	36211
			(21.6)	(29.73)		(0.02)	(78.40)	(70.26)
Assam	28608	30708	16420	18242	—	3934	12188	8532
			(57.4)	(59.40)		(12.81)	(42.6)	(27.78)
Manipur	15154	15154	1370	1463	4170	4171	9614	9520
			(9.04)	(9.65)	(27.52)	(27.52)	(63.44)	(62.82)
Meghalaya	8528	9496	706	981	103	12	7719	8503
			(8.28)	(10.33)	(1.21)	(0.13)	(90.51)	(89.54)
Mizoram	12233	15935	7127	7127	—	3568	5106	5240
			(58.26)	(44.73)		(22.39)	(41.74)	(32.88)
Nagaland	2876	8629	286	86	518	507	2072	8036
			(9.95)	(1.00)	(18.01)	(5.88)	(72.04)	(93.13)
Tripura	6011	6293	3942	3588	2069	509	—	2196
			(65.58)	(57.02)	(34.42)	(8.09)		(34.90)
NER	124950	137755	40982	46808	6861	12709	77107	78238
			(32.8)	(33.98)	(5.49)	(9.23)	(61.71)	(56.80)

Source: Basic Statistics of North-Eastern Region, various issues.

Power in North-East India

Power is an important source of energy and essential for the establishment and running of industries as well as better civic life. Now-a-days one cannot think of civic life without power. Though North-Eastern states have great potential for generating electricity, till now, all the states face shortage of power especially during the peak demand period. The capacity of power generation also varies across the states. According to CEA estimates (1978-87), the hydroelectric power potential of Arunachal Pradesh is tremendous and it alone can generate more than 27000 MW hydroelectricity, which is around 32 per cent of country's total hydroelectric potential of 84000 MW. Table 8 shows the changes in installed capacity during 1980 to 1999 across the North-Eastern states.

The table shows that out of 1709.71 MW total capacities in 1999 in the North-Eastern region, 593.3 MW comes from hydro-electricity projects, 300 MW are thermal and only 74.25 MW from diesel and the rest i.e., 742.16 from gas turbine. Most of the gas turbines are located in Assam and Tripura. There has been a notable change in the installed power generation project since 1980. A number of projects are ongoing and a number of projects have been approved for meeting the deficit and growing expected future demand for electricity in the region. Till now the states of the region have to import power from other states or neighbouring country like Nepal. Major portion of the power produced in the region is going to meet the domestic requirement and a limited amount is supplied to different industries located in the region. At present Assam is producing maximum electricity in the region, followed by Meghalaya and Tripura.

In the year 2000 total installed capacity in Nagaland was 93.46 MW and NEEPCO has also commissioned a 75 MW hydroelectric project in Doyang. In Tripura total installed capacity in 2002 is 178.46 MW. NEEPCO has also started one 84 MW gas based project near Agartala recently (Ministry of Power, Govt. of India). Total installed capacity of Mizoram on 30-4-2002 was 86.30 MW and there, NEEPCO has started a 60 MW Tuirial hydro-project. In Meghalaya total installed capacity in 2002 is 285.96 MW and one each of hydro and thermal power project are being installed for meeting the excess demand for

Table-8 : Installed Power Capacity in the North-Eastern Region (in MW)

State	Thermal		Hydro		Diesel		Gas	Total	
	31-3-1980	31-3-1999	31-3-1980	31-3-1999	31-3-1980	31-3-1999	31-3-1999	31-3-1980	31-3-1999
Arunachal Pradesh	—	—	8.4	23.60	2.4	15.8	—	10.8	39.40
Assam	141.5	300.0	—	2.00	23.3	20.69	299.0	164.8	621.69
Manipur	—	—	0.6	2.80	20.8	9.30	—	21.4	12.10
Meghalaya	2.5	—	125.9	185.20	1.9	—	—	130.3	185.20
Mizoram	—	—	—	5.40	3.5	19.10	—	3.5	24.50
Nagaland	—	—	1.5	3.30	3.6	3.26	—	5.1	6.56
Tripura	—	—	10.0	16.00	5.2	6.10	64.50	15.2	86.60
Total	144.0	300.0	146.4	593.3*	60.7	74.25	742.16*	351.1	1709.71

Sources: Power and Energy Division, Planning Commission and NEREB, Shillong.

Note: * implies that the data includes the installed capacity of the central sector also. Data corresponding to different states represents state sectors only.

power in the state. Manipur's present total power production capacity is 154.11 MW and Loktak hydroelectric power project of 90 MW capacitity has recently been inaugurated by the President of India. Total power production capacity of Assam and Arunachal Pradesh in 2002 are 597 MW and 162.43 MW respectively. Now 6 different projects of estimated capacity of 505 MW in Assam and 13 others, of which, 4 are ongoing and 9 are proposed with total 2610 and 18385 MW capacity in Arunachal Pradesh have been undertaken for raising the power production and improving the power situation in the region (NEDFi Databank Quarterly, Report and CEA statistics, Ministry of Power, Govt. of India). Though there has been a significant improvement of power situation in the region, it is still lacking in the generation of power to meet the industrial demand. While importing the power from other region, total transmission loss incurred is estimated to be 35 per cent. At present average per capita power consumption of the region is very low compared to the national average consumption of 360 KWH per year (NEDFi, July 2002).

Human Resource

Let us now consider the human resource of the region. The size and structure of population determine the supply of other primary factor labour, which is of great importance for the industrial production. But it is not only the quantity of population which is important for the development, rather it is the quality of human being consisting of the level of education, age composition, sex etc., which determines the efficiency of working population. As population grows, supply of labour and use of resources increase, raising the level of production and improvement of standard of living. However huge population growth may become a burden for the society if the extra population cannot be absorbed in gainful employment. In that case it would cause overexploitation and degradation of resources and thus may hamper the developmental prospects. Education can help in building better human resources and people can plan and implement different programmes in a better way to utilise resources in a sustainable manner. Spread of education especially among women also helps controlling population growth and thus assumed to be the best antidote to population explosion.

Table-9 : Changes in Literacy Rate, Density of Population and Sex Ratio in North-East India during 1971 to 2001

	Literacy Rate		Density of Population		Sex Ratio (Female per 1000 male)	
	1971	**2001**	**1971**	**2001**	**1971**	**2001**
Arunachal Pradesh	11.3	54.74	6	13	861	901
Assam	28.1	64.28	186	340	896	932
Manipur	32.9	68.87	48	107	980	978
Meghalaya	29.5	63.31	45	103	942	975
Mizoram	53.8	88.49	16	42	942	938
Nagaland	27.4	67.11	31	120	871	909
Tripura	31.0	73.66	149	304	943	950
North-East India	-	-	77	149	906	937
All India	29.5	65.38	177	324	930	933

Source: Basic Statistics of North-Eastern Region, various issues.

Table-10 : Number of Educational Institutions in the States of North Eastern Region

	Arunachal Pradesh		Assam		Manipur		Meghalaya	
Institution	**1978**	**1996**	**1978**	**1996**	**1978**	**1996**	**1978**	**1996**
University	-	1	3	5	*	2	1	1
General College	1	6	136	247	21	50	13	28
Engineering College	-	1	3	3	-	-	-	-
Medical College	-	-	3	7	1	1	-	-
Agricultural College	-	-	1	2	1	1	-	-
Veterinary College	-	-	1	1	-	-	-	-
Teachers Training College	-	-	8	22	3	2	1	1
Junior Colleges (+2 Stage)	-	-	9	70	-	22	-	-
HS School	8	67	112	588	13	52	-	28
High School	25	90	1694	3757	239	501	172	403
Middle School	109	301	3656	7237	381	555	392	851
Primary School	841	1256	21615	30140	3516	2548	3477	4235
Pre-primary School	35	137	262	482	1	1	384	-
Teachers Training School	-	-	32	1	4	-	9	10
Polytechnics	-	1	7	9	1	3	1	1
Technical and Industrial school	3	2	25	32	22	6	3	3
University	*	1#	*	1	*	1	4	12#
General College	6	29	7	23	6	14	190	397
Engineering College	-	-	-	-	1	1	4	5
Medical College	-	-	-	-	-	-	4	8
Agricultural College	-	-	1	1	-	-	3	4
Veterinary College	-	-	-	-	-	-	1	1
Teachers Training College	1	2	1	1	4	1	18	29
Junior Colleges (+2 Stage)	-	29	-	3	-	-	9	124
HS School	-	16	-	4	52	188	185	943
High School	114	330	101	240	102	370	2447	5691
Middle School	239	702	288	416	292	411	5357	10473
Primary School	518	1263	1114	1414	1572	2045	32653	42901
Pre-primary School	-	-	-	-	590	3406	1272	4026
Teachers Training School	2	1	3	2	-	2	50	16
Polytechnics	-	1	1	1	1	1	11	17
Technical and Industrial school	1	1	1	3	2	4	57	51

Note: # data relates to 2001, * means Post Graduate centres of different universities.

Source: Basic Statistics of North Eastern Region, various issues.

As already noted, spread of education enhances the productive capacity of human being. Growth of higher education and scientific research raise the inventive and innovative capability. Also education raises the leadership quality of the people and their capability of management. Finally, education and training can help developing entrepreneurial capacity of a person and hence generate conditions for industrial development. Therefore, a state having better human resource may be more developed even without having much natural resources than another having more natural resource but poor quality of human resources.

Literacy rate has been increased significantly in all the states during the period 1971-2001. The growth rate of literacy has been the highest in Arunachal Pradesh that started from a very low base. In the region, Mizoram has the highest literacy rate and it stands second in the country. Table 9 shows that density of population has increased by almost 100 percent. The density is very small in Arunachal Pradesh. It is the highest in Assam and followed by Tripura. Average population density of the region is however much lower than the national average. Excepting Assam, density of all the North-Eastern states are much lower than the national average. In spite of having smallest population density Arunachal Pradesh is the poorest state of the region. Lower level of education may be one of the important reasons for this. Sex ratio also increased in almost all the North-Eastern states and the average of the region is higher than that of the country. Excepting Arunachal Pradesh, Assam and Nagaland, other states of the region have better sex ratio than that of all India average.

During the last few decades educational infrastructure has been improved and the enrolment at different levels has also increased. Table 10 shows the growth of educational institutions in different states of North-East India during 1978 to 1996. It is observed that number of different educational institutions has increased many times during this period. Earlier, students from the North-East India were compelled to go to outside the region mainly for their higher studies. But now most of them have access to higher education locally. Thus those who could not avail higher studies earlier because of financial reason and communication problem now find it feasible. Therefore enrolment at different level has increased many times. However, in spite of that drop out rates at different levels are much higher in North-Eastern region. This is clear from the NSS Fifty-second Round Survey. The drop-out level is also higher in case of females than the males and it is higher in rural areas than the urban areas. Among the North-Eastern states, the over all drop-out is the highest in Arunachal Pradesh. Out of 1000 students, the drop-out rate is 810 in rural areas and 383 in urban areas (average 756). Where as the drop-out rate is minimum in Meghalaya. The figures are 359 and 373 for rural and urban areas respectively. The average is 360. Most of the dropouts occur at the primary level. In spite of creation of facilities for higher education, research and technical education and producing a number of educated and technical persons each year, the region is still dependent on the experts from outside the region at different spheres, whether it is an educational institution or an industry.

Table 11 shows the sector-wise distribution of main workers in North-East India and its change over time. Overall work participation rate in the North-East has increased slightly during 1971 to 1991. Whereas the participation rate has decreased significantly in the states of Arunachal Pradesh, Nagaland and slightly in Meghalaya and Mizoram

Table-11 : Changes in Work Participation Rate and Sector-wise Distribution of Main Workers from 1971 to 1991

	Workers % of Total Population		% of Main Workers in Primary Sector		% of Main Workers in Secondary Sector		% of Main Workers Tertiary in Sector	
State	1971	1991	1971	1991	1971	1991	1971	1991
Arunachal Pradesh	57.65	46.24	80.44	67.44	0.45	8.66	19.11	23.96
Assam	27.95	36.09	77.04	73.99	4.20	5.56	17.86	20.45
Manipur	34.57	42.18	71.30	70.00	12.24	9.66	16.46	20.34
Meghalaya	44.17	42.67	81.84	74.81	3.30	3.74	14.86	21.46
Mizoram	45.61	48.91	84.17	65.99	1.76	5.07	14.07	28.94
Nagaland	50.75	42.68	79.46	75.26	2.38	3.48	18.16	21.26
Tripura	27.79	31.14	76.58	64.08	4.25	6.41	19.17	29.51
N-E India	30.75	33.19	77.45	72.61	4.93	5.78	17.62	21.61
All India	32.91	37.46	72.56	67.5	10.69	12.0	16.75	20.5

Source: *Census of India*, Various Issues.

indicating that the rate of population growth has not matched with the rising scope of opportunity. As agriculture in these agro-economic states primarily based on shifting cultivation, with limited modernisation and without significant changes in employment scenario in the industrial sector, scope for increase in work participation rate has been limited. Moreover, there is the discrepancy in male-female employment opportunities. Though in tribal societies females are hardworking and engaged in several socio-economic activities, still there is a gender bias (Census Reports). In contrast, work participation rate has increased in Assam, Manipur and Tripura but not significantly. These are due to the sluggish growth of industrial sector and rapid population growth. This is clear from very low percentage of main workers engaged in secondary sector and the figure is around only 4 per cent for the North-Eastern region according to 1991 census report. The figure ranges from 1.71 per cent in Nagaland to 4.94 per cent in Tripura (where large-scale industry is non-existent). Not only that, the percentage of main workers engaged in secondary sector has decreased slightly during the period. During last few decades however it is the tertiary sector that has grown remarkably and percentage of main workers engaged in service sector has increased in all the North-Eastern states like the other regions of India.

Industrial Structure

Small-scale industries occupy the central position in the industrial structure of the region. Most of the few large scale and medium scale industries in the region are located in Assam. Most of the industries in the region produce commodities on the basis of the inputs available locally and primarily to meet the regional demand. A few handloom and handicraft items are exported to other regions of the country. Though the region is endowed with vast natural resources like minerals, flora and fauna; it failed to utilise those resources effectively. Industries are mostly of small scale and operate with the help of traditional and simple labour intensive technology.

Table-12 : Number and Growth of Large and Medium Scale Industries in North-East India during 1980 to 1998

	Number of Units	% of Total Industries in the Region	Number of Units	% of Total Industries in the Region
State	1980		1998	
Arunachal Pradesh	2	3.23	17	9.6
Assam	48	77.42	128	72.3
Manipur	1	1.61	12	6.8
Meghalaya	3	4.84	10	5.6
Mizoram	2	3.23	1	0.6
Nagaland	4	6.45	7	4.0
Tripura	1	1.61	2	1.1
N-E India	62	100	177	100

Note: Out of those industries, one paper mill in Assam and Nagaland, one oil refinery in Assam, one hard board industry in Nagaland and one spun silk mill in Manipur were under construction at that time.
Source: as in table2

Table-12 shows that total number of large and medium scale industries in the region was 62 in 1980 and has increased to 177. Most of them are located in Assam. Most of the industries were either agro-based or forest based and a few are mineral based. The forest-based industries are plywood and other wood products; paper-mill, hard board etc. and the agro-based industries are mainly sugar factory, jute mill, spun silk mill, muga silk, rubber and tea. The mineral-based industries are mainly oil refinery, cement factory, chemical industry, and distillery projects. Though one jute-mill and one sugar mill were established in Tripura to utilise the local raw materials and to meet the state's requirement, they are now defunct. It is because of the inefficiency and exorbitant cost of production compared to the other regions. Similarly a large number of saw mills and plywood and other wood based industries mostly located in Assam, Arunachal Pradesh and Tripura have been closed after the ruling of Supreme Court on non-felling of trees in 1997. That has led to the increase in unemployment and grievances among the mill owners as well as instigated corruption and malpractices in the forest management. Rather it would be better to impose conditions of reinvestment for the regeneration of forest by the forest users at an equal rate of exploitation/destruction caused by them. That way the level of forest based industrialisation could sustain and it would be possible to utilise the knowledge and expertise of the local people to use the herbs and other forest resources, for the development of medicines, artistic as well as other necessary consumer products, for the well being of the people along with the maintenance of the forest. The conditions of the mineral-based industries are also similar. Because of the exhaustibility of crude mineral, the rate of production will be slow (though the rate is maintained till now) unless new oil deposits are found in the region. However if advances of technology permits and innovations take place in the potential gas based industrial projects then the future problem that may arise due to exhaustibility of mineral oil may be solved to a certain extent.

Table-13 : Development of Small Scale Industries in North-East India during 1971 to 98

	Number of Establishments				Employment in Number				% of Capacity Utilisation
State	1971	1981	1991	1998	1971	1981	1991	1998	1998
Arunachal Pradesh	11	189	525	2280	187	—	—	2771	51.23
Assam	1648	4152	12805	20035	19652	—	—	34475	19.31
Manipur	485	3422	4059	5188	3409	—	—	10216	65.37
Meghalaya	164	393	1368	2079	1188	—	—	3780	55.25
Mizoram	61	599	2478	3466	336	—	—	4223	71.88
Nagaland	38	366	615	749	446	—	—	3059	46.29
Tripura	246	1188	4967	7512	1698	—	—	10069	40.76
Total NER	2653	10309	26817	41309	26910	—	—	68593	27.32
INDIA	139577	—	—	582368	1653178	—	—	3665810	50.89

Source: *Basic Statistics of North Eastern Region*, Various Issues.
NEDFi, Databank Quarterly, July, 2002.

Small Scale Industries

Table 13 shows that number of Small-scale industries (SSIs) in North-East India has increased from 2653 in 1971 to 41309 in 1998 i.e., it increased to about 16 times. Employment also increased from 26910 to 68593 during the same period i.e., it increased to around 2.5 times. This indicates that though number of establishments has increased by several times, the employment has not expanded at the same pace. Moreover, the last column shows that the capacity utilisation of the SSIs in the North-East in 1998 was below 30 per cent, which is much lower than the national average of 50.89 percent capacity utilisation. So the increase of small-scale establishments does not ensure the growth of employment unless it is properly managed and run. Among the North-Eastern states, the rate of capacity utilisation in Mizoram and Manipur was much higher than that of the national average, where as it was just over the national average in Arunachal Pradesh and Meghalaya. In other states the rate of utilisation was well below the national average.

Capital is one of the important barrier for the growth of small industries in the region. Though there has been a significant growth of banking system to help the small-scale industries to grow, during 1994 to 1999, only 25 per cent of total SSIs were set up with the help of bank finance in North-East India. It also varies across the states. It ranges from 16.5 per cent in Meghalaya to around 45 per cent in Arunachal Pradesh during 1994 to 1999. Also it is to be noted that, only 636 persons had the approval for bank finance in total, which was around half the trained persons (1256) who had applied for that (*Basic Statistics of NER*, 2000).

Khadi and Village industries also play an important role in the generation of employment and income in the region. It mainly operates in the handloom and handicraft sector that requires less capital compared to other industries. The employment and output of these industries in total are given in table-14. In spite of being a small state, the performance of this sector in Manipur is the best among all the North-Eastern states. The employment in this sector in Manipur is 0.42 lakh, which is, of course, lower than the employment in Assam (1.25 lakh). But production of those industries in Manipur is higher than that of Assam. Performance of Arunachal Pradesh is the worst in terms of employment and production in khadi and village industries.

In addition to the above, there are sericulture-based industries, which have good reputation. But the progress of this sector also has not been significant in spite of its historical background. There is also much scope for the development of plantation-based industries in the region. Some tea industries are there in the region but rubber-based and fruit processing industries are very limited compared to the potential of the region. Lastly, we may name the tourism industry that earns a good amount of revenue each year. Though it has a good prospect in the region because of its geographical and natural beauties, it has suffered a lot in the last few decades because of much talked insurgency and thereby security reasons.

Table-14 : Employment and Production of the Khadi & Village Industries in North-East India in 1998-99

State	Employment (Lakh)	Production (Lakh Rs.)
Arunachal Pradesh	—	35.91
Assam	1.25	4379.30
Manipur	0.42	4457.27
Meghalaya	0.11	1202.98
Mizoram	0.15	2412.76
Nagaland	0.19	1816.92
Tripura	0.23	1186.89
Total NER	2.35	15492.03
INDIA	58.29	511237.46

Source: Khadi & Village Industries Commission NE Zone, Guwahati.

Resource Industry Linkages

Just by looking at the number of industries and the availability of resources, it is very difficult to explain the nature of resource-industry linkage in any region. This is primarily because of the nature and extents of input requirements are different in different industry. Also industries vary in their size and capacity of production. In addition to that the input requirement of the industries even producing the same commodity may vary due to variation in their technology. Due to the heterogeneity of different industries and because of lack of data on input used by different industries, it is very difficult to estimate the total use of different resources available in the region and hence it is very difficult to find the correlation between the availability of resources and their utilisation in the existing industries in the region. Even if it is possible and we observe a strong correlation between the availability of resources and the industrial output, it may not be an indication of resource-industry linage in the region as the strong correlation may also be observed in case of a region having low industrial base as well as low resource base. Sometimes it may be observed that the industries of a region are using the resources available in other region. Similarly, resources from one region may be exported to the industries of other region.

However, there is a wide gap between the resource-base and industrial structure in the North-Eastern states of India. Though the region is endowed with ample natural resources, it failed to make use of that natural advantage to industrialise herself. Even in many cases it is observed that the raw materials of the region are being utilised in the industries located in other parts of the country or outside the country. For example, a good amount of coal of Assam and Meghalaya are being transported and utilised in the Durgapur and Bokaro steel plants located in West Bengal and Bihar. Similarly, a part of limestone is exported to cement factory located in Bangladesh. In spite of having huge potential of producing bamboo there is only one paper mill in Cachar region of Assam and none in Tripura. Till now the region imports major portion of paper and allied products from the other parts of the country.

Studies are available on resource base and the potential of industrial development in the region (NCAER, 1967, IIE, 1996). As mentioned earlier, there are several categories of potential for industrial development. Such as mineral based industries, agro-based industries, plantation and forest-based industries, demand-based industries and, tourism and human resource based industries. Despite having many natural resources, growth of industries have not taken place at the desired pace and thus there is a very low linkage between existence of resource bases and the industrial development.

Two major reasons may be assigned to the lack of industrial development in the region. Firstly, the lack of proper infrastructure and communication in the region. High transport cost leads to high cost of the production which make the products uncompetitive. Due to inaccessibility, many of the potential forest and mineral resources remain unexplored and thus could not be utilised. Secondly, there is the insurgency problem that hampers the growth of all kinds of developmental activities. Due to the insecurity, much of the rich human resources drained out each year to other region. Also the investors are not interested in many cases in this vulnerable region, in spite of governments' industrial policy to encourage investment through tax concession, subsidised loan, land allocation and other incentives. In addition to these, there is a lack of entrepreneurship skill and competitive attitude among the local inhabitants, for which, till now the industrial sector of the region is dependent upon the initiative of the entrepreneurs from other region.

As already mentioned, infrastructure facilities like banking, transport, power are the other hindrances of industrial development and thus responsible for the poor linkages between the availability of useful resources and their use in the development of industries in the region. Until now, the banking system failed to provide adequate financial support to the potential small entrepreneurs. The communication system is very weak and there is a lack of adequate preservation facility which hamper the marketing of region's agro, horticulture and floricultural products.

Role of Market and the States

Market is very important from the point of view of the development of industries in any region. For big business establishment, size of the markets and their location plays a crucial role, as the quantum of potential demand for the products determines the extent of productive capacity of the industries to be unutilised or the potential inventory of the product of the concerned industry. It acts as potential incentive and thus sets one of the preconditions for any industrial establishment. Size of the local market and hence local demand is more important in this regard. Even if the inputs are abundant in a particular location, the industry that intensively use that resource as input may not increase, if the local demand is too meagre and more so when it is very difficult to export the same to the other region. Thus Heckscher-Ohlin comparative advantage rule does not work in this case for the development of locally available input-intensive industrial development.

In this regard one may mention the doll industry of Taiwan, whose internal demand is very negligible compared to total annual production. The technology in this case is so rich and its external demand is so high that it can produce and export at a comparatively cheaper rate than the importing countries.

Moreover, due to inaccessibility and communication problem, lack of understanding with neighbouring Bangladesh to utilise their seaports it has become very difficult to export region's products to the outside market.

In the present phase of privatisation and globalisation, the scope of integration of local markets with the world market has increased and those who are technically in better position and resourceful, can take full advantage of it in expanding their industrial and business activities. However there is always a fear that in the early phase, the stiff external competition may ruin and hamper the growth of budding industries of the region and the import of those articles that can be produced indigenously would capture even the local market.

Governments' role in this case is of two types. On the one hand, as already initiated in the new industrial policy, the government of India has taken several measures to promote industrialisation in the region. A five-year tax holiday has already been announced for those, who will invest in industries in the North-Eastern region. The state governments have already promised to provide adequate land to the interested industrialists, to give loans at subsidised interest to make adequate fund available especially to the small industries, to develop infrastructure like construction of roads, training centres etc.

Policy Prescription

For the all-round development of the North-Eastern states, priority should be given on industrial development on the basis of sustainable exploitation of natural resources. It is well known that for rapid and sustainable progress of an economy, industrialisation is essential. For adequate industrial growth, proper use of natural resources, formation of capital in different forms is required. Also it needs a healthy environment in which the agents of economic change can work freely and systematically. For this, change in the attitude of the people is a must.

Education should be the first priority that brings a change in the attitude of the people. Though there has been significant growth of educational institutions in number, the quality of education has not improved keeping pace with that number. Most of the institutions in the region are severely suffering from lack of infrastructure like number of teachers, staffs, inadequate teaching facilities etc. and attention should be given for the improvement of those basic things.

It is perceptible that the rate of exploitation of natural resources in the region is well below to that of the other developed regions and hence the rate of growth of industrial production, employment and overall economic progress are also lower for the region. The industries of North-East has been lagging in the use of updated technology and hence incur relatively higher cost in the production and efficiency is relatively low. Thus they face the problem of survival from the stiff competition from improved technology users of the other region. Hence, steps should be taken to remove the technological barriers and to switch over from the traditional way of production to the modern method of industrial operation.

Agriculture, which is still the dominant sector in all the states of North-East India, should be modernised to generate sufficient surplus that can be utilised in the industrial development. Proper infrastructural development, formation of human capital and proper use of funds are highly desired.

REFERENCES

Becker, R.A. (1982), "Intergenerational Equity: The Capital-Environment Trade-off", *Journal of environmental Economics and Management*, Vol.9, No.2, pp.165-85.

Basic Statistics of North-Eastern Region, various issues, Shillong.

Census of India, various issues.

Clark, C. (1940), *The Conditions of Economic Progress, Macmillan.*

Datta, P.S. (1991), *Economic Development of Arunachal Pradesh - A Case Study of North-Eastern Council's Role,* Har Anand Publications, New Delhi.

De, U. K. (2002), "Economic Incentive and Environmental Management - A Study of Forestry in North-East India" presented in the Seminar on *The Mother-Earth* organised by NEICSSR, Shillong on 5th June, 2002.

Deka, P. (1998), *Industrial Development* (A Study of Resource and Opportunities in the Land of Seven Sisters), vol. I and vol. 2, Omsons Publications, New Delhi.

Hanley N., J. F. Shogren and B. White (1997), *Environmental Economics*, Macmillan.

Govt. of India, *Economic Survey*, Various issues.

Ministry of Environment and Forest, Government of India, *Forest Survey of India*, New Delhi.

Ministry of Power, Government of India.

National Council of Applied Economic Research (1967), *Techno-Economic Survey of NEFA*, New Delhi.

North-Eastern Council, Ministry of Home Affairs, Govt. of India, *Compendium on the Coal Occurrences of North-Eastern Region,* vol. II, March, 1991.

North Eastern Development Finance Corporation, (2002), *Quarterly Journal of North* Eastern States Economy, vol. 1, Issue 1, July.

Reddy, R. et al. (2001), "Forest Degradation in India: Extent and Determinants", *Indian Journal of Agricultural Economics*, Vol.56, No.4, Oct.-Dec., pp. 631-51.

Times of India Publication, Databank, 1987.

10

Public Resource and Its Utilization : Implications for Development of North-Eastern Region

—B. Mishra

Introduction

The attainment of rapid economic development remains as one of the major problems in a developing economy. The developmental theorists argue in general that the obvious requirement for development is a steady and rapid rate of capital accumulation. If, capital accumulation is taken as a pre-condition for the economy to take off then the related question that arises how can capital accumulation be achieved? Unlike the developed economies, where most of the capital accumulation takes place through the market mechanism in the presence of a huge amount of capital goods, capital accumulation in a developing economy, does not usually take place through any such market mechanism, because, capital goods do not flow constantly to the market in the absence of a sound infrastructural footing. Therefore, it is often argued that their governments must be responsible for most of the capital accumulation. The investment in the basic infrastructural set up, as Goode (1963)[1] argues, constitutes as a necessary pre-condition for rapid increase in innovation and capital formation in manufacturing, commerce and agriculture, necessitating large quantum of capital deployment do not result in quick and direct returns as to attract private individuals to come forward to invest, thereby shouldering a part of Government's responsibility in this regard.

One important corollary that follows from the above argument is that, the Government, in a developing economy, has to play a decisive role not only in the front of mobilization of adequate resources but also in its judicious utilization so as to achieve the desired social goals.

For augmenting the pace of economic development, it is necessary that resources should be generated through various fiscal measures. Resource for development purposes may be obtained either from internal or external sources, or from both. Under the given economic base of the developing countries, it obliges them to pay greater attention to the maximum possible exploitation of internal resources. In the light of the above discussion, we think it imperative to confine our discussion to the fiscal problems associated with mobilizing resources from internal sources. The alternative ways of augmenting internal sources are: (i) increase the savings voluntarily through a reduction in current consumption (ii) increase the savings involuntarily through additional taxation (iii) compulsory lending to the Government, or "forced savings" through inflation, (iv) by the utilization of the `disguised unemployed labour' in the productive work and, (v) through a combination of all these schemes.

However, in an economy like ours where the average income per head stays at a lower level, mobilization of resources either through voluntary reduction in current consumption or forced savings through inflation remains elusive. Further, high marginal propensity to consume and presence of a large non-monetized sector in the economy has created considerable difficulties in the mobilization of resources from compulsory lending and utilization of the 'disguised unemployed labour' in the productive work.

We are thus left with the instrument of additional taxation as the feasible method of resource mobilization for an economy like India for the purposes of development. We must make it clear at this juncture that, over the last three decades, the tax system, both in its direct and indirect levies, has been overhauled and refashioned so as to make it a suitable instrument for furthering the objectives of economic development[2].

In a federal set up, the financing of the state development plans depends to a large extent on the willingness and the capacity to mobilize adequate resources by the state Governments mainly through an effective exercise of their power of taxation. Since, the capacity to mobilize adequate resources on the part of the state governments depends on the level of development of the state in question; problems relating to resource mobilization differ from state to state. As a matter of fact, efforts made in this direction from time to time have not uniformly succeeded. Being federal in structure, the state Governments has limited statutory powers to levy taxes to finance its various infrastructural facilities and welfare programmes. This may be ascribed to the fact that while bulk of the federal revenue has been derived from more elastic sources, implying that the revenue from these taxes increases proportionately, if not faster than income, the sources of the state Government are relatively less elastic, as reported by Rao (1992)[3].

With the expansion of the Governmental activities, the magnitude of public expenditures of the state Governments have increased tremendously which in turn has given rise to the need for a rapid increase in revenue or tapping of additional resources. It is expected that the sources of revenue should grow automatically at the required rate. But the experiences of most of the state Governments in India negate the above proposition. As a result of which, this has created a widening gap between the state's expenditure responsibilities on the one hand and available resources on the other, thereby giving rise to the problem of attaining an appropriate degree of financial self-reliance on the part of the most of the state Governments in India. Thus, it can be argued that the financial problems of the states arise owing to lack of efforts on their own part to raise additional resources.

The financial constraints imposed on state Governments in India under the practice of fiscal federalism define their options more narrowly. In India, the emergence of a situation has arisen in which, some states are excessively dependent on federal transfers, while others resort extensively to overdrafts, which could be attributed either to the failure on the part of the state Governments in tapping all the productive sources of revenue or to the fact that a 'critical limit' as regards to tax effort as well as taxable capacity has already reached in case of most the states. This excessive dependence of the states on the centre is not all conducive to the development of sound federal fiscal conventions. This scenario makes a strong case for analysing the states fiscal condition in the context of North-eastern Region of India.

With this background in mind, an attempt has been made in this paper to study the intricacies of state's finance from two angles.

Firstly, the Federal Government has signaled a general resource crunch in the recent times. This has necessiated reduction on outlays on the centrally sponsored development schemes in the states on the one hand and, on the other, this has led to a major cut in subsidies and grants to the states. Thus, the outlays of the states have been substantially affected, thereby forcing the State Governments to postpone some of its developmental plan programmes. This has no doubt slowed down the process of economic development of the states. Thus the existing pattern of resource allocation of the financial resources between the union of India and its constituent units has generated imbalances between the revenue capacities and the needs of the States much to the disadvantage of the backward states of India. In this particular context, we have made an attempt at enquiring into the nature, causes and dimensions of such maladjustments and imbalances, taking North-Eastern Regions as typically backward states.

Secondly, the state's fiscal position in general has not been encouraging all together. Most distressing feature of state's finances has been growing deficit in recent years in most of the states for which such an analysis was undertaken. A recent study by Rao[4], shows that most of these states had surplus of about 1.2 percent of States' Domestic Product till mid-seventies. But, in late eighties, most of the states have shown deficit of about 1 percent of State Domestic Product. This study, which includes almost all the States of Indian Union, shows that the situation from the surplus to the deficit might have been resulted for the following two reasons: (i) these states have shown high growth of revenue expenditure of about 18 percent per annum. This may be attributed to increasing subsidies, both direct and indirect, increasing Wage Bills complemented by increased expenditure on goods and services utilized by State Governments, (ii) the interest liability of these states has been growing at an alarming average rate of about 23 percent per annum. The study attributes this trend to an emphasis on having large plan outlays without commensurate resources, which resulted in financing plans through borrowings. As a result, most of these states have experienced explosive cycles of revenue-expenditure growth. To counter balance this, we believe, that the State Governments may have to resort to either greater mobilization of adequate resources or to the stringent measures of resource utilization. We believe that the second option in the context of the underdeveloped economies may generate strong impediments to efficiency, the expansion of the economy, the growth of the resource base and finally the achievement of the developmental objectives. Further we may add that the utilization of public resources and its judicious use depends on the societal value judgment and the ideologies of the political party in power. So the related question that arises in this context is how to achieve a reasonable degree of resource mobilization in the face of rising demand for public expenditure? And what have been the consequences of resource utilization in the North-eastern States over the years?

To what extent, the State's Government can achieve or have already achieved this objective is an open question. Therefore, the present study is a modest effort in this direction to find out a suitable answer to the above question, by taking into account this aspect of the problem of States' finances.

Problem Formulation

It is evident from the above discussion that most of the State Governments in Indian Federation face severe budgetary pressures with rising demand for expenditures. Further, it is generally argued that the financial problems of the States arise from their lack of tax efforts, i.e., their failure to mobilise adequate resources from sources within their own jurisdiction. As a result of which, the financial dependence of the States on the Union Government has been on the increase in recent years. However, it is felt that, the resources available to the States under present dispensation are not adequate for meeting their requirements. We intend to accomplish this by analysing fiscal position of Northeastern states from the angles of resource mobilisation (level of revenue) and its utilization (level of public expenditure)

North-Eastern region is comparatively a background region, where agriculture is the predominant sector providing means of livelihood to more than 85 percent of the population. Though significant development has taken place in some sphere since Independence, access to opportunities for a 'reasonably minimum' standard of living in this region is one of the lowest in the country. The fiscal health of the states in this region is by no means encouraging at all, where the States' Own Tax Revenue contributes hardly 17 percent of the total tax receipts of the states. Further, the tax revenue constitutes near about 13 percent of the aggregate revenue of the states. In these states, where the states' own tax revenue contributes no more than 10 percent of the state's income and the aggregate Government expenditures constitutes about 115 percent of the state's income. It is, therefore, worthwhile to study the various aspects of the effects of state taxation and expenditures and the dimensions of its movements over the years.

Thus, the overall picture that emerges is that, the tax generating capacity of the North-Eastern states does not cope up with its increased public expenditure programmes, for achieving a desirable rate of economic progress. This exhibits clearly the low level of tax effort measures on the part of the state governments in the overall scheme of resource mobilization for developmental purposes. As a result of which, economic backwardness has been the resultant outcome.

Based on the above logic, a basic argument underlying this study is that if North-Eastern states' tax policy is to serve the ends of economic development, it should aim to attain at least two objectives. The tax system as an instrument of resource mobilisation should aim at (i) in siphoning off into the state exchequer as much revenues as can be gathered in the tax net (without endangering the incentives for private savings and investment) and (ii) in helping to release resources for private (or public) investment by reducing current consumption.

We thought it imperative to apply six indicators to assess North-Eastern states' performance with respect to the above two objectives. These indicators are: the buoyancy and elasticity, the compound growth rate and the marginal tax rate, the tax ratio and tax effort. Of these six indicators, elasticity and buoyancy coefficients are considered to be less significant in the present context as our main objective is to study the intricacies of resource mobilisation and utilization and since this is not the root that we have chosen for our study. Among the remaining four measures, the tax ratio and the tax effort measures generally do not indicate, the efficacy of the revenue structure of the states' government as they do not take into account taxable capacity. Thus, we are left to the choice of applying the compound growth rate and marginal tax rates to the tax structure so as to assess directly the efficiency of state tax measure. So, it is clear that, if the state's tax structure satisfies two conditions, namely, that: (i) the marginal tax rate increases with every increase in per capita income; and (ii) average tax rate responds positively to the changes in tax base, then it can be said that the states tax system/ resource mobilization programmes have performed satisfactorily, given its relative taxable capacity. The effectiveness of North-Eastern states' tax system is assessed in the context of these two norms. Ultimately, we believe, it is the quantum of public expenditures and taxation that the community looks to. No doubt, social, economic and political passion about the level of public expenditures and taxation always run high. But under the policy controversies, a fundamental question about the actual behaviors of the quantum of public expenditures and taxation awaits unruffled analysis. This is what has set out in this study.

All those points noted above provide a solid ground for the necessity and the desirability of undertaking an anatomy of public expenditure and taxation for the states of North-Eastern Region. The two major research questions that we have touched upon in this context are:

(1) To find out the trend of public Revenue (public resources) and expenditure (resource utilization) growth taking place in the States of North-Eastern region for the last thirty years.
(2) To study the changing compositional pattern of public revenue and expenditure over the years and find out the factors responsible for the changing compositional pattern of public revenue and expenditure.

Scope and Objectives

The study covered a period of 38 years from 1963 to 2001. This is a period during which the North-Eastern States' economy has passed through phases of both upswing and downswing owing to wide fluctuations in their agricultural sector as well as political instability and social tensions. Further, this entire period witnessed political instability and social tensions leading to substantial changes both in its expenditure and taxation policies in the entire North-eastern States. It may be mentioned here that for the purpose of inter state comparison within the North-Eastern region, we thought it imperative to take two representative states, namely Meghalaya and Nagaland as the area of our study. The reason for choosing these two states is one fold. It is observed that in recent years, the state of Meghalaya has preferred to maintain a surplus budget while that of the state of Nagaland continues to have a deficit budget over the years. Thus, we believe that inter state comparison between these two representative states may throw some light on the scope of additional resource mobilisation and the resultant patterns of its utilization in other different states of North-Eastern region. Keeping these general problems in view, an attempt has been made in this work to study in detail the following aspects of states' public expenditure and taxation.

(1) An assessment of the overall success of government measures to increase revenue.
(2) Analysis of the growth of tax and expenditure consequent on the growth of NSDP and to determine the extent to which North-Eastern states fiscal system is responsive to a change in state income over time.
(3) To measure the extent to which the revenue capacity of these states' tax system have been realized.

However the main focus of our study as mentioned earlier will be the analysis of the trends and compositional patterns of public expenditure and taxation as a whole and each item of public expenditure and taxation.

Sources and Limitation of Data

The study has been based primarily on the secondary sources of data. The main sources of data are; Annual budgets/Finance account of the various state governments including their memorandum submitted to the various finance commissions for the period covered by our study. Whenever possible, the budgetary data relating to India published in CMIE and RBI annual reports on Currency and Finance were used and consulted. For the state of Nagaland, we made use of the actual figures from the above sources for the 38 years (1962-63 to 2000-2001) covered by our study. The relevant data pertaining to the state of Meghalaya have been collected for a period of 30 years (1972-73 to 2001-2002) We have also used wherever possible the budgetary data relating to India as published from time to time in the Reserve Bank Bulletin and the RBI annual reports on Currency and Finance.

It may be pointed out it here that while tabulating the relevant data, we noticed certain discrepancies and differences in the actual figures of expenditure and revenue under certain heads in the different official sources. Even though all these are published by the respective state governments and their various official agencies. Wherever possible, care was taken to correct these discrepancies and differences by assimilating them with the primary sources of data viz; states' annual budgets and their various memorandums submitted to different Finance Commissions. In some cases where the discrepancy could not be assimilated and the differences could not be detected we have pointed it out in the relevant table.

Methodology

The data has been analyzed with the help of suitable statistical techniques and the results obtained have been subjected to relevant economic logic.

Simple regression equations are fitted to the data (by the method of least square) to estimate the trends and fluctuations in revenues and expenditures of the two representative states of North-Eastern region for the period under study. To study the shifts in the relative shares of various taxes and non-tax sources in states' own revenue, we have made use of the statistical technique of time series analysis. Specific techniques and measures are described fully as and when used. To analyze the relative growth of different sources of tax and non-tax revenues, exponential growth rates were calculated by using the formula:

$$Y = ae^{rt}$$

Where, Y is the revenue from a particular tax or non-tax source as the case might be and 't' is the time period and 'r' is the growth rate. The least square estimate of the above formula has been worked out to arrive at the exponential growth rate figures.

As the main focus of our study is on the analysis of States' taxation and public expenditures, the proposed method has been geared to that purpose.

Work Plan

The topical analysis of the present work is as follows. For the purpose of expositional covering and systematic analysis, the work is divided into three sections.

Section-I is an attempt to examine the problems and prospects of resources of the states. The purpose of this is to present an overview of all the states' finance for determining the degree of financial dependency of the state on the Union government. An attempt has also been made in this section to determine the extent to which North-Eastern region's economy is financially self-reliant in mobilizing adequate resources from sources within its own jurisdiction

Section-II is concerned with the critical analysis of public expenditure (utilization of public resources) where we made an attempt to assess the overall utilization pattern of the states' financial resources for the entire 38 years covered by our study. We have also carried out a brief analysis of the growth of public expenditure consequent upon the growth of Gross State Domestic Product in order to ascertain its degree of variation with respect to states' income.

In Section-III, the summary of the study have been reported and conclusion following from it. We have also made an evaluation of its implication in the light of our study.

I

It has already been pointed out that higher growth of expenditures in relation to the growth of receipts has resulted in an explosive cycle of expenditure growth. This has necessitated the state governments to increase its tax revenues to a considerable extent. The willingness and capacity of the government to respond to this need has been an important determinant to its capacity to carry forward developmental plan programmes. Further, economic progress in the underdeveloped economies like Meghalaya and Nagaland requires that in the initial stages of their development, higher proportion of the incremental income be channelised into productive investment through various measures of taxation. As such, tax structure should be so designed as to prevent consumption from increasing proportionately with income in the earlier stages of development. To accomplish this objective, a major question arises; what should be the economic capacity of taxation? Of course, we may not give a definite answer to this question. As M. Douglas (1953)[5] argues, "the elements of taxable capacity prove a closer examination to be so contingent, subjective and variable - to be so much a matter of circumstances of time and place, of institutional arrangements, and public attitude - that they defy generalization, and any conclusion expressed in absolute a final terms is bound to misrepresent the very nature of the problem itself." On the other hand, according to F. Due (1973)[6] "the actual efforts of taxation as source of revenue depend upon the type of tax structure the relationship of marginal to average tax rates, the reaction of the tax payers to the high rates, and the height of the period the high rates are effective, etc.".

However, in the absence of any consistent long-term policy objectives accompanied by non-significant structural changes and the absence of flexibility and adaptability in these economies, the resource problem has remained a major policy issue.

Thrust of the Problem

Therefore, an attempt is made in this section to examine the problem of resource constraint and prospects of internal resource mobilization in the state during the last thirty-eight years of planning covered by our study. We would explain the revenue constraints and the problem of resource mobilization in terms of existing contribution of different taxes by reflecting their share in the Net State Domestic Product (NSDP) and compositional structural character of different taxes on the basis of ratios and trends as well.

Problem of Internal Resource Mobilization

In the following paragraphs, an attempt is made to examine the trends in the revenue yields from different taxes and also their relative place in the system of taxation.

We intend to study the composition of tax revenues or the relative importance of the specified individual taxes in the tax system in terms of either the percentage of different taxes in total tax revenue or the ratio of these taxes to Net State Domestic Product as these two aspects of changes are interrelated. It is believed that an enquiry of this nature besides throwing some light on the underlining forces at work would be found useful in evaluating actual and potential performances of the state governments in the matter of resource mobilization.

Feasible Trends in Tax Effort

Before going into the details of the individual tax items of the state and the Union (shared taxes), an examination of their combined yields vis-à-vis state income is essential, because these give an overall idea about the extent to which the state government has been able to mobilise additional resources into the public sector savings. This, no doubt, will exhibit the relative tax effort of the government. Tables 1 and 2 facilitate such an analysis for the state of Nagaland and Meghalaya respectively.

The compound growth rates were worked out using the exponential function of the type:

$$Y = ae^{rt}$$

Where, t = time, Y= the dependent variable and r = growth rate.

Tables 1 and 2 give us year wise figures of tax revenues and state income at current prices for the period covered by the study.

Column 1 of both the tables indicates the State's Own Tax revenue. This shows that during the span of thirty-eight years plan period, State's Own Tax revenue in case of Nagaland has increased in absolute terms, roughly one hundred and thirty one fold, from Rs.0.6 crores in 1963-64 to Rs.79.00 crores in 2000-01 where as in case of Meghalaya, State's own tax revenue has increased in absolute terms more than a hundred and sixteen fold, from Rs. 1.21 crores in 1972-73 to Rs. 140.45 crores in 2001-02. Judged by the familiar growth rate, Nagaland's Own Tax revenue has registered a growth rate of 16.92 per cent per annum over the years. Similarly, the growth rate of own tax revenue for Meghalaya has registered a growth rate of 16.71 per cent per annum during the period of our study. Thus the growth rates of the own tax revenue in both the states follows more or less the similar pattern and magnitude. This increase in State's Own Tax revenue over the years was mainly due to large receipts under Sales Tax, State Excise Duty, Professional Tax and tax on income and expenditures, all of which have increased considerably over these years. The increase in absolute terms of these taxes may be attributed to the extension of tax base and tax coverage of these taxes and also due to an upward revision of the tax rates during these years.

Table 1 : Tax Revenue and State Income of Nagaland, 1963-64 to 2000-2001 (Rs.in crores)

0	1	2	3	4	5	6
Year	State's Own Tax Revenue	Total Tax Revenue	State Income	As a % of Col. 1 to Col. 3	As a % of Col. 2 to Col.3	Ratio of Col. 1 Col. 2
1963-64	0.06	0.09	5.90	1.00	1.50	0.66
1964-65	0.24	0.32	8.70	2.70	3.60	0.75
1965-66	0.32	0.44	13.80	2.30	3.10	0.72
1966-67	0.26	0.42	16.10	1.60	2.60	0.61
1967-68	0.35	0.52	18.40	1.90	2.80	0.67
1968-69	0.33	0.55	20.90	1.50	2.60	0.60
1969-70	0.46	0.71	22.10	2.00	3.20	0.64
1970-71	0.61	0.93	24.80	2.40	3.70	0.65
1971-72	0.75	1.05	28.30	2.60	3.80	0.68
1972-73	1.36	1.73	35.60	3.80	4.80	0.78
1973-74	1.94	2.41	41.50	4.60	5.80	0.80
1974-75	1.93	2.69	49.20	3.90	5.40	0.71
1975-76	2.86	3.75	56.70	5.00	6.60	0.76
1976-77	5.59	3.64	63.90	4.00	5.60	0.71
1977-78	2.87	4.00	73.20	3.90	5.40	0.71
1978-79	3.35	4.62	86.60	3.80	5.30	0.72
1979-80	4.19	6.58	109.20	3.30	6.00	0.63
1980-81	5.19	7.83	132.30	3.90	5.90	0.66
1981-82	6.36	9.45	163.30	3.80	5.70	0.67
1982-83	7.45	10.79	207.50	3.50	5.20	0.69
1983-84	10.46	14.34	255.10	4.10	5.60	0.72
1984-85	12.46	16.72	231.40	5.30	7.20	0.74
1985-86	15.39	80.51	261.10	5.80	30.83	0.19
1986-87	15.69	86.46	293.90	4.60	29.00	0.18
1987-88	20.25	105.74	337.90	6.00	31.00	0.90
1988-89	19.49	130.79	361.20	5.30	36.20	0.14
1989-90	17.44	93.78	432.90	4.00	21.60	0.18
1990-91	18.64	138.46	662.50	2.80	20.80	0.13
1991-92	21.61	161.50	761.50	2.80	21.20	0.13
1992-93	19.75	186.87	841.50	2.30	22.20	0.10
1993-94	25.08	192.05	879.50	2.80	21.80	0.13
1994-95	25.72	213.23	1258.70	2.00	16.90	0.12
1995-96	43.28	209.33	1655.90	2.60	12.60	0.20
1996-97	57.06	307.30	1848.50	3.00	16.60	0.18
1997-98	71.07	452.03	2136.80	3.30	21.10	0.15
1998-99	61.96	472.91	2183.82	2.80	21.60	0.13
1999-00	71.04	548.06	–	–	–	0.12
2000-01	79.00	620.94	–	–	–	0.12

Sources: Government of Nagaland, Finance Account (1963-64 to 1997-98; Statistical Abstract of Nagaland, 1966, 1975, 1990, 2000; Estimate of Net State Domestic Product 2000.

Growth rate: Column 1 = 18.5707 + e.16927t $R^2 = 0.96$
Growth rate: Column 2 = 228.606 + e.3883t $R^2 = 0.17$
Growth rate: Column 3 = 2025.308 + e0.038t $R^2 = 0.14$

Column 2 of the Table exhibits the trend of total tax revenue of the States during the period covered by our study. It is to be noted that the annual compound rate of growth of total tax revenue during the period under consideration was approximately 38.89 and 18.59 per cent for the states of Nagaland and Meghalaya respectively.

Table 2 : Tax Revenue and State Income of Meghalaya (1972-73 to 2001-2002) (Rs.in crores)

Year	State Own Tax	Total Tax Revenue	State Income	Column 1 as a % of Column 3	Column 2 as a % of Column 3	Column 1 as a ratio of Column 2
0	1	2	3	4	5	6
1972-73	1.21	3.33	105.09	1.15	3.17	0.36
1973-74	1.55	3.86	108.36	1.43	3.56	0.40
1974-75	1.95	4.18	111.97	1.74	3.73	0.47
1975-76	2.18	5.10	115.51	1.89	4.42	0.43
1976-77	2.48	5.57	120.08	2.07	4.64	0.45
1977-78	2.58	5.82	134.75	1.91	4.32	0.44
1978-79	3.39	6.97	149.77	2.26	4.65	0.49
1979-80	4.04	10.56	165.46	2.44	6.38	0.38
1980-81	4.88	12.07	179.62	2.72	6.72	0.40
1981-82	6.20	14.23	205.84	3.01	6.91	0.44
1982-83	7.37	16.09	227.10	3.25	7.08	0.46
1983-84	9.50	19.36	263.14	3.61	7.36	0.49
1984-85	12.24	22.91	302.27	4.05	7.58	0.53
1985-86	14.93	60.45	341.53	4.37	17.70	0.25
1986-87	17.74	73.00	386.25	4.59	18.90	0.24
1987-88	19.61	84.91	466.86	4.20	18.19	0.23
1988-89	27.72	110.19	505.96	5.48	21.78	0.25
1989-90	32.26	97.52	659.78	4.88	14.78	0.33
1990-91	36.01	116.37	767.35	4.69	15.17	0.31
1991-92	42.54	147.81	884.22	4.81	16.72	0.29
1992-93	44.18	169.82	978.54	4.51	17.35	0.26
1993-94	47.93	175.75	1133.38	4.23	15.51	0.27
1994-95	56.27	200.90	1258.04	4.47	15.97	0.28
1995-96	66.26	225.97	1380.31	4.80	16.37	0.29
1996-97	77.37	294.94	1485.28	5.21	19.86	0.26
1997-98	73.55	360.32	1690.42	4.35	21.32	0.20
1998-99	88.36	388.91	2079.25	4.25	18.70	0.23
1999-00	102.98	444.74	2467.13	4.17	18.03	0.23
2000-01	132.48®	296.73	2806.20	4.72	10.57	0.45
2001-02	140.45©	323.61	3267.36	4.30	9.90	0.43

Source: Budget in Brief, Government of Meghalaya: 1974-75; 1977-78; 1978-79; 1982-83; 1983-84

Budget at a Glance, Government of Meghalaya: 1984-85; 1989-90; 1994-95; 1996-97; 1998-99; 2001-02

Estimates of State Domestic Product of Meghalaya, 1980-81 to 1995-96, Government of Meghalaya, Directorate of Economics and Statistics, Meghalaya, Shillong,

State Economy, Government of Meghalaya, Directorate of Economics and Statistics

*Note: Net State Domestic Product figures are in current prices.

® = Revised Estimate

© = Budget Estimate

Rate of Growth: Column 1 = 0.1711e 0.1671t, R^2 = 0.9882
Column 2 = 0.9657e 0.1859t, R^2 = 0.9628
Column 3 = 23.7504e0.1468t, R^2 = 0.9851

Both the tables indicate a rising trend of the total tax revenue over the years for both the states. Since the total tax revenue includes shared taxes, the higher exponential growth rate may be ascribed to the better tax mobilization efforts made by the Central Government from time to time. Further, higher growth of total taxes in Nagaland's situation indicates the degree of elasticity and buoyancy that are inherent in the shared taxes resulting in a larger devolution of resources from the Centre to the State by way of higher share in the Central taxes.

The data presented in column 3 of the above tables is the aggregate of the sector-wise estimates by industrial origin of the State Domestic Product at factor cost at current prices. Although the state Domestic Product in both these two states had increased in absolute terms, the exponential growth rates give some dis-tressing results. While the exponential growth rate of Nagaland's state domestic product stays at a lower level of 3.8 percent, the exponential growth rate of state domestic product in case of Meghalaya comes to be around 12.61 percent over the years.

If, we express the relationship between the tax revenues and state income in the conventional tax-income ratio terms, Tables 1 and 2 reveal some interesting results.

Column 4 of the same Tables presents the percentage of State's own tax revenue to the net state domestic product over the years. The percentage of State's own tax revenue to net state domestic product in the state of Meghalaya, which was 1.15 per cent in 1972-73, increased slowly over the years and stood at 4.30 per cent in 2001-02. Similarly, in case of Nagaland, the percentage of own tax revenue to net state domestic product has almost remained comparatively static over the years. If, we judge the performances of the State's own tax revenue on the basis of its contribution to the net state domestic product, then the performances of the State's own tax revenue in both the states present a poor picture altogether. The observed trend indicate the failures of both the state governments in mobilising adequate resources from its own taxation measures.

Column 5, shows the percentage of total tax revenue to the state income. This reveals a continuous increase in percentage share of total tax revenue in the state income over the years in both the states. This shows that over the years, a sizeable share in incremental income has been transferred to the public exchequer.

Column 6 of the above tables shows the ratio of the State's Own Tax revenue to the total tax revenues as accruing to the states during these years. A distressing feature in Naglannd is that the ratio, which was 0.66 in the year 1963-64, has decreased to 0.12 in the year 2000-01. This decreasing ratio of State's Own Tax revenue to state's total tax revenue would seem to indicate that the state has not put in greater efforts than before in raising its own tax revenue in much more official way during the period from 1985-86 to 2000-01 and has not tapped more resources from the state economy thereby not increasing the avenues for financing its own expenditure. Meghalay's experience to this effect is no way different to the observed trend in the state of Nagaland. Table 2 shows that the ratio which was 0.36 in the year 1972-73 remained more or less stagnant over the years with the ratio of 0.43 in the year 2001-02. The stagnant ratio of the State's own tax revenue to the State's total tax revenue during the period of our study indicates that the State has not put in extra efforts with the passage of time in raising its own tax revenue in a much more efficient way during the thirty year period of our study and also has not made any sincere effort to tap more resources.

Thus, the inferences that follow from the above analysis are as follows:

1. There has been an increase in NSDP in both the states but the rate of increase is less than the rate of increase in State's own tax revenue and much less than the rate of increase of the total tax revenue over the period.
2. The role of the State's own tax revenue as a component of NSDP over the period of our study has not been proportionate to the likely coerce for additional taxation as a source of revenue for the State. This is substantiated by the fact that the percentage share of the State's own tax revenue in the NSDP has increased at a much slower rate than the velocity ascribed to total tax revenue.

Table 3 : Percentage Shares of State's Own Tax Revenue, Shared Taxes and Non-Tax Revenue of Nagaland, 1963-2000 (in crores)

Year	State Own Tax Revenue	Non Tax Revenue	Shared Taxes	Total Revenue	As % of Col. 1 to Col. 4	As % of Col. 2 to Col. 4	As % of Col. 3 to Col. 4
	0	1	2	3	4	5	6
7							
1963-64	0.06	0.13	0.03	0.22	27.27	59.09	13.64
1964-65	0.24	0.35	0.08	0.67	35.82	52.23	11.95
1965-66	0.32	0.42	0.12	0.86	37.20	48.83	13.97
1966-67	0.26	0.61	0.16	1.03	25.24	59.22	15.54
1967-68	0.35	0.59	0.17	1.11	31.53	53.15	15.32
1968-69	0.33	0.64	0.22	1.14	28.94	56.14	14.92
1969-70	0.46	1.06	0.25	1.77	25.98	59.88	14.14
1970-71	0.61	1.16	0.32	2.09	21.18	55.50	15.32
1971-72	0.75	1.19	0.34	2.28	32.89	52.19	14.92
1972-73	1.36	1.71	0.37	3.44	39.53	49.70	10.77
1973-74	1.94	1.82	0.47	4.23	45.86	43.02	11.12
1974-75	1.93	2.02	0.76	4.71	40.97	42.88	16.15
1975-76	2.86	2.31	0.89	6.06	47.20	38.11	14.69
1976-77	2.59	3.02	1.05	6.66	38.88	45.34	15.77
1977-78	2.87	3.35	1.13	7.35	39.04	45.57	15.39
1978-79	3.35	3.54	1.27	8.16	41.05	43.38	15.57
1979-80	4.19	4.34	2.39	10.92	38.36	39.74	21.09
1980-81	5.19	4.92	2.64	12.75	40.70	38.58	20.72
1981-82	6.36	6.31	3.09	15.76	40.35	40.03	19.62
1982-83	7.45	9.26	3.34	20.05	37.15	46.18	16.67
1983-84	10.46	11.07	3.88	25.41	41.16	43.56	15.28
1984-85	12.46	14.81	4.26	31.53	39.51	46.97	13.52
1985-86	15.39	18.78	65.12	99.29	15.50	18.91	65.59
1986-87	15.69	24.13	70.77	110.59	14.18	21.19	64.63
1987-88	20.25	25.34	85.49	131.08	15.44	19.33	65.23
1988-89	19.49	27.17	111.30	157.96	12.33	17.20	60.48
1989-90	17.44	35.03	76.34	128.81	13.53	27.19	59.28
1990-91	18.64	31.35	119.82	169.81	10.97	18.46	70.57
1991-92	21.61	32.07	139.89	193.57	11.16	16.56	72.28
1992-93	19.75	27.37	167.12	214.24	9.21	12.77	78.02
1993-94	25.08	24.77	166.97	216.82	11.56	11.42	77.02
1994-95	25.72	85.19	187.51	298.42	8.61	28.54	62.85
1995-96	43.28	35.05	166.05	244.38	17.71	14.34	67.95
1996-97	57.06	32.55	250.24	339.85	16.78	9.57	73.65
1997-98	71.07	45.03	380.96	497.06	14.29	9.05	76.66
1998-99	61.96	44.09	410.95	519.00	11.98	8.52	79.05
1999-00	71.04	49.00	477.02	597.06	11.89	8.20	79.91
2000-01	79.00	50.08	541.94	671.02	11.77	7.46	80.77

Sources: Government of Nagaland, Finance Account (1963-64 to 1997-98);

Growth rate: Column 2 = 53.3834 + *e*.1243t $R^2 = 0.56$
Growth rate: Column 3 = 26.850 + *e*.1705t$R^2 = 0.45$
Growth rate: Column 4 = 70.7161 + *e*.1695t $R^2 = 0.51$

3. If, we consider tax-income ratio as the simplest measure of tax burden or sacrifice, the information given in the forgone tables reveal that both the states under consideration fare rather poorly on this count, and
4. Lastly, it indicates the greater reliance of the states on shared taxes for the purpose of resource mobilization.

All the above trends are corroborated by the observations that we may feel tempted to make on the basis of our analysis of Table 3 and 4.

Table 4: Percentage Shares of State's Own Tax Revenue, Shared Taxes and Non-Tax Revenue of Meghalaya (Rupees in crores)

(Rupees in Crores)

Year	State Own Tax	Non-Tax Revenue	Shared Taxes	Total Revenue	Column 2 As a % of Column 5	Column 3 As a % of Column 5	Column 4 As a % of Column 5
0	1	2	3	4	5	6	7
1972-73	1.21	0.93	2.12	4.26	28.40	21.83	49.77
1973-74	1.55	1.27	2.31	5.13	30.21	24.76	45.03
1974-75	1.95	1.98	2.23	6.16	31.66	32.14	36.20
1975-76	2.18	3.04	2.92	8.14	26.78	37.35	35.87
1976-77	2.48	2.14	3.09	7.71	32.17	27.76	40.07
1977-78	2.58	2.04	3.24	7.86	32.83	25.95	41.22
1978-79	3.39	4.14	3.58	11.11	30.51	37.27	32.22
1979-80	4.04	3.65	6.52	14.21	28.43	25.69	45.88
1980-81	4.88	21.93	7.18	33.99	14.36	64.52	21.12
1981-82	6.20	6.34	8.02	20.56	30.15	30.84	39.01
1982-83	7.37	5.99	8.72	22.08	33.38	27.13	39.49
1983-84	9.50	7.21	9.86	26.57	35.75	27.14	37.11
1984-85	12.24	9.79	10.67	32.70	37.43	29.94	32.63
1985-86	14.93	11.51	45.52	71.96	20.75	15.99	63.26
1986-87	17.74	14.11	55.27	87.12	20.36	16.20	63.44
1987-88	19.61	17.26	65.29	102.16	19.19	16.90	63.91
1988-89	27.72	20.90	82.47	131.09	21.15	15.94	62.91
1989-90	32.26	18.85	65.17	116.28	27.74	16.21	56.05
1990-91	36.01	18.71	80.36	135.08	26.66	13.85	59.49
1991-92	42.54	22.62	105.27	170.43	24.96	13.27	61.77
1992-93	44.18	18.08	125.64	187.90	23.51	9.62	66.87
1993-94	47.93	28.40	127.83	204.16	23.48	13.91	62.61
1994-95	56.27	38.64	144.63	239.54	23.49	16.13	60.38
1995-96	66.26	66.92	159.71	292.89	22.62	22.85	54.53
1996-97	77.37	47.47	217.56	342.40	22.60	13.86	63.54
1997-98	73.55	29.85	286.77	390.17	18.85	7.65	73.50
1998-99	88.36	51.46	300.55	440.37	20.06	11.69	68.25
1999-00	102.98	83.86	341.76	528.60	19.48	15.87	64.65
2000-01	132.48	95.48	164.25	392.21	33.78	24.34	41.88
2001-02	140.45	105.35	183.16	428.96	32.74	24.56	42.70

Source: *Budget in Brief,* Government of Meghalaya:: 1974-75; 1977-78; 1978-79; 1982-83; 1983-84

Budget at a Glance, Government of Meghalaya:: 1984-85; 1989-90; 1994-95; 1996-97; 1998-99; 2001-02

Rate of Growth: Column 2 = 1.3438 e0.1444t $R^2 = 0.9191$
Column 3 = 1.4510 e0.1955t $R^2 = 0.9385$
Column 4 = 4.0045 e0.1761t $R^2 = 0.9673$

It is observed from the foregoing Table 3 and 4 that the rate of growth of State's Own Tax revenue is much lower than the rate of growth of the state's share in central taxes. Yet, the increasing importance of tax revenue as an element of state income has been clearly apparent over the period in question.

Tables 3 and 4 bring out the significance of trend of shared taxes for the state of Nagaland and Meghalaya for the stipulated period covered by the study. It is observed that the share of shared taxes in the total revenue of the states have increased steadily over the years in both the states. However, a look at the column 5 and 7 of the above tables reveal that the relative importance of states' own taxes have been much less than it has been in the case of shared taxes as an element of total revenue of the states over the period in question.

Further, it is interesting to note that the relative importance of states' own tax revenue have established a somewhat erratic behavior though it has registered a trend towards an increase in both the states under consideration. It may be added here that both the states of Nagaland and Meghalaya depend much more heavily on the shared taxes as the most plausible source of resource mobilisation as evident from the exponential growth rate figures of the respective states. This clearly shows the increasing dependence of the states on the central devolutions that they adhere to when compared to its otherwise increasing pressure on its own tax revenue. Thus, judged from the angle of the states' own effort, the states' revenue performance have been rather dismal in the sense that both the states raised a lower proportion of revenue in relation to the other sources of revenue, viz., shared taxes and non tax revenue.

AVERAGE AND MARGINAL TAX RATE

In order to have a more meaningful analysis of the changing tax-income ratio, we thought it imperative to relate the Average Tax Rate with the Marginal Tax Rate. The purpose of relating these two measures of the tax-income ratio is two fold.

First, the concept of marginal rate of taxation is useful in relation to a discussion on the appropriateness of the disposition of additional national income among several uses in any given country[7]. The marginal tax rate determines whether, and how fast, the tax ratio increases in the context of an increase in income over time. It is usually hypothesized that a high marginal tax rate is a product of higher per capita income.

Second, the Average Tax Rate of the base period is likely to influence the marginal rate in so far as it is possible for a given tax system to take out the same fraction from the incremental income as that from the original income base. Further, this will indicate the degree of variations in the tax revenue with respect to changes in the tax base.

The Average Tax rates have been calculated by the following formula:

Amount of taxes collected/Size of the taxable base

The formula may be described symbolically as follows:

If, RAj and PBj are the actual revenue and the potential base respectively for the jth tax in the state, then, the average tax rate is:

$$ARj = \frac{RA_j}{PB_j}$$

able 5 : Average and Marginal Rates of taxation in Nagaland from 1963-64 to 1998-99 (in crores)

0	1	2	3	4	5	6
ear	Average Tax Rate on			Marginal Tax Rate on		
	Total Tax Rev,	State'a Own Tax. Rev.	Shared Taxes	Total Tax Rev.	State's Own Tax Rev.	Shared Taxes
63-64	1.50	1.00	0.50	–	–	–
64-65	3.60	2.70	0.90	7.93	6.20	1.73
65-66	3.10	2.30	0.80	2.30	1.50	0.80
66-67	2.60	1.60	1.00	-0.86	-2.60	1.73
67-68	2.80	1.90	0.90	4.30	3.90	0.40
68-69	2.60	1.50	1.10	1.20	-0.08	2.00
69-70	3.20	2.00	1.20	13.32	10.83	2.50
70-71	3.70	2.40	1.30	8.14	5.55	2.59
71-72	3.80	2.60	1.20	4.50	4.00	0.50
72-73	4.80	3.80	1.00	8.76	8.30	0.46
73-74	5.80	4.60	1.10	11.52	9.80	1.72
74-75	5.40	3.90	1.50	3.60	-0.12	3.72
75-76	6.60	5.00	1.50	14.11	12.40	1.71
76-77	5.60	4.00	1.60	-1.52	-3.70	2.18
77-78	5.40	3.90	1.50	0.80	3.00	0.80
78-79	5.30	3.80	1.40	4.60	3.50	1.10
79-80	6.00	3.80	2.10	8.60	3.70	4.85
80-81	5.90	3.90	1.90	5.40	4.30	1.10
81-82	5.70	3.80	1.80	5.22	3.70	1.52
82-83	5.20	3.50	1.60	3.60	2.40	1.20
83-84	5.60	4.10	1.50	7.45	6.30	1.15
84-85	7.20	5.30	1.80	–	–	–
85-86	31.00	5.80	25.20	214.78	9.80	204.98
86-87	29.00	4.60	24.40	18.14	0.09	18.05
87-88	31.20	6.00	25.30	45.04	10.36	34.68
88-89	36.20	5.30	30.80	107.56	-3.20	110.71
89-90	21.16	4.00	17.60	-51.60	-2.80	-48.80
90-91	20.80	2.80	18.00	19.40	0.52	18.88
91-92	21.12	2.80	18.30	23.20	3.00	20.20
92-93	22.20	2.30	19.80	31.71	2.32	29.39
93-94	21.80	2.80	18.90	13.60	14.02	-0.42
94-95	16.90	2.00	14.80	5.58	0.16	5.42
95-96	12.60	2.60	10.00	-0.98	4.42	-5.40
96-97	16.60	3.00	13.50	50.86	7.15	43.71
97-98	21.10	3.30	17.80	50.20	4.85	45.35
98-99	21.60	2.80	18.80	44.40	-19.37	63.77

urces: Table 1 and 3.

Table 6 :Average and Marginal Rates of Taxation in meghalaya for the Period 1972-73 to 200 2002

Year	Average Rate on			Marginal Rate on		
	Total Tax Revenue	State's Own Tax Revenue	Shared Taxes	Total Tax Revenue	State's Own Tax Revenue	Shared Taxes
(1)	(2)	(3)	(4)	(5)	(6)	(7)
1972-73	3.17	1.15	2.02	16.21	10.40	5.81
1973-74	3.56	1.43	2.13	8.86	11.08	- 2.22
1974-75	3.73	1.74	1.99	25.99	6.50	19.49
1975-76	4.42	1.89	2.53	10.28	6.56	3.72
1976-77	4.64	2.07	2.57	1.70	0.68	1.02
1977-78	4.32	1.91	2.41	7.66	5.39	2.27
1978-79	4.65	2.26	2.39	22.88	4.14	18.74
1979-80	6.38	2.44	3.94	10.66	5.93	4.73
1980-81	6.72	2.72	4.00	8.24	5.03	3.21
1981-82	6.91	3.01	3.90	8.75	5.50	3.25
1982-83	7.08	3.25	3.83	9.07	5.91	3.16
1983-84	7.36	3.61	3.75	9.07	7.00	2.07
1984-85	7.58	4.05	3.53	95.62	6.85	88.77
1985-86	17.70	4.37	13.33	28.06	6.28	21.78
1986-87	18.90	4.59	14.31	14.77	2.32	12.45
1987-88	18.19	4.20	13.99	64.65	20.74	43.91
1988-89	21.78	5.48	16.30	- 8.24	2.26	10.50
1989-90	14.78	4.73	10.05	17.52	4.47	13.05
1990-91	15.17	4.69	10.48	26.90	5.59	21.31
1991-92	16.72	4.81	11.91	23.34	1.74	21.60
1992-93	17.35	4.51	12.84	14.21	2.42	11.79
1993-94	15.51	4.23	11.28	4.76	6.69	- 1.93
1994-95	15.97	4.47	11.50	20.50	8.17	12.33
1995-96	16.37	4.80	11.57	65.70	10.58	55.12
1996-97	19.86	5.21	14.65	31.87	- 1.86	33.74
1997-98	21.32	4.35	16.97	7.35 3	81	3.54
1998-99	18.70	4.25	14.45	14.39	3.77	10.62
1999-00	18.03	4.17	13.86	- 43.65	8.70	- 52.35
2000-01	10.57	4.72	5.85	5.83	1.73	4.10
2001-02	9.90	4.30	5.60			

Note: Calculations are based on Tables 2 and 4.

On the other hand, for estimating the Marginal Tax Rate[8], the formula used in th case is Absolute change in Tax Revenue / Absolute change in Tax Base or, symbolically, we can put it:

$$MTR = \frac{\Delta TR}{\Delta TB}$$

Where, MTR = Marginal Tax Rate

Δ TR = change in Tax Revenue, and

Δ TB = change in Tax Base.

Tables 5 and 6 are an attempt to present the average and marginal tax rate not only r aggregate revenue but also for shared taxes and state's own tax revenues. We consider ese two tables as an improvement of the previous tables as they provide some further sight into the changing tax-income ratio over a period of time.

A closer perusal of the above Tables suggests that there existed a shift in the pattern tax revenue of both the states. For instance, the Average Tax Rate in both the states ems to have registered a moderate increase for the state's own tax revenue and a ectacular increase for the shared taxes.

Further, the division of the total tax revenues into those accruing to the State's own xes and shared taxes, clearly shows that in case of both the states, the bulk of the crease in the total tax revenue is accounted for by the shared taxes.

A closer look at column 2 of the Table 6 indicates that of the 18.03 per cent of the net ate domestic product taken away by the State of Meghalaya and the Centre in the year 99-2000 towards resource mobilisations, 13.86 per cent is by the Centre alone, and the st 4.17 per cent by the State government. In other words, the Union Government has llected more than 77 per cent of the total revenue, and the contribution of the State self is only 23 per cent. It can be seen that throughout the thirty year period of our udy, only the year 1984-85 witnessed the contribution of the State's own taxes to be ghtly higher than the contribution of shared taxes. This means that, the contribution the State's own taxes declined from 36.28 per cent in the year 1972-73 to 23.13 per cent 1999-2000. We may note it here that although, the year 2000-2001 and 2001-2002, perienced some improvements in these tax rates, we can not draw any definite conclusion t of it, due to the fact that, figures represented against this particular year was the idget estimate. And, to that extent, our conclusion, if drawn, might be adversely affected.

On the other hand, for the state of Nagaland, the division of the total tax revenue to those accruing to the State's Own Taxes and shared taxes, respectively, clearly ggests that the bulk of the increase in the overall revenues has to be accounted for ared taxes. Of the 21.60 per cent of the state's income (column 2 of table 5) taken away the State and the Union Government in the year 1998-99, 18.80 per cent was by the nion Government alone and the rest 2.80 per cent by the State Government. In other ords, the Union has collected more than 87 per cent of the total revenue, and the ntribution of the State, itself, was only 13 per cent.

Thus, the results obtained from the above exercises suggest that during the specific eriod covered by the study for the states of Nagaland and Meghalaya, consistent and eliberate efforts on the part of the central government in comparison to the state overnments, which has accounted for a substantial part of variations in the marginal x rate.

The findings based on the above observations suggest that the increased tax burden both the states during the period of study has come primarily through the central overment. Thus, if we look at the problem from the point of view of Average and Marginal ax Rate, it may be concluded that both the states have made relatively lower tax efforts mobilise adequate internal resources to meet its growing developmental needs.

Thus, it is evident that both the states have performed rather poorly in mobilizing lequate resources from their internal sources for the purpose of carrying out their own evelopmental plan programmes. This trend no doubt talks about the poor resource base these two economies. Therefore, in the absence of additional means to mop up adequate revenue, both the states are far from goal of financial self-reliance, which has necessita them, to depend much more heavily on the federal transfer to meet the growing dema for public expenditure. As a result of the intensified adherence to the principle of fis deficiency, the states of Meghalaya and Nagaland have shown a distinct trend of rapi growing financial dependence on federal transfers. Bearing in mind this ground real an attempt is made to ascertain the compositional magnitude of the total Central transf in the over all State finances. Given the poor resource base of these two representat states, we think it imperative to study the quantitative implications of federal transf to these two states in order to find out how far the relative yield of various components public resources has remained consistent with the requirements of rapid econor development. Accordingly, an attempt is made in the following paragraphs to exam the magnitude and the components of federal transfers to the states in order to find their relative size and importance in the overall fiscal structure of the state.

Table 7 : Total Transfer of Financial Resources from the Union to the State of Nagaland (196 64 to 2000-01) (Rs. in crores)

	III Plan 1963-64 to 1965-66	IV Plan 1069-70 to 1973-74	V Plan 1974-75 to 1978-79	VI Plan 1980-81 to 1984-85	VII Plan 1985-86 to 1989-90	VIII Plan 1992-93 to 1996-97	IX Pl 1997- 2000-
1. share of Divisible taxes and Duties	0.07(1)	0.35(1)	1.02(1.85)	3.44(2)	81.80(23)	187.57(30)	452.71(4
2. Grants-in-aid	7.42(98)	26.21(82)	46.69(84)	120.99(62)	213.02(62)	397.59(59)	538.10(4
(a) Statutory (within the purview of Finance Commission)	1.96(26)	16.66(64)	29.67	59.20(49)	46.38(21)	143.43(36)	
(b) Other grants (Within the purview of Planning Commission and F.C.)	5.46(72)	12.11(36)	17.02(36.46)	61.79(51)	166.63(79)	254.15(64)	
3. Loan	1.00(1)	5.30(17)	7.31(14.15)	17.98(13)	48.51(15)	85.12(11)	127.19(1
4. Total Federal Transfer	7.50(100)	31.86(100)	55.02(100)	142.41 (100)	343.43 (100)	670.98 (100)	1118.((10
5. Total statutory transfer	2.03(27)	17.01(53)	30.69(95)	62.64(44)	128.18 (37)	331.09(49)	
6. Total non-Statutory Transfer	5.47(73)	14.85(47)	24.33(45)	79.77(56)	215.14 (630)	339.97(51)	
7. State's own Resources (Tax and Non Tax).	0.50	2.40	5.56	17.68	43.74	70.01	117.8
8. Aggregate state's Expecnditure	9.13	35.43	83.96	186.31	421.20	948.63	1428.(
9. Total Resources transfer to	82%	90%	65%	76%	81.15%	70%	78

Note : Figures in parentheses indicate the proportion to total.

Sources : Finance Accounts of Nagaland (1963-64 to 1969-70 and 1976-77 to 1998-1999), CMIE, 2000 and Statistical Abstract of Nagaland, 1968, 1970, 1975, 2000.

Trends and Patterns of Federal Transfers

The intention here is to examine the trends in the composition of federal transfers with reference to its main components, namely, (i) tax devolution, that is state's share of the central taxes as determined by the recommendations of the Finance Commission, (ii) grants-in aid of different categories and (iii) central loans. This exercise is carried out with a motive to determine and ascertain the total quantum of resources that are made available to the respective state governments in order to carry out their various developmental plan programmes.

Table 8 : Transfer of Financial Resources from the Union to the State of Meghalaya

(Rupees in Crores)

Year.	Shared taxes	Total statutory grants	Loans & Advances from the Centre	Total Resources transferred	State's Total Own Resources (Tax & Non-tax)	Aggregate State's Expenditure	Total Resource Transferred to Aggregate State's Expenditure	State's Total Own Resources to Aggregate State's Expenditure
1	2	3	4	5	6	7	8	9
1972-73	2.12	13.23	5.36	20.71	2.14	33.25	62.29	6.44
	(10.24)	(63.88)	(25.88)	(100.00)				
1973-74	2.31	12.18	5.46	19.95	2.82	26.86	74.27	10.50
	(11.58)	(61.05)	(27.37)	(100.00)				
1974-75	2.23	23.39	0.64	26.26	3.92	32.69	80.33	11.99
	(8.49)	(89.07)	(2.44)	(100.00)				
1975-76	2.92	25.19	1.00	29.11	5.22	35.44	82.14	14.73
	(10.03)	(86.53)	(3.44)	(100.00)				
1976-77	3.09	30.82	1.94	35.85	4.62	40.95	87.55	11.28
	(8.62)	(85.97)	(5.41)	(100.00)				
1977-78	3.24	33.46	2.50	39.20	4.62	56.18	69.78	8.22
	(8.26)	(85.36)	(6.38)	(100.00)				
1978-79	3.59	43.90	2.33	49.82	7.53	55.29	90.11	13.62
	(7.21)	(88.12)	(4.67)	(100.00)				
1979-80	6.52	46.19	1.90	54.61	7.69	64.19	85.08	11.98
	(11.94)	(84.58)	(3.48)	(100.00)				
1980-81	7.19	55.94	4.05	67.18	26.81	101.94	65.90	26.30
	(10.70)	(83.27)	(6.03)	(100.00)				
1981-82	8.03	61.81	5.06	74.90	12.54	136.57	54.84	9.18
	(10.72)	(82.52)	(6.76)	(100.00)				
1982-83	8.73	74.71	24.67	108.11	13.36	124.71	86.69	10.71
	(8.08)	(69.10)	(22.82)	(100.00)				
1983-84	9.86	98.39	9.89	118.14	16.71	147.01	80.36	11.37
	(8.35)	(83.28)	(8.37)	(100.00)				
1984-85	10.67	115.28	10.83	136.78	22.03	178.29	76.72	12.36
	(7.80)	(84.28)	(7.92)	(100.00)				
1985-86	45.52	111.02	13.00	169.54	26.44	191.93	88.33	13.78
	(26.85)	(65.48)	(7.67)	(100.00)				

contd.

1986-87	55.27	127.54	13.18	195.99	31.85	230.22	85.13	13.83
	(28.20)	(65.07)	(6.73)	(100.00)				
1987-88	65.29	154.29	15.78	235.36	36.88	264.36	89.03	13.95
	(27.74)	(65.55)	(6.71)	(100.00)				
1988-89	82.47	171.18	22.79	276.44	48.62	318.05	86.92	15.29
	(29.83)	(61.92)	(8.25)	(100.00)				
1989-90	65.17	192.82	36.02	294.01	50.05	350.69	83.84	14.27
	(22.17)	(65.58)	(12.25)	(100.00)				
1990-91	80.36	217.89	27.87	326.12	54.72	405.65	80.39	13.49
	(24.64)	(66.81)	(8.55)	(100.00)				
1991-92	105.27	238.25	20.74	364.26	65.17	492.29	73.99	13.24
	(28.90)	(65.41)	(5.69)	(100.00)				
1992-93	125.64	240.60	22.19	388.43	62.26	588.60	65.99	10.58
	(32.35)	(61.94)	(5.71)	(100.00)				
1993-94	127.82	296.63	105.41	529.86	76.33	909.08	58.29	8.40
	(24.12)	(55.98)	(19.90)	(100.00)				
1994-95	144.63	290.76	37.50	472.89	94.92	796.20	59.39	11.92
	(30.58)	(61.49)	(7.93)	(100.00)				
1995-96	159.71	391.00	20.87	571.58	133.18	796.41	71.77	16.72
	(27.94)	(68.41)	(3.65)	(100.00)				
1996-97	217.57	388.06	28.53	634.16	124.84	813.58	77.95	15.34
	(34.31)	(61.19)	(4.50)	(100.00)				
1997-98	286.77	306.58	39.42	632.77	103.40	850.72	74.38	12.15
	(45.32)	(48.45)	(6.23)	(100.00)				
1998-99	300.55	392.32	48.88	741.75	139.82	1022.93	72.51	13.67
	(40.52)	(52.89)	(6.59)	(100.00)				
1999-00	341.76	415.04	50.76	807.56	186.85	1195.40	67.56	15.63
	(42.32)	(51.39)	(6.29)	(100.00)				
2000-01*	164.25	845.01	61.31	1070.57	227.96	1601.89	66.83	14.23
	(15.34)	(78.93)	(5.73)	(100.00)				
2001-02**	183.16	892.17	60.88	1136.21	245.80	1785.15	63.65	13.77
	(16.12)	(78.52)	(5.36)	(100.00)				

Note : * = Revised Estimate
** = Budget Estimate

Shared taxes include (i) share of income tax proceeds, and (ii) share of proceeds from Union excise duties.

Source : Budget in Brief, Government of Meghalaya:: 1974-75; 1977-78; 1978-79; 1982-83; 1983-84;
Budget at a Glance, Government of Meghalaya:: 1984-85; 1986-87; 1989-90; 1996-97; 2000-01; 2001-2002

Tables 7 and 8 give a picture of the total resources transferred from the Union to the State of Nagaland and Meghalaya respectively during the period under consideration. The total Central resources transferred to the State of Meghalaya in absolute terms were Rs. 20.71 crores in 1972-73, which increased to Rs. 1136.21 crores in 2001-02. Similarly, the total resources transferred to the state of Nagaland, which was Rs.7.50 crores during the Third plan period increased to Rs.1118 crores during the IX plan period. The ratio of Union resources transferred to aggregate State's expenditure no doubt suggests a state of apathy towards the resource mobilisation capacity of the individual states. Looking at the problem from this angle itself speaks out the internal resource constraints that the North-Eastern States experience in recent years. The ratio of Union resources transferred to aggregate states' expenditure in Meghalaya which was at 62.29 per cent in 1972-73 increased to 63.65 per cent in 2001-

02. This ratio which was at 82 percent in Nagaland during the 3rd plan period slightly decreased to 78 percent during the 9th Plan period.

If the pattern of the composition of federal transfers is to be taken as the yardstick to measure the relative degree of self-reliance of the States, then the findings of the foregoing Tables corroborate the inferences drawn earlier that the degree of self-reliance in North-Eastern states is exceptionally low. This is further supported by two representative states' (Nagaland and Meghalaya) remarkably high dependence on grants, the high and increasing share of tax devolution, and the relatively small share of their own taxes and non-tax revenue in the overall resource mobilisation effort of the State.

Given the resource constraints imposed on these two states by their failures to mobilise adequate internal resources, a reprisal of the utilisation patterns of the public resources in terms its compositional patterns and the direction of change have much significance. This, we intend to accomplish in the next Section.

II

In this section, an attempt is made to discuss the utilisation pattern of public resources in the states of Nagaland and Meghalaya. Such an analysis is sought in terms of the patterns of public expenditure /public investment outlays and their growth over the years.

The observed phenomenon in the North-Eastern region's context exhibits a tremendous increase in public investment outlays over the years. In order to understand the intricacies of the problem of resource utlisation in the context of the two representative states of North-East, it is proper to analyse first the trends of public expenditure or the direction in which it has moved. Keeping this in mind, an attempt is made here to discuss the growth of total public expenditure both revenue and capital accounts of the two states for the period under investigation.

The following Tables 9 and 10 present the trend of the growth of total public expenditure for the states of Nagaland and Meghalaya respectively.

A close perusal at Column 1 of the above tables exhibits that total public expenditure in case of both the states has increased several folds over the years. The average annual rate of increase in the total public expenditure worked out to be 1362 percent and 117.65 percent for the state of Nagaland and Meghalaya respectively.

Column 2 of the above tables shows the growth of net state domestic product which has increased from Rs. 105.09 crores in 1972-73 to Rs. 3267.36 crores in 2001-02 maintaining an average annual rate of increase of 100.30 per cent in the state of Meghalaya. On the other hand, there has been a tremendous increase in Nagaland's State domestic product from 5.9 crores to 2183.8 crores thereby registering an average annual rate of increase of 971 percent.

Thus, it may be inferred that the average annual rate of increase of total public expenditure in both the states outweigh the average annual rate of increase in net state domestic product. Thus, we find that Government expenditure has grown at a faster rate than the State income.

Table 9 : Total Receipts and Expenditures and State Income of Nagaland (in crores)

Year	*Total Expenditures*	*NSDP*	*% of (1) to (2)*
(0)	(1)	(2)	(3)
1963-64	2.89	5.9	48.9
1964-65	10.55	8.7	121.2
1965-66	13.96	13.8	101.1
1966-67	16.37	16.1	10.16
1967-68	21.38	18.4	116.1
1968-69	23.81	20.9	113.9
1969-70	26.38	22.1	119.3
1970-71	31.83	24.8	128.3
1971-72	38.20	28.3	134.9
1972-73	40.36	35.6	113.3
1973-74	40.40	41.5	97.3
1974-75	48.60	49.2	9.87
1975-76	67.99	56.7	119.9
1976-77	84.58	63.9	132.3
1977-78	98.01	73.2	133.8
1978-79	120.64	86.6	139.3
1979-80	107.43	109.2	98.3
1980-81	137.09	132.3	103.6
1981-82	158.46	163.3	97.0
1982-83	245.15	207.5	118.1
1983-84	310.31	255.1	121.6
1984-85	243.52	231.4	105.2
1985-86	344.65	261.1	131.9
1986-87	385.33	293.9	131.1
1987-88	439.93	337.9	130.1
1988-89	469.05	361.2	129.8
1989-90	517.07	432.9	119.4
1990-91	548.42	662.5	82.7
1991-92	716.45	761.50	09.0
1992-93	776.94	841.5	92.3
1993-94	905.37	879.5	102.9
1994-95	853.83	1258.7	67.8
1995-96	1079.22	1655.9	65.1
1996-97	1127.83	1848.5	61.0
1997-98	1230.30	2136.8	57.5
1998-99	1490.50	2183.8	68.2
1999-00	1494.90	–	–
2000-01	1498.80	–	–

Source: Finance Accounts of Nagaland; Statistical Handbook of Nagaland, 1968, 1970,1975,1980, 1986, 1990, 1996, 1997, 2000; and Estimates of Net State Domestic Poduct 2000.

Table 10 : Growth of Total Public Expenditure of the State of Meghalaya (both Revenue and Capital Account)

Year	State's Total Expenditure (Te) (Rs. Crore)	Net State Domestic Product (Rs. Crore)	Column 2 as a percentage of Col. 3
(0)	(1)	(2)	(3)
1972-73	33.25	105.09	31.64
1973-74	26.86	108.36	24.79
1974-75	32.69	111.97	29.20
1975-76	35.44	115.51	30.68
1976-77	40.95	120.08	34.10
1977-78	56.18	134.75	41.69
1978-79	55.29	149.77	36.92
1979-80	64.19	165.46	38.79
1980-81	101.94	179.62	56.75
1981-82	136.57	205.84	66.35
1982-83	124.71	227.10	54.91
1983-84	147.01	263.14	55.87
1984-85	178.30	302.27	58.99
1985-86	191.93	341.53	56.20
1986-87	230.22	386.25	59.60
1987-88	264.36	466.86	56.63
1988-89	318.05	505.96	62.86
1989-90	350.69	659.78	53.15
1990-91	405.65	767.35	52.86
1991-92	492.29	884.22	55.68
1992-93	588.60	978.54	60.15
1993-94	909.08	1133.38	80.21
1994-95	777.97	1258.04	61.84
1995-96	796.42	1380.31	57.70
1996-97	813.58	1485.28	54.78
1997-98	850.72	1690.42	50.33
1998-99	1022.93	2079.25	49.20
1999-00	1195.40	2467.13	48.45
2000-01	1601.89 (R.E)	2806.20	57.08
2001-02	1785.15 (B.E)	3267.36	54.64

Source: *Budget in Brief*, Government of Meghalaya, 1974-75; 1977-78; 1978-79, *Budget at a Glance*, Government of Meghalaya:: 1984-85; 1986-87; 1987-88; 1989-90; 1992-93; 1993-94; 1994-95; 1996-97;1998-99; 2001-2002,*Statistical Hand Book*, Meghalaya,1976.

Estimates of State Domestic Product of Meghalaya, 1980-81 to 1995-96, Government of Meghalaya, Directorate of Economics and Statistics, Meghalaya, Shillong.

State Economy, Government of Meghalaya, Directorate of Economics and Statistics.

Column 3 of the above tables indicates total public expenditure as a percentage of net state domestic product. It is interesting to note that while the percentage share of total public expenditure to state domestic prduct gives an erratic trend in case of Nagaland, a smooth trend is observed to this effect in case of the state of Meghalaya. In absolute terms, although the ratio of total public expenditure to state domestic product has increased several folds from 48.9 percent to 68.2 and 31.64 to 54.64 in case of the states of Nagaland and Meghalaya respectively, in relative terms, both the percentages have increased more or less in same proportions and in same magnitudes.

The growth in public expenditure as seen above may be explained by the intensive development efforts made by the government through comprehensive economic planning. Therefore, the former is closely related to the latter. In other words, if the plan is more comprehensive, it tries to develop the sub-sectors of the economy simultaneously.

The factors responsible for expanding public sector activities in the States' economy can be explained through two distinct approaches. The first approach relates to the increasing pressure on the demand for public services due to low level of monetization and high population growth, and its subsequent impact on the density of population and urbanization.

The second approach is based on the supply factor. In an economy where the private sector's active participation is underdeveloped, the public sector has to play a decisive role in shaping and re-shaping the structure of the economy. Thus, both demand and supply factors taken together might have made a decisive influence on expanding the size of the public sector in these economies.

Further, an attempt is made to calculate the exponential growth rate of the economic variables presented in the above tables by using the earlier method ($Y=ae^{rt}$). The compound growth rates for both the total expenditure and state domestic product are presented below for comparative purposes.

Nagaland

$Te = 906.62^{e0.146896t}$, $R^2 = 0.97$

$NSDP = 2025.308 + e0.038t$, $R^2 = 0.14$

Meghalaya

$Te = 23.7504^{e0.1468t}$; $R^2 = 0.9851$

$NSDP = 66.2490^{e0.1261t}$; $R^2 = 0.9889$

It is observed from the above estimating equations that the exponential growth rate of the total public expenditure in both the states surpasses the growth of state income during the period covered by our study..

Since the growth of aggregate public expenditure does not tell us about the direction of compositional pattern of public expenditure, we thought it imperative to segregate the total public outlays into Revenue and Capital outlays for the purpose of getting a clear picture about the direction of change in the compositional patterns of total public outlays.

Keeping this in view, an attempt is made in the following paragraphs to present the composition and the growth of revenue expenditure of the state under three heads namely, General services, Social services, and Economic services. The compositional pattern of the revenue expenditure for the state of Meghalaya and Nagaland are presented in Table 11 and 12 respectively.

Table 11 : Sectorwise Revenue Expenditure of Meghalaya

(Rupees in Crore)

Year	General Services	Social Services	Economic Services
0	1	2	3
1972-73	5.01	6.15	7.02
1973-74	4.96	6.62	7.97
1974-75	7.61	7.00	10.42
1975-76	8.98	7.91	10.47
1976-77	8.61	9.00	12.51
1977-78	12.69	13.03	15.49
1978-79	10.72	12.28	17.40
1979-80	11.52	14.29	20.14
1980-81	16.71	19.49	25.62
1981-82	21.94	24.81	27.53
1982-83	28.10	29.07	27.85
1983-84	27.61	37.89	34.22
1984-85	30.78	31.78	44.76
1985-86	38.07	44.30	52.60
1986-87	47.98	48.86	59.58
1987-88	57.60	56.82	75.19
1988-89	68.38	76.61	79.59
1989-90	78.58	94.86	85.33
1990-91	87.58	112.65	110.59
1991-92	102.86	137.55	127.64
1992-93	123.89	145.65	140.75
1993-94	149.04	177.91	155.91
1994-95	158.25	162.50	136.20
1995-96	188.42	209.01	182.96
1996-97	205.62	324.40	186.94
1997-98	197.82	253.64	195.22
1998-99	280.34	299.95	235.15
1999-00	337.44	356.04	234.32
2000-01	435.00 (R.E.)	448.64 (R.E.)	309.22 (R.E.)
2001-02	510.48 (B.E.)	498.18 (B.E.)	346.17 (B.E.)

Source: *Budget in Brief*, Government of Meghalaya, 1978-79; *Budget at a Glance,* Government of Meghalaya:: 1984-85; 1986-87; 1989-90; 1994-95; 1998-99; 2000-01; 2001-02.

Table 12 : Sector-wise Revenue Expenditure of Nagaland (in crores)

Years	*General Services*	*Social Services*	*Economic Services*
1963-64	1.08 (44)	0.70 (29)	0.65 (28)
1964-65	4.97 (58)	2.05 (24)	1.47 (18)
1965-66	5.83 (61)	2.79 (28)	1.16 (11)
1966-67	6.54 (50)	3.43 (26)	3.08 (24)
1967-68	7.10 (48)	4.20 (26)	3.46 (24)
1968-69	7.80 (41)	5.23 (27)	5.92 (32)
1969-70	9.69 (46)	6.42 (30)	4.77 (24)
1970-71	10.56 (43	7.03 (29)	7.01 (28)
1971-72	10.98 (38)	8.70 (30)	8.72 (32)
1972-73	12.26 (41)	9.56 (31)	8.56 (28)
1973-74	13.19 (42)	10.86 (35)	7.00 (23)
1974-75	13.53 (38)	11.49 (32)	10.47 (20)
1975-76	16.49 (39)	13.39 (31)	12.72 (30)
1976-77	16.39 (35)	13.86 (30)	16.21 (35)
1977-78	19.44 (36)	15.59 (30)	18.25 (34)
1978-79	25.34 (36)	24.23 (32)	24.26 (32)
1979-80	24.48 (35)	21.36 (31)	22.67 (34)
1980-81	32.87 (36)	29.53 (32)	28.97 (32)
1981-82	34.15 (34)	30.46 (30)	36.03 (36)
1982-83	48.24 (38)	39.66 (30)	42.95 (32)
1983-84	64.78 (40)	48.45 (29)	51.98 (31)
1985-86	88.83 (38)	75.95 (33)	63.28 (29)
1986-87	103.05 (38)	79.75 (30)	85.90 (32)
1987-88	124.99 (38)	94.30 (28)	109.73 (34)
1988-89	130.91 (36)	102.42 (28)	131.75 (36)
1989-90	144.58 (38)	123.84 (32)	112.09 (30)
1990-91	143.97 (34)	119.81 (28)	156.69 (38)
1991-92	174.62 (36)	127.95 (26)	179.31 (38)
1992-93	163.01 (40)	129.04 (32)	109.26 (28)
1993-94	214.10 (40)	158.94 (29)	175.70 (31)
1994-95	280.62 (49)	168.79 (28)	135.21 (23)
1995-96	336.58 (40)	248.44 (29)	249.46 (31)
1996-97	352.90 (42)	242.56 (28)	251.84 (30)
1997-98	419.40 (41)	250.10 (25)	334.30 (34)
1998-99	463.80 (44)	279.30 (26)	306.00 (30)
1999-2000	540.20 (45)	326.00 (27)	314.10 (28)
2000-01	576.60 (45)	348.60 (27)	331.70 (28)

Sources: Finance Accounts of Nagaland 1963-64 to 1997-98; Statistical Abstract of Nagaland; CMIE, March 2001.

Note: Figures as shown within brackets are the average plan percentage of each sector to total revenue expenditure of the state

It is evident from Tables 11 and 12 that the revenue expenditures under the various heads in both the states have increased tremendously over the years. An anatomy of the revenue expenditures exhibits the following specific directions.

It is evident from the above tables a major portion of total revenue expenditure has entered into the non-developmental expenditure under General Services where it stayed at near about 46 percent of the total revenue expenditure. The reasons for the tremendous increase of non-developmental expenditure being the expansion of the state administrative machinery; the steady increase in the emoluments of government servants necessitated by rise in prices and the mounting interest payments and servicing of debts, etc. The observed trend indicates the rapid expansion of the service sector which has taken place in both the states over the years.

Column 2 of above tables indicate the revenue expenditures on social services. The relative share of total revenue expenditure under this head suggests that the social welfare oriented activities has remained an important programme of the respective state governments throughout. If developmental expenditure on social services will presumably be taken to reflect public expenditure on human capital then, experiences of these two states negate the above functional relationship as economic backwardness coupled with a reasonable degree of poverty make its presence felt in these states of North-Eastern region.

Column 3 of the table brings out the data of revenue expenditure on Economic Services. A close look at the above tables indicates that although there has been an increase in revenue expenditure under this particular head over the years, spectacular development in agriculture and allied services, industry and minining still remains a day dream for these regions of the North-Eastern part of the economy.

We have made an attempt to calculate the exponential growth rate of revenue expenditure sector wise by following the similar procedure ($Y = ae^{rt}$). The results of the estimated equations are presented below for the two states.

	Nagaland	Meghalaya
1.	$G_S = 281.755\, e^{.142517t}$ $R^2 = .97$	$Gs = 4.2354e^{0.1578t}$, $R2 = .9939$
2.	$S_S = 193.281\, e^{.145200t}$ $R^2 = .97$	$Ss = 4.6786e^{0.1593t}$, $R2 = .9922$
3.	$E_S = 158.353\, e^{.154161t}$ $R^2 = .96$	$Es = 7.0426e^{0.1341t}$, $R2 = .9877$

where, G_S = General Services;

S_S = Social Services;

E_S = Economic Services.

These results suggest that comparatively, the growth rate of revenue expenditure on economic services in Nagaland is higher, i.e. 15 percent, whereas in case of Meghalaya, it is the social sector which accorded the highest priority. The growth rates further indicate that over the years, the economic policy of the government of Nagaland has tilted towards the development of the agriculture and allied services, community development, power development and transport and communication. In contrast to it, economic policy in the state of Meghalaya has tilted towards the development of the service sectors over the years.

No doubt, that the revenue budget so far we discussed gives a partial picture of the aggregate resource utilisation position of the state governments. In order to have an in-depth understanding of the intricacies of the state resource utilisation, an analysis of the capital budget becomes imperative. This is what has been set out in the following paragraphs.

Table 13: Sectorwise Capital Outlay in Meghalaya.

(Rupees in crores)

Year	General Services	Social Services	Economic Services	% of (1) to TCO	% of (2) to TCO	% of (3) to TCO
0	1	2	3	4	5	6
1972-73	0.35	....	2.75	2.32	....	18.25
1973-74	0.27	....	3.21	3.69	....	43.91
1974-75	0.93	1.44	3.72	12.14	18.80	48.56
1975-76	0.46	1.61	5.12	5.69	19.90	63.29
1976-77	0.30	1.49	4.46	2.56	12.72	38.09
1977-78	0.71	2.02	5.99	4.44	12.63	37.44
1978-79	0.70	3.28	8.20	4.70	22.03	55.07
1979-80	0.70	6.95	8.65	3.84	38.10	47.42
1980-81	0.74	10.08	10.28	1.76	23.96	24.41
1981-82	1.52	9.46	12.42	2.44	15.19	19.94
1982-83	2.24	10.17	13.91	5.64	25.62	35.05
1983-84	3.35	15.72	14.54	7.00	32.85	30.39
1984-85	3.04	11.39	16.71	4.94	18.53	27.18
1985-86	2.92	17.80	17.44	5.13	31.26	30.62
1986-87	4.95	22.03	24.34	6.71	29.85	32.99
1987-88	3.72	22.05	27.78	4.98	29.50	37.16
1988-89	6.44	21.48	33.06	6.89	22.98	35.37
1989-90	4.66	23.40	39.49	5.07	25.46	42.96
1990-91	6.32	23.52	45.11	6.66	24.79	47.54
1991-92	6.17	26.80	50.44	4.97	21.57	40.60
1992-93	5.84	31.66	65.08	3.28	17.76	36.50
1993-94	8.72	29.63	66.91	2.05	6.95	15.70
1994-95	5.10	29.07	68.65	1.50	8.57	20.24
1995-96	8.06	35.48	90.61	3.73	16.43	41.95
1996-97	6.08	46.38	72.39	3.09	23.59	36.82
1997-98	4.77	42.49	78.62	2.88	25.66	47.47
1998-99	5.98	50.13	88.39	2.88	24.16	42.60
1999-00	9.46	53.76	101.95	3.54	20.09	38.10
2000-01	12.97*	120.45*	125.65*	3.17	29.45	30.72
2001-02	14.49**	118.14**	132.80**	3.37	27.45	30.86

Note: * = Revised Estimate; **=Budget Estimate; TCO = Total Capital Outlay

Source: *Budget a Glance,* Government of Meghalaya:: 1974-75; 1977-78; 1984-85; 1989-90; 1994-95;1998-99;2001-02.

$Gs = 1.0892e^{0.1061t}$, $R^2 = 0.7823$

$Ss = 4.6786e^{0.1593t}$, $R^2 = 0.9922$

$Es = 7.0426e^{0.1341t}$, $R^2 = 0.9877$

The sector wise capital outlay exhibits some interesting results. Although the total capital outlays on general services, social services and economic services have increased over the years, the increase in capital outlay on economic services was accorded with the highest priority followed by the social services. Capital outlay on general services is

Table 14: Sector-wise Capital Outlay in Nagaland

(in crores)

Year	*General Services*	*Social Services*	*Economic Services*	*% of (1) to TCO*	*% of (2) to TCO*	*% of (3) to TCO*
(0)	(1)	(2)	(3)	(4)	(5)	(6)
1963-64	0.5	0.10	0.31	10.86	21.73	67.41
1964-65	0.10	0.16	1.18	4.84	7.76	87.4
1965-66	0.11	0.19	3.63	2.80	4.83	92.37
1966-67	0.02	0.16	2.88	0.66	5.22	94.12
1967-68	0.05	0.20	6.07	0.8	3.16	96.04
1968-69	0.21	0.21	4.05	4.70	4.70	90.6
1969-70	0.24	0.67	4.59	4.36	12.18	83.46
1970-71	0.24	0.98	5.66	3.48	14.24	82.28
1971-72	0.23	0.68	8.49	2.44	7.23	90.33
1972-73	0.18	0.74	7.78	2.06	8.50	89.44
1973-74	0.26	0.46	6.73	3.48	6.17	90.35
1974-75	0.42	2.84	7.89	3.76	25.47	70.77
1975-76	0.54	2.98	7.93	4.71	26.02	69.27
1976-77	0.68	3.24	7.06	6.19	29.50	64.31
1977-78	0.33	3.87	11.54	2.09	24.58	73.33
1978-79	0.55	5.62	13.41	2.80	28.70	68.5
1979-80	0.79	6.52	14.95	3.54	30.00	66.46
1980-81	0.92	7.79	16.99	3.57	30.31	66.12
1981-82	1.19	8.79	17.84	4.27	31.6	64.13
1982-83	1.88	10.37	22.19	5.45	30.11	64.44
1983-84	3.40	13.01	20.66	9.17	35.09	55.74
1984-85	2.45	21.28	8.41	7.62	66.21	26.17
1985-86	5.07	17.01	22.39	11.40	38.25	50.35
1986-87	7.50	17.97	34.10	12.60	30.16	57.24
1987-88	8.73	19.27	46.21	11.76	25.96	62.28
1988-89	10.34	25.62	38.25	13.93	34.52	51.55
1989-90	9.20	30.85	45.39	10.76	36.10	53.14
1990-91	8.83	26.54	51.58	10.15	30.52	59.33
1991-92	10.44	27.67	58.81	10.77	28.54	60.69
1992-93	15.19	17.67	46.42	19.05	22.23	58.64
1993-94	9.09	27.15	59.93	9.45	28.23	62.32
1994-95	3.17	6.48	34.41	7.19	14.70	78.11
1995-96	11.93	30.41	101.40	8.30	21.15	70.55
1996-97	13.14	57.09	134.61	6.41	27.87	65.72
1997-98	16.50	74.00	94.90	8.90	40.00	51.1
1998-99	14.90	89.10	113.50	6.85	40.93	52.22
1999-2000	12.90	82.00	110.80	6.28	39.84	53.88
2000-01	12.90	77.30	99.50	6.80	40.74	52.48

Source: Finance Accounts of Nagaland; Statistical abstract of Nagaland; CMIE, March 2001.

$G_s = 4.9981\, e^{.17025t}$ $\quad R^2 = .91$

$S_s = 16.8886\, e^{.1759t}$ $\quad R^2 = .90$

$E_s = 181.473\, e^{.11472t}$ $\quad R^2 = .89$

presented in Column 1 of the tables 13 and 14 indicates that the general services received the least attention in the state of Meghalaya where it is the economic services which received least treatment in Nagaland over the years. Column 1 of the table further exhibits a fluctuating trend of capital outlay on general services over the years.

Column 3 of the tables 13 and 14 presents the capital outlay on economic services. The above tables clearly indicates the priorities of the government for the development of agriculture and allied services, community development, transport and communication, housing, rural and urban development, public health and power development, etc. over the years.

In order to substantiate the above findings, we have calculated the percentage share of the sector-wise capital outlay to the total capital outlays and have presented the same in column 5, 6 and 7 of the above tables. The percentage share of capital outlay on general services remained more or less static during the period as evident from column 5 of the tables 13 and 14.

Whereas, the percentage share of capital outlay on social services showed a decreasing trend right from 1964-65 till the year 1973-74. Then, the percentage share picks up to an upward trend from the year 1974-75 and remained almost static till 1990-91. Thereafter, the percentage share showed a downward trend from 1991-92 to 1996-97. Nevertheless, the percentage share of capital outlay on social services reported a considerable increase from 1997-98 and remained static till 2000-01 for the state of Nagaland. On the other hand, the percentage share of capital outlay on social services increased from the third plan average till the sixth plan average. But beginning from the seventh plan average, its percentage share started declining up to the eight-plan average. And in the following plan i.e. ninth plan average, its percentage share picks up to 40 per cent.

On the other hand, the percentage share of capital outlay on economic services exhibited an upward trend beginning from 1963-64 to the year 1973-74. The percentage share however remained at a lower level and remained almost static for the rest of the years i.e. from 1974-75 till the year 2000-01, the last year of our study. The plan average percentage share which was 89.30 per cent in the third plan average increased to 93.90 per cent in the following three year annual plan average i.e.1966-67 to 1968-69. Thereafter, its percentage share started declining in the rest of the plan periods except a minor increase in the two-year annual plan average i.e.1990-91 to 1991-92 and eight plan average. And finally, the percentage share saddled at 52.41 per cent in the ninth plan average.

The above study clearly indicates that the capital outlay on public works in the states has not been consistent over the years. Though, public works remained an area where capital is being spent, it is becoming more of maintaining the already created capital asset rather than undertaking new projects. The social welfare services continue to remain an important activity of the state over the years. Although the capital outlay on economic services shared the substantial capital expenditure of the states in its real terms, there has been constant fluctuation of capital investment on this sector. Rather, a decreasing trend of its percentage share to total capital outlays has been the feature of capital investment on economic services. This implies the slowing down of economic development in both the states.

Thus, to sum up, it may be argued that both the states follow more or less a similar pattern of resource mobilization and also a similar pattern of resource utilization although they have opted for different budgetary controls.

III

In the foregoing sections we tried to spotlight various aspects of North-Eastern Region's fiscal system by taking two representative states for the purpose and tried to indicate the sphere in which problems have arisen and solutions are necessary. It may be mentioned here that although we tried to raise the issues concerned very exhaustively, we failed to treat those issues in an extensive manner. We must confess it here that we have neither undertaken an elaborate study of each of the aspects of the problem that we have raised nor have we gone in minute details into the considerable statistical materials presented in the tables.

With these limitations in mind an attempt is made in the following paragraphs to present a comprehensive account of the major findings of the study. The important findings of the study are as follows.

An analysis of the percentage share of state's total tax revenue and shared taxes in the net state domestic product exhibited some disturbing results. The percentage of State's own tax revenue to net state domestic product, increased slowly over the years in case of both the states. If, we judge the performances of the State's own tax revenue on the basis of its contribution to State income, then the performances of the State's own tax revenue presents a poor picture altogether. From this point of view, the State's own tax revenue has been increasing at a very slow rate during the period of our study. If we visualize tax-income ratio as the simplest measure of tax burden or sacrifice then the analysis revealed that the ratio has marginally increased in both the states of Nagaland and Meghalaya implying thereby the existence of a static tax structure over the years. This only proves that the States of North-Eastern region fare rather poorly on this count.

The analysis of the ratio of the State's own tax revenue to the total tax revenues accruing to the State was an attempt to ascertain the degree of tax efforts of the government during these years. It is quite disheartening to note that the ratio has nearly remained stagnant during the period of our study. In the light of the above finding, we may conclude that the States had neither put in extra efforts in raising its own tax revenue in a much more efficient way nor had it made any sincere effort to tap more resources during the period covered by our study. We believe, this might have been one of the factors responsible for the explosive cycles of public expenditure growth.

From the above findings, we may be tempted to draw two inferences. First, in the absence of any cohesive additional domestic resource mobilization programmes, financing of ever increasing public expenditure has led to the dependency syndrome of the State on the Centre for higher grants-in-aid. Secondly, the non-existence of a vibrant tax structure in order to finance the increased volume of public expenditure has placed the State at the mercy of market forces in terms of public borrowings. Judged from the angle of sound fiscal ethics, the performance of the State government to this effect seems to be unreasonable.

In order to find out the extent of dependency of the State on the contribution of Central taxes, an analysis of the shared taxes in the total tax revenue of the State revealed that the shared taxes have increased in both the states on an average from 30.02 per cent in the year 1972-73 to 71.85 per cent in the year 1998-1999. A striking feature of the State's taxation as revealed by our analysis was the phenomenal increase in contribution of the shared taxes to the total tax revenue of the State. It was observed that over the years, there has been a continual outpacing of the State's own tax revenue by the shared taxes. This indicated that the relative importance of the State's own taxes has been much less than it has been in the case of shared taxes as a component of total tax revenue of the State during the period of our study. As a result, the States have cut a poor figure with regard to the efforts put in by it during the last thirty years of our study to mop up additional resources from its own sources. The increasing dependence of the State on the share of Central taxes might partly be due to the ever-increasing pressure of the State on the Central Government to widen the pool of shareable taxes and partly due to the greater in-built flexibility and in-built responsiveness that have been brought into these taxes thereby making them more elastic and buoyant than the State's own taxes.

Based on the above exercises, we may be tempted to conclude that, the trend observed from the pattern of the composition of the State's taxes is not at all warranted from the point of view of a healthy fiscal economy. The reverse would have been commendable in the context of the State's efforts at achieving self-reliance with regard to resource mobilization of adequate resources for implementing several developmental programmes.

From the above analysis, one could see the dismal performance of the State governments in generating adequate resources from the sources at its disposal. Hence, an attempt was made to analyze the amount of funds transferred from the Centre to the States in order to find out the extent of dependency of the State on the Union Government. The ratio of Union resources transferred to aggregate State's expenditure was 62.29 per cent in the year 1972-73 which increased to 63.65 per cent in the year 2001-02 for the state of Meghalaya. Whereas, Nagaland's experience shows that this ratio is around 78 percent. The State's share of divisible taxes and duties has increased both in absolute and in relative terms. This trend has brought about a plausible deleterious effect on the growth and sustenance of the resource mobilisation efforts of the States in recent times. Given the level of resource mobilization effort of the States and given its degree of dependence on the Centre, we can hypothesize that the State will continue to depend heavily on the Central transfers, in the years to come unless it goes for an immediate rationalization of its tax structure. Therefore, in the absence of additional means to mop up adequate revenue, the States of North-East are far from the goal of financial self-reliance.

It is evident from the above discussions that the two representatives State have failed miserably on the front of internal resource mobilization thereby giving rise to a situation of explosive cycle of expenditure growth.

Keeping in mind the constraints of the growth of States' tax revenues over the years, which we believed has given rise to an explosive cycle of public expenditure growth, an appraisal of the constituent expenditure instruments in terms of its growth and compositional pattern assumes great importance. Section-II was an attempt in this direction.

The major findings of Section II are as follows:

The analysis of the average annual growth rates of total public expenditure, net state domestic product showed that over the years, the average annual rate of increase of total public expenditure has surpassed the average annual rate of increase of net state domestic product and per capita expenditure. The extraordinary growth of public expenditure in relation to the net state domestic product may be attributed to the massive involvement of the governments in their over all developmental activities of the state in the presence of a highly expanded service sector and a non-existence industrial sector. In the states where the average annual rate of growth of public expenditure tends to be near about double than the average rate of growth of net state domestic product, raises serious doubt about the productivity and efficiency of the public expenditure programmes in the face of a subsistence agricultural sector and low per capita income.

Further, the analysis on the revenue expenditure exhibited an increasing trend during the entire period covered by our study. When revenue expenditure was taken as a percentage to total public expenditure, it was found that for most of the years, revenue expenditure constituted on an average more than 70 per cent of total public expenditure. This increase of revenue expenditure of the State governments clearly exhibited the pattern and direction of public expenditure whereby the States had failed miserably in building up its capital base for further development. This clearly shows that over the years, a large chunk of public investment has entered into the unproductive channels, as it is evident from its high percentage share in net state domestic product.

The analysis of capital outlay as a percentage of total public expenditure enabled us to find the trend of public investment taking place in the States during the period of our study. It was observed that capital expenditure on an average constituted less than 30 per cent of total expenditure for most of the years covered by our study. A distressing feature that emerged from the analysis was the declining trend of capital expenditure over the years. This only proves that the State has not been able to pursue expenditure policies in consonance with the achievement of long term goals and objectives.

The analysis of the pattern of public expenditure in the State of Meghalaya, based on the sector-wise analysis of revenue expenditure indicated that the expenditures on social services accounted for the maximum annual compound rate of growth of 15.93 per cent while the general services recorded 15.78 per cent and the economic services showed 13.41 per cent. The above growth rates indicate that the revenue expenditures on social services account for the maximum rate of growth followed by the revenue expenditures on general services and economic services. This has resulted in a disproportionate growth of the service sector. The disproportionate growth of the social sector has not only absorbed most of the public investment funds over the years, but also has given rise to a weaker linkage between the different sectors of the economy. The weak linkage is not a healthy sign from the point of view of sustainable economic development and also from the point of view of domestic resource mobilization. Similarly, the exponential growth rates of the sectorwise revenue expenditure in the context of Nagaland exhibits that the state does not markedly differ from the state of Meghalaya.

Further, the analysis on the sector-wise capital expenditure indicated that the capital outlay on social services accounted for the maximum annual compound rate of growth of 15.93 per cent followed by the capital outlay on general services which recorded 10.61 per cent and economic services exhibited 13.41 per cent. This trend no doubt substantiate our earlier finding that it is the social sector which has received much attention in the various plan periods of the State. This indicates that the Government has followed a policy of appeasement by providing immediate employment opportunities without taking proper measures to expand the industrial sector and the industrial base of the economy. It may be argued that it is the deliberate policy accomplishment of the government, which is responsible for the deplorable condition of the economic sector. We believe that this lop-sided planning has given a serious blow to the development of agriculture, trade and industries in the state.

REFERENCES

1. Goode, R. B.; "Taxation and Economic Development", in Morgan, T.; Betz, G. W.; and Choudhary, N. (eds); *Readings in Economic Development*, Belmont; wordsworth publishing Co., 1963.
2. The committees which (and individuals, who) investigated the Indian tax system such as, the Taxation Enquiry Commission in 1954, Nicholas Kaldor in 1956, the Central Excise Reorganization Committee in 1963, S. Boothalingam in 1968, the Direct Taxes Enquiry Committee in 1971, Raj committee in 1972, Indirect Taxation Enquiry committee in 1976,Chokshi Committee Report in 1978, Jha Committee Report in 1983, Chelliah committee Report in 1987, Kelkar committee Report in 2002 all these had the restructuring of the Indian tax system as the object of their exercise so as to make it the potent and flexible instrument of plan implementation and revision in the manifold interpretations of the terms.
3. Rao, M. G.; "Proposal for State Level Budgetary Reforms", paper presented at IIDs seminar on Fiscal Discipline and Fiscal Consolidation at the central and state level, IIDs, Calcutta, February 19, 1992 (mimeo).
4. Ibid.,; pp. 7-10.
5. Douglas, M; 'Taxable Capacity and British and Canadian Experience', in *Limits of Taxable Capacity* (Princeton, N.J., Tax Institute, Inc. (1953).
6. Due, J.F. and Fiedlsender, A.F.; *Government Finance : Economics of the Public Sector*, Richard d. Irwin, Inc. Hornewood, Illionois, Irwin Dorsey Limited, Georgetown, Onterio, (1973).
7. Chellioh, Raja J. - Trends in Taxation in Developing countries, in Richard M. Bird and Oliver Oldman (edt.), *Readings on Taxation in Developing Countries*, London, The Johns Hopkins University Press, 1975, p. 109.
8. An accurate measure of the marginal rate can be obtained only by using time-series data through a regression of tax revenue on income. It may be pointed out here that the marginal tax rate formula that we are using here is based on an observations at two points in time and to that extent they are only rough estimate.

11

Resource Anxieties and Development Arbitrariness : Paradoxes of Modernity in the Northeastern Region

—*B.S. Butola*

Using common sense, for many the 'Northeast' conveys an idea of territoriality or geographical location of a region. But, the case of the North-Eastern Region of India is far more complex than what meets the eyes. In order to understand the region and decipher appropriate meanings from its identity one needs to transcend the realms of common sense and delve into the political economy of identity formation in a post colonial country in general and its peripheral region like the Northeast in particular. Quintessentially, the region's geographical identity is not that entirely important if one wishes to contextualise it within the larger canvas of modernity, development and postcoloniality. Looking through the spectacles of marginality, the region emerges as an economically, culturally, ideologically hegemonised identity for some and a counter hegemonic identity for others. And above all it is also a power relation that is protean, ambiguous as well as full of apparent and real contradictions.

Its identity is too specific to be compared to any other regional, cultural and historical identity. Take for example, the concept like the 'North' has specific meanings in the discourses on development. It is considered synonymous to developed regions (Hirschman: 1981). Similarly the concept 'East' (Orient) symbolises a subordinated and hegemonised identity. In the postcolonial discourses 'East' is considered an epitome of Occident's greatest, richest and oldest colonies (Said: 2001). Moreover, it is a relationship of power, domination and of varying degree of a complex hegemony (Said: 2001). However, this particular identity is by far the most appropriate to comprehend the objectivity of the Northeastern region of India. It is a region that symbolises the negation of Hirschman's 'North' and epitomises an extreme case of Said's 'Orient'. Consequently, this region does not only form the geographical periphery of India but it also represents the economic, political and cultural periphery of the same. It is a region that has been hegemonised near perfection. The magnitude of peripheralisation is so intense and pronounced that some scholars preferred to identify this region with a classic case of marginalisation leading to internal colonisation (Saikia: 1995). Today, it is included among the laggard regions of the country and every single indicator of development, empowerment and freedom draws the bottom most values. Moreover, its strategically sensitive location at the confluence of varying economic, cultural, philosophical and ideological regimes on the one hand and continuing volatile politico-social climate right from the days of India's independence on the other has repeatedly send warning signals to the power centres at different levels many a times in the past (Butola: 1997). It is an irony that most often these warnings were misinterpreted in a binary logic and it was considered as a choice between the rational versus irrational, development versus backwardness, nationalist versus antinationalist or modern verses archaic etc. at the power centres. The Northeast, particularly its political economy and ethos were considered not only irrational but also impediments in its progress and dynamism of the entire country. Little scopes were made available for moderation on either side. Most often, it was the unilateral decision of the power centres that the irrational, backward, archaic and to some extent secessionist if not entirely antinationalist Northeast has to give ways to the so-called rational, modern and Pan-Indian National interests. Thus, there was always an impasse between the aspirations of the people of the region and the response it received from the power elites at the centre. Consequently, the situation has become so alarming that it now threatens the unity and integrity of the country. Now, it has become a major issue of concern to many nationalists and development theoreticians alike. Scholars have expressed their anxieties over the prevailing state of affairs in the region. They have also tried to suggest models and strategies for ameliorating the ills of the region. Some of the often-quoted anxieties about the region are:

NATURAL RESOURCE ANXIETY IN THE NORTHEAST: A REGION OF NATURAL RESOURCE OPPULANCE AND HUMAN RESOURCE SQUALOR

This is perhaps the most crucial of all the anxieties of the region. Scholars of all shades have unanimous opinions about the vivid and rich natural resource base of the region. They opined that the northeastern region is one of the richest natural resource regions of India. To substantiate their claims these scholars have taken help form the data available through various government publications. Some of the important resources and data pertaining to these, often cited by the scholars are as follows:

Land Resources

Land has an enhanced importance among various other natural resources of the region. It can be considered as the source resources in a predominantly extensive subsistence economy dominated by "*Jhum*" cultivation. The region has approximately 7.76 percent of the total geographical area of the country and it accounts for less than 3 percent of the total population of the same. Thus, this region has relatively low density of population as compared to the other states in the country. To be more precise, with the exceptions of Tripura and Assam with density of population 262 and 284 persons per sq. km. respectively all the other states in the region have very low density of population. It is as low as 10 persons per sq. km. in Arunachal Pradesh followed by 33 in Mizoram. So, this particular attribute of the region's resource base has enormous potentials for the future development and well being in the region (Tahir: 1998). The data given in Table 1 is often quoted to strengthen this argument further. It is evident from the data that all the states in the region can be considered well placed as far as availability of land is concerned. With the exception of Assam and Tripura all the other states in the region have recorded higher per capita land availability than the national average of 0.36 hectares per capita. For other states the value ranges between 6.36 hectares in Arunachal and 1.20 hectares in Manipur. Availability of such a rich land resource and favourable climatic conditions have huge potentials to make agricultural, horticultural, animal husbandry etc. economic enterprises in the region. Moreover, success story of tea plantation for over 150 years is also a testimony to prove that with suitable technology, skill, capital and adequate infrastructure the region has the potential to become a leader in some of the agricultural products.

Table 1 : Per Capita Availability of Land

States/Region/India	1991 Per Capita Land (Sq. Km.)
Arunachal Pradesh	6.36
Assam	0.35
Manipur	1.2
Meghalaya	1.26
Mizoram	3.03
Nagaland	1.28
Tripura	0.38
NER	0.71
India	0.36

Source: Basic Statistics of Northeast published by Northeastern council, Shillong.

Forest Resources

Forests are one of the richest and most diversified resources in the region. It has approximately 164010 sq. km. area under forest, which is approximately 65.9 percent of the total geographical area of the region. These figures get enhanced importance once placed against the low i.e. 19.5 percent of the total geographical area under forest at the national level. Moreover, the region has a distinction of accounting for more than 53.92 percent of total area under natural vegetation identified as dense forest i.e. more than 40 percent density (Mohapatra: 2000).

Table 2 : Area Under Forest as Percentage of total Geographical Area (1989-99)

State	Percentage to total Geographical area	Dense forests as Percentage to total forested area	Open forest as Percentage to total forested area
Arunachal	82.21	83.89	16.11
Assam	30.20	61.28	38.72
Manipur	77.86	34.15	65.85
Meghalaya	69.70	37.90	62.10
Mizoram	86.99	20.65	79.35
Nagaland	85.43	36.27	63.73
Tripura	54.79	38.78	61.22
All-India	19.38	59.22	40.02

Source: Forest Survey of India, Ministry of Environment and Forest, Government of India, New Delhi (1998-99).

There are states like Arunachal Pradesh, Manipur, Mizoram and Nagaland where area under forest is more than 80 percent of their geographical area. Moreover, forests in the region are not only an attribute of nature but these are also the expressions of the rich socio-cultural and economic heritages of the region with certain distinct features. Some of the important characteristics features of the vegetation in the region that make forest special in the life and economy of the region are:

- There are more than 400 varieties of rare orchids found in the region. Occurrence of so many varieties of orchids along with other vegetations in such a smaller area make it one of the sixteen hot spots in the world from the point of bio-diversity.
- Some of the tallest trees of India are also found in the evergreen forest of this region. *Makari Sal* also known as *Shorea Assamica* grows up to the height of 60-70mt. is one of the tallest tree species found in the region.
- The vegetation of the region has a variety of *carnivorous* plants like *pitcher plant*, *bludderwart* and *sursjneor* and also a variety of *saprophytic*, *epiphytic* and *parasitic* plants that have immense potentials in the promotion of eco-tourism in the region.
- The vegetation types of the region are also enriched by innumerable reserves of medicinal plants that constitute the valuable treasure of the traditional knowledge of the numerous indigenous communities in the region.
- Apart from these the region is also the native land of one the world famous *aromatic beverage tea plant*.
- The rich and luxurious natural vegetation cover of the region provides an ideal habitat for the sustenance of a large variety of animals. Together with these the region has rich potentials for the development of eco-tourism.
- This is perhaps one of the few regions in the world that has as many as 28 national parks and wildlife sanctuaries. *Kaziranga National Park* known for *One Horned India Rhinoceroses*, the Great Indian Elephants and Wild Buffaloes have special attraction for the national as well as international tourists.

Table 3 : Some of the well-known national parks, wildlife sanctuaries and bio-reserves of the region:

Name	Districts	Important Species
Kaziranga National Park	Golaghat	One-horned Rhinoceros, wild elephants, pelican, hoolock gibbon etc.
Keibul Lamjao National Park	Loktak	Thamin (rare wild goat) and Sangai (brow antlered Deer).
Mauling National Park	West Siang	Takin, coral and Serow varieties of Goat Antelopes.
Manas Wildlife Sanctuary and Project Tiger	Barpeta	Royal Bengal Tiger project, golden langur.
Sonai-Rupali Wildlife Sanctuary	Sonitpur	Royal Bengal Tiger, Imperial pigeon, elephants etc.
Orang Wildlife Sanctuary	Darang	Rhinoceros, wild buffaloes and migratory pelicans etc.
Pabitara Wildlife Sanctuary	Marigaon	Rhinoceros, leopards etc.
Laokhowa Wildlife Sanctuary	Nagaon	Rhinoceros, wild buffaloes, swamp deer etc.
Garampani Wildlife Sanctuary	Golaghat	Elephants, leopards and hoolock gibbons etc.
Pabha Wildlife Sanctuary	Lakhimpur	Wild buffaloes also referred as Milroy buffalo sanctuary.
Baranadi Wildlife Sanctuary	Darang	Pigmy hog hispid hare etc.
Didru-Saikhowa Wildlife Sanctuary	Tinsukia	Deohanh (white winged duck)
Nameri Wildlife Sanctuary	Sonitpur	Elephants, Royal Bengal Tiger, capped langur etc.
Pakhul Wildlife Sanctuary	East Kameng	Haven for nature Lovers, Royal Bengal Tiger, Leopard, bison etc.

(Contd...)

Balpakram Wildlife Sanctuary	Garo Hills	Elephants, antelope etc.
Intaki Wildlife Sanctuary	Nagaland	Clouded leopard, barking deer, elephants, bison etc.
Dampa Wildlife Sanctuary	Aizawl	Elephants, leopards, tiger etc.
Trisshna Wildlife Sanctuary	Tripura	Indian Gaur.
Sampara-Bardalani and Bardoibam-bilmukh Bird Sanctuary	Lakhimpur	Florican, king fisher, hornbill.
Yangou Pokpi Lokchaw Sanctuary	Chandel	Rare species of birds.
Sipahijala Sanctuary	Tripura	Rare species of Birds and Animals
Barnali and North Cachar Wildlife Sanctuary (proposed)	Cachar	Clouded leopard, leopard, hoolock gibbon etc.
Dhaleswari Reserve Forest (proposed)	Cachar	Slow loris, pig tailed monkey, Royal Bengal tiger etc.
Keilam Hill Sanctuary (proposed)	Churanchandpur	Sabeng (wild goats).
Juko Valley National Park (proposed)	Senapati	Wild goats.
Siroi Kasong National Park (proposed)	Ukhrul	Orchids and lilies (siroi lily).
Namdapha Tiger Project	Changlang	Panda, Royal Bengal tiger, Flying squirrel etc.
Deepar Beel Bird Sanctuary	Kamrup	Migratory birds.

Apart from these there are some biosphere reserves like Dehang, Dibang (Arunachal Pradesh), Manas, Dibru, Saikhowa (Assam) and Nokrek (Meghalaya) and Wild life Sanctuaries like D'Ering Memorial (Itanagar), Eaglenest, Kane, Kamlang, Sessa Orchid Sanctuary, Dibang Valley and Tale (Arunachal), Wameri and Sonai Rupai (Assam) that have large potential for the development of ecotourism in the region.

Water Resources

Water is another most important natural resource of the region. This is one of the richest regions of the country in this particular resource. Water in the form of precipitation, surface runoff and ground water is considered to be in abundance in the region. The average annual rainfall for the region is estimated to be approximately 250 cm. But there are areas like Cherapunjee and Mawsynram in the region that receive more than 1200 cm. average annual rainfall. Nearly 80 percent of precipitation received in the region is mostly confined to 4 to 6 summer months from April to September. Apart from this, fair amount of precipitation also occurs in other seasons. This region also receives 10-15 percent precipitation in the winter months from the western disturbances. It is only in exceptional circumstances that the region as a whole or any part of it can be considered as draught prone. However, there are instances that crops like tea get adversely affected due to relatively long dry spells extending beyond 20 to 30 days at a stretch. Suffice to state that the plain areas of the region have a distinction of relatively higher ground water table and at places the zone of saturation is much above the surface. These are the areas that were once marshy and swampy, thus considered unsuitable for sustainable agriculture, but with the introduction of new techniques of marshy land reclamation in the recent past these have emerged among the important rice and fish producing areas in the region.

Apart from the rain and ground water, surface water is another important natural resource in the region. Brahmaputra is the major river in the region. Nearly 70 percent of the total area of the region falls within the catchments of this mighty river. Smaller river and tributaries of Barak, Chindwin, Kaladan, Karnaphuli, Fenny and Gumti share the remaining 30 percent basin area. River Brahmaputra is the major lifeline of the region. It has economic, cultural, spiritual, strategic and aesthetic significance in the life, polity and natural environment of the region. It has always been the single most uniting factor in the regional culture and civilization and it enjoys similar aesthetic and spiritual significance in the life of the people of the region as is done by river Ganga to the people in North India and Godavary in South India. Moreover, it also provides an easy and cheap mode of transportation and interaction among various communities of people living along the banks of the river. It was expected that with the introduction of modern modes of transportation the importance of Brahmaputra as a means of transportation will get reduced but on the contrary, its importance has increased over the years and even in the first decade of 21st century there are only four rail and road bridges that link the areas on the opposite banks of the river. Its mighty waters offer huge potentials for the development of fresh water fishing and eco-system, internal navigation, adventure tourism etc. Apart from all these, the river and its tributaries also possess huge potentials for the development of hydroelectric power. Some of the important hydroelectric power generation projects in the region are enlisted in Table 4.

As stated earlier the region receives fairly sufficient amount of precipitation and the ground water potential too are favourable in most parts of the region. Consequently, the demand for irrigation is less pressing than many other parts of the country. Most of the areas where ground water situation is less favourable are the mountainous and plateau areas of the region where Jhumming is the most dominant form of extensive subsistence form of agriculture. Thus, use of the rich irrigation potentials of river water for irrigation is far below than the potentials utilisation levels. It had only 22.50 percent of the total agricultural area under irrigation. Most of the Medium Level Irrigation Schemes are located in the state of Assam; while the other states like Tripura, Meghalaya, Manipur etc. have mostly small or minor irrigation projects. Most of these are seasonal in nature and controlled and maintained either by individuals or communities.

Table 4 : Important Hydroelectric Power Projects in the Region, their Capacity and Status

NAME	SITUATION	INSTALLED CAPACITY MW.	STATUS
Umtru	Ri-Bhoi	11.50	Completed 1957
Umium	East Kahsi hill	54.00	Completed 1963
Kyrdemkalai	Ri-Bhoi	60.00	Completed 1963
Nangalbibra	West Garo Hill	5.00	Completed
Loktak	Imphal	105.00	Completed
Leinmakhong	Manipur central	1.16	Completed
Nunghangkhong	Ukrul	1.50	Completed
Tipaimukh	Manipur-Mizoram Border	200.00	
Juja Mini	Kohima	2.00	Commissioned 1978
Daiyang	Wokha	105.00	Under construction
Dikhow	Mon-Tuensang	1.00	Under construction
Dhaleswari	Mizoram	75.00	
Gomti	Tripura	10.00	Incomplete
Maharani	Tripura	1.00	Incomplete
Kameng	Arunachal Pradesh	600.00	Construction to begin
Ranga Nadi	Lower subansiri	505.00	Under construction
Damwe	Lohit	1000.00	Under construction
Pakke	East Kameng	90.00	Under construction
Kopili	Meghalaya-Assam	150.00	Part completed
Karbi-Langpi	Karbi	120.00	Under construction
Bardikhari	Assam	200.00	Under construction

Source: Basic Statistics of Northeast, published by the North-eastern Council, Shillong 1995.

Other Natural Resources

The scholars are equally enthusiastic about the opulence of some of the strategic natural resources like ***Petroleum*** and ***Natural Gas*** that can contribute in the development of the region. Table 5 gives a conservative estimate of some of the natural resources of the region.

It is evident from Table 5 that the region has huge natural resource base and with suitable techno-institutional networking, the region possesses enormous potentials for development in future. However, there are already a few resources like oil and natural gas in which this region contributes more than 50 percent of the total national production.

Table 5 : Major Mineral Reserves in the North-East India (Estimated 2002)

Mineral	Important States	Reserve (million tonnes)
Crude Oil	Assam	70.46
Natural Gas	Assam	23000.00(million cubic metres)
	Tripura	25000.00(million cubic metres)
	Total	**48000.00 million cubic metres)**
Coal	Assam	371.00
	Meghalaya	564.00
	Arunachal Pradesh	91.000
	Nagaland	17.200
	Total	**1043.20**
Lime Stone	Assam	463.00
	Meghalaya	4147.00
	Arunachal Pradesh	350.00
	Manipur East	6.40
	Nagaland	357.00
	Total	**5323.40**
Kaoline	**Meghalaya**	**5.24**
Clay	Meghalaya	28.00
	Tripura	0.5
	Total	**28.5**
Dolomite	**Arunachal Pradesh**	**247.00**
Graphite	**Arunachal Pradesh**	**85.00**
Quartzite	Arunachal Pradesh	3.00
	Assam	17.00
	Total	**20.00**
Sillimonite	**Assam**	**50.00**
White Clay (Fuller's Earth)	**Assam**	**20.00**

Source: NEDFi Databank Quarterly, July 2002. Basic Statistics of North Eastern Region, Published by Northeast Council, Shillong, 1990 and updated with NEDFi databank, 2002.

Similarly, the scholars also have anxiety about the other natural resources. But unfortunately, their anxiety is predominantly due to the typical mind-set that has dawned on most of us mainly by virtue of accepting the development propaganda circulated through the world market and world wide net-work of governmentality. Most of the scholars have failed to look at the development-modernisation ideologies critically. The annals of world history teach us that there are evidences from the experiences of areas, regions, countries and communities to prove that there is an inverse relationship between rich resource base and levels of development and modernisation. Most developed and modernised regions/countries of the world have chronic deficiency of the so-called natural resources and at the other extreme there are the most backward regions/countries of the world that have rich reserves of the natural resources. Moreover, the resource rich regions/countries/ communities are also the most backward and poverty stricken. To tell the history of colonisation and neo-colonisation in one sentence it can be safely stated that rich resource base makes one vulnerable to interventions, manipulations and manoeuvres by the external forces particularly the forces of world market and globalisation. The North-Eastern Region of India is not an exception to this harsh reality. No region can be rich or poor as far as resource potentials are concerned. In fact, *resources are not a thing but a function in which the substances of our surroundings both physical and meta-physical take part. It is function that can satisfy certain needs that is economically feasible, technologically accessible, culturally acceptable and environmentally sustainable*. It is unfortunate that most of the scholars seem to be governed by the ruling ethics of the time i.e. 'nothing succeeds like success'. Since, something has partially succeeded somewhere it does not justify its emulation everywhere. It is also unfortunate because, the scholars are not only trying to assess the resource potentials of the region from the point of view of rationalist development oriented mindset but they have also failed to make an inventory of the alternative resource potentials of the region. An important omission in this respect is that of the vivid cultural and social capital resources of the region.

Cultural and Social Capital Resources

The North-eastern region is perhaps one of the few regions not only in India but also in the world that possesses such great diversity of cultures and civilisations. There are more than 500 known and well-defined cultural groups and communities inhabiting in the region with their distinct ways of life and views about the world. They still possess their distinct culture, customs, values, costumes, ways of articulation and expressions. They are also unique as far as their traditional knowledge and social and cultural capitals are concerned. These aspects of the regional resource base have enhanced importance in the agc of globalisation, privatisation and liberalisation. Today, the dominant world economies are in search of new colonies for resource mobilisation and realisation of their profits. Capitalism has been transformed from the classical commodity market relations to knowledge and information technology dominated market relations. Use of brute and barbaric methods of physical, economic and politico-cultural domination and control over the subjects have been replaced by the techniques of hegemonic control through subterranean capillary power relations. In the changed circumstances the organism itself has become the target of the forces of colonisation. Rich bio-diversity of the region makes it one of the most important destinations of global capital. Appropriation of the cultural and social capitals and indigenous resources including traditional knowledge resulting into generalised estrangement of the communities and individuals have set into motion the process of globalisation and corporate trans-national capitalism in the region.

This is by far the most formidable challenge and crisis faced by numerous communities living in the region. Scholars interested in proper development of the region will have to take cognisance of these crucial attributes of the regional resource base and attempts should be made to initiate the resource inventory and mapping intra-regional diversities properly. Thus, proper regional development exercise in the North-eastern Region will have to move away from the traditional ways of looking at Resource-Industry Inter Linkages and take resort into Culture-Society-Economy-Environment-Inter Linkages.

Liberalisation-Globalisation has brought an end to the age of Commodity Market Relations and it has set into motion the Information-Technology-Resource-Industry-Inter-Linkages. It is the age of biotechnology, genetic engineering and genome research. The obsession of the scholars with the out dated modes of development is likely to prove detrimental to the development of the region. An aggressive resource inventory of the genetic and cultural resources is an imperative if the region wishes to resist the processes of neo-colonialism that targets colonisation of life itself.

SCIENTIFIC RESEARCH AND DATA ANXIETY

Modernist mindset is most active among the scholars and planners that are claiming to carry a scientific, objective and rational research in the region. According to them to be scientific, objective and rational means to be instrumental and factual. There is a secular obsession among most of the scholars to quantify or look for factual information (data) for a meaningful research. Consequently, it is observed that instrumental rationality has pushed the practical and emancipatory human rationality into the margins of most of the discourses. The ascendancy of the instrumental rationality to the position of a universal rationality has been possible through the active participation of the modern state. Most often than not, it is noticed that rationality thus constructed only reflects the mirror image of the dominant material conditions of the society. To this extent rationality emerges as a constructed entity.

In the age of modernity, the Leviathan state along with its various organs and apparatuses pontificates in carrying the noble task of manufacturing and dissemination of such rationality. To accomplish this task the modern state creates a network of organisations and institutions to construct and publish factual information popularly known as 'Data'. Therefore, the underlying assumptions that remain valid are 'data are over and above the policy statements of the power elites that control the material social conditions and use the state to pursue their sectarian interests'. It is the handiwork of a Foucauldian state which is primarily an agency of moulding, using, ingesting, directing the collective capacities of its' citizens/subjects and fashioning it into the most powerful tool of collective action called the 'Governmentality'[1]. This is in diametrical opposition to a constitutional state, which primarily upholds the rule of law (Andrew Feenberg: 1996). The nature, quantity and quality of data published by the state and its various institutions also reflect the philosophy of the ruling elites. The process of data production is part and parcel of the hegemonic control that manufactures and circulates the information with a trademark of objectivity, legitimacy and authenticity.

In recent times right to information has become as one of the founding principles of people's empowerment and freedom but unfortunately the issues at stake are not just that of right to information alone. On the contrary, the cardinal issues include: What constitutes the information itself? What is the interrelationship between ideology and information? How to inculcate a critical insight among the subjects/citizens that will help them to isolate the ideology from the information? In a class society as that of today where wisdom is replaced by knowledge and knowledge by information, to be rational means to have more information. Moreover, a person endowed with more information is also considered both rational and legitimate. However, it would be wrong to say that the process of using information for these purposes is a unique feature of last two centuries only. In fact the process is as old as the days of the French Revolution.

In the aftermath of the French Revolution when "people: the subject" were transformed into "people: the citizens" and in turn they became the sole possessors and also the only legitimisers of real power under democracy they became the central theme of concern for the rulers. Thus, it was mandatory for the ruling classes to invent new ways and means to manage and control the consent and attitudes of the people itself. In order to manipulate the subject in better ways and more effectively it was necessary to know them in totality. Thus, it became imperative to assess and enumerate them through better data management. Once it succeeded in 'knowing' the people in a particular way, thereafter, every thing was quantified and transformed into database. Henceforth, people were reduced to subjects and amalgamated with other positivities. Their morals, values and preferences too became manageable and predictable. Hereafter, human beings became an experimental entity and man became the subject of experimental sciences. In order to institutionalise these operations new branches of knowledge emerged. Positivism emerged as new branch of knowledge to study human beings in a scientific manner (Foucault: 1994). This also gave birth to scientific racism and disciplines like Eugenic that professed the rationality of healthy individual more desirable than those are unhealthy (Rose: 2001).

The point here is not to cry foul about data per se but to be cautious about the data and the ideology mingled with it. Many scholars may be under the illusion that data are facts and these are neutral to value judgements and class ideology. Therefore, there is hardly any need to be aversive to data per se. However, as a precautionary measure one could obtain desired objectives by deconstructing the data supplied by such institutions. Thus, it will be possible to achieve similar objectives by appropriating the data and drawing diametrically opposite conclusions.

Taking such a position can at its best be interpreted as a wishful thinking. It is so because, is it necessary to give legitimacy to the channels of hegemonic control in order to attain the desired objectives and reach at politically correct conclusions? Therefore, the choice is not between to use and not to use the data but between to legitimise or not the capillary power relations in the age of governmentality.

The North-Eastern region is hardly an exception to these manipulations and manoeuvres carried on the name of data generations and management. Most of the scholars opined that one of the serious handicap in conducting a serious and meaningful research in the region is paucity of authentic data. They also opined this region is a laggard not only in terms of its development and modernisation but also deficient in making objective evaluation possible for want of up-to-date data and adequate information. Therefore, for modernisation availability of data is a must and most of the efforts of the state are geared towards bridging the gulf by building a sound database. As a consequence the major emphasis of most of the state and central government organisations in the region is on data generation or manufacturing rather than the well being of the people.

Technology as Anxiety

Human beings are considered to be the tool making animals. There is a lot of sense in saying that 'human are such stuffs as tools and technologies have made them'. Human beings make tools but repeated and sustained use of these over generations also make human beings. Technology does not only bring in physiological and anatomic changes/ modifications in human beings but the same is also responsible for changing him as a social and political being that needs to evolve various social institutions in order to put these tools into operation. Thus, technology serves well as a servant than as a master. But the real crises emerges when technology or tools do not only get deeply entrenched into ones being and start dominating and dictating terms but also become the sole basis of a legitimate and rational human action. In other words, when technology get accepted as the criterion for defining human ontology and epistemology that signals total triumph of tools over the humans. A human endowed with such a technological rationality is likely to radiate greater disaster than done a barbaric tyrant so far.

Often one comes across writing on the North-Eastern region emphasising the need of a technological revolution as the panacea to overcome the development modernisation impediments that the region is at present confronted with. There can be no disagreement about it that technology is an imperative to break open the nature of stagnation which most of the communities in the region are at present in. Once again, the real issue at stake is not the need for technology but that of proper and just technology. What the region is in need at present is not just any technology but one that strengthens and complements the human practical rationality, restores the fast disappearing organic links among the members of the community and between human beings and their immediate environment and above all one that can halt and alter the processes of secular alienation.

Choice of technology has special significance in the age of information technology because today the choices of technology are made on the basis of two prime considerations. The first and foremost consideration is the scope and margins of profitability and the other being technology for governmentality. Today, in the name of technological sophistication and precision, life and organism have been brought within the ambit of market relations and super surveillance. Use of Remote Sensing Techniques like the Aerial Photographs, Landsat Imageries, Geographical Information System (GIS) and Geographical Position Systems (GPS) etc. are in vogue for making an inventory of resources in the region. As far as the North-Eastern Region is concerned most of the scholars both within and outside the region consider these developments either path breaking technological innovations or paradigm shifts in the regional resource inventory. They often forget to notice the underlying social, economic and power relations of the same. It is hardly a secret to notice that, with every new technological innovation there emerges a new power relation. The development in the technology of observation and monitoring are no exception to these. In a 'Panoptic Society' or 'Society of the Spectacles' these have become the indispensable components in Governmentality. These new techniques have successfully widened the optical gaze for evaluation, assessment, management and control of resources and populace in the age of super-surveillance. These are developed and deployed ubiquitously to acquire wide spectrum view of the subject including for the purpose of mapping the macro and micro environmental variations with greater precision in order to gain continuous and uninterrupted access to the subject for the purpose of effective manipulation and manoeuvrings. The annals of contemporary history and geography have many evidences to prove these assertions. The Americans successfully used these during the War in Vietnam, Nicaragua, Cuba and Afghanistan and Iraq etc., the Russian too in Afghanistan and Chechiniya, and other World Powers along with other superpowers are using these for clandestine monitoring of the resistance movements and dissentions activities on a global scale. The sovereign nation states use these techniques for evaluating their natural resources, monitoring its territory and also the subjects particularly that have become the epitome of unity between the geographical and social marginalisation and are threatening the very unity and integrity of these Nation states. The Srilankan Government uses these to monitor the movements of the Liberation Tigers of Tamil Ellam (LTTE) in the Northern and Eastern Provinces of Sri Lanka; India too uses these to monitor the insurgent movements in Jammu and Kashmir and in the Northeast Region. The Americans and its Western Allies are still using these for effective monitoring, manoeuvring and control everywhere particularly Iraq, Cuba, North Korea, Pakistan, Afghanistan and other countries. The interface of the super surveillance technologies along with the Geographical Information System (GIS) and Geographical Positioning System (GPS) have helped in the optimisation of resource exploitation including time in executing the control more effectively and lethally with greater precision.

However, the control would be useless and incomplete unless the view obtained through the 'Wide Spectrum Telescopic Optical Gaze' is supported and supplemented by the 'Microscopic Precision Optical Gaze' particularly one that can transcend the limits encountered by the 'Traditional Optics'. It is necessary because, in the changed circumstances the body and the organisms have become the site of powers contest. In order to intervene into the body space and the organism the 'Surveillance Gaze' needs to be Trans-Opaque particularly one that successfully defies the limitations of the ocularcentricism. Uses of CAT Scanners, X-rays, Ultra Sounders, Genetic and DNA mappings etc. have been done to gain access to the body space of the organisms. With the introduction of these techniques the dialectics of interior and the exterior has collapsed into one-dimensional entity i.e. "the Ulterior". Thus, the 'One-Dimensional Man' of Herbert Marcuse disappears into oblivion and it has been replaced by technologically constructed and Genetically Mapped body spaces that are available for appropriation by the wider public only after duly acknowledging the rights of the patent holders. Therefore, it is difficult to conceive of representations made by using the sophisticated techniques like the Land-sat etc. without motives. The phenomena thus represented have neither the exterior nor the interior but only the Ulterior dimensions.

Once again the point here is not to argue against the use of modern technology but to put up a case for the use of an alternative technology, one that is liberating rather than alienating. What the people in the region need today is not the technology that will improve their economic efficiency and sharpen their competitiveness and brings in ruptures in their community life and symbiotic human- nature relationships. They need technologies that will minimize the trauma of redundancy and obsolescence that have become the characteristic features of the so-called modernization and development in the region. Moreover, what the region needs most urgently is a change in the mindset of people that consider the region as a chronic case of development handicaps for want of an immediate technological revolution. However, the truth is that the Northeast is not a pathological case. Therefore, suggesting prescriptions and advising administration of externally induced higher doses of technology is likely to prove more detrimental for the development of the region. The region needs a technology that will empower its people and reduce the chances of redundancies among the communities.

Anxiety about an Entrepreneurial State

Development of the Northeast has been one of the most complex and intriguing processes right from the inception of planned development in India. The new born nation already struggling with the birth pangs encountered formidable challenges in the realisation of its triple objectives of sovereignty, economic development and national integration in the region. The leaders of freedom struggle had expected that the people of the region would respond very much like those in the other parts of the country and they would also feel more liberated and independent in a free India. They also expected that the people of the region would embrace their new and broader identity by joining the so-called national mainstream and rejoice the same without too many reservations. But, to the surprise of many, most of the communities in the region did not only show indifference but they also offered stiff resistance to such ideas and policies. Since, most of the tribal communities living in the hilly and mountainous areas of the region were apprehensive about the new national identity that was being superimposed upon them, it was but natural of them to resist any such move. They were possessive of their hard yet simple and independent tribal ways of living. For them incorporation in the so-called national mainstream and common national identity was nothing more than loss of their identity and secluded ways of life. Thus, they refused to participate in the so-called civilising missions carried by the colonisers for a long time and to the envy of many they were still proud of their independent existence. But, existence of tradition tribal ways of life right up to the middle of twentieth century were in no way desirable and sustainable particularly in the mids falling paradigms and emerging new world order that was pontificating on the celebrations of gigantism. In a global theatre where might was increasingly taking over the just and right, the small was also considered weak and miserable. It was also the beginning of new episteme and reasoning. Hereafter, small may be beautiful but not useful and definitely it was neither compatible nor sustainable. On the contrary, the small was interpreted either as a handicap or lack of requisite inertia to continue if not equal to nothingness.

There are over five hundred small communities living in the region that have become the replica of timelessness and ossified communities. Their reluctance largely emanated from their ignorance of the wonders that modernity has placed before the mankind. The achievements made in science, society, culture and economy were conspicuous by their absence in the difficult and hard life of the tribal and backward people in the region. Lack of enthusiasm and vehement opposition to the magic mantra of national development programmes among the people of the region on a sustained basis over a long time period became the cause of worry and anxiety to many.

Scholars and planners came up with their own model to over come these challenges. State regulated, managed and sponsored development were one of the many such models. It was believed that development is a lopsided process. Since the determining factors both natural and social are in favour of uneven development then the developed areas and centres are likely to attract more of these opportunities at the expense of other areas. So, if development is left to the interplay of the market forces alone then regional inequalities are likely to be more alarming. Widening regional disparities in case of India will make it difficult to realise the other two objectives outlined in the preamble of the planning philosophy of India. Therefore, it was suggested that state should not only regulate and sponsor development in the region but it should also become an entrepreneur in undertaking the developmental activities. And above all it was also the responsibility of the state to carry developmental activities forward along with creating the requisite infrastructure and institutional framework that will guide these communities to find their ways in the otherwise fiercely competitive world.

Apart from the anxieties mentioned above there are some other equally important ones. Anxiety about conspicuous absence of infrastructure, market, entrepreneurial skill, institutional supports and capital etc. are considered some other important banes of development in the region. According to these scholars the North-Eastern region will have to transform all the above-mentioned odds and evens into its favour before it finds itself on the road to development. Based on these misplaced anxieties, the development priorities suggested by these scholars too degenerates into development arbitrariness. Some of the important ones are:

Development Arbitrariness in the Region or Development as the Reason of the State

Today, there is hardly any other concept like development that has so many different meanings to so many people. 'It serves many purposes including as a reason of state, as a legitimiser of regimes, as a component of vision of a good society and above all, as a shorthand term for the need of the poor and the needy' (Nandi: 2000). Looking at the vision of development suggested by most of the scholars to the northeast it is almost unanimous that the region needs to break open its age-old shackles of stagnation and low levels of economic efficiency. To begin with it needs to adopt resource specific development strategies for proper development.

Development as Social Differentiation

As mentioned earlier land is the most abundant and widely used natural resource in the region. It is abundant from every possible yardsticks of measurement. Land is in abundance not only because of its extensive uses but it is also due to the fact that it forms the basis of the livelihood of more than 85 percent of the total population in the region. Therefore, social distribution of land and particularly the land tenure system also epitomises the most prominent site of social contradictions in the region. Broadly speaking, the land ownership pattern in the region particularly among the hill and tribal people was much different from what it was among the plain people. The land tenure system among the tribes of the region was based on village-community ownership. The individual family ownership was confined mostly to the homestead land. Traditionally, the village councils under the headship of Village Headmen (*Gaonburas*) were the custodians of village land. They used to give plots of land to the individual family for the purpose of cultivation. Though, there were minor intra and inter-tribe variations yet such a system of land tenure was practiced among most of the hill tribes. For example, the district was divided into revenue units called *Hill Mauzas* among the Garos of Meghalaya and each Mauza was further divided into ***Akings***. Each Aking under an *Aking Nokma* was the custodian of the village land and he used to own the village land on behalf of his clansmen. The *Aking Nokma* had the authority to distribute the land among his clansmen for cultivation. Other tribes in Meghalaya followed similar practices. Among the Khasis, the *Syiem* was authorised to distribute the land among the cultivators through the Village Headman *(Rangbah Shnong)* and the Village Council *(Village Darbar)*. This was also the practice among the Mizos before the independence when the *'Lal'* was vested with the authority of distributing the land among the villagers. But after the independence the Village Council plays the role of distributing the land among the cultivators. Thus, one occasionally came across the cases of landlessness and intra-tribal disputes about the distribution of land and its resources in the past.

The situation is much different now. In the name of development one witnesses that there has been erosions in the authority of the traditional institutions particularly in relation to their control over the common property resources of the village. Land today is the most sought for commodity among the tribes of the region. It has become the basis of socio-economic differentiation. There are ample examples of land concentrations in few hands and large-scale landlessness in the region. The so-called egalitarian society of the yester years has been replaced by a class society. Today, land related disputes have taken precedence over all other social conflicts in the region. The intensity of social differentiation has also cast its serious repercussions on the environment and use of community resources in the region. It has been noticed that the Jhum cycle in most of the areas has been limited to 2-3 years period. This has considerably depleted the soil fertility and all bio-mass of the area. Which in turn has placed enormous stress on the social fabric. The so-called egalitarian subsistence societies of yester years are reeling under chronic poverty, malnutrition, ill health and improper hygienic conditions.

Development as Strategic Action

Development is the reason of the state. Every action initiated in the name of development differentiates the society into at least four segments arranged in hierarchical order. The state and the economy occupy the top position and the life world comprised of the public and the private spheres are placed at the bottom of the hierarchy in that order. The state continuously manufactures the rationalities desired by the logic of the economy and with the cooperation of various organs of the state and civil society and the state in its turn disseminates the same into the public and the individuals. Thus, the strategic action assumes the status of the philosophy and ideology of the state and replaces the communicative or practical action of the subject. This has many repercussions as far as empowerment of the subject is concerned. It places them at the highest stage of their alienation and hegemonisation. They become the object of development rather than the subject of the same. Consequently, diversity gets interpreted as obstacle and differences as disloyalty. Uniqueness is interpreted as an aberration and stereotypes as rational and legitimate. Resistance to strategic action is treated as an act of treason and dealt with severe punishments including physical dissipation. Ironically enough, such a process of marginalisation of the subject is often valorised as development.

The north-eastern region is in the limelight for many years for being the hotbeds of communities voicing their differences. Unfortunately, their activities have been interpreted as an act of treason within the stringent development discourses. There are some scholars who reduce these turmoils to simple problems of law and order. Yet, there are a few others that think that these ethnic resentments are part of a global conspiracy against an emerging world power i.e. India. There are a few more that believe that widening regional disparities due to wrong implementation of development policies are responsible for all that is happening in the region. But, there are very few who find it difficult to accept that the problems in the region are deeply entrenched into to reason of the state itself. Every community in the region has reservation against this particular reason but they are not in a position to articulate for want of adequate conjunctural requirements. However, there are communities in the northeast that have succeeded in articulating and sustaining their resentments due to a combination of favourable circumstantial factors including their strategic locations. But, it is an irony that most of these have so far failed to come up with its own model of change and empowerment. Thus, they find it difficult to put up a sound case for the protection of their cultural rights and social capitals.

Development as Antithetical to Social and Cultural Capital Formations

Strategic action involves in gaining access to the life and body of the individual. It is an important aspect of development. It has much wider and lethal repercussions in case of the North-eastern region. The tribal communities in the region have a rich and vivid stock of social and cultural capitals. There are certain specific features of their social beings such as trust, norms, and networks that have always improved the efficiency of the community by facilitating cooperation and coordination among all the members of the society (Putnam 1993). Social associatedness and community concerns are some of the richest treasures of tribal life in the region. Prevalence of community work, mutual help and services in every spheres of their life constitutes the rich stock of the social capital of most of the tribal communities in the region. The practice of *Zawlbook* (Youth

Dormitory), youth clubs, Naga Mothers' Associations, Village and District Council etc. are components of their rich social capital. The traditional tribal communities of the region were not only relatively more egalitarian but they were also less alienated from their products, their labour, themselves and their species, in the past. Their lives were more organised and organically composed around the norms of their social associatedness in the past. Development has broken both the bonds of their social interdependence and exposed them to unprecedented degree of generalised and universal alienation.

Similarly, the traditional knowledge of the indigenous communities regarding the attributes of their environment and resources, cultural practices like songs, dances, cuisine, traditional skill, craft and design etc. all form part of the cultural capital of various communities in the region. Their ethics centred social life thriving on the intricate relationships with their immediate environment over centuries has endowed them as the repository of traditional knowledge. Any activity that aims at achieving development based on people's empowerment will have to rely on the strength of the social and cultural capital stocks of the region. This is perhaps the way out from the present impasses.

RESOURCE-INDUSTRY INTER-LINKAGES AND DEVELOPMENT: THE MAGICAL TRIDENT

The concept "development" has mesmerising effects on the modern minds. It is opium of the modern man. There are perhaps very few other concepts like development that have unleashed such a colossal damage to our society, culture and environment. And above all millions of people continue to be sacrificed every day at the holy altar of development throughout the length and width of the world. It was/is perhaps the single most potent ideological force that was/is responsible for the mass annihilation of Red Indians and other races in the American continents, enslavement of black races and colonisation, marginalisation and exploitations of others on a world scale (Bigelow: 1991). However, there are still a large number of scholars that consider development as the prerequisite for human freedom and empowerment (Sen: 2001)2. In his famous book *Development as Freedom* Sen has placed unconditional commitment in favour of development. To quote him "*Development can be seen, ..., as a process of expanding the real freedom that people enjoy*" (Sen: 2001). Illustrating his argument further he sees a positive "correlation between income per head and longevity" (Sen: 2001) on the one hand and democracy and development on the other. At another place he writes, "no substantial famine has ever occurred in a democratic country, no matter how poor" (Sen: 2001). However, it goes without saying that famines are not the only calamity that human beings face in their social existence. Human history is a witness to the facts that most of the wars, displacement and ghettoisation of the masses have taken place not by the dictators alone but by the champions of democracy and protagonists of development.

The argument placed here is not an attempt to equate dictatorship with democracies. On the contrary, democracies are decidedly preferable to any dictatorships including the one by the proletariats. But, this does not absolve the democracies from the agonies these have caused to millions on a global scale. World continues to bleed, colonised and recolonised by the apostles of democracy and development. In the recent times the Soviets colonised the Afghanistan for the same purpose. The Americans and its Western allies mostly the advanced capitalist countries and their puppets in the Middle-East pushed the Soviets out of Afghanistan and placed the Taliban in their place for the same purpose.

Once again they pushed the Taliban and installed their puppets for the same reasons. Today similar things are taking place in Iraq. The American and the British forces along with the allied troops have devastated one of the ancient civilisations of the world in the name of democracy and development.

Scholars may have reservations about drawing parallels to situations that are quite dissimilar from each other. They may also think that, it has happened in 'x' and 'y' places and 'x' and 'y' communities and it may not happen elsewhere. But, unfortunately this is only a wishful thinking and it will continue to happen, may be in different forms and on different pretexts. Because uneven development, displacement, estrangement, ghettoisation and annihilation are the logical outcomes of the logic of the structure of capitalist development.

Therefore, to talk of resources-industry inter-linkages and development within the over arching capitalist world order is nothing but a new myth for the old ills. The agonies of the northeastern region is intricately linked with its peripheral and marginal positions within the framework of global capitalism. The political, economic, cultural and environmental problems of the region and its people will multiply many folds once the trident of globalisation, liberalisation and privatisation are in full swing. A fully globalised, liberalised and privatised India and particularly the Northeast will only radiate disaster triumph.

CONCLUSION

To sum-up the forgoing discussions, it can be said that the so-called rich natural resource bases in the northeast has so far failed to provide development incentives in the region. On the contrary, there is much sense in saying that for want of other necessary conditions the rich natural resource base is largely responsible for the prevailing state of affairs in the region. To initiate meaningful and desired development, change in the mind-set is imperative. Which in its turn is intricately linked with the logic of the structure of capitalist development. Therefore, to remove the ills of the region, transformative rather than reformative measures are a must. The logic of commodity market mechanism is unlikely to cut much ice in the otherwise marginalised and peripheralised regional political economy. In the age of information technology and knowledge-centred market relations the emphasis of development in case of the region should be on forging unity between social and cultural capital resources of the region. These two also form the core of identity and development in the region and any thing other than these will continue to create wedge between economy and culture. Finally, if development is for the empowerment of the people then research and development in evolving organic links among the culture, economy and environment provides the vital clues. This will also reduce people's alienation by opening up new opportunities of realising their creative potentials. Isolation and insulation of the region and its people will be suicidal for the regions, its culture, environment and polity. They will have to think globally and act locally.

REFERENCES

Edward W. Said (1995) : *Orientalism : Western Conceptions of the Orient,* Penguin books India.

Ashis Nandi (2000) : *The Savage Freud and other Essays on Possible and Retrievable Selves,* Oxford India Paperbacks, Oxford University Press, New Delhi.

Amartya Sen (2001) : *Development as Freedom,* Oxford India Paperbacks, Oxford University Press, New Delhi.

Anup Saikia (1995) : Regional Development of the North Eastern Region of India: Export Base Theory, Government Policy and Underdevelopment (Ph.D. Thesis Department of Geography North Eastern Hill University Shillong, Unpublished).

B.S. Butola (1997) : "Crisis of Hegemony and Counter Hegemonic Insurgency in North East India" *Insurgency in North-Eastern India* (Ed.) B. Pakem, Omsons Publications, New Delhi.

Hans Knoing (1991) : *Columbus : His Enterprise Exploding the myth,* Monthly Review Press, New York.

Michel Foucault (1994) : *The Order of Things an Archaeology of Human Sciences,* Vintage Books, Random House, New York.

Michel Foucault (1990) : *History of Sexuality,* Vol. I, Penguin Books, Harmondsworth.

Andrew Feenberg (1996) : "Marcuse or Habermas : Two Critiques of Technology', in *Inquiry,* Vol. 39.

K.N. Panikkar (2002) : *An Agenda for Cultural Action and Other Essay,* Three Essays, New Delhi.

M. Taher and P. Ahmed (1998) : *Geography of North-East India,* El-Dorado Publications, Guwahati.

A. C. Mohapatra, *et. a.,* (2000) : *Man and Environment,* Star Publishing House, Shillong.

David G. Smith (1992) : "Modernisation, Hyperliteracy, and the Colonization of the Word", in *Alternatives,* Vol. 17.

Albert O. Hirschman (1981) : *Essays in Trespassing Economics to Politics and Beyond,* Cambridge University Press Cambridge, England.

Roby Rajan (1992) : *"Pathological Rationality / Rational Pathologies",* in *Alternatives,* Vol. 17.

Ivan Illich (1981) : *"The De-linking of Peace and Development", Gandhi Marg,* New Delhi.

Ron Martin (1999) : "The new 'geographical turn' in economics : Some critical reflections" *Cambridge Journal of Economics,* vol. 23.

Andrew Feenberg (1996) : "Marcuse or Habermas : Two Critiques of Technology", *Inquiry,* Vol. 39.

Christopher Noris (1995) : "Truth, Science and the Growth of Knowledge", in *New Left Review,* 210 Mach-April.

Shiv Viswanathan (2001) : "Democracy, Governance and Science : Strange case of the Missing Discipline", in *Economic and Political Weekly,* Vol. 36 No. 39.

Graham Burchell, *et. al.* (1991) : *The Foucault Effect : Studies in Governmentality,* Harvester Wheatsheaf, Hertfordshire.

Nikolas Rose (2001): "The Politics of Life Itself", in *Theory, Culture & Society,* Vol. 18(6).

Bill Bigelow (1991) : Hans Knoing (1991): *Columbus : His Enterprise Exploding the myth, Monthly Review Press, New York.*

---

[1] Governmentality means three things:

a. The ensemble formed by the institutions, procedures, analysis and reflections, the calculations and tactics that allow the exercise of this very specific albeit complex form of power which has as its target population, as its principal form of knowledge political economy, and as its essential technical means apparatuses of security.

b. The tendency which, over a long period and throughout the West, has steadily led towards the preeminence over all other forms (sovereignty, discipline, etc.) of this type of power which may be termed government, resulting, on the one hand, in the formation of a whole series of specific governmental apparatuses, and, on the other, in the development of a whole complex of saviors.

c. The process, or rather the result of the process, through which the state of justice of the Middle Ages, transformed into the administrative state during the fifteenth and sixteenth centuries, gradually becomes 'governmentalised'.

[2] "Indeed, the democractic poor centuries sometimes have had much large decline in the production and supply of food, and also sharper collapse of the purchasing power of substantial sections of the population, than some nondemocratic countries. But while the dictatorial countries had major famines, the democratic ones managed to avert famines altogether despite the worse food situation. (Sen : 2001.178.9)

12

What Ails Development in North-East India?

Rabindra N. Bhattacharya

Introduction

The north-eastern (N.E) states of India are characterized by a high rate of population growth; a restricted range of resources (natural and human), labour immobility (out-migration in particular); poor infrastructure, incomplete land market; restricted access to credit, insurance and capital markets; volatile and uncertain social environment ; and largely subsistence economies. Assam has more diversified resource-base and, hence, is kept outside the purview of our discussion here.

Agriculture and other biomass-based subsistence activities dominate the life of most of the people in most of these economies. Households or extended family units and, in some instances, communal work (organized, for instance, on a village or tribal/ethnic basis) are the prevalent social organizations of production in the subsistence sector.

It is not implied here, that all production in these economies is carried out in the subsistence sector. Dual social arrangements may emerge when advanced economic sectors develop. However, production for markets beyond the respective state boundaries and for national and for international markets depends primarily upon a narrow range of primary products and natural resources (exhaustible as well as regenerative) and in the subsistence sector traditional arrangements are still likely to persist. In many instances, clan and social arrangements have undergone changes as a consequence of exposure to the market economy and with the national and transnational contracts. Due to limited range and quantum of production most of these states depend heavily on the central government for economic assistance and other forms of concessions.

Given the ongoing process of globalisation and the above context, the paper has the following structure. Considering each state of North-East India as a small open agrarian economy, Section II attempts to identify some important problem areas that are ailing (or likely to do so in future) these states in the process of economic transformation. Section III draws some useful insights from the theory of endogenous growth incorporating natural resources (capital) and social and institutional issues that have bearing on the possibility of (sustainable) development of the North-Eastern states. Finally, based on the insights drawn from the earlier sections, Section IV draws certain conclusions that are pertinent to economies of North-East India.

I

Problem Areas

With the process of exposing these economies to the rest of the country and the rest of the world, some of these economies may come to depend on the export of extractive non-renewable resources-oil, coal and other minerals and/or renewable natural resources, like forests (e.g. forests of Arunachal). Sometimes, state-run enterprises extract and sell natural resources. In others, resources may be privately owned by national or transnational enterprises.

Suppose an enterprise is charged with selling non-renewable natural resource on the world market so that the discounted net profits are maximized. For a small economy that is, one that sells its natural resources on world markets but that does not have a large enough market share to be able to influence world prices (a so-called price-taker).

The principle of opportunity cost is particularly an important guide to the rate of extraction. A ton of coal extracted and sold today is a ton unavailable in the future. In deciding whether to extract and sell an additional ton today, the extractor must consider not only the cost of extracting the ton, but also the cost of foregoing the highest profit that could have been earned if the coal had instead been extracted and sold in the future. It is optimal to adjust extraction in any given period until this 'more inclusive' definition of marginal cost (m.c.), or "augmented marginal cost," equals the market price (p), i.e., p = m.c. + opportunity cost.

This rule implies that the current extraction rate of a private owner of a natural resource depends not only on the current price (as in the standard theory) but also on expectations about future prices. These price expectations determine the opportunity cost of additional current extraction. Extracting a resource based on p = m.c. would imply over exploitation because it fails to account for the profit foregone when an additional ton is extracted today.

Even this elementary analysis illuminates questions having important bearing for N-E states. Private enterprises, be it national or transnational, operating in an uncertain and volatile sociopolitical environment in N-E states may not have any expectation about future prices and as such opportunity cost of current extraction may be negligible to them. And this may indeed induce them to over-extract the resource leading to its early exhaustion. The process is likely to be quicker should the enterprises be transnationals operating in an uncertain environment. The fall-out of this exhaustion of resources could be traumatic for the area.

Some of these N-E states like Arunachal have abundance of regenerative natural forests to generate income in the early stages of development. If a large share of that income is saved, natural wealth can be converted into human and human made capital such as an educated workforce, infrastructures, productive agriculture, industry and other assets. Yet, if we allow for the depletion of the resource base with development, the performance of these specific resource-rich states would seem to be discouraging and unsustainable. Why should this be the outcome? If regenerative resources are depleted at rates faster than they can be replenished or substituted by human-made capital, development will be 'unsustainable.' Moreover, resources like natural forests regenerate over long periods and second-growth forests are likely to be different from native stands. Furthermore, if harvesting greatly alters the habitat, regeneration can take longer time or become impossible. The process may generate irreversible damages. However, with global marketization, it is these resources that are more likely to become exportable and more susceptible to external shocks.

Theory tells us that before harvesting begins, the stock of tree biomass in a virgin forest is large and cannot grow rapidly because its supply of nutrients is limited. When harvesting begins the trees can replenish their numbers more rapidly. But as the harvesting effort increases, this process reaches a peak, after which the annual growth of the stock declines and so does the sustainable harvest. If the harvest effort continues to grow, the forest biomass may be so small or so scattered that regeneration cannot replace the harvest at any level, this leads to extinction. The stock becomes too small to replace the rate of harvest.

Once overharvesting becomes apparent, harvesters might adjust by reducing their effort. However, the concept of minimum biologically viable population is, in effect, a counter argument. Besides this, consider a multinational/national logger in north-east India operating in an environment of uncertain future (due to perceived or real social tensions). His cost of logging will probably be quite low (particularly because of low labour cost in these labour-surplus insulated economies) while the international price of log is really very high. In the absence of future expectation, benefits of preservation will not accrue to him. Hence there is little incentive to desist the operator from over-exploitation (Bhattacharya, 2002)

It may be profitable for a private enterprise to exploit a resource fully now rather than defer this exploitation. Furthermore, the government of a state/ country facing this predicament may support the side of profitable exploitation by private enterprise now. It can be politically worthwhile for governments to sacrifice long-term goals in order to obtain comparatively short-lived gains for the community. Apart from the political expediency of myopia (Buchanan and Tullock 1962), it may also be that governments or ruling elites are largely dominated by the interests of large private enterprises.

Again, in the process of exploitating the renewable and non-renewable resources, the economy may reduce the quality or availability of other resources (negative externality), such as agricultural land, which are inputs in the production of the subsistence goods. Consequently the economic and social catastrophe may be much more severe.

The dependence of poor people of N-E on their natural resources, such as soil and its cover, water, forests, animals and fisheries are self-evident. The rural folk of these bio-mass-based subsistence economies eke out a living from products obtained directly from plants and animals. For poor people, some environmental regenerative natural resources in danger of exhaustion from overuse are often complementary to other goods and services (e.g., livestock and grazing land) while other environmental resources supplement income, most especially in times of acute economic stress. So erosion of the environmental resource base can make certain categories of people destitute (Dasgupta, 1993).

Dasgupta (1993) draws our attention to another very important dimension of the problem. When shadow prices of environmental resources are not properly taken account of, resource-based goods can be assumed to be underpriced in the market. Again, unidirectional externalities, such as deforestation in the uplands inflicting damages on the low lands in integrated watersheds, have a special significance in this context. When unidirectional externalities are present in regions that export primary products there is an implicit subsidy on such products. It is the poor peasants, forest dwellers, pastoral people etc. who, in the ultimate analysis, really pay this subsidy, since common law de facto recognizes the polluter's rights (Dasgupta, 1991).

Extent of common property resources to total assets of rural communities is likely to be substantial in N-E. Here common property resources imply local commons like village ponds and tanks, pastures and threshing grounds, watersheds, river beds, sources of fuelwoods, medicinal herbs, bamboo, resin etc. Local commons are open only to those having historical rights, kinship ties, community membership etc.

A series of policy intervention along with market forces are likely to be unleashed in the wake of opening up and globalisation. This will alter the land use and tenurial system (directed to institutionalization of modem private property) with serious environmental and social consequences to both private and communal property resources. Bypassing the transitional task of creating an environment for the evolution of co-operation-based new 'common property resource management' (CPRM) institutions may further aggravate the already prevailing unquite environment of India's north-east (Bhattacharya, 2002)

In open agrarian economies (like the N-E states) prices of inputs and outputs are set in the world market, so the level of real income is determined by factors that lie outside the control of the indigenous agents of the economy (Perrings,1997). Relative price shifts (adverse terms of trade) can induce a process in which increasing levels of activity by the agents operating near minimum subsistence level may lead directly to deepening poverty and resource degradation. This is likely to happen because of the exhaustible nature of the basic resource in agriculture or pastoral activities - land. Perrings (1997) has developed a formal model of the intensification of subsistence production within a defined technological horizon in terms of exogenous shocks incorporating the exhaustible nature of natural resources exploited by rural producers. Arable or pastoral land is only renewable if agrarian activity does not involve overuse leading to irreversible change that makes land useless under the technology applied. If it does experience such change it is for all practical purposes exhaustible. Perring's work (1997) suggests that the impact of any change in the economic environment of an open agrarian economy will vary both with the level of activity (the intensity of resources use within the existing technological horizon), and the sensitivity of natural environment to change in that level.

Anthropological studies indicate that the apparent stability of the closed agrarian economies was the outcome of a variety of institutional control mechanisms designed to cope up with an uncertain environment by restricting investment to sustainable levels (Nash, 1967, and Sahlins, 1974).

The opening of agrarian economies to national and world markets is likely to change the characteristics of these economies (like N-E economies) in significant ways. Certain input and output prices are now set by forces external to these economies. The link between real income, saving and local natural environment will be snapped or will at least become tenuous. The role of traditional institutions in regulating resource use pattern will be weakened with implications both for the incentive effects of traditional communal or common property, and for the way that uncertainty is taken care of (Perrings, 1997). The sources of uncertainty now are the environment and the external market. Rural producers' response will then be function of the methods chosen to minimize risk in both states.

In agrarian and pastoral economies, strategies for minimizing risk hinge on decisions in two areas: the traditional choice as to the optimal level of activity; and a new choice between production either for direct consumption or for the market (Livingstone, 1981). However, neither the market risk nor the direct consumption risks of harvest failure are insurable except through the decisions taken by agrarian producers in these two areas (Perrings, 1997). Subsistence-constrained producers, under such situations tend to adopt what Lipton (1968) has called 'Survival algorithms'. They tend to adopt low market value but environmentally less susceptible crops or livestocks suitable for both market production and direct consumption. The important point here is that the production and consumption decision of the risk minimizing producers in the open agrarian economies have a bias in favour of tried practices and traditional products, and against technological innovations. The costs of such technological conservatism, in terms of specialization losses of trade, are implicitly accepted as a part of the premium to be paid for the risk exposure to the world market (Perrings, 1997).

Similar kind of considerations influence saving behaviour of agrarian producers. Saving in financial assets may tend to be limited by the availability of financial institutions. However, the absence of such institutions may very well be a consequence of the fact that the safety-oriented survival algorithms employed by households favour savings in real assets. Savings in real asset provide both a means of direct consumption in the case of crop failure (insurance against direct entitlement failure) and a degree of protection against product price volatility (insurance against trade entitlement failure). An important implication of this is that capital in such an economy is not freely mobile and as a result structural change in such economies is likely to be very slow.

III

Sustainable Development: Resource, Institutions and Endogenous Growth

What are the various economic policies and instruments available to economies of N-E India for ensuring that an economy is able to meet the need of the present generation without compromising the ability of the economic system, including its environmental resource base, to meet the need of future generations? This concern for any type of economy is now widely recognized as the economics of sustainable development (SD).

An important conceptual basis for understanding the role of environment in SD is to view the way in which natural resources and environments provide economic benefits as being similar to the way in which any valuable asset provides 'services' an economy. Along with physical and human capital environmental resources should be viewed as important economic assets which can be called natural capital (Pearce and Barbier, 2000)

Human-made, or physical capital (KP), natural capital (KN), and human capital (KH) all contribute to human welfare through supporting the production of goods and services in the economic process. We know about the role of KP; KN is used for material and energy inputs into production, acts as a sink for emitted wastes from the economic process, and provides a variety of ecological services to sustain production, such as nutrient recycling, watershed protection and catchment functions and climate regulation; and KH includes human skills necessary for advanced production process and for research and development activities that usher in technical innovations. All three forms of capital also contribute directly to human welfare independently of their contributions through the economic process. For example, KN includes aesthetic values, and provides a variety of ecological services that are essential for supporting life.

One of the recent advances in the economics literature with implications for SD is the emergence of endogenous or new growth theory. This is expected to have some important implications for the economies of N-E India. A key component of these models (unlike conventional neoclassical model) is that technological innovation is endogenously determined by private and public sector choices within the economic system (Romar, 1990; Lucas 1988; Rebelo 1991).

One of the important implications that emerge from endogenous growth literature (e.g. Barro and Sala-I-Martin, 1995) is that the property of conditional convergence (i.e., as the economy develops its growth rate should eventually diminish until it reaches its steady state growth rate) does not necessarily mean that poorer countries/regions should display higher rate of growth than richer countries/regions. Empirical studies of Barrow and Sala-I-Martin (1995) tend to suggest that once the adverse effects of government distortions and poor institutions across countries are accounted for - as reflected in such indicators as the ratio of government consumption to GDP, corruption, political instability and lack of enforcement of contracts - then growth does appear to be negatively correlated with the initial level of per capita income. The implication is that persistently bad government policies and ineffective institutions are inhibiting the long growth prospects of low-income countries. This also, to an extent, explains why the growth rate of N-E economies remain secularly low.

According to the endogenous growth school, the lack of stable and credible economic policies and institutions in poor countries inhibit the generation of use of new technological ideas to reap greater economic opportunities, thus limiting economic growth and development. Romer (1993) predicts "the feature that will increasingly differentiate one geographic area....from another will be the quality of public institutions. The most successful areas will be the ones with the most competent and effective mechanisms for supporting collective interests, especially in the production of new ideas." As a consequence, the inability of poor regions to take off economically can be attributed to institutional and policy failures.

Apart from institutional and policy failures another important factor may be the structural economic dependence of these economies on their natural resource (KN) endowments (Pearce & Barbier, 2000). Barbier (1994) shows that countries displaying low or stagnant growth rates are highly resource dependent. Matsuyama (1992) shows that trade liberalization in a land-intensive economy could slow down economic growth by inducing the economy to shift resources away from manufacturing (which produces learning-induced growth) towards agriculture (which does not).

Endogenous growth theorists have not shown much concern about the contribution of natural resources to growth or with the role of innovation in overcoming resource scarcity. However, focusing simply on policy and institutions to foster improved innovation in the advanced economic sectors of low-income economies may not be sufficient. As these economies are highly dependent on natural resource base for economic growth and development over the medium term, the takeoff into higher growth rates and economic development will be directly related to the ability of these economies to manage their natural resources efficiently and sustainably over the medium to long term.

Homer-Dixon (1995) identifies social ingenuity as a precursor to technical ingenuity. He suggests two mechanisms by which resource scarcity can limit both the total supply and the rate of supply of ingenuity. First, resource scarcity often provokes competitive action by powerful elite groups and narrow social coalitions to defend their interests or to make gains out of scarcity through rent-seeking behaviour. These can hinder efforts to create and modernize institutions and can generally hinder to coordinate human activities, talents and resources in response to scarcity. Severe scarcity may sometime cause social turmoil and violence that can directly impede the functioning of ingenuity-generating institutions. Second, Homer-Dixon argues that resource scarcity often reduces the availability of human and financial capital (so essential for endogenous growth) for the production of ingenuity by shifting investments from long-term growth to immediate tasks of scarcity management. These problems and failures in turn undermine the innovation process in particular by disrupting the abilities of the core economy to generate sufficient human capital, develop research and development capacities, utilize existing technological knowledge, and to produce and disseminate new technology throughout the economy.

There are some evidences that in many poor agrarian economies depletion and degradation of natural resources - such as agricultural land, forests, fresh water and fisheries - may be a contributing factor in social processes that destabilizes the institutional and economic conditions necessary for innovation and growth (Barbier & Homer-Dixon, 1999). Evidences have also been found across a wide cross-section of low income countries that social and political instability is highly correlated both with low levels of productive investments and resource scarcity. We can draw some evidences like these from N-E of India too.

V

Conclusion

In sum, our foregoing discussions in sections II & III and recent application of endogenous growth theory suggest that resource dependency need not be an absolute barrier to low income resource dependent N-E states of India for achieving both long term growth and SD. However, it needs to be emphasized that it is not sufficient for these economies to focus exclusively on policies and institutions to foster improved innovation in their relatively advanced economic sectors. On the contrary, the take-off into higher growth rates and sustainable economic development will be directly related to the ability of these economies to manage their natural resources efficiently and sustainably over the medium to long term (Pearce & Barbier, 2000).

REFERENCES

Barbier, E.B., (1994), 'Natural Capital and Economics of Environment and Development'; In Jansson, A.M., Hammer, M, Folke, C and Costanza, R (eds), *Investing in Natural Capital: The Ecological Economics Approach to Sustainability*, Island Press, Washington DC.

________ and Homer-Dixon, T., (1999), 'Resource Scarcity and Innovation: Can Poor countries Attain Endogenous Growth?' AMBIO, Vol 26, No. 1.

Barro, R.J. and Martin S.I., (1995), *Economic Growth*, McGraw-Hill, N.Y.

Bhattacharya, R.N., (1999), 'Economies of India's North East, Natural Resource Base and Globalization' in Banerjee A. and Kar, B. (eds), *Economic Planning and Development of North Eastern States*, Kanishka, New Delhi.

Buchnan, J. and Tullock, G., (1962), *The Calculus of Consent*, Michigan Press.

Dasgupta, P., (1993), *An Inquiry into Well-Being and Destitution*, Oxford: Clarendon.

Homer-Dixon, T.F., (1995), 'The Ingenuity Gap: Can Poor Countries Adapt to Resource Scarcity?' Population and Development Review, Vol. 21.

Lipton, M., (1968), 'The Theory of the Optimizing Peasant', Journal of Development Studies

Livingstone, I., (1981). 'Supply Responses of Peasants Producers: The Effect of Own-Account Consumption on the Supply of Marketed Output,' in *Development Economics and Policy: Readings*, George Allen & Urwin, London.

Lucas, R.E., (1988), 'On the Mechanics of Economic Development', Journal of Forestry Economics, Vol. 22.

Matsuyama, K., (1992), 'Agricultural Productivity, Comparative Advantage and Economic Growth', Journal of Economic Theory, Vol. 58.

Nash, M., (1967), 'The Social Context of Economic Choice in a Small Society' in G.Dalton (ed.), *Tribal and Peasant Economies*, Austin.

Pearce, D. and Barbier, E., (2000), *Blue Print for a Sustainable Economics*, Earth scan, London.

Perrings, C., (1997), *Economics of Ecological Resources*, Edward Elgar, UK

Rebelo, S., (1991), 'Long-Run Policy Analysis and Long-Run Growth', Journal of Political Economy, Vol 99.

Romer, P., (1990), 'Endogenous Technological Change', Journal of Political Economy, Vol. 98.

Sachs, I.D. and Warner, A.M., (1995), *Natural Resource Abundance and Economic Growth*, Development Discussion Paper No 517a, Harvard Institute for International Development.

Sahlins, M., (1974), *Stone Age Economics*, Tavistock Press, London.

13

Structural Change and Resource-Industry Linkages in India's North-East : Some Policy Imperatives

—Gurudas Das

Structural change in an economy is what a barometer is to weather. It exhibits the internal health of an economy. It indicates the direction towards which the economy is heading. It also sensitises the planners and other economic agents about policy interventions needed to keep the economy in the desired track. As an analysis of structural change essentially captures the sectoral performances over time, it is of immense use in identifying the areas of stress and strain through which different sectors and sub-sectors undergo. As a result, any long-term strategy of economic development of an area must factor into this dimension. In fact, structural change in an economy provides the clues for making a road map for development.

This paper makes a preliminary attempt to understand the nature of structural change that is taking place in the states of North-east India and seeks to extend some plausible explanation for this. An attempt has also been made to fathom out the policy implications for this change. The analysis is based on simplistic three-tier sectoral classification of the economies of north-eastern states. A more in-depth study can only reveal the various dimensions of the change.

Main features of structural change

(1) The share of primary sector to NSDP in most states of North-east is steadily declining. This is, indeed, a sign of structural progression (Table 1).

(2) The percentage share of main workforce engaged in the primary sector is also gradually declining. However, there are a few instances of reverse decadal movement of occupational structure in the primary sector to that of its share to NSDP. For example, in Nagaland, while NSDP share of the primary sector steadily declined from 48.09 percent in 1971 to

42.86 percent in 1981 and then to 29.07 percent in 1991; the share of main workers engaged in the primary sector has declined from 78.95 percent in 1971 to 72.03 percent in 1981, it again gone up to 73.01 percent in 1991 indicating what is known as "structural retrogression".

Table 1: Structural Change

State		Sectoral share of NSDP (%)			Occupational distribution of working population (%)		
		1971	1981	1991	1971	1981	1991
Arunachal Pradesh	P	59.19	47.28	46.19	80.44	75.28	67.44
	S	20.34	22.21	21.56	0.44	8.92	8.66
	T	20.47	30.51	32.25	19.12	15.80	23.90
Assam	P	49.14	53.85	35.47*	77.65	NA	73.99
	S	20.39	11.76	21.53*	5.10	NA	5.56
	T	30.47	34.39	43.00*	17.85	NA	20.45
Manipur	P	47.99	49.10	38.02	71.29	69.60	70.00
	S	16.82	7.65	10.20	12.23	13.35	9.66
	T	35.19	43.25	51.78	16.48	17.05	20.34
Meghalaya	P	65.11	44.62	33.58	81.84	79.76	74.81
	S	7.05	19.95	17.00	3.30	4.23	3.74
	T	27.84	35.43	49.42	14.86	16.01	21.45
Nagaland	P	48.09	42.86	29.07	78.95	72.03	73.01
	S	10.54	14.86	12.14	1.05	1.46	1.41
	T	41.37	42.26	58.77	19.99	26.51	25.57
Tripura	P	70.02	60.22	38.01*	76.58	70.18	64.08
	S	7.01	8.50	8.20*	4.25	7.40	6.37
	T	22.97	31.28	53.79*	19.17	22.42	29.55
India	P	47.78	41.30	34.08	72.1	68.7	66.8
	S	21.16	23.00	26.65	11.2	13.5	12.7
	T	31.06	35.70	39.27	16.7	17.8	20.5

Source: Various issues of Economic Review and Statistical Handbooks of Arunachal Pradesh, Assam, Manipur, Meghalaya, Nagaland and Tripura

Note: NSDP data are not strictly comparable as the base years are different. NSDP data at constant price are not available for Mizoram.

* relate to 1993-94

(3) Although the overall occupational change during 1971-1991 is in the same direction as the share of the primary sector to NSDP, it is not of the same dimension. Between 1971 and 1991, whereas the primary sector's share to NSDP in Manipur has declined by 20.78 percentage point, the share of main workers engaged in this sector has only declined by 1.81 percentage point (Table 2). This huge difference between these two is no doubt a major concern for the future progress of the economy of Assam, Manipur, Meghalaya and Tripura. However, this difference is not a major cause of concern in case of Arunachal Pradesh and Nagaland (Table 2). This difference indicates that the labour-productivity in the primary sector is declining perhaps due to overcrowding.

Table 2: Structural Change: Primary Sector

State	Primary Sector's Share to NSDP (%)			Main Workers engaged in Primary Sector (%)		
	1971	1991	% Change	1971	1991	% Change
Arunachal Pradesh	59.19	46.19	(-) 21.96	80.44	67.44	(-) 16.16
Assam	49.14	35.47	(-) 27.82	77.65	73.99	(-) 4.71
Manipur	47.99	38.02	(-)20.78	71.29	70.00	(-) 1.81
Meghalaya	65.11	33.58	(-) 48.43	81.84	74.81	(-) 8.59
Nagaland	48.09	42.86	(-) 10.87	78.95	73.01	(-) 7.52
Tripura	70.02	38.01	(-) 45.71	76.58	64.08	(-) 16.32

Source: Various issues of Statistical Handbooks of the Staties of worth cent and various census reports.

(4) While the NSDP share of the primary sector in most states has steadily declined between 1971 and 1991, the compensating rise of the share of secondary sector was not steady. Although between 1971 and 1981, all the states, except Assam and Manipur, under consideration have experienced a positive growth of the secondary sector both in terms of its share to NSDP and percentage of main workers engaged in it (Table 1), this trend has reversed between 1981 and 1991.

(5) The decline in the share of primary sector to NSDP between 1971 and 1991 has largely been compensated by the rise in the share of tertiary sector in all the states. In Arunachal Pradesh tertiary sector compensated 90.62 percent of the fall in the primary sector, the same for Assam, Meghalaya, Nagaland and Tripura amount to 68.44, 91.48, 96.28 and 91.66 percent respectively. Secondary sector played a significant role only in Meghalaya by compensating 31.56 percent of the fall in the share of primary sector to NSDP. Thus, except Meghalaya, the secondary sector did not experience any significant growth during the two decades (1971-1991). In case of Manipur, both the share of primary and secondary sectors declined by 9.97 and 6.62 percentage points respectively. The tertiary sector alone has compensated both the declines.

(6) Although secondary sector's share in NSDP has steadily increased between 1971 and 1981 as well as between 1981 and 1991 at the national level, its share in NSDP in north-eastern states has increased between 1971 and 1981 but except Assam, Manipur, declined between 1981 and 1991 (Table 1). An investigation of the causes of this decline necessitates further study of the sub-sectors of the secondary sector.

(7) A decomposition of the secondary sector and the proportional contributions of the sub-sectors to the former's share in NSDP in Meghalaya reveals (Table 3):

Table 3 : Percentage share of the sub-sectors to total secondary sector income of Meghalaya

Sub-sector	1973-74	1980-81	1990-91	1999-2000 (Q)
Manufacturing	36.88	22.15	17.66	15.76
Construction	34.71	64.03	69.96	76.76
Electricity & Water Supply	28.41	13.82	12.38	7.48
Total Secondary Sector Income (in crores)	4.61	29.80	135.11	309.21

Source : Various issues of Statistical Handbooks of Meghalaya.

(i) the contribution of 'manufacturing' has steadily declined from 36.88 percent in 1973-74 to 15.76 percent in 1999-2000,

(ii) the share of 'construction' to total secondary sector contribution has steadily increased from 34.71 percent in 1973-74 to 76.76 percent in 1999-2000,

(iii) the contribution from 'electricity and water supply' has also steadily declined from 28.41 percent in 1973-74 to 7.48 percent in 1999-2000.

These trends indicate that, since inception, the state is undergoing through a process of de-industrialisation. The relatively higher contribution of the secondary sector to NSDP in Meghalaya is in no way reflects its better industrial base. Rather it is the construction activities that play the key role. The positive growth of the secondary sector between 1971 and 1981 was due to the spurt in construction activities following the conferment of statehood to Meghalaya. The rise in the share of construction outweighed the fall in the share of manufacture as well as electricity and water between 1973-74 and 1980-81. However, the momentum of growth of 'construction' activities slowed down between 1980-81 and 1990-91. In spite of positive growth, the rise in the share of construction could not outweigh the combined fall in the share of manufacture as well as electricity and water supply. And hence the share of secondary sector in NSDP of Meghalaya has declined between 1981-1991.

(8) However, Northeastern states did not experience the structural retrogression in the secondary sector as had been observed in case of national economy between 1981 and 1991. While the NDP share of the secondary sector increased from 23 percent in 1981 to 26.65 percent in 1991, employment in this sector had declined from 13.5 percent to 12.5 percent showing a clear sign of structural retrogression. For the north-eastern states, both the variables moves in the same direction.

(9) During this two decades (1971-1991), tertiary sector in the North-eastern states grew much faster than the national trend (Table 1). However, unlike elsewhere, the progress registered in tertiary sector's share in NSDP and employment in Northeastern states seems to be primarily because of higher public expenditure.

(10) The snapshots of the features are:

(i) Except Tripura, the percentage of main workers engaged in the primary sector in Northeastern states is higher than that of national average. Hence, some policy measures are needed to boost up the non-agricultural sector so that its capacity to draw and absorb additional workforce rises.

(ii) The manufacturing bases in all the Northeastern states remain very weak. The shares of manufacturing in NSDP as well as workforce are negligible. Given the resource-bases of the northeastern states, it appears that the potential in this area is yet to be tapped. Hence special policy measures are, indeed, needed to boost up this sub-sector.

(iii) In all the states of North-east, there has been a spectacular growth of the tertiary sector. The share of this sector both in NSDP as well as workforce have steadily increased over the two decades (Table 1). The structural change that these Northeastern states are undergoing indicates a shift from the primary to tertiary sector bypassing the secondary sector.

Implications of structural change

Foregoing discussion leads to two important questions: (i) what is wrong if structural change flows from the primary to tertiary sector bypassing the secondary sector as has been happening in the economies of northeastern states? (ii) why the secondary sector is being bypassed in the process of development?

Let us take on the first question first. There are quite a few deeper implications of the structural change that flows from the primary to tertiary sector bypassing the secondary sector.

(a) If the secondary sector does not grow, the inter-sectoral linkages between agriculture and manufacturing will remain weak, which in turn, will rule out the transition of agriculture from tradition to modernity. This is evident from the features and performances of agriculture in the northeastern states.

(b) Secondary sector provides the necessary base on which tertiary activities grow. In fact, the scale of manufacturing in a way delimits the outer perimeter of tertiarisation in an economy. The grafted growth of tertiary sector not only suffers from lack of self-sustenance but also breeds socio-political tensions as the workforce trained in it could hardly be absorbed in non-agricultural sector.

(c) With very weak manufacturing base, the economies of the north eastern states resemble a two-sector economy having primary and tertiary sectors. The primary sector mainly produces food crops, other agro-forest based products and minerals. For agricultural inputs it has to depend on outside supply. Whatever is produced, after local consumption, if there is any marketable surplus, it has to be sent outside without any value addition because of the absence of manufacturing/processing facilities. If the outside market is far away that involves high transportation cost, in that case, market signals will not encourage surplus production. The primary sector will then run on subsistence level and the workforce therein will earn only subsistence wage. In that case, services produced in the tertiary sector will have a few takers. The economy will be caught into a low-level equilibrium showing the signs of underdevelopment and stagnation. This will, then, no doubt, add to social tension as there is not enough scope for the people to earn a decent living.

Let us now consider the second question: Why the secondary sector is being bypassed in the process of development? In fact, as has already been pointed out, it is the manufacturing, which is experiencing a steady decline over the years in the north-eastern states, and thereby pulling down the share of the secondary sector in NSDP. Hence, to put the question precisely: why do the manufacturing bases in north-eastern states remain weak? Why the region is passing through a process of de-industrialisation? Does the region lack in resources?

The Resource-base

The resource-bases of the states have already been portrayed in the state-specific status papers. Whatever resource mapping has already been done, it is evident that the region is one of the resource-rich areas in the country. It is the store house of crude oil (70.46 mt in Assam), natural gas (48000 mcm in Assam and Tripura), coal (1043 mt in Assam, Meghalaya, Arunachal Pradesh and Nagaland), limestone (5323 mt in Assam, Meghalaya, Arunachal Pradesh, Manipur and Nagaland), clay (28.5 mt in Meghalaya and Tripura), dolomite (247 mt in Arunachal Pradesh) and graphite (85 mt in Arunachal Pradesh). Apart from these, commercially viable reserves of minerals like kaolin, sillimanite, glass sand, quartz, feldspar, uranium reserves have also been found in the region.

Besides minerals, the region is having huge water resource. As per the estimate of Central Water Commission, the average annual run-off (AAR) of all the river basins of our country is 1869 billion cubic metre (bcm). Of this only 690 bcm, i.e., 3.92

percent is utilisable. The two-river systems of northeast India, i.e., the Brahmaputra and Barak, together have the highest average annual run-off of 585.60 bcm, i.e., 31 percent of the country's total surface water/run-off.

However, the hilly physiographical setting of the region, heavy annual precipitation, narrow basins of the tributaries of the Brahmaputra have reduced the scope of utilisation of this run-off to a great extent. It has been estimated that out of 585.60 bcm of AAR, only 24 bcm is the utilisable flow in the Brahmaputra and Barak river basins (BBRB). The ratio of utilisable flow to AAR for BBRB is only 4 percent while the same for the Indus and the Ganga are 63 and 48 percent respectively.

The live storage capacity of the utilisable flow is a very important indicator of water resource management. So far, only 1.10 bcm capacity for live storage has been created through completed projects in the catchment area of BBRB, while the same for the Indus is 13.83 bcm and for the Ganga is 36.84 bcm.

The total replenishable ground water potential in the country is estimated at 432 bcm per year. The same for BBRB is roughly 45.39 bcm per year. For the Indus and the Ganga, this estimate stands at 26.49 and 170.99 bcm per year respectively.

Thus a total of 69.39 bcm water resources including both surface and ground are available in BBRB which accounts for 6 percent of total utilisable water resources of the country.

However, the water resource potential of North-East Region will be a bit higher than that has been projected for BBRB as the physical boundaries of the region and BBRB do not coincide. Besides BBRB, the region also contains other small river basins draining into Bangladesh and Myanmar.

Besides agriculture, the implications of this water resource for the growth of other sectors of North East Region are many. As per an estimate of Central Electricity Authority (CEA), the hydro-electric power potential (at 60 % load factor) in all the major river basins in the country is assessed at 84000 MW. Of this, the Brahmaputra basin alone has the potential of 35000 MW, i.e., 42 percent of the total potential in the country. The Indus and the Ganga basins have the potential for 20000 MW and 11000 MW respectively. However, a revised estimate puts this potential at 31,857 MW (at 60% load factor). The maximum potential lays with the north bank tributaries of Brahmaputra which pass through Arunachal Pradesh. State-wise hydro-power potential assessed for North East Region is given below:

Table 4: Hydro-Power Potential in NER

States	Potential at 60 percent load factor (MW)
Arunachal Pradesh	26755
Assam	351
Manipur	1176
Meghalaya	1070
Mizoram	1040
Nagaland	1455
Tripura	10
NER	31857

Note: Assessed potential excludes plants of 2 MW and below

Source: Hydro-Electric Power Potential of India, CEA, 1988, taken from "Report on Power Perspectives for the North Eastern Region", July 1994.

However, this huge hydro potential of NER is yet to be tapped. As on 31.03.93, a total of 19,354 MW capacity has been installed in the country which accounts for about 23 percent of the total potential. The tapping of the same in NER at that time was only 1.44 percent (Table 5).

Table 5: Region-wise Hydro-Potential and Tapping (in MW)

Region	Assessed Potential (at 60% load factor)	Installed Capacity as on 31.3.1993	Percentage of Tapping
Northern	30154	6304	20.91
Western	5679	2644	46.56
Southern	10763	8360	77.67
Eastern	5591	1588	28.40
North-Eastern	31857	458*	1.44
India	84044	19354	23.03

* - 487 MW including micro hydels (as per NERB Annual Report, 1992-93).

Note: Figures of installed capacity cover plants under CEA monitoring.

Source: Hydro-Electric Power Potential of India, CEA, December 1988; CEA Bulletin, March 1993.

The region, thus, in spite of having the highest hydro-power potential in the country, generates only negligible share of it. Its per capita power consumption is very low compared to national average. While at the national level the per capita consumption of electricity in agriculture is 60.1 Kwh, the same for NER is 1.7 Kwh (1991). With its vast potential, while the region could have generated enough power that could have revolutionised its economy, it has perpetually remained as the net importer.

Table 6: Forest and Cultivable Areas in NER: 1996-97

(000 hectares)

State	Geographical Area	Forest Area	Forest Area as Percent of Geographical Area	Cultivable Land	Cultivable Land as Percent of Geographical Area
Arunachal Pradesh	8374	5154	61.55	293	3.50
Assam	7844	1930	24.60	3257	41.52
Manipur	2233	602	26.96	164	7.35
Meghalaya	2243	935	41.68	1082	48.24
Mizoram	2108	1598	75.81	446	21.16
Nagaland	1658	863	52.05	614	37.03
Tripura	1049	606	57.77	310	29.55
North East Region	25509	11688	45.82	6166	24.17
India	328726	68750	20.91	183545	55.83

Source: Ministry of Agriculture, Government of India, Land Use Statistics, 1995-96 to 1996-97

Apart from minerals, water and hydro-electric power potentials, NER is also rich in forest resources. About 46 percent of the total geographical area of the region is under forest, which is much higher than that of the national average (Table 6). Moreover, the forest in this region is rich in bio-diversity having a large number of rare species of flora. Although compared to national average, the region does not have much cultivable land, but the most part of the landscape constitutes in-situ resource for its charming scenic beauty.

It is, thus, evident from the above account that resource unavailability is not the cause of meagre growth of the manufacturing sector in the region and its subsequent de-industrialisation. Rather a study of the industrial structures as has been done in the state specific papers presented in this seminar, reveals a very weak resource-industry linkages in all the northeastern states. Resource-use in this region is basically extractive in nature. Even that too is done at large scale only in cases of critical minerals like crude oil where sizeable public sector investment has been undertaken for national interest. There exists a wide gap between the resource-base and industrial structure in the region. While the resource base is strong enough to support variety of industries at all scales-large, medium and small-the existing industrial structure, dominated by the small scale demand-based units, is lagging far behind. An obvious question arises as to why does this resource-industry linkage remain so weak in the regional economy?

Political Economy of Weak Resource-Industry Linkages

The reasons for this may be traced to the peripheral location of this region in relation to national market. Indeed, there is no denying of the fact that the partition of the country has made the region land-locked, robbed her traditional channels of communication and positioned her at the geographical periphery of the country. This has raised the transportation cost manifold, which, in turn, has made most of the production activities in the region non-competitive. Moreover, the region's loss of market in erstwhile East Bengal, now Bangladesh, has not been compensated in terms of either the growth of a regional market within or strong integration with the national market. Although the access of the region's produce to national market no longer remains cost-effective, produces of other regions have competed out their local counterparts. This has eroded the base of the traditional manufacturing in the region. The region is, thus, exposed to the backwash effects of national development and hence experiencing some sort of de-industrialisation in the post-colonial era.

Thus, this "lack of access to market" has been one of the main causes for under utilisation of the available resources as well as weak resource-industry linkages in the region. The small and segregated internal market of the region has been the major hindrance that makes the better use of her rich natural resources commercially unviable. The resource exploitation here warrants first the scarcity of a particular natural resource product to go up to such a level that can justify the higher price at which it can be supplied in the national market by using the resources from the peripheral states of northeast. Market signals emanating from the operation of the national economy are not strong enough to bring the resources of the region, except critical ones, into immediate use. Here lies the theoretical rationale to look beyond the framework of the national economy and the state-centric mindset while formulating the development strategy for the border areas like the north eastern region.

Policy Options

What are the policy options, one can think of, which will accelerate the use of resources and strengthen the resource-industry linkages in the region?

Firstly, a policy framework may be thought of to situate the region within the broad canvas of South Asia and South-East Asia which can provide the necessary access for the local produce to the markets of the neighbouring countries. This will then remove the handicap of market inaccessibility from which the region is suffering since independence. The region's geo-economic advantages of being the gateway to the South-East Asian markets, which has not been reaped so long, may, then, break her isolation and bring an end to her peripheral status.

Secondly, any strategy for development of the north eastern region should aim at reduction of transportation costs. For this to happen, all the modes of transportation - roadways, railways, waterways and airways-need to be strengthened within as well as between the regions on the one hand and an interlinking needs to be established between the communication systems of India and Bangladesh on the other. In fact, the Bangladesh corridor can play a major role in reducing the to and fro transport cost between the north eastern and eastern region of India.

Thirdly, an effective regulatory framework needs to be put in place in order to protect the local manufacturing from the outside competition. In view of the fact that structural impediments are far stronger than the incentives provided to local industries, more teeth need to be added to the special industrial policy devised by the Central Government for the industrial development of the region.

Fourthly, as the strengthening of resource-industry linkages requires large-scale operations involving the use of sophisticated technology, highly trained manpower, huge investment and above all, use of resource belt that cuts across the boundaries of north eastern states, activism on the part of the central agencies can only ensure these goals.

Concluding Remarks

The resource-industry linkages, once strengthened, will add to resilience of the regional economy and make economic progress self-sustaining. With the growth of manufacturing, this sub-sector, then, will be in a position to absorb a part of the labour force tied in the primary sector. This will, then, reduce the population pressure on agriculture. This will enable the agricultural sector to transform itself from tradition to modernity leading to a rise in productivity. An increase in productivity will fetch more income and hence more demand for goods and services produced in the non-agricultural sector. The inter-sectoral dynamics, once set in motion, will propel the economy towards higher stages of development.

❑❑❑

Index

J

K

L

M

N

S

T

U

●●●